JANE EYRE ON STAGE, 1848–1898

For Colin,
who has always believed in me

Jane Eyre on Stage, 1848–1898

An Illustrated Edition of Eight Plays with Contextual Notes

PATSY STONEMAN
University of Hull, UK

ASHGATE

Published by
Ashgate Publishing Limited
Gower House
Croft Road
Aldershot
Hampshire GU11 3HR
England

Ashgate Publishing Company
Suite 420
101 Cherry Street
Burlington, VT 05401-4405
USA

Ashgate website: http://www.ashgate.com

British Library Cataloguing in Publication Data
Jane Eyre on stage, 1848-1898 : an illustrated edition of eight plays with contextual notes.
– (The nineteenth century)
    1. Bronte, Charlotte, 1816-1855. Jane Eyre 2. Bronte, Charlotte, 1816-1855 – Adaptations
    3. Eyre, Jane (Fictitious character) – Drama I. Stoneman, Patsy
    822.8'080351

Library of Congress Cataloging-in-Publication Data
Jane Eyre on stage, 1848-1898 : an illustrated edition of eight plays with contextual notes /
    [edited] by Patsy Stoneman.
    p. cm. — (The nineteenth century series)
    Includes bibliographical references (p.   ) and index.
    ISBN 978-0-7546-0348-1 (alk. paper)
    1. English drama—19th century. 2. Brontk, Charlotte, 1816-1855—Adaptations. 3. Eyre,
Jane (Fictitious character)—Drama. 4. Governesses—Drama. I. Stoneman, Patsy. II. Brontk,
Charlotte, 1816-1855.
Jane Eyre.

    PR1271.J36 2007
    822'.808351—dc22

2006033508

ISBN: 978-0-7546-0348-1

Printed and bound in Great Britain by MPG Books Ltd, Bodmin, Cornwall.

14787217

fw

Contents

The Nineteenth Century Series
General Editors' Preface

The aim of the series is to reflect, develop and extend the great burgeoning of interest in the nineteenth century that has been an inevitable feature of recent years, as that former epoch has come more sharply into focus as a locus for our understanding not only of the past but of the contours of our modernity. It centres primarily upon major authors and subjects within Romantic and Victorian literature. It also includes studies of other British writers and issues, where these are matters of current debate: for example, biography and autobiography, journalism, periodical literature, travel writing, book production, gender, non-canonical writing. We are dedicated principally to publishing original monographs and symposia; our policy is to embrace a broad scope in chronology, approach and range of concern and both to recognize and cut innovatively across such parameters as those suggested by the designations 'Romantic' and 'Victorian'. We welcome new ideas and theories, while valuing traditional scholarship. It is hoped that the world which predates yet so forcibly predicts and engages our own will emerge in parts, in the wider sweep, and in the lively streams of disputation and change that are so manifest an aspect of its intellectual, artistic and social landscape.

Vincent Newey
Joanne Shattock
University of Leicester

Abbreviations and References

Abbreviations: used for archives and journals frequently cited in footnotes.

References: Short references in footnotes (normally authors' last names) can be expanded by consulting the 'List of Works Cited' at the end of this book.

Please note that where journal articles are referred to archive sources rather than the original journals, the bibliographic details may be incomplete or even missing if the archive clipping is not fully identified.

BPM	Brontë Parsonage Museum
CLSL: HC	Camden Local Studies Library: Heal Collection
DNB	Online *Oxford Dictionary of National Biography*
EA&A	*The Era Almanack and Annual*
ILN	*The Illustrated London News*
ISDN	*The Illustrated Sporting and Dramatic News*
HTC	Harvard Theatre Collection
NYPLPA: BRTC	New York Public Library for the Performing Arts: Billy Rose Theatre Collection
NYST	*New York Spirit of the Times*
NYT	*New York Times*
SLSL	Southwark Local Studies Library

List of Illustrations

Acknowledgements

First and last, I must acknowledge my gratitude to Sarah Cheesmond, who in 1990 alerted me to the existence of these plays, and to the Leverhulme Trust for awarding an Emeritus Fellowship which enabled me to complete this research in 2005.

In between, I have been indebted to many individuals and institutions for different kinds of assistance. Hull University's Faculty of Arts Research Executive enabled me to stay in London to begin the transcription. Sue Lonoff was immensely generous in facilitating my visit to New York and searching sources in Harvard. Jean Chothia helped introduce me to theatrical criticism. Shirley Baslow provided a clue to Leeds performances which I would not have found without her, and Ted Bottle has offered enthusiastic help in relation to the Coventry play. Judith Smith has searched sources in New York, and Sarah Fermi in Cambridge. My sister, Barbara Jean Frick, has provided essential help in researching and translating German sources. Sabine Vanacker and Philip Holmes have helped with Danish and Norwegian references.

Librarians in the Billy Rose Collection of the New York Public Library for the Performing Arts, the British Library Manuscript Room, the Brontë Parsonage Museum, Harvard College Library, the Houghton Collection of Harvard University and the London Theatre Museum, together with Local Studies Librarians in Bradford, Camden, Coventry, Leeds, Oldham and Southwark, and the Yorkshire Archaeological Society, have provided essential help.

Formal acknowledgement is due to the institutions who have given me permission to reproduce the images in my illustrations: to the Billy Rose Theatre Collection, The New York Public Library for the Performing Arts, Lenox and Tilden Foundations for the 1848 Courtney playbill, the anonymous 1867 playbill, the portraits of John Brougham and Laura Keene, the etched scene from Brougham's play and the 1873 photograph of Charlotte Thompson; to the British Library for manuscript pages from the plays by Hering, Paul, Willing and Wills; to the Harvard Theatre Collection, The Houghton Library for the Coburg Looking-Glass Curtain and the etched scene from Charlotte Thompson's 1873 performance; and to V&A Images/Victoria and Albert Museum for the poster for the National Standard Theatre. Detailed credits will be found in the List of Illustrations and with each figure in the text.

I am grateful to Camden Local Studies and Archives Centre, for providing images of the Park Theatre, J.T. Douglass, and Stella Brereton, and to Hull University Photographic Services for providing images of the 'View in the New Cut', the Surrey Theatre, the etched scene from *Nobody's Child*, the Globe Theatre and Mrs Bernard-Beere. Although all the images from Camden and Hull were published more than a hundred years ago, it is just possible that artists' copyright might still apply. I have not been able to trace the owners, but if anyone claims copyright, they should apply to the publishers of this work.

Introduction

Such then is a sample of what amuses the Metropolitan populace![1]

Charlotte Brontë's bemused, if not horrified, response to a *Jane Eyre* which was on stage in London only three months after the publication of her novel is well known. Until recently, however, nothing was known about the play, its author or the circumstances of its performance, although the information was not hard to find.[2] The reason seems to be that before the advent of cultural studies, this kind of theatrical event fell between the traditional fields of literary and dramatic scholarship. Literary critics, focused on the unique qualities of Charlotte Brontë's novel, saw adaptations only as travesties of her text, while for theatre critics, adaptations by definition lacked dramatic authenticity.

Two shifts in academic focus have altered the status of such ephemeral texts. From the perspective of sociology and politics, the discipline of cultural studies has revealed the ideological importance of popular culture. From the perspective of linguistic theory, poststructuralism has challenged the traditional separation of high from low culture by arguing for the cultural interconnectedness of all textual production. Despite its potentially leveling implications, a theory of intertextuality is not necessarily at odds with traditional aesthetic values. The classic status of a text such as *Jane Eyre* is sometimes measured by its 'excess of meaning': a richness and complexity which finds responses in different communities and generates widely differing readings. Ephemeral derivatives, such as the plays in this volume, collectively testify to the fruitful excess of their classic pre-text while individually they act as unique markers of social and ideological change.

When, more than twenty years ago, I began collecting material for my book, *Brontë Transformations: The cultural dissemination of 'Jane Eyre' and 'Wuthering Heights'*, I was fascinated by the processes which transform famous texts into common cultural property. Even so, I did not think of looking for the play that Charlotte Brontë mentions. It was a talented postgraduate student who told me that not just one, but several stage versions of *Jane Eyre* could be found in the Lord Chamberlain's collection of manuscript plays in the British Library.[3] Prompted by the variety and liveliness of what I encountered, I conceived the twofold ambition which lies behind this book: to transcribe and edit the play-texts in order to preserve them and make them available;

---

[1] Charlotte Brontë in Smith, Vol. 2, p. 27; quoted in full in the section on the reception of John Courtney's play, below. *Jane Eyre* was first published in October, 1847.

[2] As far as I know, Donna Marie Nudd (*Jane Eyre*) was the first person to identify the playwright as John Courtney and the theatre as the Victoria.

[3] I shall always be grateful to Sarah Cheesmond for setting me off on this research.

and to propose some hypotheses which might explain, in social and ideological terms, the many changes, sometimes bizarre and outrageous, which the playwrights made to Charlotte Brontë's novel.

Ironically, we owe the preservation of these plays to British censorship. From 1843 to 1968 every play performed in public in Britain had to be submitted to the Lord Chamberlain for approval; the Lord Chamberlain's Plays, therefore, form an almost complete record of theatrical performances for more than a century.[4] I found six versions of *Jane Eyre* in the Lord Chamberlain's Plays, performed between 1848 and 1882; there are also two plays from the same period which were performed and published in New York. Although some of the plays were being performed until the end of the century, no new play seems to have been written until 1909.[5] These plays, therefore, form a natural group. In chronological order, they are:

1848	'John Courtney' [John Fuller]	*Jane Eyre* or *the Secrets of Thornfield Manor*	Victoria Theatre, London
1849	John Brougham	*Jane Eyre*	Bowery Theatre, New York
1867	Anon.	*Jane Eyre*	New Surrey Theatre, London
1870	Charlotte Birch-Pfeiffer	*Jane Eyre* or *the Orphan of Lowood*	Fourteenth Street Theatre, New York
1877	Mme von Heringen Hering	*Jane Eyre*	Theatre Royal, Coventry
1879	'James Willing' [J.T. Douglass]	*Jane Eyre* or *Poor Relations*	Park Theatre, Camden Town, London
1879	T.H. Paul	*Jane Eyre*	Adelphi Theatre, Oldham
1882	W.G. Wills	*Jane Eyre*	Globe Theatre, Strand, London

In this book, the edited text of each play is preceded by five head-notes:

- on the original text and the principles on which it has been edited;[6]
- on the playwright;
- on the original theatre(s) and performance(s);
- on the reception of the play (I have tried to reserve this section for comments on the play as an adaptation of *Jane Eyre*, separating these from comments on the actors or staging, which will be found under 'theatres and performances');

---

4   See Booth et al., Vol. 6, pp. 40–42, for information on the Licensing Laws.
5   Miron Leffingwell, *Jane Eyre*, 1909. Morton Collection ts 316, University of Chicago.
6   It is unlikely that any of these manuscripts has authorial status, although I have not been able to check them against an authorial holograph. Some are in several hands. Stephens suggests that the Lord Chamberlain's copy was often made by a poorly-paid 'drudge', though 'in some cases the author's MS was used for this purpose' (*Profession*, p. 187).

- a brief list of distinctive features for each play (Table 1 shows how the action of each play is distributed in comparison with the locations in the novel).

The head-notes to the plays provide all the detailed information I have been able to find about the individual plays. This introduction, however, allows me to consider the plays as a group – firstly to place them in their theatrical context, and secondly to consider how their various revisions of the novel relate to the social and ideological context in which they were performed.

The Theatrical Context

None of the eight plays was performed at a prestigious West-End theatre. They were written to meet the insatiable popular demand for domestic melodrama which particularly characterized the 'transpontine' theatres – so called because they were 'across the bridge' on the unfashionable south or Surrey side of the Thames. The first two British plays in this collection (1848 and 1867) were performed at the principal transpontine theatres – the Victoria and the Surrey – appealing to huge and rowdy audiences.[7] The last play in the group, however (1882), was performed at the smaller, more genteel Globe Theatre, off the Strand;[8] it is a more thoughtful, less sensational play, and clearly appeals to a more middle-class audience. This group of plays thus spans, and demonstrates, that period of significant change in theatrical history called the 'gentrification' of the theatre.

The early years of the nineteenth century saw an unprecedented increase in the population of London and an equivalent demand for amusement at prices that working people could afford. Large numbers of theatres were built during this time,[9] many of them with a capacity of thousands in the low-priced pit and gallery seats, and, according to Mayhew, the more prosperous working people were able to go to the theatre several times a week. The evening's entertainment would last for up to six hours, with many different items included. Theatres needed to be resourceful to meet this level of demand from a mostly local audience. At the beginning of this period, most theatres kept a 'stock company' with a repertory of plays, and expected to change their programmes fairly often. Thus there was a 'constant demand from managers for new pieces at very short notice, perhaps as little as twenty-four hours',[10] and since playwrights were paid at pitifully low rates, the adaptation of popular novels was an obvious and labour-saving choice.[11] The demand also led to widespread piracy,

---

[7] See head-notes for details.

[8] Not to be confused either with Shakespeare's Globe or with the Globe Theatre on Shaftesbury Avenue.

[9] Most South Bank and East End theatres had been built by 1843 (Booth et al., Vol. 6, p. 33); few theatres were built between 1843 and 1860 (Rowell, p. 13).

[10] Stephens, *Profession*, p. xii.

[11] Novelists were paid between ten and a hundred times more than playwrights of the period (Booth et al., Vol. 6, pp. 51–4).

Table 1   Locations used in the plays

Blank areas indicate locations not used

Charlotte Brontë 1847	'John Courtney' [John Fuller] 1848	John Brougham 1849	Anon 1867	Charlotte Birch-Pfeiffer (US) 1870	Mme Heringen von Hering 1877	'James Willing' [J.T. Douglass] and Leonard Rae 1879	[T.H. Paul] 1879	[W.G. Wills] 1882
Gateshead		Act I	Prologue Sc 1–7	Act I Sc 1–6	Prologue			
Lowood	Act I Sc. 1–2	Act I Sc 1					Act I Sc 1–2	
Thornfield	Act I Sc 3–5 Act II Sc 1—6 Act III Sc 1–2	Act I Sc 2 Act II Sc 1 Act III Sc 1–3 Act IV Sc 1–3	Act II	Act I Sc 1–6 Act II Sc 1–12 Act III Sc 1–7	Act II Sc 1–6 Act III Sc 2–12 Act IV Sc 1–9	Act I Sc 1–3 Act II Sc 1	Act II Sc 1 Act III Sc 1–3	Act I Act II Act III
Morton	Act III Sc 3–4	Act V Sc 1				Act III Sc 1–4		
Ferndean	Act III Sc 5–6	Act V Sc 2–3				Act IV Sc 1		Act IV

especially of foreign plays, and the 1867 play in this collection must have been pirated, either from a performance, or from a prompt-book, since its German source was not printed until 1870.[12]

Although there are clear differences between the earliest and the latest plays in this group, they all fall into the most popular theatrical genre of the nineteenth century – melodrama. The word literally means 'music drama' and its history in Britain was also directly shaped by the theatre licensing laws.[13] Before the Theatre Regulating Act of 1843, only two theatres in England – Covent Garden and Drury Lane – were licensed to produce serious drama carried by the spoken word.[14] We still speak of the 'legitimate' drama with this meaning. All the other, so-called 'minor', theatres had at least to appear to be offering something different. Horse-riding, clowning, acrobatics, dumb-shows, water-tanks and firework displays were some possibilities. Sensational visual effects were as important as spoken words; a scene in Paul's *Jane Eyre*, for instance, ends with the 'Maniac' on the parapet of Thornfield against a background of flames, while Jane points to her, naming Rochester's duty: 'save your wife!' The conventions of dumb-show persist in scenes which end with a 'picture' or 'tableau' in which the characters strike a pose to reinforce its moral impact. In the 1867 play, for instance, Jane's denunciation of Aunt Reed is frozen into a 'picture'. It was, however, the provision of music that had the magical effect of transforming, for legal purposes, what was essentially a spoken play into something else, often defined vaguely as a 'burletta'.[15] By 1843 the minor theatres had become skilled in evading the law by such means, and melodrama took its distinctive form from the need to combine a spoken text with musical accompaniment.

Theatres often had 'sizeable' orchestras which provided an 'almost continuous' accompaniment to plays, and 'often played *with*, or at least *under* an actor's voice'.[16] The 1848 and 1867 manuscripts of *Jane Eyre* do not mention music (although it is credited on the 1867 playbill), but the fact that music is not mentioned does not mean that it was not used; on the contrary, 'music was such an integral part of performance that by the 1850s few critics mentioned it, and few scripts indicate its inclusion'.[17] In the other *Jane Eyre* plays, music is specified variously for social events (Brougham) or to heighten emotion (Hering), and theatre orchestras would have a stock of '"hurry music", "combat music" and "love music" applicable to many plays'.[18] The playbills for the later American plays specify a medley of light classics, but the W.G. Wills play

---

12   Stephens, *Profession*, gives details of how the dialogue of plays in performance was copied by teams of pirates (p. 86).
13   Booth et al., Vol. 6, p. 44.
14   Booth, M., *Theatre*, p. 151.
15   Rowell and Jackson, p. 9.
16   Booth, M., *Theatre*, p. 123. Mayer (pp. 51–2) gives details of leit-motifs etc and (pp. 56–61) includes facsimile scores with spoken cues.
17   Taylor, p. 124.
18   Robertson Davies, in Booth et al., Vol. 6, p. 266.

in this collection is superior in having music specially composed by a well-regarded composer.[19]

Speaking over music 'inevitably led to a heightened, deliberate and passionate mode of delivery', with many pauses to allow the words to carry; actors emphasised their words by facial and bodily gestures 'on an almost balletic scale'.[20] Acting manuals instructed actors in the precise coding of emotion by gestures indicating horror, despair or rapture,[21] conventions which survive not only into silent films but in present-day staging of nineteenth-century opera and ballet.[22] Other hybrid theatrical forms also merged with melodrama, so that such plays often offered slap-stick comedy, grotesque costumes and tumbling, elaborate scene-painting and sensational effects requiring real animals, fireworks, water-scenes or stage machinery.[23] In a 'stock' company, members specialized in 'stock' characters (who were sometimes 'colour coded' – 'black villain, scarlet woman, spotless maiden and motley fool'[24]) and stock situations, including marital squabbles in which the woman comes off best.[25] In Brougham's play, the servant John marries Grace Poole in order to introduce scenes of this kind.

The licensing laws thus lay behind many features of melodrama. A drama with musical accompaniment, dumb show and visual sensation needed strong and simple moral contrasts, in which good and evil are clearly differentiated and motivations are unambiguous. This drama was so well attuned to the tastes of the time, however, that when the Theatre Regulating Act of 1843 finally abolished the monopoly of the patent theatres, there was no immediate change in the kind of drama provided in all the others.[26] On the contrary, the legitimate theatres had themselves already yielded to the demand for melodrama, which remained the predominant theatrical form for most of the century.

The gradual process of gentrification, however, meant that some smaller theatres were built (such as the Park and Globe Theatres where Willing's and Wills's plays first appeared), and in existing theatres the pit benches were gradually replaced by stalls, and thus changed from the cheerful province of cut-price hecklers to a more genteel area.[27] Figure 7 shows the New Surrey Theatre in 1866, with its pit filled with backless benches, although it did have 'two rows of stalls'.[28] Michael Booth writes that 'by 1880 the middle-class conquest of the theatre auditorium, and consequently

---

19   See headnotes to the plays for details. Taylor (p. 125) quotes Charles Reade's account of the importance of an accomplished dramatic musical director.

20   Taylor, pp. 125, 129; see also Booth, M., 'Acting', pp. 31–6.

21   James, p. 7; Taylor, pp. 38–9.

22   See Robertson Davies, in Booth et al., Vol. 6, p. 269.

23   See head-notes to the 1867 play for stage effects and to Willing for scene-painting.

24   Taylor, p. 122.

25   Booth, M., 'Acting', p. 37.

26   Taylor, p. 16.

27   Booth et al., Vol. 6, p. 18.

28   *ILN*, 20 January 1866, p. 2163.

of the drama itself, was complete'.[29] The Park and National Standard Theatres, however, where Willing's play was performed in 1879 and 1881, aimed at a mixed audience, and compromised, with stalls at the front and benches at the back (Figures 16 and 18).[30]

By the 1860s, play runs in London were being lengthened by an influx of audiences who travelled from the country by train.[31] At the same time, provincial repertory companies yielded to touring groups who could perform the same play many times over by moving from town to town.[32] The 1877 play in this collection was performed by a company on a 'six nights' engagement' in Coventry (though it is not clear whether the tour continued) and both the Willing and Wills plays were performed in the north of England after their London beginnings. The extensive American career of Birch-Pfeiffer's play also depended on touring companies. Birch-Pfeiffer's play itself passed easily into the sphere of silent film, which was the natural inheritor of melodramatic gestures and effects.

The Plays as Versions of 'Jane Eyre', in their Social and Political Context

The emergence of melodrama was not purely a functional response to theatrical legislation; it was also a way of dealing with social change. Peter Brooks argues that melodrama began in France as an ideological vehicle for revolutionary protest, and Michael Booth confirms that in the mid-nineteenth century it was still 'anti-aristocratic, anti-employer, anti-landlord, anti-landowner and anti-wealth, often violently so'.[33] The plays in this collection, however, show that heightened indignation can co-exist, as in Dickens, with a general acceptance of class structures. Henry Mayhew records that the Chartists who filled the Victoria Theatre had only the vaguest ideas about social organization;[34] they were content to accept landowners so long as they were benevolent, and were much more eager for the come-uppance of hypocritical parsons, cheating shop-keepers and sadistic policemen – the 'rich' classes they had most to do with. The social order in melodrama is not overthrown but purged of its wickedness; melodrama is most vividly democratic in showing the oppressed poor as the arbiters of good and evil.[35]

The 1848 version of *Jane Eyre* is a good example. John Courtney's play gives prominence to the servants at Lowood School, newly invented characters named Joe

---

29 Booth et al., Vol. 6, p. 21.
30 See headnotes for more detail. Figure 21 shows the Globe Theatre in 1869, with mixed stalls and benches, though it may have changed by the date of Wills's play (1882).
31 Booth et al., Vol. 6, p. 19.
32 Jackson, p. 81.
33 Brooks, p. 14; Booth et al., Vol. 6, p. 33.
34 Mayhew, Vol. 1, p. 20; see head-note to Courtney's play for details.
35 Brooks, pp. 17, 44. The main interest of Paul's play, which may never have been performed, is its use of stock melodramatic motifs – satire against hypocrisy and greed, and defence of virtue.

Joker, Betty Bunce and Sally Suds. They are tired of the low pay and bad conditions, and cause so much trouble that Mr Brocklehurst has to call in the forces of the law. The clever servants, however, make their escape, tricking the constable and the beadle into diving through a window into a water-butt. The play opens with these scenes at Lowood School, where Jane is already a teacher, and the comedy conveys much explicit criticism of charity school management.

The Victoria Theatre had made a speciality of plays dealing with servants,[36] but the introduction of servants into the *Jane Eyre* plot is not just a commercial accretion; it reorientates our perspective on the novel. We see the initial scenes from the servants' point of view, and it is Betty Bunce who introduces the play by telling us (in a curious kind of Cockney Yorkshire) that most of the 'scholars' at Lowood 'are orphans with cruel uncles and aunts who send them out of the way to be thumped, bumped and consumptionized.' Betty's description of the school, with its thumping and bumping, evokes the more brutal oppression of Dotheboys Hall,[37] and by sympathizing with the orphans, she makes it clear that she and the other servants are aligned with Jane as victims of oppression. Jane herself publicly denounces Brocklehurst: 'Charity! Oh, 'tis a monstrous mockery of it, 'tis persecution upon the helpless and unprotected – and I tell you, sir, that you should blush to own such feelings as inhabit your cold and uncharitable heart'. She leaves Lowood at the same time as Joe and Betty, so that her departure appears less the solitary flight of a Romantic individualist than part of a concerted rebellion of class victims. The class enemy, moreover, is represented not by Rochester's upper-class friends, who do not appear in this play, but by Brocklehurst and Jehediah Piper, a comic predatory shopman who cheats in an election and tries to seduce Betty.

1848, the year of this play, is, of course, the year of *The Communist Manifesto*, the final Chartist petition, and the 'year of revolutions' in Europe, and it is tempting to see revolutionary meanings in the play's innovations,[38] but the play is not revolutionary in its outcome. Jane marries Rochester just as Cinderella gets her Prince, and the rebellious servants from Lowood sink happily into the less oppressive servitude of Thornfield Hall. Nevertheless the play as a whole supports Peter Brooks's argument that the assertive rhetoric of melodrama is 'in all cases radically democratic'. If, as Brooks argues, the essence of melodrama is 'the dramaturgy of virtue misprized and eventually recognized',[39] then in this play it is the virtue and resourcefulness of servants and victims – the class from which the audience is drawn – which is recognized by a benevolent superior (Rochester), while the devious and parasitic middle classes are exposed as the real class enemy.

---

[36] See the head-note to the play for details.
[37] In Dickens's *Nicholas Nickleby* (1839).
[38] Barker (*passim*) warns against the dangers of drawing facile conclusions.
[39] Brooks, pp. 15, 27.

John Brougham's play was written for New York's Bowery Theatre, equivalent in class terms to the transpontine London theatres, where comedy was an essential part of the entertainment. The direction of Brougham's comedy, however, was different from Courtney's. While Courtney ignores the aristocrats, reducing them to off-stage shadows, Brougham puts them in the limelight and relentlessly mocks their inanity. In this version, Jane confronts Rochester's guests before his arrival and, therefore, without his protection, highlighting her vulnerable position. She is, however, more than adequate to the occasion. When Lord Ingram makes a clumsy pass at her – 'do you know, Jane, that you're devilish pretty?' – he finds himself 'Snubbed, by Jove!' and the curtain falls on '*Tableaux of astonishment*'. Jane's indignation is expressed in a bitter soliloquy:

> Shame, shame upon their cruelty; [...] Better, a thousand times better, my solitary cell once more, than be gibed and mocked at by the vulgar-wealthy; to have the badge of servitude engraved upon my very heart, and know that tyrant circumstance has placed me in a world all prison, where every human being is a watchful jailor, and where you must endure the unceasing lash of insolence, the certain punishment of that statuteless but unforgiven crime, poverty.

Moments like this, inviting what Peter Brooks calls 'the admiration of virtue', are at the heart of melodrama.[40] Jane is initially left to face the enemy alone, but is finally surrounded by admiration. While the aristocrats have to be forced unwillingly to recognize her qualities, the servants 'cluster round' in approval, and Jane and Rochester' final reconciliation is greeted by cheering peasants. Once again, a lower-class audience is entertained by seeing class enemies mocked, while the play as a whole re-establishes social harmony by focusing on virtuous individuals.

For Charlotte Brontë's first readers, Jane Eyre was above all an independent woman, and, indeed, it is her spirited self-reliance which makes her an ideal heroine of melodrama. Courtney and Brougham revel in the emphatic display of Jane's virtue, but the melodramatic ideal does not easily map onto modern ideas of feminism. Donna Marie Nudd, in her pioneering study of *Jane Eyre* adaptations, lists ways in which the nineteenth-century male playwrights 'edit out' Brontë's feminism;[41] she contrasts them unfavourably with Birch-Pfeiffer, whose play emphasizes Jane's talents and the equality of the lovers.[42] Nudd's argument, however, shows signs of special pleading. It is true that in Courtney's play, Jane promises faithful support to Rochester before she could possibly know him, and in Wills's play, he only pretends to be dependent on Jane after his fall from the horse, but these incidents do not negate the effect of Jane's independent spirit. In five of these eight plays, Jane saves Rochester from the bedroom fire, as in the novel, and none of them shows the reverse, although in Brougham and Wills Jane faints when confronted with the murderous madwoman. Six of the plays

---

40 Brooks, p. 25.
41 Nudd, *Jane Eyre*, pp. 39–51.
42 Nudd, *Jane Eyre*, pp. 73–83.

reproduce Jane's 'equal as we are' speech very much as in the novel, and though Willing shows Rochester proposing to Jane, this is to highlight his seductive culpability.[43] The need for a happy ending does mean that the plays' assertive indignation is mollified and deflected into conventional gender-harmony.[44] Despite Nudd's argument, however, it is the Birch-Pfeiffer group which most blatantly shows Rochester as unblemished hero, with Jane in need of his protection.

These three plays (1867, 1870 and 1877) are all versions of one originally written in German by Charlotte Birch-Pfeiffer, and have certain things in common. They emphasise gender-relations, but in a conservative atmosphere. Although Jane is still an outspoken victim, the emphasis is less on her ability to defend herself and more on the importance of her having a strong and virtuous defender. These plays, whose sub-title is *The Orphan of Lowood*, begin with a Prologue in which Jane is still a child at Gateshead, where the pathos of an orphan betrayed by her guardian quickly evolves into righteous indignation. Jane's Uncle Reed, we learn, had exacted a promise from his wife that she would take care of Jane after his death. Aunt Reed has, of course, not fulfilled this promise and Jane deeply resents the treatment she has received from this so-called 'benefactress'.

In Charlotte Brontë's novel, Jane pours out her bitterness as she leaves to go to Lowood, but her outburst is heard only by Aunt Reed, and her accusations are ineffectual. In the Birch-Pfeiffer plays, Jane speaks in the presence of Mr Brocklehurst – and, of course, the audience – and threatens her aunt with divine retribution. In the 1867 play she asks her aunt:

> did you not whilst grasping the death hand of my uncle swear to use me as though I were your own child – never to forsake me? How have you kept that oath? At another tribunal you will meet my uncle again – he will say, 'Where is the orphan girl I confided to your care? What have you made of her – how fulfilled thy vow?' Answer – 'I have persecuted – beaten her, banished her from my roof – to the stranger bequeathed her as a pauper homeless and friendless' –

and, turning to Brocklehurst, she concludes, 'now Sir, I am yours!'. This is a spectacular instance of what Brooks calls 'the desire to express all', in which Jane appears as the typical melodrama heroine, 'femme étonnante' – astonishing woman – 'because her demonstration, her representation, of virtue strikes with almost physical force, astounding and convincing. The melodramatic moment of astonishment is a moment of ethical evidence and recognition'.[45] Later in the play we find that this moment of 'ethical evidence' has indeed made its mark on Aunt Reed.

---

[43]   The proposal scene is missing from Paul's manuscript.

[44]   Although Helena Michie argues that Willing's representation of sisterhood between Jane and Blanche challenges the normal heterosexual denouement.

[45]   Brooks, pp. 4, 26.

One innovation of the Birch-Pfeiffer plays is that the Reed family, grown up, take the place of Charlotte Brontë's Ingrams, and Georgina (or Georgine) Reed appears as Lady Claremont (1867), Clarens (1870) or Clarence (1877), a scheming widow, in the place of Blanche Ingram. In the Thornfield scenes, where Mrs Reed is confronted with the adult Jane, she appears almost as a tragic figure (certainly a rewarding part for an actress), unable to reconcile herself to the dependent whom she has wronged, yet whose passionate denunciation has poisoned her peace of mind. In these plays, although the young Jane is indignant, the adult Jane is particularly virtuous and long-suffering, freely forgiving her aunt and almost obtusely denying herself recognition of Rochester's regard.

Birch-Pfeiffer's play has some feminist elements. She presents Jane as not just a virtuous victim but a gifted one, whose talents are overlooked because of her class obscurity. Rochester is first drawn to her because he admires her paintings, which are prominent in the plot. Her talent is, however, sufficiently recognized by this kind 'protector' and does not call for any revision of gender relations. Birch-Pfeiffer's play is also conservative in class terms, particularly in its deference to aristocratic status. Brougham's play suggests that Rochester is the 'farmer's friend', who outspokenly prefers his governess to 'such as ye' (that is, Lady Ingram). Birch-Pfeiffer's Rochester, by contrast, is elevated to 'Sir Rowland Rochester' (1867) or even 'Lord Rowland Rochester'.

1867, the year in which the first English version of Birch-Pfeiffer's play was performed, was the year in which Disraeli came to power on a platform of 'noblesse oblige'. It was also the year of the Second Parliamentary Reform Bill, which enfranchised most middle-class men, raising debate about the responsibilities of power. John Stuart Mill's women's suffrage amendment was defeated, the established view being that women did not need to vote because women's interests were always 'covered' by the protection of a male relative. This question of male responsibility for women and children is central to all the Birch-Pfeiffer versions of *Jane Eyre* – a responsibility which extends beyond the immediate family, so that Rochester is described as a 'father to the neighbourhood'.

A man with Rochester's past, however, might not seem fit to follow the saintly Uncle Reed as Jane's protector; and accordingly the Birch-Pfeiffer plays share another innovation to the plot. The madwoman in the attic is revealed to be – no! not Rochester's wife, but the wife of his dead brother, whom he has taken in out of the goodness of his heart. Adèle is her daughter conceived out of wedlock, whom Rochester has adopted. To the question 'how have you treated the orphan child?', Rochester could thus answer without a blush. He also has the arrogance of virtue, telling Jane, in the 1877 version, 'I will have you, and no other!' to which Jane replies 'Ah Rowland, my lord – my world – I am yours!' and she 'throws herself into his arms'. Rochester then announces the marriage to the assembled party, 'embracing Jane with one arm and stretching the other towards heaven' while 'Jane has clasped her hands, and seems to pray'. The overall effect is to excite the audience's sympathies with the couple's evident sexual energies whilst at the same time confining them within a conformist matrix.

The rather sickening virtue of both the protagonists in the Birch-Pfeiffer plays gives way in our final three plays to a much more critical representation of Rochester. Although there are considerable differences among the plays by Willing, Paul and Wills, they all present Jane as a sexual object, to be ogled and subjected to compliments, sincere and otherwise. In Willing and Paul, she is also a financial object, since her inheritance is known from early on, and the Reed family, especially John Reed, is active in trying to trick her out of it. The presentation of Jane as an heiress so early in the play might seem a curious change, since it counteracts the victim status and vulnerability which were the stock in trade of the earlier melodramas. This group of plays, however, appeared at the time of public debate about the second Married Women's Property Act, which was finally passed in 1882. Before this date the whole of a single woman's capital would pass into her husband's ownership on marriage. In these later plays, then, a woman's ownership of money makes her vulnerable in a different way from the poor orphans of the earlier plays.[46]

The 1879 play by 'James Willing' follows the Birch-Pfeiffer pattern in some respects; it has a Gateshead Prologue, for instance, although in this play Jane is already meek and virtuous as child, and forgives her aunt for her bad treatment before leaving her house. Like the Birch-Pfeiffer plays, this one also jumps to Thornfield, where Rochester's guests include a grown-up John Reed. Here, however, the similarities end. The rest of the guests are Ingrams and Eshtons, as in the novel, and John Reed presents himself as Rochester's rival for Blanche Ingram. In the novel, John Reed appears only as a child and we hear of his later dissipation only indirectly. In this play, however, he reappears at Thornfield, and if Rochester is a 'reformed rake', John Reed reminds us what a rake might look like in action; he becomes the stereotypical villain of melodrama.

The most startling innovation in this play is that John Reed seduces Blanche by staging a false marriage which acts as a parallel to Rochester's own attempted deception. While Jane flees, explicitly to protect her 'honour', Blanche succumbs and is then abandoned by the unrepentant Reed. Mr Brocklehurst is also enlisted in this play to give a comic dimension to this theme. After Jane's flight from Thornfield, it is Brocklehurst who takes her in and, from a hypocritical mixture of financial and sexual motives, offers her marriage. Jane, however, settles for the post of village schoolmistress, and scarcely has she established herself when Blanche, now barefoot and starving, arrives on her doorstep begging for a crust. In the manner of melodramas, the parallels and contrasts between them are made explicit. Blanche complains, of John Reed, 'he promised marriage – I, too credulous dupe, believed him, trusted him – loved him – but he robbed me of the choicest jewel of a woman's life – and then flung aside the empty casket'. Jane explains that she too has been deceived, 'cruelly – but –' and Blanche bitterly ends her sentence for her 'not – fallen – you would say'.

46	It may be an accident that the *Daily News* advertisement for Wills's *Jane Eyre* on 21 February 1883 appears next to an advertisement for Mrs Holdsworth's guide to *The Married Women's Property Act of 1882*.

Blanche has already spelled out for the audience the meaning of the word 'fallen':

> a cast off mistress – a woman of the streets – the woman, who suffers all the degradation, losing position, friends, station, is an outcast whose momentary sin no repentance can palliate, no reparation condone – the man, the betrayer, whose base passion has ruined the heart he should have cherished, society receives with open arms – he is free to ruin other homes, and send more innocent souls to perdition.

Jane, who already knows she is an heiress, now demonstrates true magnanimity by offering to share her fortune with Blanche, whom she calls 'sister'.[47] When Jane and Rochester finally get together, Blanche is still with them, a surprising indication of what women might choose to do with independently owned money.

Earlier in Willing's play, when Blanche is trying to choose between Rochester and Reed, one of her arguments for choosing Reed is the old saying, 'a reformed rake generally makes the most devoted of husbands'. Blanche does not know that the maxim would apply just as well to Rochester, but Brontë's novel itself seems to endorse the maxim. It is interesting, therefore, that the play by W.G. Wills, performed in 1882, harshly condemns Rochester as 'reformed rake'. This play is the only one in this collection to begin at Thornfield, with no Gateshead or Lowood scenes. Jane's unhappy childhood and orphan status are conveyed only through her conversation with Rochester, whose laconic tone replaces the indignant rhetoric of the earlier plays. Moreover, she has come to Thornfield not direct from Lowood, but from a safe home with good friends, the Rev. Prior and his mother (invented for this play). Mr Prior continues to monitor Jane's welfare (his only drawback being his unwelcome proposals of marriage), and he is there to take her away when she decides she must leave Thornfield. Although there is much emphasis on the Ingrams' sneering at Jane, her education and calm demeanour protect her, while Rochester's love appears to provide a final vindication. There is a sensational scene where the maniac suddenly appears intent on killing Jane, but there is no foreboding laughter or other building of suspense. Much of the normal machinery of melodrama is thus absent; the tone of the play is quiet, and Jane is not a notable victim either in class terms, or as an orphan, or as the fearful occupant of a 'haunted' house. She is not even vulnerable as an heiress, since there is no mention of her legacy in this play.

Jane's vulnerability in this play lies, in fact, entirely in her sex, and its most surprising feature is the way in which this aligns her with other women across class divisions. While in Charlotte's novel and in most of the plays Jane is presented as friendless apart from Rochester,[48] in this last play by W.G. Wills she has the support

---

[47] It is possible that this playwright was influenced by reading Elizabeth Gaskell's *Life of Charlotte Brontë* (1857), in which Gaskell describes 'a village girl that had been betrayed some little time before, but who had found a holy sister in Charlotte' (Oxford World's Classics, 2001, p. 456).

[48] Nudd, *Jane Eyre* (p. 42) remarks on the playwrights' excision of female friends such as Helen Burns, Miss Temple and the Rivers sisters.

not only of Mr Prior and his mother, but also of most of the other women in the play. At one point or another Mrs Fairfax, Blanche Ingram and her mother, Grace Poole and even the madwoman herself warn Jane to leave the house at once, either because of Rochester's known affairs or because of his first marriage. In this version it is Blanche Ingram, who was herself deceived by Rochester, who reveals to Jane the existence of his first wife.

When Blanche describes Rochester as 'a dishonourable, despicable, unprincipled man whose life has been one system of hypocrisy', Jane at first defends him. But when Grace Poole corroborates Blanche's accusations, Jane herself rather startlingly turns against Rochester. In a truly melodramatic scene, where Rochester talks wildly in an attempt to justify himself, Jane grimly repeats one question: 'Is that Woman Your Wife?'. When Rochester finally replies, Jane turns to leave with this parting speech:

> what have I to say! but that I have been a poor truthful vain fool, and you have purposed to destroy me, without pity or warning. What have I to say, but that you spread your net well, and I could detect [no] false ring in all your kindness. Oh! Sir, in whom am I to believe, when the one I could have worshipped has proved an enemy? (*Rochester sits with pale face in hands, affected.*) You have done me a bitter wrong, that will follow me through life. Henceforth I'll distrust everything I love, I'll think everything happy must be hollow.

Rochester's punishment in this play is unusually severe. He is subject to wracking pains of conscience, and where Courtney and Willing restore his sight at the end, here there is no mitigation of his injuries, and he is left alone in poverty. The final reconciliation between Jane and Rochester is, as in the novel, entirely between themselves, and despite the final coming together, the point is made that Rochester is not innocent. If he had succeeded in his deception he would have done Jane a real injury.

The change from the saintly hero of the Birch-Pfeiffer plays to the bowed Rochester of Wills's play is striking, and it may be relevant that 1882, the date of Wills's play, saw the culmination of 'The Women's Revolt' – the lengthy and highly-publicized feminist agitation for the repeal of the Contagious Diseases Acts. These Acts, intended to check the spread of sexually transmitted diseases, were perceived by feminists as a licence to humiliate and degrade women, since they allowed the police to arrest and examine any woman suspected of being a prostitute. Josephine Butler's campaign to repeal the Acts exposed the fact that apparently respectable men could behave in sexually irresponsible ways with impunity, while the penalties, in terms of disease and opprobrium, were borne by women.

My interpretation of these plays assumes that they act as readings of *Jane Eyre* which incorporate current discourses, whether they be class consciousness, or debate about the financial and sexual situation of women. Such meanings were, however, far from overt, and were not recognized by any contemporary reviewers. About 1848, the time of the first play in this collection, one of Mayhew's costermongers declared that 'love and murder suits us best, sir',[49] and in 1882, the date of the last play, William

---

[49]   Mayhew, Vol. 1, p. 15.

Archer was complaining that 'a drama which opens the slightest intellectual, moral, or political question is certain to fail. The public will accept open vice, but it will have nothing to do with a moral problem'.[50] Michael Booth finds the reason simple:

> the Lord Chamberlain and his Examiner of Plays acted throughout our period as governmental arbiters of taste, which is basically why the English drama from 1737 until nearly the twentieth century has not been, and could not be, concerned with sex, politics and religion.[51]

'Sex, politics and religion' can, however, shape the rhetoric and structure of plays without appearing to pose 'a moral problem'. Melodrama derives its power not from intellectual debate but from the violent expression of feelings fermented by injustice. Such expression can hardly avoid being 'political', though it may require the perspective of another age to interpret its meanings. If, as poststructuralists argue, ideology is most effective when it masquerades as common sense or common knowledge, then the unexamined indignation of the melodrama was a more powerful political medium than the 'problem plays' of Archer's hero, Shaw.

In literary terms, these plays are debased versions of Charlotte Brontë's novel. Their very distortions, however, may shed light on their famous pre-text. Nowadays we read *Jane Eyre* primarily as the story of an individual remarkable for her inward complexity. The ambiguities of the novel (which can be read as revolutionary or as conservative) contribute to that sense of endless possibilities which is one of the marks of literary greatness. Studies which place the novel in its historical context in terms of the 'status incongruence' of governesses, the link between landed British wealth and colonial slavery, or the social causes of female madness, confirm what Terry Eagleton calls the 'overdetermination' of the individual's unique situation at the intersection of class, gender and racial structures.[52] The Victorian plays, by contrast, simplify and narrow the novel's focus. In place of a subtly ambiguous Jane we have the stereotypes of melodrama – orphan victim, spotless maiden, 'astounding woman'. In place of Rochester's painful dilemma we have the stainless hero of the Birch-Pfeiffer plays or Wills's culpable deceiver.

These changes of focus, however, can play a temporary spotlight on aspects of the novel which might not otherwise seize our attention. When Courtney aligns his heroine with the servants, it diminishes her individuality, and distorts the realities of class stratification, but its exaggeration of Jane's lowly status emphasizes her class effrontery in daring to claim equality with the gentry. It is intriguing to speculate whether Lady Eastlake (who wrote her famous review of *Jane Eyre* in the same year

---

50 Quoted in Booth et al., Vol. 6, p. 36.
51 Booth et al., Vol. 6, p. 40. Playwrights subject to the Lord Chamberlain seem to have practised self-censorship; none of the plays in this collection needed censorship apart from substitutions of single words, such as 'goodness' for 'God' in phrases like 'Thank God!'.
52 Eagleton, p. 8.

as this play) took fright at the story's popularity at the Victoria Theatre, a known Chartist hotbed. Eastlake declares 'that the tone of the mind and thought which has overthrown authority and violated every code human and divine abroad, and fostered Chartism and rebellion at home, is the same which has also written Jane Eyre'.[53] Her denunciation has seemed laughably extreme to modern ears, but Courtney's play, with its comically insolent subversion of authority, shows us how the novel might be read in this way.

Willing's invention of the sub-plot in which John Reed seduces Blanche Ingram similarly reduces these characters to the stock figures of villain and fallen woman; nevertheless this insistent parallel, with its histrionic placing of the fallen woman, highlights for us the enormity of Rochester's deception. In a present-day climate of sexual permissiveness, readers can be impatient with Jane's failure to flout social ostracism and follow her heart. Willing's play insists that we take a hard look at the dangers of illicit union. Wills's play raises even more uncomfortable questions which are wholly overlooked in the novel. A man who has had sexual relations with at least four women of loose virtue (Bertha, Clara, Giacinta and Céline) would have had a good chance of acquiring a sexual disease, and female novelists of a later generation did not shrink from this knowledge.[54] In 1847 it was impossible for Charlotte Brontë to address this factor, but it is there, submerged in the novel's potential meanings. Wills's play insists that it be placed in the balance, considerably diminishing Rochester's moral status.

Examples such as these show that the relationship between a classic text and its ephemeral derivatives can be as much a dialogue as a one-way traffic, with the lesser work casting back questions for its distinguished pre-text. Indeed, a work like *Jane Eyre*, which impresses us with a sense of its literary value, does so partly because

> it has exceeded the conjuncture of its production, has engaged with altered ideological contexts and been reproduced in different contemporary readings. […] The greater the text, the more we are compelled to read it through a palimpsest of other interpretations.[55]

The plays in this collection have not formed part of any well-known 'palimpsest' of textual accretions around *Jane Eyre* because for more than a hundred years they have rested in the unvisited grave of the British Library's Manuscript Room. Now that they are available, I hope that they will open up new debates about the potential meanings of Charlotte Brontë's text or – at least – about the ways in which her Victorian readers received it.

---

53   *Quarterly Review* (December 1848) Vol. 84, pp. 153–85, p. 174.
54   Sarah Grand's *The Heavenly Twins* (1893), in which a young mother dies together with her disfigured baby after contracting a disease from her husband, is a good example.
55   Easthope, pp. 57, 59.

Jane Eyre

or

The Secrets of Thornfield Manor

by

John Courtney

1848

Editor's Notes

The Text

The play exists in a single hand-written copy in the Lord Chamberlain's Collection of Plays in the Manuscript Room of the British Library (Add. MS 43009). The manuscript is written on both sides of small pages of badly browned paper, pasted into a large volume which is numbered consecutively from p. 566; the Courtney play occupies pp. 595–629. The edges of the paper are in good condition and the script is regular and legible. The hand appears the same throughout, although the title page is in a more formal hand. At p. 608 the cream/brown paper gives way to paler, blue/white and less discoloured paper. The manuscript is prefaced by the following letter:

> To the Examiner of Theatrical Entertainments:
> Sir
> With permission of the Lord Chamberlain of Her Majesty's household the accompanying Drama will be represented at the Victoria Theatre on Monday Jany 31st next
>   D W. Osbaldiston
> To J.M. Kemble Esq^u
> Victoria Theatre
> Jan'y 21. 1848

The play is marked as 'Licensed by the Lord Chamberlain's Office, 1848'. The Lord Chamberlain's Day Book has no further information except 'Date of Licence 27: Jan 1848'.

Few of the speeches have final punctuation, and I have introduced final stops, question marks and exclamation marks. Dashes are used more frequently than any other mark, and I have left as many of these as are consistent with intelligibility, but have changed some to commas or full stops. I have introduced some 'bracketting' commas; for instance: 'for the Lowood Institution as they calls it, aint no better' becomes 'for the Lowood Institution, as they calls it, ain't no better'. Where the writer uses commas to create 'comma splices', however, I have substituted a dash as being consistent with his practice elsewhere and less offensive to the modern sense of correctness. I have introduced apostrophes for possessives such as *Jane's* and contractions such as *it's* and *don't*. I have expanded abbreviations and contractions such as *tho'* and *y^r* and have standardized abbreviations of speakers' names. I have removed some capital letters from the middles of sentences. I have substituted 'Joe Joker' for 'Jem Joker' in the first scene, since he is called 'Joe' for the rest of the play.

The Playwright

The author is not named on the manuscript, which was for some time misattributed to John Brougham, despite the fact that the manuscript play is quite different from Brougham's published text. The manuscript does, however, specify a performance at the Victoria Theatre on 31 January 1848, and the New York playbill for that

performance states that 'The Drama [was] written expressly for this Theatre, by Mr.
J. Courtney' (see Figure 1a).[1]

'John Courtney' was the author of more than sixty other plays listed in the Lord
Chamberlain's Collection, and the 'Backstage' website lists eleven playbills for plays
by Courtney. In 1853, he was described as 'stock author' for the Surrey Theatre,[2]
which had links with the Victoria through its manager, David Osbaldiston. Boase
cites 'John Courtney' as the stage name of John Fuller, who was born on 29 August
1804, appeared as an actor at various London theatres between 1829 and 1852,
wrote a number of plays for the Olympic, Haymarket and other theatres, and died in
Camberwell, London, 17 February 1865.[3] H. Davenport Adams, however, records
1813 as Courtney's date of birth and does not remark on the pseudonym.[4] Boase does
not include *Jane Eyre* in his list of Courtney's works.

The Theatre and Performances

The only surviving playbills for this play are for the Royal Victoria Theatre, London,
on 31 January, 1848, announcing for the 'First Time, an entirely New Drama (in
Four Acts) [...] founded on the Celebrated Work of the same name, by Currer Bell'
(little more than three months after the publication of her novel in October, 1847). An
advertisement appeared in *The Era* for two days in February, and Charlotte Brontë
speculates about the play in a letter dated 5 February (see 'Reception', below).[5] *The
Era* has a further advertisement on 13 February, but the play then disappears.

The Victoria Theatre was built, as the 'Coburg', on the south bank of the Thames
in 1818, and was renamed 'Victoria' in 1833. It was a large theatre, holding more
than 2,000 people, built in response to an expansion of population in the area, and
also to the improved cross-river access provided by Waterloo Bridge.[6] Figure 2,
'View in the New Cut', shows the theatre surrounded by street vendors, and in
1859, George Sala described the New Cut as 'one of the most unpleasant samples
of London', its tenements filled with 'an unwashed, unkempt, wretched humanity'.[7]
John Hollingshead, manager of another theatre, gives this account of an evening at
the Old Vic:

---

1   There are two surviving playbills: one in NYPLPA: BRTC (Figures 1a and 1b), and a
     shorter one, not including the name of the playwright, in the University of Bristol Theatre
     Collection.
2   Stephens, *Profession*, p. 96.
3   Boas, Vol. 4, p. 774.
4   Adams, Vol. 1, p. 345.
5   *Era*, 6 February 1848, p. 8, referring to 8 and 10 February.
6   Davis and Emeljanow, pp. 3, 24. Thornbury and Walford say the potential capacity was
     2,800 (p. 398).
7   Quoted in Davis and Emeljanow, p. 10.

The gallery of the Victoria was a huge amphitheatre, probably containing about fifteen hundred perspiring creatures; most of the men in shirt-sleeves, and most of the women bare-headed, with coloured handkerchiefs round their shoulders, called 'bandanna wipes' in the slang of the district, and probably stolen from the pockets of old gentlemen who were given to snuff-taking. This 'chickaleary' audience was always thirsty – and not ashamed. It tied handkerchiefs together – of which it always seemed to have plenty – until they formed a rope, which was used to haul up large stone bottles of beer from the pit, and occasionally hats that had been dropped below.[8]

Charles Mathews, yet another manager, gives a similar description of how 'the lower orders rush there in mobs' to 'applaud frantically, drink ginger-beer, munch apples, crack nuts, call the actors by their Christian names, and throw them orange-peel and apples by way of bouquets'.[9]

Henry Mayhew, in *London Labour and the London Poor*, gives an extended account of the gallery audience, with vivid details about the noise, the pressure, the stench and the heat. Mayhew deals with the Victoria Theatre in his section on costermongers, since 'three times a week is an average attendance at theatres and dances by the more prosperous costermongers',[10] and 'on a good attractive night, the rush of costers to the threepenny gallery of [...] "the Vic" is peculiar and almost awful'. 'There are few grown-up men that go to the "Vic" gallery', he reports.

The generality of the visitors are lads from about twelve to three-and-twenty, and though a few black-faced sweeps or whitey-brown dustmen may be among the throng, the gallery audience consists mainly of costermongers. Young girls, too, are very plentiful, only one-third of whom now take their babies, owing to the new regulation of charging half-price for infants.[11]

The prevalence of costermongers in this audience helps to explain the comic scenes in Courtney's play, since costermongers were particularly hostile to the police, who were forever 'moving them on'. Mayhew includes 'Policemen' in his section on 'The Politics of Costermongers', since 'the notion of the police is so intimately blended with what may be called the politics of the costermongers'. Costers, he says, 'are nearly all Chartists', although often 'without understanding anything about the six points', and 'with their opinion of the police, all the more ignorant unite that of the governing power.' The reason why Rochester's aristocratic friends do not appear in Courtney's play may be that such people scarcely appeared on the horizon of this audience:

the costermongers have very vague notions of an aristocracy; they call the more prosperous of their own body 'aristocrats'. Their notions of an aristocracy of birth or wealth seem to be formed on their opinion of the rich, or reputed rich salesmen with whom they deal.

---

8   John Hollingshead, *My Lifetime* (1895), quoted in Booth, J., p. 50.
9   Quoted in Baker, p. 399.
10 Mayhew, Vol. 1, p. 15.
11 Mayhew, Vol. 1, p. 18.

Figure 1a   Playbill for John Courtney's *Jane Eyre* at the Victoria Theatre,
              1848, showing the elaborate scene descriptions for which David
              Osbaldiston, the Victoria Theatre manager, was famous. This unique
              copy is reproduced by permission of Billy Rose Theatre Collection, The
              New York Public Library for the Performing Arts, Lenox and Tilden
              Foundations

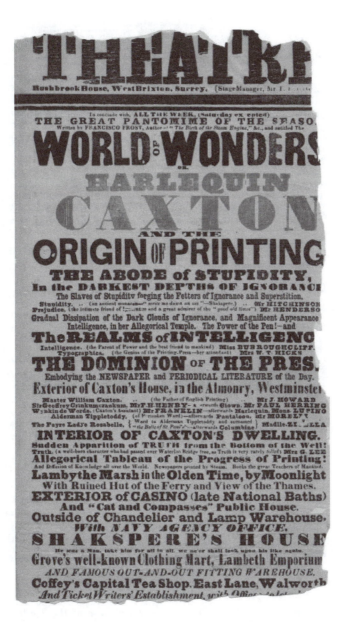

Figure 1b   Playbill for John Courtney's *Jane Eyre* at the Victoria Theatre, 1848, showing the elaborate scene descriptions for which David Osbaldiston, the Victoria Theatre manager, was famous. This unique copy is reproduced by permission of Billy Rose Theatre Collection, The New York Public Library for the Performing Arts, Lenox and Tilden Foundations

Figure 2 'View in the New Cut', showing the Victoria Theatre as part of a busy street scene: from G.W. Thornbury and E. Walford, Old and New London, 1879. Image supplied by Hull University Photographic Service

Because the police represented power in general, they were the immediate target for political attack; Mayhew is 'assured that in case of a political riot every "coster" would seize his policeman'.[12] Accordingly, 'to serve out a policeman is the bravest act by which a costermonger can distinguish himself. Some lads have been imprisoned upwards of a dozen times for this offence; and are consequently looked upon by their companions as martyrs'.[13]

Such an audience would relish Courtney's humiliation of the constable, the beadle and the self-serving 'shopman', Jehediah Piper, and Charles Dickens, in 1850, suggests that the audience was fairly homogenous in class terms (see Figure 3):

> The company in the pit were not very clean or sweet-savoured, but there were some good-humoured young mechanics among them, with their wives. These were generally accompanied by 'the baby', insomuch that the pit was a perfect nursery. [...] There were a good many cold fried soles in the pit, besides; and a variety of flat stone bottles, of all portable sizes.
>
> The audience in the boxes was of much the same character (babies and fish excepted) as the audience in the pit. A private in the Foot Guards sat in the next box; and a personage who wore pins on his coat instead of buttons, and was in such a damp habit of living as to be quite mouldy, was our nearest neighbour.[14]

The Victoria Theatre, together with its neighbour, the Surrey, fostered a theatrical style which West End critics disparagingly called 'transpontine' (across the river), and the Victoria Theatre in the 1830s 'touched new depths in spine-chilling melodrama'.[15] Although its extravagance 'furnished the burlesque-writer with endless fun',[16] the managers were also seriously blamed for this low taste, and the management of David Osbaldiston in the 1840s 'was actually referred to in print as "the most degraded in London"'.[17] Charles Knight, writing in 1846, complains,

> Look at our theatres; look at the houses all around them. Have they not given a taint to the very districts they belong to? The Coburg Theatre, now called the Victoria, and the Surrey, what are they? At Christmas time, at each of these minor theatres, may be seen such an appalling amount of loathsome vice and depravity as goes beyond Eugene Sue, and justifies the most astounding revelations of Smollett.[18]

In 1847, *The Theatrical Times* complains that the Victoria tries only to please a degraded audience:

---

12   Mayhew, Vol. 1, p. 20.
13   Mayhew, Vol. 1, p. 16.
14   Dickens, p. 14.
15   Rahill, p. 140.
16   Baker, p. 399.
17   Booth, J., p. 52.
18   Quoted in Booth, J., p. 53.

Figure 3   The audience at the Victoria Theatre. This drawing shows the audience
reflected in the famous 'looking-glass curtain' in 1822, when the theatre
was called the Coburg. The mirror curtain had gone by 1848, when
Jane Eyre was performed there, but the class division of the audience
by gallery, circle and pit was still in force. Reproduced by permission
of the The Harvard Theatre Collection, The Houghton Library

The vulgar and the ignorant, such as those who throng to the Victoria to witness atrocious melodramas fit only for an audience of felons, care not what an actor is so long as he is but vociferous and tears a passion to rags. If a fellow without sense or education can but bellow like a coster-monger, it is sufficient to please in that elegant locality.[19]

In 1850, however, Dickens uses the very first issue of *Household Words* to defend the theatres, and the Victoria in particular, arguing that theatregoing is beneficial for an uneducated audience:

Joe Whelks, of the New Cut, Lambeth, is not much of a reader, has no great store of books, no very commodious room to read in, no very decided inclination to read, and no power at all of presenting vividly before his mind's eye what he reads about. But, put Joe in the gallery of the Victoria Theatre; show him doors and windows in the scene that will open and shut, and that people can get in and out of; tell him a story with these aids, and by the help of live men and women dressed up, confiding to him their innermost secrets, in voices audible half a mile off; and Joe will unravel a story through all its entanglements, and sit there as long after midnight as you have anything left to show him. Accordingly, the Theatres to which Mr Whelks resorts, are always full; and whatever changes of fashion the drama knows elsewhere, it is always fashionable in the New Cut.[20]

By 1859, George Sala surprisingly describes Victoria's plays as 'highly healthful and beneficial',[21] and despite the adverse opinions, it is possible to attribute this positive change to the efforts of David Osbaldiston and Eliza Vincent, local actors who managed the theatre from 1841. Vincent was to play the lead parts in both *Susan Hopley*, the management's big success, and in Courtney's version of *Jane Eyre*. [22] Under Osbaldiston, the Victoria became famous for homely melodrama and (in his own words) 'the Representation of those Affecting Scenes of Real Life, which come so closely and so touchingly home to the Hearts of all'.[23] He

recognized that this playhouse stood in the middle of one of London's roughest and most squalid neighbourhoods. Its only hope of survival lay in giving a tough local public theatrical goods that had no pretensions of passing over their heads. [He] inaugurated a house policy that was at least consistent in that the theatre became known as the home of domestic melodrama (more properly melodramas of domestics) like *Susan Hopley*, or *The Vicissitudes of a Servant Girl* and *Mary Clifford, the Foundling Apprentice Girl*.[24]

---

[19]   Quoted in Booth, J., p. 54.

[20]   Dickens, p. 13.

[21]   Quoted in Davis and Emeljanow, p. 10.

[22]   After Osbaldiston's death in 1851, Vincent managed the theatre alone (Davis and Emeljanow, p. 36). Howard says Osbaldiston was manager '29.9.1843–7.1.1851' (Howard, p. 164). Osbaldiston was born in 1794; Vincent was born in 1815 and died, as Mrs Benjamin Crowther, in 1856 (Wearing).

[23]   Quoted in Booth, J., p. 49.

[24]   Roberts, p. 26.

Susan Hopley (1841), by G. Dibdin Pitt, was the play which established a reputation for Osbaldiston and Vincent, and its success explains the prominence of the servant characters in Courtney's *Jane Eyre.*

Jane Eyre was Osbaldiston's swan-song at the Vic, according to John Booth, who reports that it 'had good scenery and "some really excellent acting"'.[25] A unique copy of Osbaldiston's playbill survives in the New York Public Library (see Figures 1a and 1b). It shows that *Jane Eyre* was in a supporting role to 'The Great Pantomime of the Season [–] World of Wonders or Harlequin Caxton and the Origin of Printing', presenting 'The Abode of Stupidity', 'The Dominion of the Press', 'Shakspere's House' and so on. The scene painter and the maker of the stage machinery are given the same prominence as the playwright. Osbaldiston's playbills were 'long flimsy sheets with plenty of big black lettering',[26] and a former audience member recalls that

> however gingerly you handled those bills some of the black came off on you, and so it happened that when you wiped away a sympathetic tear with your finger you frequently left a black streak down your cheek. I once saw the audience turn out of the 'Old Vic' – after the performance of an old-fashioned drama of the weepy-weepy order, and the faces of the crowd were a study in black and white.[27]

These playbills were also famous for their detail and for their emotional exhortations. The playbill for *Susan Hopley* invited the audience to 'look around, and behold the moist tear of compassion, flowing from the o'ercharged heart. Who can restrain these, the best feelings of our nature, at the representation of such Domestic Woe?'[28] The large playbill for *Jane Eyre*, originally printed in red and black, gives not only an extended synopsis of the plot, but also exclamatory descriptions of the different scenes of the play, emphasizing the spectacle presented by grand rooms and broad landscapes, with quotations from the play and summaries of its moral dilemmas – 'Perilous Situation of Jane!'; 'A Night of Terror!!!'; 'The Struggle between Love and Duty!'.

Charles Kingsley described Osbaldiston's Old Vic as 'a licensed pit of darkness, a trap of temptation, profligacy and ruin, triumphantly yawning night after night', where prostitutes were freely allowed into the theatre, and Peter Roberts argues that 'in the light of these known facts, Osbaldiston's long-winded playbills', with their references to domestic virtue, 'positively radiate hypocrisy'.[29] Edwin Fagg, on the other hand, claims that 'the Vic became the recognized scapegoat in theatrical London for publicists who probably were never inside the theatre'.[30]

Fagg suggests that 'the domestic dramas were really one way of utilizing Miss

---

[25]   Booth, J., pp. 51–2.

[26]   Booth, J., p. 55.

[27]   George R. Sims, 'My Life' (1916), quoted in Booth, J., p. 55.

[28]   Quoted in Fagg, p. 85.

[29]   Roberts, pp. 26–7.

[30]   Fagg, p. 98.

Vincent'. Vincent, who played the part of Jane, had been on the stage since the age of eight[31] and was an actress of some repute. H. Barton Baker (1904) confirms that although the 'suburban minor theatres' such as the Victoria 'arose at a time when the histrionic art was a mere bundle of traditions and conventionalities', nevertheless many of their actors 'possessed considerable real dramatic power'. Miss Vincent, according to Baker, 'might have stood beside' the best West End performers.[32]

Reception of the Play

The Era predictably compares this *Jane Eyre* with Osbaldiston's great success, *Susan Hopley*, and also invokes the current scandal about 'the Yorkshire schools' by comparing Lowood School with 'Mr Squeers's establishment' (in *Nicholas Nickleby*). The review consists mostly of a summary of the plot, emphasizing that Rochester 'would have perished but for the exertions of his faithful servant Joe Joker'. It concludes that the play is 'certain to be attractive', since 'Miss Vincent as Jane, played well throughout, "The Heroine of Domestic Drama" having exactly the part to suit her; she displayed much feeling and good taste, and was loudly applauded'. Part of the 'attractiveness', however, is clearly of a lower kind: 'There is, of course, a comic underplot, in which Joe Joker and Betty Buner [sic] keep the house in a roar'.[33] This review suggests that the play was relatively successful, especially when compared with the attitudes of 'the most intelligent man' that Mayhew met among the costermongers, who said that 'love and murder suits us best, sir'; they liked tragedy, but 'the high words in a tragedy we call jaw-breakers, and say we can't tumble to that barrikin'.[34] Mayhew's conclusion is that 'the "Vic" gallery is not to be moved by sentiment', and he gives numerous examples to show that 'they prefer vigorous exercize to any emotional speech'.[35] Edwin Fagg, however, gives a long account of the staging and reception of *Susan Hopley* which suggests that the tastes of the audience did include sentiment.[36]

There is, alas, no record of the account written of Courtney's play for Charlotte Brontë herself by William Smith Williams, who had been a theatre critic before joining the firm of Smith, Elder and Co. (Charlotte's publishers), and offered to see the play and report on it to her. Charlotte speculates that

> A representation of 'Jane Eyre' at a Minor Theatre would no doubt be a rather afflicting spectacle to the author of that work: I suppose all would be wofully exaggerated and painfully vulgarized by the actors and actresses on such a stage. What – I cannot help asking myself – would they make of Mr Rochester? And the picture my fancy conjures up

---

31   Fagg, pp. 87, 100.
32   Baker, p. 354.
33   *Era*, 6 February 1848, p. 11.
34   Mayhew, Vol. 1, p. 15.
35   Mayhew, Vol. 1, p. 19.
36   Fagg, p. 86.

by way of reply is a somewhat humiliating one. What would they make of Jane Eyre? I see something very pert and very affected as an answer to that query.[37]

Although Williams's description of Courtney's *Jane Eyre* seems to be lost, we do have Charlotte's response to it. She said, 'you… have shewn me a glimpse of what I might call *loathsome*, but which I prefer calling *strange*. Such then is a sample of what amuses the Metropolitan populace! Such is a view of one of their haunts!'[38]

Distinctive Features of the Play

- There is an additional invented cast of comic servant characters and Betty Bunce has her virtue threatened by a comic, predatory shopman.
- The aristocrats, though mentioned, do not appear.
- Jane is a teacher at Lowood at the start; there is much emphasis on the scandal of school management.
- Coverage is fairly complete, including the Rivers family.
- The servant, Joe, rescues Rochester from the fire.
- Richard Mason runs mad at the end to provide a little business.
- Rochester's sight is restored.

---

[37] Smith, Vol. 2, p. 25.
[38] Smith, Vol. 2, p. 27.

Jane Eyre by John Courtney

Act I

Scene 1

Schoolroom

Betty Bunce discovered

Betty: Dear me, what a life is mine – servant of all work to a charity school – for the Lowood Institution, as they calls it, ain't no better than a charity school – £15 won't pay the board and teaching of they poor girls, so they makes the rest up by subscriptions and such like – poor things. I'm afraid most of our scholars are not sent to be edicated – they are sent out of the way by fathers and mothers that can't very well account for their being in the way – or else the poor things are orphans with cruel uncles and aunts who send them out of the way to be thumped, bumped and consumptionized – they none of them look half-fed and half-fed they are not either.

Enter Joe Joker

Betty: Well, Joe, how do you get on?

Joe: Not at all and it ain't very likely I shall, if I don't get out of this.

Betty: It's not very promising living here, is it?

Joe: You've heard of Buchan's Domestic Medicine haven't you? Well that tells you how to kill yourself without paying a doctor to do it; this is Domestic Transportation – visiting Botany Bay or Norfolk Island without crossing the herring pond.

Betty: What have you got there?

Joe: Oh this is the bread basket – here's slices, here's a breakfast for a growing girl after an hour's run in the grounds on a frosty morning, washed down too with a basin of burnt skilagilee.

Betty: Why it's horrid!

Joe: And yet Mr Naomi Brocklehurst, the manager and treasurer, calls himself a saint.

Betty: He's a tall, lanky, parchment-skinned, frowning old hunks.

Joe: I'll give warning – I can't stand it any longer. Look at this jacket and this waistcoat – would you believe that they were once a fit? They hang, Betty, and if I stay here another month I shall have to have a shirt covered with fish-hooks to hang em by. I shall cut the Lowood Institution – if I don't I shall die of domestic starvation – I shan't see the world. Therefore I'm determined to make a rush and get out before I go out like a rush light.   *(Exit)*

Betty: Hang me if I don't follow his example – what's £5 a year and no perquisites and half starved into the bargain? I like that Joe Joker – I wonder if he has ever thought of taking a wife? (*Bell*) Oh, there's the warning for breakfast and here comes the young girl Jane Eyre they made teacher of, because she had no friends to go to when she had done all her learning – good morning, Miss.

Enter Jane Eyre

Jane: Good morning. I see everything is ready.
Betty: Yes Miss, I've swept and dusted, and Jem has brought in the bread – Poor thing, how pale and serious she looks – ah, she has long borne a heavy heart.   (*Exit*)

Jane: Cold and chill, will my spirit bear on this bleak and cheerless fate? Infancy passed in a dull lethargy – girlhood encountering every day the frowns and scoffs of those who should have cherished and caressed me, and now womanhood dawns with a still darker prospect. Eight years have passed away since as a care-stricken child I quitted my aunt Reed for this place and from that hour, no friendly letter or inquiry has reached me – no mother's caress or father's kindly regard lives in my memory. I am as one dead to the world save that I live and move, for even my aunt sent with me evil reports, painted me in the blackest dye to Mr Brocklehurst. Oh, what hope have I but in flight – should my advertisement for a situation fail I must linger here till death shall end my suffering – they come – let me dry my tears.

Enter Schoolgirls – Miss Temple – Miss Scatchard

Miss Temple: Monitors, bring in the breakfast. (*The oldest girls bring in bowls and hand them round etc.*) Monitors, serve out the bread.
Girl: What horrible stuff!
Others: Dreadful!
Miss Scatchard: Silence, girls, or I'll report you to the Manager – how dare you, Miss, turn up your nose at such healthy and nourishing food!

Enter Betty

Betty: If you please, Miss Temple, Mr Naomi Brocklehurst is coming to visit the school – his carriage is at the door.
Miss Scatchard: Girls, finish your breakfast and prepare yourselves to greet your benefactor with propriety – teacher Jane Eyre, take your slate and note complaints with orders for amendment.

Enter Mr Brocklehurst

Brock:	Good morning, Miss Temple – why does that girl turn out her toes like a profane and unhallowed dancer? turn 'em in! Miss Scatchard! that girl in the dark hair squints – put her eye straight, Miss Scatchard!
Miss S:	She squinted when she came, sir.
Brock:	Nonsense, it's all obstinacy, I'll not allow squinting here, it's a wicked habit. You got the packet of thread I sent you, Miss Temple? It struck me it would be just the quality for the calico chemises and I sorted the needles to match – you shall have some darning needles next week – mind on no account give more than one to each girl and if they lose them correct them accordingly – and I wish the woollen stockings to be better looked to – I just now examined the clothes drying in the kitchen garden – there was a number of black hose in a very bad state and from the size of the hole I should say they hadn't seen a needle for a month!
Miss T:	They shall be looked to.
Brock:	Mind they are; and ma'am, the laundress tells me some of the girls have two tuckers in the week – it's too many by half, the rules don't allow of such extravagance – and there's another thing which really astonishes me, shocks me – I find in settling accounts with the housekeeper that a lunch consisting of bread and cheese has twice been served out to the girls during the past fortnight – it's a dangerous innovation on our rules.
Miss T:	I must be responsible for that – the breakfast was so ill prepared that the pupils could not possibly eat it, and I dared not allow them to remain fainting till dinner time.
Brock:	Madam, you will allow me to say, my plan in bringing up these girls, is to render them hardy, patient and self-denying, to encourage them to endure fortitude under temporary privations – madam, when you put bread and cheese into these children's mouths, you may indeed feed their bodies but you little think how you starve their immortal souls – and, Miss Temple, what is that girl with curled hair, curled – curled all over!
Miss :	It is Julia Severn.
Brock:	And why has she or any other girl curled hair?
Miss :	Her hair curls naturally.
Brock:	That girl's hair must be cut off entirely – I'll send a barber to-morrow – and I see others have the same excrescence – that tall girl, tell her to turn round – tell em all to turn round. (*Girls do – stifling laughter*) All those top-knots must be cut off.
Miss T:	Teacher, make a mem[orandum] of the aforesaid.

Jane has been lost in reverie – slate falls and is broken

Brock:	Abominable carelessness – Junior Teacher, stand forth – I have long had something to say to you – girls attend to me: teachers and pupils, you all see this young girl – would you believe it, the evil [one] has found a servant and an agent in her – you must shun her example, avoid her company – teachers, you must watch her, keep your eyes on her movements, weigh well all her words, scrutinize her actions, punish her body to save her soul – for I have it from her best of friends, her dear kind and loving aunt, that she is a liar. I learned it from her whose generosity she repaid so ill, that this good aunt was compelled to separate her from her own young ones – she has sent her here to be healed and teachers, girls, I beg you not to allow the waters to stagnate around her – do you see that, she has the audacity to shed tears – crocodile tears!
Miss T:	'Tis really dreadful, sir.
Brock:	It's abominable – Junior Teacher, stand where you are the whole day without food – we must mortify the spirit – let no one speak to her.
Jane:	I will not stand here, sir, as you desire!
Brock:	You won't? Miss Scatchard, do you hear that!
Miss S:	I do, sir, and weep to hear it.
Brock:	Why you ungrateful –
Jane:	Stay, sir!
Brock:	Silence, Miss –
Jane:	I will be heard, for my pent-up feelings must have vent. For eight years I have endured all that falls to the lot of the poor orphan girl, discarded by those that should protect her and cast upon the cold care of an unfeeling world – all that I could do in patience, suffering, industry and obedience to those above I have done. You sir, by the munificence of others, are placed here as our protector. Instead of kindness from you, I and those around me meet but scorn. In place of the bland smile and mild reproval for our errors we meet but your continuous frown, your determined opposition. Charity! Oh, 'tis a monstrous mockery of it, 'tis persecution upon the helpless and unprotected – and I tell you, sir, that you should blush to own such feelings as inhabit your cold and uncharitable heart.
Brock:	And dare you talk thus to your kind protector?
Jane:	I do, and tell you too that the time will come when those who dispense their wealth for the instruction of their poorer fellow beings will see more closely into the conduct of those into whose hands they place their trust.

Some of the girls express joy etc.

Brock:	Do you hear that, Miss Scatchard – put that girl with the curly hair upon the high stool.

Enter Joe Joker

Joe Joker:	I say, governor!
Brock:	Governor!
Joe:	I've come to give you warning for this day month – Oh, Miss Jane! What's the matter – crying?
Brock:	Don't approach that girl, sir.
Joe:	I shall if I like.
Brock:	Scoundrel!
Joe:	Holloa, I say, don't that come again –
Brock:	Dare you interfere with my authority?
Joe:	Yours or anybody else's if he don't know how to use it – here, Miss Jane, here's a letter for you.
Brock:	Here, coachman, John, come here and turn this scoundrel out!

Coachman and John enter

Joe:	Oh, that's your game is it! (*Business*)
Jane:	Nay, for my sake!
Brock:	Seize him, lock him up! (*Scuffle*)

Enter Betty Bunce

Betty	Stand off – if you lay hands upon him I'll lay this broom about your heads!
Jane:	Nay, Betty, Joseph! (*General bustle etc.*)

Scene 2

Apartment

Enter Miss Scatchard

Miss S:	What depravity – I must run for a constable – but I'm really so nervous that I can't go myself – here, Sally Suds, are you in the laundry?

Enter Sally Suds

Sally:	No miss I'm in the washus, and them gals do make their clothes so dirty I really must have more soap.
Miss S:	Never mind the soap now – put on your bonnet and run to Lowood for a constable – Joe Joker is murdering Mr Brocklehurst!
Sally:	That's just what I've long longed to see, for his stingy ways – he says soda is better than soap – let him try it, that's all – I call him old save-soap.

Miss S:	And you won't go for a constable?
Sally:	Not a bit of it, my place is in the washus – he's a prying cross old hunks, and I've sworn if he comes into the washus again I'll dab some suds in his face – he shall [have] soap enough for once – Joe has given him a whacking and I'll give him a lathering (*Exit*)
Miss S:	The house is turned upside down, and if I stay here much longer I shall be served the same. (*Exit*)

Enter Joe Joker

Joe:	Well I don't think old Brocklehurst will like to tackle Joe Joker again! Where are you going to, Betty?

Enter Betty

Betty:	To card my boxes, for I've discharged myself upon the spot.
Joe:	Betty, you are a trump, you stood up manfully in my defence! Where are you going?
Betty:	I don't care where I go so long as I go from here – Jane Eyre is going too.
Joe:	Where, poor girl?
Betty:	That letter you brought her from the post office was an answer to an advertisement she had put in the paper for a situation – it is a situation as governess at £25 a year, and Miss Temple asked Mr Brocklehurst to let her go and give her a recommendation.
Joe:	Which, of course, he gave her.
Betty:	He did, and was very glad to get rid of her, for fear his conduct to the poor girl should reach the ears of the subscribers – she goes in a few minutes as the coach comes by the gate.
Joe:	I wish her success – poor girl, she's alone in the world.
Betty:	So am I, it's very awkward, isn't it, Joseph?
Joe:	What makes you call me Joseph, my dear?
Betty:	What makes you call me my dear, Joseph?
Joe:	Why, I don't know, but there has been an imperceptible something creeping over me, ever since you came to defend me – I say, how is your book? – do you take the field or the favourite?
Betty:	I don't know what you mean, but I'd back you.
Joe:	Then I'm the favourite.
Betty:	You are my favourite.
Joe:	And you'd back me through life?
Betty:	That I would!
Joe:	Come to my arms!

Enter Beadle and Constable

Joe:	What do you want, old nob stick?
Beadle:	To take you up for an assault and battery of a worthy and respected man – constable, I charge you to aid and assist!
Const:	By virtue of my office and this here staff I does – prisoner, surrender!
Betty:	Now, Joseph! (*Business – Scuffle etc.*)
Beadle and Const:	Help, murder!
Betty:	Be quiet – here, this cupboard – no – the window – the cistern is beneath!
Joe:	Throw it up, Betty – they shall have a bath – now – out with you!
Both:	Mercy – murder!
Betty:	Silence! (*Business*)
Both outside:	Help, murder, robbery, drowning!
Joe:	Ha, ha – now, Betty, let's seek our fortunes together. (*Exeunt*)

Scene 3

Apartment in Thornfield Hall

Rochester discovered

Roch:	The night is rough, and the wind shakes the gables of these old towers I love. Thornfield [is] still my boyhood's home – and yet staying by the old beech trunk, a hag stood by me and with a loud laugh, exclaimed – 'Like it if you can, like it if you dare!' – [Perhaps] 'twas my bewildered brain that pictured the wild form – no- I will like, I dare like it!

Enter Mrs Fairfax and Jane Eyre

Mrs F:	Here is the new governess, Miss Eyre, sir.
Jane:	'Tis the gentleman whom I assisted when thrown from his horse just now on my journey hither.
Mrs F:	You expect your guests tonight, I believe, sir.
Roch:	Yes – let the governess approach me – you will not find your pupil, Miss Adèle, very bright – you come from –
Jane:	From Lowood school, sir.
Roch:	Ah, I know – a charitable concern – how long were you there?
Jane:	Eight years, sir.
Roch:	Eight years and not dead – I know you again – when you assisted me on my way here I thought by that face of yours that you had bewitched my horse to throw me – who were your parents?
Jane:	I have none.
Roch:	And your home?

Jane:	I have none.
Roch:	Where do your brothers and sisters live?
Jane:	I have no brothers or sisters.
Roch:	Who recommended you to come here?
Jane:	I advertised and Mrs Fairfax answered the advertisement.

Enter Sam

Sam:	Sir, your guests have arrived. Mrs Ingram and her daughter, Colonel Dent and –
Roch:	I'll go – Mrs Fairfax, you can stay here with Miss Eyre – now sir – (*Exit with servant*)

Jane:	Mr Rochester seems very abrupt.
Mrs F:	No doubt he appears so to you. He has enough to harass him – family troubles – he lost his elder brother a few years since.
Jane:	Was he so fond of his brother, as to be still inconsolable for his loss?
Mrs F:	Oh no, perhaps not – for he prejudiced his father against Mr Rochester to keep the estate wholly in his hands – so they both contrived to bring our master into a painful position, as he calls it, for the sake of making his fortune abroad. He brought the little girl Adèle with him from abroad – who she is I cannot tell you. I don't think he has resided at Thornfield a fortnight together since the death of his brother, and indeed I do not wonder he shuns the old place.
Jane:	Why should he shun it?
Mrs F:	Why – because – come now – I must not talk any more or perhaps I may be saying too much. I must run and see after the lady guests – you can stay here till I return. (*Exit*)
Jane:	I feel a thrill of fear, spite of the appearance of wealth and comfort that surrounds me. (*A distant scream and wild laugh*) Great heaven, what was that – what can it mean? This old house, the woman's mystery, the master's strange manner – he is here!

Enter Rochester

Roch:	So, now I have played the part of a good host, put my guests into the way of amusing each other; I am at liberty to attend to my own pleasures. Miss Eyre, draw a chair and sit by me. Now look at me – do think me handsome?
Jane:	No, sir.
Roch:	Well – that's plain and blunt! What fault do you find with me – do you think me stern and unforgiving?
Jane:	Oh sir, far from it – that face bespeaks kindness I am sure.

| Roch: | But I am not kind – time and circumstances make us other than we would or should be. When I was your age I was kindly and feeling, but fortune has knocked me up and down since then. Ah, I might have been other than I am, I might have been as good as you, wiser, and almost as stainless. |

Noise and enter Sam

Roch:	What now, sir?
Sam:	A stranger sir – a rough weather-worn looking man, has demanded entrance and is now sitting amongst your guests in the drawing room.
Roch:	A stranger?
Sam:	To me sir, but he said he had known you long.
Roch:	His name?
Sam:	He said he'd tell that to you – he comes, I think I heard him say, from Spanish Town in the West Indies.
Roch:	Ha! should it be – go sir, I'll be with him soon – the West Indies –
Jane:	You are ill, sir – take my hand.
Roch:	Oh! this blow!
Jane:	Lean on me, sir.
Roch:	Jane, you offered me your hand, let me have it now. My little friend, would I were in a quiet island but with you and all trouble and hideous recollection banished from me.
Jane:	Can I help you, sir – oh tell me how and with my life –
Roch:	Jane, I have guests in the drawing room waiting my presence – were they all to spurn me, what would you do? Were they to leave me one by one, what would you do?
Jane:	Remain more firmly by you, sir.
Roch:	To comfort me?
Jane:	Yes, sir, to comfort you.
Roch:	Could you dare censure for my sake?
Jane:	For any friends who merited my just regards, as I am sure you do now.
Mason (without):	Don't tell me – I'll stay no longer – I must and will see him!
Roch:	That voice!

Enter Mason

| Mason: | So, old friend, we meet again. |
| Roch: | 'Tis he and all is over. (*A loud scream and wild laugh – picture*) |

Scene 4

Corridor

Enter Sam

Sam:	Well, this is a mysterious affair – this stranger has forced his way into Mr Rochester's presence, and there has been the deuce to pay in the drawing room – there's something very mysterious about our master.

Enter Mrs Fairfax

Mrs F:	Sam, the gentlemen are all waiting to be conducted to their rooms.
Sam:	Very well – this is a strange affair, Mrs Fairfax, with this mysterious stranger.
Mrs F:	It's very mysterious that you can't mind your own business.
Sam:	Mrs F, you are a crabbed old Guy as knows nothing and won't be teached. (*Exit*)

Enter Jane Eyre

Mrs F:	Has Mr Rochester recovered his alarm?
Jane:	He has, ma'am, and I believe has conducted the stranger to a sleeping apartment.
Mrs F:	What – does he stay here?
Jane:	Oh yes, I heard him say he came to visit Thornfield for some weeks. Tell me, pray pardon me the question, but twice tonight have I heard a wild scream that made me thrill with fear!
Mrs F:	You must not heed that, 'tis merely the loud laugh of a vulgar woman who is kept here for needle-work in the upper part of the mansion. There is no harm in her but it sounds – by the bye here she comes.

Enter Grace Poole

Mrs F:	Well, Grace, have you got your supper beer?
Grace:	Yes.
Mrs F:	Oh, Mrs Grace – I hope you will restrain that loud laugh of yours – it sounds so through the old galleries, that people imagine it some fiend's rather a woman's.
Grace:	I can't help it sounding – people must laugh sometimes – or the devil's in it. (*Exit*)
Jane:	A strange creature – why does Mr Rochester employ so odd a person?
Mrs F:	She is useful and gets through a deal of work, but I must to the guests

	to see to their rooms – you doubtless are tired and ready for bed – you know your room, good night.　　　　　　　　　　　　　(*Exit*)
Jane:	Good night – What airy vision floats around me? – in a short time a world has passed before me of hopes and fears surely never to be realized – oh no, kindly as Mr Rochester spoke to me, I am still his servant, no more – why then does his vision haunt me – and then the mystery of this stranger, his pallid cheek on his appearance. Then his questions to me – what can it mean – I am alone – I hear nothing but the footfalls of those who are retiring to rest. I seem spell-bound by a strange fear. (*Laugh and shriek*) Oh, let me fly to my room and there offer up my orphan prayer to him who ever shields the lone and unprotected!

Scene 5

Gallery – Stairs leading off R and L to sleeping rooms

Enter Sam

Sam:	Well, I have shown the people to their rooms and now I'll show myself to my room – there's something uncommon mysterious about Master and his friend – eh, here come Master and his friend – I'll watch. (*Hides*)

Enter Rochester and Mason

Roch:	Now we understand each other – you will not blab?
Mason:	Oh no – she is safe, you say?
Roch:	Perfectly, and attended to with care.
Mason:	'Tis well, now show me to my room.
Roch:	This way.　　　　　　　　　　　　　　　　　　　　(*Exeunt*)

Sam comes down

Sam:	Now what the devil can I make out of that? (*Shriek*) Oh lord, oh dear, I've lost all my curiosity, I don't want to know what that is!
	(*Exit*)

A tall female appears, above in the gallery, with dark hair, hanging loose behind, in a white dress. She makes various gesticulations – looks from landing on to stage – feels along wall as for an entrance then passes off – when off, shriek and laugh heard.

Enter Jane

Jane:	Heavens, that shriek, it seemed at my very door, what can it be – again! (*Noise*)

Mason (without): Help – help – save me, save me!
Jane: My fears are true – there is murder doing!
Mason: Rochester – Rochester, come to me for heaven's sake!
Jane: Ha, I must give the alarm – help, help – murder is doing! Help, I say!

The figure rushes along gallery – unseen by Jane, with shriek. Enter Guests.

All: What is the matter?
Jane: There is murder doing – there!
All: What murder?

Mason runs on from entrance in gallery – wounded.

Mason: Help me – save me – Rochester, where are you?
Roch (following): Here – here, Mason!
Mason: I am dying, murdered by – *(falls)*.
All: By whom?

Rochester, to Jane, places his finger to his lips as if to entreat silence. Wild shrieks and laughter.

Tableau
End of Act I

Act II

Scene 1

Room in Thornfield Hall

Mason discovered faint and pale in a chair – Carter binding up his arm – Rochester and Jane Eyre by him

Roch: Now, my good fellow, how are you?
Mason: She's done for me, I fear.
Roch: Not a whit – in a few days you'll not be any the worse for it – Carter, assure him there's no danger.
Carter: I can do that conscientiously – only I wish I had got here sooner, he would not have lost so much blood – the flesh on the shoulder is torn as well as cut, the wound was not done by a knife but by teeth.
Mason: She bit me, worried like a tigress!
Roch: You should have grappled with her.
Mason: She said she'd drain my heart.

Roch:	Be silent – you will soon be out of the country – when you are in Spanish Town, you may think of her as dead, or rather you need not think of her at all.
Mason:	Impossible to forget last night.
Roch:	Pshaw, have some energy, man. There, Carter has done with you. Jane, was anyone stirring just now, when I sent you to my room?
Jane:	No sir, all was still.
Roch:	Now get on your feet – come, try! Carter, take him under the other shoulder – be of good cheer, Richard, step out – Jane, place the cloak around him.
Mason:	I do feel better.
Roch:	I am sure you do. Now, Jane, unbolt that side door leading to back stairs and if you hear anyone about, come to the foot of the stairs and call. Now, Mason, we'll hand you to the chaise – take care of him, Carter, and keep him at your house till he is quite well – goodbye, Dick!
Mason:	One word – let her be taken care of, let her be treated tenderly, let her –
Roch:	I do my best, have done it, and will do it. (*Exeunt*)
Jane:	What am I to think? Mr Rochester, to pacify his guests, said it was a mere dream and they retired – the female they speak of and who inflicted this wound, who and what can she be, and why was I employed by Mr Rochester to assist the night through in such a mystery? – he returns, I will to my room.

Enter Rochester

Roch:	Would to heaven there was an end of this – Jane!
Jane:	Sir?
Roch:	You have passed a strange night and you look pale – very pale. Were you afraid when I left you alone with Mason?
Jane:	I was afraid of some one coming out of the inner room, sir.
Roch:	Ah – but I had fastened the door, I should have been a careless shepherd if I had left a lamb so near a wolfish den unguarded.
Jane:	Will the strange woman, Grace Poole, live here still, sir?
Roch:	Yes, yes, have no fear of her.
Jane:	Yet your life is hardly safe while she stays – this Mason too.
Roch:	He would not willingly injure me – ever since I have known him I have had but to say, do that, and the thing has been done – Jane, you are my little friend?
Jane:	I like to serve you, sir, in all that is right.
Roch:	Jane, listen, you have power over me and might injure me, yet dare I not shew you where I am vulnerable, lest faithful and friendly as you are, you bring me on to ruin.

Jane:	Oh sir, this pains me – I would not be inquisitive, and should not seek to learn the secrets of my master – still the confidence you have placed in me this night emboldens me to ask – can I by any means, consistent with my sex, my station, or my means, relieve your griefs? for heavy they are, I can see.
Roch:	Look at me and tell me, are you at ease – not fearing that I err in detaining you, or that you err in listening to me?
Jane:	I do not fear.
Roch:	Picture to yourself a well reared boy, but wild from childhood upward, then place him in a foreign land committing error – no matter of what nature – mark, I say not crime, I speak not of shedding blood – I speak of error, through which hope quits him. He wanders here and there seeking rest in exile, searching for happiness in pleasure, such pleasure as blights all feeling and makes the heart a sepulchre. Soul-withered he returns – after years of banishment he meets a being fair without soil or taint – he feels better days come back, his mind fills with purer thoughts. Tell me, is the wandering and sinful but now rest-seeking and repentant man justified in overleaping custom, in daring the world's opinion, to attach to him forever this gentle, gracious, genial stranger?
Jane:	Oh sir, 'tis impossible for me, a simple girl, to answer. A wanderer's repose or a sinner's reformation depends not upon his fellow-creature, he should look higher for strength to amend and for solace to heal.
Roch:	Jane, I have been a wordly, dissipated, restless – but no crime-stained man, yet I believe I have found the instrument of my cure in –
Jane:	What, sir?
Roch:	You – you do not curse me.
Jane:	Sir – I – no sir.
Roch:	Your hand in confirmation thereof – oh memory, memory *(rushes out)*.
Jane:	He suffers heavily – has error led so near to crime as to – Oh no, let me at least hope that his soul is without stain.

Enter Joe Joker and Sam

Sam:	Now you really can't come in here.
Joe:	Oh, humbug!
Jane:	Is that you Joseph?
Joe:	Eh – Ah I said I was right, how do you do Miss Jane, Miss Temple told me where you had come to, and I came here on purpose, to see you, but this chap told me I mustn't come in.
Sam:	We ain't none on us allowed no followers.
Joe:	If his conduct to you, Miss Jane, requires licking into shape, I'm the man.
Sam:	Vulgar wretch *(aside and exit)*.

Jane: I'm very glad to see you, Joseph, but what brought you here so soon?

Joe: Why, they sent the beadle and constable after me – however, with Betty's assistance, I pitched em both into the water-butt – after that we thought it best to take to our legs and off we came together.

Jane: And where is Betty?

Joe: She's got a place in the little Town of Millcote close by, and I'm not perticlar, anything so long as it's honest. You see, Miss, a chap must not be too precise as has got no more independence than an independent spirit – but still I'm independent of father, mother, or relations, for I never knowed any of em, it seems to me I comed up all on a sudden – I never could make how it was, well hunger soon sharpened my wits and I got a job and it got me something to eat. From getting jobs I got a place, and from one place to another I got at last to old Brocklehurst's and if I hadn't dropped his acquaintance I should soon have dropped into my grave, for he starved body and smalls.

Jane: We have both need to thank the chance that sent us from such a home – come, you will breakfast with me – Mrs Fairfax will be glad to entertain one who, like you, has befriended me.

Joe: Do you mean, Miss, to introduce me as an acquaintance with such clothes as these – look at my jacket!

Jane: I introduce you, not your attire – 'tis your heart I estimate, your clothes I heed not – come.

Joe: Well I never!   (*Exeunt*)

Scene 2

Room at Mr Jehediah Piper's

Enter Betty Bunce

Betty: Well, this is lucky, that as I got here I should get a place, and a very nice place too – nobody to attend to but the old gentleman and his shopman – he seems such a nice man, rather precise – I don't much like his not allowing any followers – oh, here he comes.

Enter Jehediah Piper

Piper: Now, my good girl, hear me, you are not aware of the onerous duties you have to perform here – in the first place my name is Jehediah Piper.

Betty: Yes sir, Jeddedidah Piper.

Piper: No, girl, Je-he-diah Piper, mark that.

Betty: Jee-he-di-ah – now I've got it – Mr Jee-hee-diah Piper.

Piper: Now there are two Pipers in this town – now Betty, mark me – we the two Pipers are of the same business, Grocers, Mealmen and Corn chandlers, and strange as it may appear we never can agree.

Betty:	Two of a trade never can.
Piper:	Betty, the other Piper's a scoundrel, for he not only set up in business against me, but succeeded, by scandal, to blacken my character and ruin my fortunes – by marrying the very lady I had intended to make an offer of my hand to, and how do you think he accomplished his base purpose Betty?
Betty:	I can't tell sir.
Piper:	I had a little shop-boy, an active, smart little fellow, no-one in the world to protect him but me, and the black-hearted villain informed the lady that this little boy – was a young Piper.
Betty:	La sir, and did she believe it? I'm sure I shouldn't, to look at you.
Piper:	It so happened, heaven knows how, but the poor boy did resemble me. From that hour the lady dropped my acquaintance and in a month became the wife of my mortal enemy. But I'll be revenged – he puts up for church-warden, so do I – I'll swamp him. I've made every voter dead drunk three times a week for this month past and I'll be at the head of the poll – he shall sneak home like a dog with a tin kettle to his tail.
Betty:	Well, sir, I wish you may get it.
Piper:	I will get it. Now, Betty, during my absence let the house be full of propriety for the least impropriety here would be my ruin should my enemies get hold of it.

Enter Tom

Tom:	Please sir, the voters with the boards is ready and the drummer too.
Piper:	Let them come in and we'll march to the Poll together.
Tom:	You must come in.

Enter two or three queer-looking fellows – each bearing a board with a placard written on

Piper:	Welcome, my friends – drummer, do you proceed before – can you play 'See the conquering hero comes'?
Drummer:	Yes, sir, but we never plays that till we wins.
Piper:	Damn it, sir, I'm sure to win, so play away – now march!
	(*Exeunt*)
Betty:	Ha ha, so you are a nice old gentleman to allow no followers –

Enter Joe

Betty:	Eh, what, I ought to know you, why what have you been about and where did you get that dress?
Joe:	I'm a gentleman's coachman now, Betty.

Betty:	But whose coachman are you?
Joe:	The gentleman's as keeps the house where Jane Eyre lives – I breakfasted with her and as he wanted a coachman, Jane popped the question, and I was coated, hired and breeched.
Betty:	Well, I declare, this is double luck, but you know I mustn't have anyone to visit me here.
Joe:	Oh yes, you must, besides I've had news of Daddy Piper, that rather raises my bilious apprehensions – I called at the Pig and Lollypop to wet my new livery and the first thing I heard was 'So old daddy Piper has got another new maid, poor thing'.
Betty:	What did they mean by poor thing?
Joe:	Ah, that's what I opened my eyes about, but I was soon satisfied for they said he never had a new maid but in a very short time he had a new young piper.
Betty:	Why, the old villain! (*Noise etc.*) Hark, what's that? why it's Mr Piper with a lot of people pelting him – you can't stay here.
Joe:	But I will!
Betty:	Nonsense, don't be silly, here he comes – here, get into this closet.
Joe:	Why, it's full of flour sacks, I shall spoil my new livery.
Betty:	Go in. (*Noise*)

Enter Piper

Piper:	Defeated, outvoted, by the very scoundrels I had swilled to their throats, the same scoundrels too would have bonnetted my brains out if I hadn't taken to my heels – I can never hold up my head again. Is that you, Betty?
Betty:	Yes, sir, how have you got on?
Piper:	My enemy has triumphed, he is churchwarden and I am nobody.
Betty:	Well sir, don't fret.
Piper:	Go to that cupboard, you'll find a bottle of brandy – give me a glass – another, thank you, come here, my dear.
Joe:	His dear.
Piper:	You pity me, don't you, Betty?
Betty:	I do, sir.
Piper:	Come and sit by me, Betty – you are sure you have no followers? I saw an ugly fellow dressed like a coachman looking at the house as I went out.
Betty:	I don't know any coachman, sir.
Piper:	That's dear Betty – ah, you don't know what I felt when I first saw you – Oh, Betty, take pity on your wretched master, let me have one faithful heart to repose upon – smile upon him – oh, Betty, suffer him to take (*about to kiss her*)
Betty:	That (*a slap*).

Piper: Oh!
Joe (from cupboard): And that as a plaister, Daddy Piper (*throws flour*).

Noise etc. – Piper's party enter with their placards torn and followed by successful party

Piper: Murder, thieves, robbery – Tom – Tom!

Enter Tom

Tom: Here I am, master!
Mob: One cheer more and a groan for Daddy Piper! (*Business. General confusion*)

Scene closes

Scene 3

Room in the Hall

Enter Jane Eyre

Jane: How happy it has made me to be enabled to serve my good old Joe. Strange the kind interest my master takes in me. Oh, he has suffered much. How is it that I, a poor girl, a creature of his bounty, should feel his equal – I do so spite of myself – it is the confidence his kindness gives to me – to own it other, would be imprudence, nay madness.

Enter Rochester

Roch: Jane.
Jane: Sir, I beg pardon, I did not see you.
Roch: No matter, how like you this house?
Jane: Oh sir –
Roch: Your pupil, little Adèle, Mrs Fairfax, how feel you towards them?
Jane: I can but love them sir – I have an affection for all here.
Roch: For all, Jane?
Jane: For all my equals, and respect for those above me.
Roch: You would be sorry to part with them?
Jane: I should indeed.
Roch: Yes, 'tis this life's curse, no sooner do we find a resting place than some harsh voice calls aloud – arise and begone!
Jane: Must I begone, sir?
Roch: I fear you must.

Jane: Well sir, I shall be ready when you say the word.

Roch: Rumour no doubt has reached you that I'm about to be married?

Jane: The lady I have heard named sir – your visitor, Miss Ingram.

Roch: Yes – Adèle must go to school, and you must get another situation. In about a month I hope to become a bridegroom and in the interim I shall seek another asylum for you, I think in Ireland.

Jane: Ireland – 'tis a long way, sir – and then the sea is a barrier.

Roch: From what Jane?

Jane: From England and from Thornfield – and –

Roch: Well?

Jane: From you, sir – What have I said? – It is a long way, sir.

Roch: It is. I am sorry to send my little friend on such weary travels, but if I can't do better, how is it to be helped? – are you anything akin to me, think you Jane?

Jane: I cannot speak or answer him.

Roch: Because I sometimes have a strange feeling with regard to you, especially when you are near me as now. And if that boisterous channel and two hundred miles of land or so come between us I'm afraid that you'd forget me.

Jane: That I never should – Oh, that I had never seen Thornfield!

Roch: Because you are sorry to leave it?

Jane: Yes, because in it I have received the only kindness in my unhappy life – the necessity of departure is like looking on the necessity of death.

Roch: Where is the necessity?

Jane: You, sir, have placed it before me, in Miss Ingram, your bride.

Roch: I have no bride.

Jane: But you will have.

Roch: Yes – I will –

Jane: Then I must go – you have said it yourself.

Roch: No you must stay. I swear it and the oath shall be kept.

Jane: Oh sir, do you think I can stay to become nothing to you? Think you because poor, I am soulless, heartless? – I have as much heart as yourself and had fate graced me with wealth and beauty – I should have made it as hard for you to leave me, as 'tis now hard for me to leave you – forgive my boldness, but 'tis my spirit that addresses your spirit – as if both had passed through the grave and stood in heaven equal – as we are!

Roch: As we are indeed, Jane.

Jane: And yet not so, for you are going to wed one inferior to you, one with whom you have no sympathy, one whom you love not – I would scorn such a union – therefore I am better than you – let me go to Ireland.

Roch: Jane, be still, don't struggle like a wild frantic bird, rending its own plumage!

Jane: I am no bird, and no net ensnares me – my will is free, which I now exert to leave you.

Roch: And your will shall decide your destiny – I offer you my hand, my heart, the share of all I possess.

Jane: Your bride stands between us.

Roch: Jane, will you marry me? – you doubt me – have not faith in me.

Jane: No.

Roch: What love have I for Miss Ingram? none – what love has she for me? none. I caused a rumour to be whispered this morning that my fortune was not a third of what was supposed – in an hour her mother and herself quitted the hall – I could not, would not marry Miss Ingram. You – you I love – you, poor, obscure and friendless as you are – I entreat to accept me as your husband.

Jane: What, I? – do you truly love me, a poor mean girl – do you sincerely wish me to become your wife?

Roch: I do – I swear it.

Jane: Then I will marry you.

Roch: My wife!

Jane: My dear husband! (*They embrace*)

Enter Mrs Fairfax

Mrs F: Gracious me –

Roch: What is the woman staring at – Mrs Fairfax!

Mrs F: Sir.

Roch: Behold my future wife – I have proposed, she has accepted, we marry tomorrow.

Mrs F: Tomorrow – the man's moonstruck!

Roch: But why this sudden surprise – why came you here?

Mrs F: To tell you that Colonel Dent and your friends are waiting to take their leave.

Roch: Ah, they've heard the rumour of my poverty – I come – Jane, I shall not be long – till then, adieu, bless you.   (*Exit*)

Mrs F: Ahem – I feel so astonished, I hardly know what to say to you, Miss Eyre. Mr Rochester has asked you to marry him, I think I heard him say so.

Jane: He did.

Mrs F: How it will answer I cannot tell – he might almost be your father. Is it really for love he's going to marry you?

Jane: Mrs Fairfax!

Mrs F: I hope all will be right in the end, but you cannot be too careful, believe me – keep Mr Rochester at a distance – distrust yourself as well as him. Gentlemen in his station are not accustomed to marry governesses – there, dry your eyes – heaven grant it may all happen for the best. (*Exit*)

Jane: Kind creature – yet how her very kindness chills my heart – why should
               he wed me as she says, a poor lone one – yet why should he not – may he
               not feel as I do? – I see that he has suffered – that his heart has throbbed
               for happiness in vain as mine has – may I not then be the ministering
               agent of his future happiness? Oh, let me chase away sad forebodings
               – he comes!

Enter Rochester

Roch: Halloa, what's the matter? – come, on with your bonnet, I have ordered
               the carriage, we'll be off to Millcote – buy your wedding array and
               tomorrow be married.
Jane: Oh pray, sir, let not such haste –
Roch: Pshaw, never let a good mind cool – come, put on your bonnet, take my
               arm – we'll have a love stroll to Millcote and buy the wedding dress
               and the ring too – don't blush, there's nothing to be ashamed of, come
               my future little wife.   (*Exeunt*)

Scene 4

Outside Stabling

Enter Joe Joker

Joe: Well I'm jiggered if I ain't raising like a balloon – here's Miss Jane
               Eyre going to be Mrs Rochester and Betty's to be her maid – we are
               all to go to London together and then to France and foreign parts and
               I'm to drive em all the way!

Enter Dick Nisi

Dick: Oh, Joseph Joker, I believe?
Joe: Yes, that's my name.
Dick: Ah then, I have the very unpleasant duty to serve you with a writ of
               action and for assault of battery [sic] against her majesty's liege subject
               Jehediah Piper of Millcote to wit, take notice therefrom and appear in
               person.
Joe: Well, what's this bit of paper about? am I to go and wallop him
               again?
Dick: Very good – assault admitted to plaintiff's attorney – you'd better
               employ an attorney, for if this action goes against you, and as you have
               admitted the fact it's sure to do, the damages will be heavy.
Joe: What fact?

Dick:	Why, throwing two handsfull of flour into the face of our worthy client Mr Piper.
Joe:	To be sure I did and I'll smother him next time.
Dick:	Very good (*writes*) 'Life in Danger' – 'threat of murder'.
Joe:	What's all this about?
Dick:	That you stand in danger of being cast in heavy damages for your treatment of the gentleman aforesaid – we have witnesses, which makes our action safe.
Joe:	And if I pitch into a chap and nobody sees me do it, how do I stand then?
Dick:	No writ of action without witnesses – can't succeed.
Joe:	Then I should be in no danger.
Dick:	Unfortunately not sir.
Joe:	Then I'll have my fun out of you at once! (*Lashes him with whip*) Now dance to the rogue's march!
Dick:	Oh Lord, murder!
Joe:	Off you go! (*He runs off*) I say, old chap, my compliments to Daddy Piper! (*Exit*)

Scene 5

Sleeping Chamber

Jane and Betty discovered

Betty:	What beautiful things, to be sure, and Mr Rochester bought all these!
Jane:	Yes, and I had trouble in preventing him buying everything in the shop. I'll place the things on this chair that I may look on them the moment I awake.
Betty:	I should take em to bed with me!
Jane:	I am not so silly as that – why, the sun has risen, how these summer nights pass. Well, Betty, this will be our wedding day – he will have it so and I can't deny him.
Betty:	La, no – I shouldn't attempt it for my part!
Jane:	Well, then, I'll say goodnight to you. You must be stirring early.
Betty:	Do you think I could lie abed when there was a wedding on? Why, I shan't sleep a wink, I know, for thinking of it. (*Exit*)
Jane:	Now to rest – oh, what a change from the unprotected orphan girl to the mistress of this mansion – a wife too of one so far above me that my head turns dizzy at the thought – oh, I shall be so happy (*the laugh heard*) ha! that laugh again – oh, that horrid Grace Poole, her laugh is unearthly and at such times too – just as one feels so happy – I'll throw myself upon the bed, a few moments may recover me. Angels protect and guard me. (*Goes to bed and sleep*)

*Bustle – Laugh – Closet door opens and the woman appears stealthily and wildly
surveying the room*

Jane (awakens): Oh, what a fearful dream. I thought too I heard a noise as of some
one in the room. (*Rises*) Betty, is that you, no – yet the rustling I thought
was here. (*Bustle – sees the woman*) Oh heaven! (*Tries to fly but is
intercepted*) Help me, heaven, help – save – sa – sa (*falls*).

The wild woman laughs loudly as the scene closes

Scene 6

The Grounds

Enter Joe Joker

Joe: I think this is doing it with all these white favors, they are all getting
up and in the bustle I see here's my Betty.

Enter Betty

Betty: Well, Joe, you are like me, up and dressed for the wedding.
Joe: Yes and when I got these favors about me I felt as though I should like
to have had a wife myself.
Betty: Ah, that can't be yet, we have no money.

Enter Sam

Sam: Mr Joseph, you are to get the carriage, Mr Rochester and his bride are
nearly ready – Miss Betty, master says how you are to dress yourself
as you are to be bridesmaid.
Betty: Me – bridesmaid!
Sam: Yes, them's his orders.   (*Exit*)
Betty: What do you think of that!
Joe: It stuns me – give me a kiss before you go.
Betty: That I will. (*Does so and Exit*)
Joe: That's nice – I wish old Brocklehurst could see me now!   (*Exit*)

Enter Rochester and Jane
Roch: Come, Jane, look up – I'll explain to you this vision – it was half dream
half reality – a woman did, I doubt not, enter the room and that woman
was Grace Poole – you call her a strange being and not without reason.
You will ask me why I keep such a woman in my house. When we have
been married a year and a day, I'll tell you – are you satisfied?

Jane:	I must perforce be on your assurance – but indeed the sight was dreadful.
Roch:	Cheer up – we shall be away shortly from this dull home amidst gayer scenes where you will laugh at these sad fancies.

Enter Sam

Sam:	The carriage is ready, sir.
Roch:	We come. (*Exit Sam*) Now Jane, from this hour my wife! (*Exeunt*)

Scene 7

Outside of Village Church

Enter Briggs

Briggs:	So our information is correct – the clergyman is robed and ready and the clerk stands by him. 'Tis well – I must inform him – ha! carriage – the wedding party. (*Exit*)

Enter Rochester, Jane Eyre, Betty and Sam followed by a few country people

Roch:	Come, let us hasten in. I hate this vulgar gaze – what is the matter?
Jane:	A cold fear, a strange presentiment seems to arrest my steps – the dream of last night – that wild woman standing as a barrier to our union!
Roch:	Pshaw – we are at the church porch, where no impediment can stay our happiness – come – (*going off*).

Enter Briggs

Briggs:	Stay! I forbid this marriage!
Roch:	You – fool, stand by!
Briggs:	Proud man – your wife still lives, I have a witness who can prove it.
Roch:	Liar – produce him!
Briggs:	He is here. (*Enter Mason*)
Roch:	Mason.
Mason:	I affirm that that man is the husband of my sister Bertha Antoinette Mason and that she is now living at Thornfield Hall. (*Jane falls*)
Roch:	Villain, Traitor, reptile! (*flies at Mason – Bustle*) Ha ha ha, devils – foiled – her curse is on me!

Tableau
End of Act 2

Act 3

Scene 1

Chamber

Jane Eyre and Betty discovered

Betty:	Now do, Miss Jane, look up – you have sat here the whole day alone and without food, I cannot bear to see you thus.
Jane:	I care not for myself, it is for him, dire calamity has struck a noble soul and truly do I pity him – leave me, Betty, I am better when alone.
Betty:	Ring if you want me – oh dear – I don't know how Joe may turn out, but I don't long half so much to be married as I did.

(Exit)

Jane:	Shall I fly from Thornfield at once, since I have wakened from this dream and found all void and vain? – ah, I can bear that – but to quit him, the only one who ever tendered me the hand of kindness – yet reason, conscience tell me that I should – must!

Enter Rochester

Roch:	Jane, I never meant to wound you thus. Oh, I know I am the husband of Bertha Mason and you are changed – Jane, listen to me – did you not know that I was not the elder son, and that my father was an avaricious grasping man?
Jane:	Mrs Fairfax, sir, informed me so.
Roch:	That father had resolved to give my elder brother the whole of his property – yet his imperious spirit could not see me poor. I must therefore be provided for by a wealthy marriage – accordingly I was married to the daughter of a rich planter of Spanish Town – fool that I was, her mother I had never seen, thought she was dead – my marriage over, I learned the truth, she was a maniac – there was a younger brother too, dumb and an idiot. My wife gave signs of incipient madness. I strove to repress the antipathy I felt towards her, but all in vain. Her malady increased with fearful rapidity, her vices sprang up fast and rank – how horrid were the curses they entailed upon me! Bertha Mason, the true daughter of an infamous mother, dragged me through all the hideous and degrading agonies which must attend a man bound to a wife at once intemperate and unchaste.
Jane:	Pray sir, calm yourself!
Roch:	Jane, for four years I suffered these agonies – I stood on the verge of despair – a broken-hearted, hopeless man. My father and my brother, who died soon after this fatal marriage, had not made it known to my

friends in England, to which country we soon sailed. Oh, 'twas a fearful voyage – she became a raving monster! I arrived at Thornfield, had her safely lodged in the third story and hired Grace Poole to tend her – she and Carter the surgeon who dressed Mason's wounds are the only two I have ever admitted to my confidence. Grace has been a good keeper but my wife is cunning and will sometimes elude her vigilance and commit those wild acts that become dangerous to my repose and safety. You have heard my story – do you pity me?

Jane:	From my soul!
Roch:	I felt assured you would. Oh, Jane you are my better angel – it was because I felt and knew your heart that I resolved to marry you, that I asked you to accept my pledge of fidelity and to give me yours. Say then, you will be mine?
Jane:	Sir –
Roch:	Jane, mean you go one way in the world and to suffer me to go another?
Jane:	I do.
Roch:	Would it then be sinful to love me?
Jane:	It would be sinful to obey you, sir.
Roch:	Jane, give one glance to my wretched life when you are gone. What then is left me – where shall I look for hope?
Jane:	Where I do – there!
Roch:	Then you will not yield?
Jane:	No.
Roch:	You condemn me to live wretched and die accu[r]sed!
Jane:	I advise you to live sinless and to die tranquil.
Roch:	Pshaw! 'tis false pride, fear of others – who in the world cares for you or will be injured by what you do?
Jane:	I care, sir, for myself – that moral principle that sustained me when a poor friendless child is all I have at this hour to stand by and there I plant my foot.
Roch:	You will leave me, Jane?
Jane:	Yes – heaven bless you, my dear master, and keep you from harm – and still reward you for past kindness to me.
Roch:	Jane –
Jane:	Farewell – farewell for ever! (*Rushes out*)
Roch:	Jane – Jane Eyre – oh lost – lost! (*Staggers back*)

Scene closes

Scene 2

Outside of Thornfield Hall

Enter Jane Eyre

Jane: I must fly temptation, even as the spirit bending over me last night instructed me, 'Daughter, fly temptation' – I will follow the instruction, and he, my kind master, he will seek me and find me gone. Ha! what will not he suffer. Oh, let me call down one blessing on him and now again the poor lone and friendless girl, conscious in integrity, seeks a home wherever heaven may direct her steps.   (*Exits*)

Enter Joe Joker

Joe: This is a queer world – a fellow's no sooner comfortable than it's all up with him – I thought I was all right yesterday and now it's all t'other way!

Enter Betty

Betty: Oh, Joe, I do feel so melancholy, I thought Miss Jane was going to be a lady and now she isn't you see – oh, you men – you are all wretches – I wouldn't have anything to do with a man after this!

Joe: Well, but you don't mean to say, because this master of ours is a rum un, that I'm like him?

Betty: You are all alike, there never was a man yet that was worth a dump!

Joe: If you come to that, men and women's much of a muchness, for you can't make a good woman without cutting her head right off – what have you got to complain of – I'm doing the thing that's right as a sweetheart and you'll find me right as a trivet when we are married!

Betty: Well, I dare say I was wrong.

Joe: Lord bless you, I should never have two wives from one of the soundest principles in nature!

Betty: I should like to see that principle – what is it, tell me?

Joe: Well, among all the women as I seed, I never seed the woman yet, as was not a match for the best man alive and as couldn't give him a little un into the bargain.

Betty: Oh Joe, you are a duck after all!

Joe: Well, woman is comfortable notwithstanding. (*A window is thrown open discovering a glaring flame. The woman appears – laugh etc.*) Holloa! what's that, the hall is on fire!

Enter Rochester

Roch: Ha! the hall on fire – where is Jane – Jane Eyre! (*Rushes up*)

Joe: Stay, sir, for heaven's sake!

Roch: Stand off – Jane, I come to rescue you! (*Rushes in*)

Betty: Oh, do not follow him!

Joe: He is our master and must not perish thus! (*Follows*)

Screams – Servants rush out etc

Roch (at window): She will perish – Jane – Jane Eyre! (*The woman appear at top of roof etc.*) The flames suffocate me!

Omnes: Ah, he will be lost!

Joe is seen bearing him off as the flames burst forth and part of Hall falls in – the female still laughing as she falls among the ruins

Tableau etc.

Scene 3

Country with Neat House

Enter Jane

Jane: What am I to do, where wend my way – oh that flash – the rain has chilled me – my limbs refuse their office – faint, cold – oh, here is shelter surely, they will not refuse me entrance till this storm shall pass away – courage, Jane! (*Knocks*)

Hannah (at door): What do you want?

Jane: I would see your mistress to beg a night's shelter.

Hann: We can't take in vagrants to lodge, it isn't likely!

Jane: I shall die if I am turned away!

Hann: Not you – I'm afraid you have some ill plans agate – if you have any followers, housebreakers, or such like, you may tell em we are not by ourselves in the house (*disappears*).

Jane: What is to be my fate – oh, this hour is horror, hope leaves me – well, I can but die!

Enter St John

St J: All must die, my poor girl, but all are not condemned to meet a lingering doom such as yours would be were you to perish here – come let me assist you (*knocks*).

Jane: Oh sir, thank you!

Hann (at door): That you, master – there has been a beggar woman – oh dear me here she is!

St J: Take this poor girl and attend her kindly.

Hann: Yes, master – come in my dear – poor thing, why she's quite faint, I declare. (*Exeunt*)

Room

Scene 4

Jane discovered, St John attending her – Diana and Mary St John on each side of her

Diana:	Oh brother, how fortunate you saw her – the poor girl might have died at our very door had you not seen her.
St J:	When you name to us the residence of your friends we can write to them and you can be restored to your home.
Jane:	I am without friends or home, not one tie links me to any living being.
St J:	Where did you last reside?
Jane:	Pardon me but that must remain a secret.
St J:	Yet if I know nothing of you I can not help you and help you need.
Jane:	I need it and seek it so far that some generous person may put me in the way of getting work.
St J:	What have you been accustomed to?
Jane:	Sir, you have rescued me by your hospitality from death and I will tell you as much of my history as I dare – I am an orphan the daughter of a clergyman – my parents died before I could know them – I was brought up and educated at a charitable institution where I passed eight years as a pupil and teacher – you may have heard of the Lowood Orphan Asylum.
St J:	I have.
Jane:	I left Lowood to become a private governess – this place I was suddenly obliged to quit – the reason of my departure, I cannot, ought not to explain.
St J:	Can it be? Lowood – you are the niece then surely of Mrs Reed of Gateshead who has died since you left her and your name Jane Eyre!
Jane:	Oh sir, you a stranger – how know you this?
St J:	By this letter which but yesterday I received – you had an uncle in Madeira who is dead and has left you rich!
Jane:	Rich?
St J:	Yes, your uncle's attorney and agent has been seeking you – your fortune is vested in the English funds – Briggs has the will and necessary documents.
Jane:	Mock not a poor girl thus.
St J:	'Tis true and more, your father was related to my mother. Your uncle also – who disinheriting myself and sister leaves his fortune to his orphan niece – a fortune of £20,000.
Jane:	It cannot be – 'tis some mistake!
St J:	No mistake.
Jane:	Your mother, then was my father's sister and my aunt!
St J:	Yes.

Jane: You and your sisters, then, are my cousins, our blood flows from the same source – and I have some one to own and to love – oh heaven, for this great blessing accept my prayers – cousins, embrace me, come to my arms, my heart!

Group around her and Scene closes

Scene 5

Country near Thornfield

Enter Briggs

Briggs: Who would be a lawyer bothered with every body's business and troubles – here's my friend Mason become a raving madman and obliged to have a keeper – and here's the niece of my late client John Eyre, to whom he has left £20,000, not to be heard of. All I can gather is that an aunt at Gateshead, now dead, had discarded her and placed her at Lowood institution to get rid of her – on enquiring there, I find she had gone to Thornfield Hall – went thither and found that she had gone off and the house was burned down – where shall I find her? I must go to the St Johns, the next of kin, and notice them – who would be in the law!   *(Exit)*

Enter Joe Joker

Joe: Here's a shut up to a fellow's ambition – burnt out – I threw off my coat in my hurry and never saw it again – my old Jacket went too and now I'm as badly off as ever!

Enter Betty

Betty: Oh dear, here's a pretty business – I've nothing left but what I stand in – and poor Jane, nobody knows whether she was burned or not for she can't be found anywhere!

Joe: Ah, that's the most shocking thing of the whole.

Betty: It is indeed – oh dear – boo-oo!

Joe: Now if you cry like that I shall bolt.

Enter Jane Eyre

Jane: Now that I am not dependent on him, I must see him once again – what do I see – Betty!

Betty: Oh, my dear Miss, how glad I am to see you!

Jane:	Mr Rochester, tell me –
Betty:	Oh, poor gentleman!
Jane:	What has befallen him? – I left the hall without leave-taking –
Joe:	Lucky you did for the hall is burned to the ground!
Jane:	And Mr Rochester?
Betty:	Oh, miss he was in great danger but Joe saved him from the flames.
Joe:	Yes Miss, he's safe, but his senses, I fear, are gone and he is blind they say.
Jane:	This is a blow indeed – but do they know the cause of the fire?
Joe:	Why they do say it was Mr Rochester's wife that he kept confined upstairs – she was mad and the woman who watched her was fond of a drop – so they think she had taken a little too much and had fallen asleep, that the mad lady had escaped and set the house on fire, for when I first saw it, she was screaming and laughing at one of the windows – a short time after she gained the roof which soon fell in and she was never seen again.
Jane:	Alas, poor creature! and where is Mr Rochester?
Joe:	At a farm close by.
Jane:	Shew me to it instantly – Joseph – Betty droop not you shall not suffer – I will provide for you – for I am now rich and will reward you!

Joe and Betty: This way, then, Miss Jane.   (*Exeunt*)

Scene 6

Farm House

Enter John Dean and Rochester

Roch:	It is dark – why do you bring me here – lead me to the light I say!
Dean	Sir, I cannot give light to eyes that have it not – lean on my arm, sir.
Roch:	Let me alone, I can walk without it.

Enter Diana and Jane

Diana:	There is the wreck of what he was.
Jane:	Edward!
Roch:	That voice – what sweet madness seizes me – where is this speaker is it Jane indeed?
Jane:	Yes, 'tis she who when fortune smiled upon you, fled, rather than encounter shame – because she could not meet you in equality and honor – but that bar removed she seeks you in your troubles, to bring you hope, peace and happiness. Now rich herself, she comes to share her riches with you, to tend you with care and love.
Roch:	What do I hear – Jane, will you – can you marry me?

Jane:	I can – I will!
Roch:	And you will love me?
Jane:	Most truly, sir!
Roch:	And can you bear with my infirmities?
Jane:	They are monstrous – I love you better now – than in your proud state of independence when you disdained every title but that of giver and protector.
Roch:	Come, my own fond girl and give life and joy to him whose life had nearly left him – Ha –
Jane:	What's that?
Roch:	'Twas like the lightning's flash – it is no fancy – I see – tree and flower the glorious light of day – what joy breaks upon me, 'tis she – she that I have idolised – do so still – my Jane – my wife!
Jane:	Oh, for this in gratitude I bow in thankful reverence!

Mason rushes in

Mason:	Ha ha! I have you, I know you, give Bertha back to me or I'll tear her from your heart! (*Noise and cries of 'Follow – follow – this way'*)
Jane:	He is mad!
Roch:	Watch – stand back!
Mason:	Bertha – where is she – you have hidden her from me – I will have her (*flies upon Rochester*)
Jane:	Help – help – Mary – John – Help! (*They enter*)

Business – Rochester is weak and as Mason is dragging him down Jane swings him round – he staggers, recovers and makes another furious rush upon them both – at this Joe Joker enters and seizing Mason by the throat shakes him

Joe:	No, you don't do anything of the kind, you rascal!

Carter with others arrive. Farm servants enter

Carter:	Secure him – pinion him – he is mad (*they do so*).

Enter Briggs

Briggs:	As a march hare, I'll affirm that fact – You, I believe, are Jane Eyre – I, as attorney for your late uncle John Reed, Merchant of the Island of Madeira, place into your hands a fortune of twenty thousand pounds, left you according to his will and testament.
Jane:	Edward, do you hear? – you are safe, and Jane Eyre the orphan girl your wife. Joseph, the preserver of my husband and myself, be happy; for I will make you so!
Joe:	Huzza!
Omnes:	Huzza!

Jane Eyre

A Drama in Five Acts

Adapted from Charlotte Bronte's Novel

by

John Brougham
1849

Editor's Notes

The Text

The play was first performed in 1849,[1] but the copy-text for this edition is that published in 1856 by Samuel French, of 121 Nassau-Street, New York, as No. CXXXVL in French's American Drama Series, 'The Acting Edition'. The title-page specifies that the play is 'As Performed at Laura Keene's Varieties' and confirms that the play has been 'entered according to Act of Congress' in 1856 'by John Brougham in the Clerk's Office of the District court of the United States for the Southern District of New York'.

An undated edition by John Dicks, of 313 Strand, London (No. 400 in 'Dicks' Standard Plays'), is identical with the French edition, even to the cast list, except that this is headed 'First performed at Laura Keene's Varieties, New York, 1856'. The play does not appear in the Lord Chamberlain's Day Book for 1852–1865. The Dicks edition has a cover illustration showing Act V Scene 1, where Jane falls asleep to the sound of music, while 'the scene becomes luminous, and Rochester is seen stretching his hand towards her' (see Figure 4). Nicoll also mentions Lacy's Acting Edition, but I have not seen this.[2]

The punctuation and stage directions differ little from modern conventions and the version printed here is lightly edited to remove some obvious errors and bring the presentation into line with the other plays in the collection.

The Playwright

John Brougham (1810–1880) was a well-known actor and playwright in both Britain and the United States (see Figure 5).[3] He was born in Dublin but made his first appearance on the stage in London in 1830, and in 1831 was working with Mme Vestris at the Olympic Theatre, beginning to write plays almost immediately. He followed Vestris and Charles Mathews to Covent Garden, but in 1840 himself became manager of the Lyceum Theatre. He wrote a huge number of plays, many of them novel adaptations, especially Dickens, and most of them performed in London.[4]

---

[1] *NYST*, 31 Mar, 1849 (Vol. 19, p. 72).
[2] Nicoll, Vol. V, pp. 80, 281.
[3] Adams cites 9 May 1810 as Brougham's date of birth (p. 216) as do the *DNB*, Bordman (p. 96) and Banham (p. 133), but Boase (Vol. 1, p. 426), and *Britannica Online* (accessed 26 May, 2005) give 9 May 1814.
[4] Nearly thirty of his plays were licensed by the Lord Chamberlain between 1840 and 1870; 'Backstage' lists nearly sixty playbills. *DNB* attributes 75 plays to Brougham, and Banham 126 (p. 133).

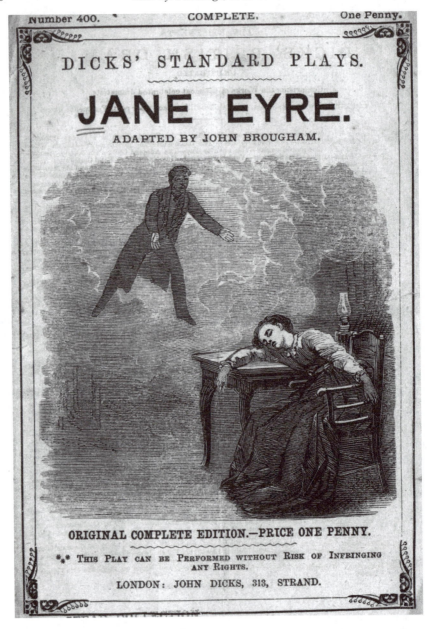

Figure 4   Jane Eyre hears Rochester calling. Title page illustration for John
Brougham's *Jane Eyre* (first performed in New York, 1849), from
Dicks' (undated) Standard Plays edition. Reproduced by permission of
Billy Rose Theatre Collection, The New York Public Library for the
Performing Arts, Lenox and Tilden Foundations

Figure 5   Photograph of John Brougham. Reproduced by permission of Billy Rose Theatre Collection, The New York Public Library for the Performing Arts, Lenox and Tilden Foundations

In 1842, he left England for the United States, worked as an actor, and opened Brougham's Lyceum on Broadway in New York in 1850. In 1856 he became manager of the Bowery Theatre, and apart from a period in England from 1860 to 1865, remained in the New York theatre world for the rest of his life.[5] He was clearly a man of great generosity of spirit, and in 1875 we find a writer in San Francisco joining forces with another in New York to praise 'that whole-souled, happy, and philosophical John Brougham', who 'has all his life been doing good by stealth, and blushes now to find it fame'.[6]

As an actor, he was famous for his comic roles. He had a robust sense of humour and was evidently a great wit and raconteur. The clipping file in New York's Billy Rose Theatre Collection is full of his bons mots and anecdotes, and where his speech is quoted directly it seems to have an Irish flavour. He would doubtless have appreciated one of his obituaries, which cites him as 'a remarkable instance of the difference existing between aristocratic England and democratic America, for while in the first he is known as Lord Brougham, in our own favoured republic he is only recognized as the distinguished dramatist and actor'. If this were true, it would cast an interesting light on the critique of aristocratic manners in his *Jane Eyre*, but the

---

5   *DNB* (accessed 9 February 2005).
6   *NYST*, 10 April 1875.

memoir is a spoof, hilariously confusing the playwright with Henry Brougham, the British statesman and social reformer.[7]

Jane Eyre does not seem to have been a particularly important play in his repertoire. The thick collection of newspaper cuttings in the Billy Rose Theatre Collection does not mention the play; neither does a whole-page, small-print article in *The New York Clipper* which mentions several other plays for 1849 and 1856.[8]

Theatres and Performances

Brougham's *Jane Eyre* was first performed at the Bowery Theatre, New York, on 26 March 1849, with Miss Catherine Wemyss and Mr John Gilbert in the lead roles.[9] The Bowery was in a rough area of New York, but in 1856 the play was produced at Laura Keene's Varieties, with Laura Keene herself in the main part (see Figure 6).[10] Laura Keene (1826?–1873) was born in England as Mary Moss,[11] and, like Brougham, began her career in London under Mme Vestris, where she excelled in comic roles such as Lydia Languish in Sheridan's *The Rivals*. After a tour of the United States in 1852 and Australia in 1854, she was prosperous enough to assume the management of her own New York theatre at 622 and 624 Broadway. Here she successfully introduced the English practice, innovative in the States, of running a play for an extended season, and was praised for her attention to detail 'as well as the well-nigh perfect acting'.[12]

Reviewers described Laura Keene as 'endowed with an unusual share of that scarcely definable quality often called personal magnetism':[13]

> Her manners were elegant and refined, her taste in dress was unexceptionable, her elocution was clear, correct, and remarkably musical, she was generally well versed in her

---

7   NYPLPA: BRTC: unidentified clipping.

8   *New York Clipper*, 19 February 1880, p. 2.

9   Leonard, p. 763; Leonard gives a complete cast list (p. 766). This performance was reviewed *NYST*, 31 March 1849.

10 Leonard gives 26 May as the opening date (p. 763). Leonard (p. 767) also lists a performance of Brougham's play at Wallack's Theatre, New York, in 1877 with Clara Morris as Jane, but it is unlikely that the 'new version' of *Jane Eyre* performed by Charlotte Thompson at the Windsor Theatre, New York, in 1882, was Brougham's, as Leonard claims (see head-note to Birch-Pfeiffer).

11 Banham gives ?1826 as her date of birth, as does an anonymous review of John Creahan, *The Life of Laura Keene*, Philadelphia: The Rodgers Publishing Company (NYPLPA: BRTC, Locke Collection, Envelope 888; clipping has no date but is marked '897'). An unidentified obituary in Envelope 888 gives 1820 as the date of birth, as does 'Laura Keene' in the *LoveToKnow* website (accessed 9 February 2005).

12 NYPLPA: BRTC, Locke Collection, envelope 888.

13 NYPLPA: BRTC clipping (MWEZ + n.c 13,400): *NYT*, June 1886.

Figure 6   Signed portrait of Laura Keene, who played Jane in Brougham's 1856
                production at Laura Keene's Varieties, New York. Reproduced by
                permission of Billy Rose Theatre Collection, The New York Public
                Library for the Performing Arts, Lenox and Tilden Foundations

parts, and she was always 'at home' in the by-play and details of the scene. In truth it was
a pleasure to see Miss Keene merely walk across the stage. All her movements were those
of an intelligent, thorough-bred lady.[14]

When her theatre opened in 1856, the New York *Spirit of the Times* dubbed her
'beyond a doubt, the […] particular "Laura" of New York, for whose smiles hundreds
of "Petrarchs" are sighing'. This reviewer, however, also praises her qualities as a
manager, in which role

> her intelligence, energy, and indefatigable perseverance, have obtained for her an enviable
> celebrity. She richly merits all the success she has achieved from the skill she has displayed,
> in first ascertaining the peculiar tastes of the New York public, and next, catering for them
> in a refined elegance of style, with which they were previously unacquainted – we confess
> something in the shape of a *penchant* for 'petticoat government' in theatrical matters;
> and when that government possesses all the energy and discrimination manifested by
> the most efficient male *empressario*, combined with those subtle elegancies felt more
> than seen, which feminine taste alone can dictate, the charm becomes the greater, and
> we unhesitatingly pronounce in favor of a lady manageress to rule the destinies of our
> amusements.

---

14   *NYST*, 15 Oct, 1855.(NYPLPA: BRTC clipping: Locke Collection, envelope 888).

Her newly built theatre is described as surpassing 'any other in New York' for 'seeing, hearing, and perfect ventilation'; its décor was 'extremely chaste – white and gold, with coloured draperies'.[15] Laura Keene was the first woman in the USA to become a theatre manager.[16]

Reception

A *Spirit of the Times* review is the only recorded response we have to the 1849 performance of Brougham's play, and I reproduce it in full:

> At the *Bowery*, a drama by Mr BROUGHAM – one of his series, evidently, of dramatic versions from popular novelists – has been produced with marked success. The novel of 'Jane Eyre' presents many incidents of a strikingly dramatic character, and there is scarce a personage in the entire work who could not be made to appear advantageously on the stage. The more prominent of these Mr Brougham has taken hold of and worked into a composition of much interest and dramatic merit. Still he labors under the disadvantage of being confined to the present time, and deprived of an opportunity of revelling in that richness of costume and scenery which forms so strong an ingredient in all pieces written for the Bowery stage. Could 'Jane Eyre' be carried back to the middle ages and honored by those nondescript dramas in vogue on the stage, the enthusiasm of the audience would have known no bounds.[17]

I have no information about the reception of the 1856 production.

Distinctive Features of the Play

- Prominence is given to the aristocrats' attempt to ridicule Jane, and her spirited self-defence.
- Relative prominence is given to named servants who expand on the 'ghost' plot; 'John' marries Grace Poole, and they have comic marital squabbles.
- There is a sensational scene in which the madwoman sets the house on fire.
- Jane faints on learning that the madwoman, who appears in the midst of the fire, is Rochester's wife.
- Jane and Rochester's final reconciliation is greeted by peasants with a garland – Rochester is 'The Farmer's Friend'.

---

15   ['Laura Keene']s New Theatre', *NYST*, 15 Nov 1856 (NYPLPA: BRTC clipping: Locke Collection, envelope 888).
16   Hartnoll and Found, p. 253.
17   *NYST*, 31 March 1849. I am grateful to Judith Smith for providing this extract.

Jane Eyre by John Brougham

Cast of the Characters

As Performed at Laura Keene's Varieties, New York

Fairfax Rochester	Mr George Jordan
Lord Theodore Ingram	" Dickerson
Colonel Dent	" H. Hall
Mr Brocklehurst	" Bass
John Downey	" T. B. Johnston
Mr Wood	" Reeve
Jane Eyre	Miss Laura Keene
The Dowager Lady Ingram	" Wells
Lady Blanche Ingram	" Kate Reynolds
Lady Mary Ingram	" Close
Miss Temple	" Walters
Mrs Gryce	Mrs Scott
Miss Scatcherd	" Lesdernier
Grace Pool	" Carpenter
Mrs Colonel Dent	Miss Macdonough
Mrs Eshton	" Johnson
The Maniac Wife	Mrs Lesdernier

Characters in the Charade

The Bride	Miss K. Reynolds
Bridesmaids	Misses Brown and Smith
Rebecca at the Well	Mrs J. R. Scott
Jacob	Mr W. Dempster
Prisoner	" Haywood
Prisoner's Wife	Miss Haywood

Costume

Rochester	1st dress, riding coat, high boots, broad h[at. 2nd,] gipsy disguise; 3rd, long grey coat, loose vest.
Ingram	Elegant evening dress.
Col. Dent	Evening dress, quaint.
Brocklehurst	Black dress.
John Downey	1st, plain livery; 2nd, country boy's dress.
Wood	Dress of clergyman.
Jane Eyre	1st, very plain dark charity school dress; 2nd, black silk; 3rd, wedding dress; 4th, plain travelling dress.

Dowager Lady Ingram	Elegant evening dress.
Lady Blanche and Mary	Ditto.
Miss Temple	⎫
Miss Gryce	⎬ Same as Jane Eyre's 1st dress.
Miss Scatcherd	⎭
Grace Pool	1st, very grotesque chambermaid's dress; 2nd, country girl's dress.

Stage Directions: Exits And Entrances

L. means *First Entrance, Left.* R. *First Entrance, Right.* S.E.L. *Second Entrance, Left.* S.E.R. *Second Entrance Right.* U.E.L. *Upper Entrance, Left.* U.E.R. *Upper Entrance, Right.* C. *Centre.* L.C. *Left of Centre.* R.C. *Right of Centre.* T.E.L. *Third Entrance, Left.* T.E.R. *Third Entrance, Right.* C. D. *Centre Door.* D. R. *Door Right.* D.L. *Door Left.* U.D.L. *Upper Door, Left.* U.D.R. *Upper Door, Right.*

The Reader is supposed to be on the Stage, facing the Audience.

[*Editor's Note*: despite this careful explanation, the stage directions in the text differ from this (e.g., 'LH2E' which presumably means 'left hand second entrance' and should be 'SEL' according to the directions above. I have therefore altered the directions to conform to the explanation above.]

Act I

Scene 1

A very plain chamber in Lowood Academy – Window practicable, but barred prison-like

Miss Gryce and Miss Temple discovered

Enter Miss Scatcherd, S.E.L.

Miss S:	Here's a fine to do! who do you think is coming here directly?
Miss T:	I cannot say, Miss Scatcherd.
Miss S:	The veritable Mr Brocklehurst himself. The generous endower of this most benevolent institution for the confusion of intellect and suppression of liberty.
Miss T:	For shame, Miss Scatcherd; you must not speak so.
Miss S:	I'll say what I think, in spite of any body. Heaven knows I'm sick enough of this dungeon.
Miss :	So indeed am I. But I must fulfill my destiny.

Miss S: Pshaw! a fig for destiny. I'm resolved when Mr Brocklehurst does come, to give him a piece of my mind. I'll say to him –

Enter Brocklehurst S.E.L.

Brock: What will you say, my dear Miss Scatcherd?

Miss S: I hope you find yourself quite well to day, sir.

Brock: Remarkably well, I thank you Miss Temple, your most obedient. I congratulate you all, ladies, upon the general appearance of your interesting pupils. But – pray be seated – I regret, and believe me, it gives me, as a man and a Christian, inexpressible pain to be obliged to reprove – I regret, I say, to find that the rules of the establishment have been, I would almost say, criminally neglected.

Miss T: I am sure, sir, not of our own –

Brock: Ah – suffer me. How is it, Madame – I address you as superintendent and controller of this place – how is it that the woollen stockings are not better attended to?

Miss T: Indeed, sir, I –

Brock: Ah – pardon me. I find also, in settling accounts with the housekeeper, that a lunch, consisting of bread and cheese, has twice been served to the girls within the last fortnight. By whose authority was this shameful innovation? May I be permitted to request an answer, direct and unequivocal?

Miss T: I must be responsible for the circumstance, sir; the breakfast was ill prepared, and –

Brock: Allow me. You are aware that my plan in bringing up these girls is, not to accustom them to habits of luxury –

Miss G: There's no doubt about that –

Brock: Miss Gryce, if you please – but on the contrary, by spare diet and wholesome exercise, to render them hardy, patient, and self-denying, and encourage them to evince fortitude, under temporary privation.

Miss G: Starvation!

Brock: Privation, Miss Gryce. That woman's deafness is very inconvenient. Oh! madam, when you put bread and cheese, instead of thin water-gruel, into those children's bodies, you little think how you starve their immortal souls.

Miss G: You are right, sir, the poor things are starved nearly.

Brock: Silence! and now, Madame, I come to the most awful dereliction of all. I observed as I passed through the school that one girl, if not more, had her hair decked in the absurd vanity of curls, absolute cork-screw curls.

Miss T: It is Julia Severn, sir. Her hair curls naturally.

Brock: *Naturally!* madame! don't attempt to hide your negligence under such a paltry plea. What have we to do with nature?

Miss G:	Nothing.
Brock:	Miss Temple, that girl's hair must be cut off. I will not have a curl or a top-knot in the school. I want those charges to become the children of grace, not the offshoots of vanity. Where is Jane Eyre?
Miss T:	She has retired to her room, sir; her health is failing under the close confinement.
Brock:	Impossible! close confinement here? Why, she must be out of her senses.
Miss G:	Nearly.
Brock:	I don't believe a word of it; it's nothing but laziness. If she does not attend to her duties to-morrow, she must seek elsewhere for a situation, and they are not to be picked up so easily; and now, ladies, I will take my leave, trusting that the reproof which conscientious feelings alone urge me to make will sink deep within your hearts, and ultimately spring up into the sweet-smelling flower of repentance and amendment. Good day. (*Exit Brocklehurst, S.E.L.*)

Enter Jane Eyre, L.

Jane:	Ah, aunt, aunt! you do not, you cannot know the bitter slavery to which your hate has doomed me; eight long years of joyless, hopeless, pitiless imprisonment – life dragged along in one unvarying level, in the very springtime of my youth – with heart and brain astir, and yearning for the love of kindred, full of bright thoughts and glorious impulses, the world and all its chances, changes, forever closed against me – it is terrible. Oh for freedom! freedom! my heart bounds like an imprisoned bird against its wiry barrier, at the mere thought – freedom – blessed freedom; those only, who lose thee, know thy worth. (*Throws open window.*) Oh, I have prayed for liberty until my loud cry seemed scattered on the passing wind. I cannot rest – I cannot think – my tortured brain, in wild confusion, whirls. Heaven send me a change, no matter what – a break to this heart-cankering monotony – a change, or I shall go mad.

Enter Miss Gryce

Miss G:	Perhaps you may have one sooner than you anticipate.
Jane:	How! speak! is there such a hope?
Miss G:	Brocklehurst has been here, and I took advantage of my slight deafness to give him a few stings.
Jane:	Poor girl, his heart is clad in steel, no mortal can reach it; but you hinted at a change; what do you mean!
Miss G:	In the first place, he says you are not sick, that it's nothing but laziness.
Jane:	The hypocrite! the false-tongued hypocrite! Go on.

Miss G:	And that unless you attend to your duties, you'll have to go.
Jane:	Where?
Miss G:	Anywhere – out into the road; he'd do it.
Jane:	He would – I know he would. What shall I do? Oh, pity me, for I need pity much. Homeless, friendless, and an orphan; what is to become of me?
Miss G:	Why don't you try and get something to do?
Jane:	Have I not done so? Have I not, in the faint hope of, at least, changing my servitude, advertised for the situation of a governess? I have served here for eight years, and I would fain *serve* elsewhere; I know it would but be an exchange of prisons, but even that variety would be a boon. A new place in a new house, with new faces – it does not sound as sweet as liberty, excitement, enjoyment; but alas! they are all equally hollow and flattering, and to me it is a mere waste of words to utter them.
Miss G:	Don't grieve so terribly; who know what this letter may contain?
Jane (starting up):	For me! Gryce. (*Fiercely.*)
Miss G:	What! don't look at me so awfully.
Jane:	You are one who would see the fire laid to the stake before you would produce the wretch's pardon.
Miss G:	I was afraid it might contain bad news.
Jane:	There is no bad news for me, the slightest change becomes an incident; a drop of water in the endless desert of my existence is as a mighty river. (*Reads.*) Oh kind, benignant Providence, my prayers are heard at last! Listen. (*Reads.*) 'If J.E. is in a condition to give satisfactory reference as to character and capacity' – (that they must not, dare not refuse me,) 'a situation can be offered to her where there is but one pupil, a little girl, under ten years of age, and where the salary –' Oh, I care not for that. 'Apply to Mrs Fairfax, Thornfield.'
Miss G:	Thornfield, why it's not more than two hours' walk from here.
Jane:	My heart is full, and forces from my eyes the unaccustomed tears. Years – long years of suffering misery are forgotten in this one moment of delight. Now my aspiring thought will have fit element to work within; high hopes and wild imaginings are crowding through my brain. I feel as though I were revelling in dream land, and as with a lightning flash, the rocky barrier is rent that kept me from communion with my kind. Oh, world! oh! bright and glorious world! thy doors are opened to me at last. (*Exit, R.*)

Scene 2

Drawing Room elegantly furnished in Mr Rochester's house

The Dowager Lady Ingram, Lady Blanche Ingram, Lady Mary Ingram, Mrs Dent, Lord Ingram, Col Dent, and Frederick Lynn, discovered

Dow: What an extraordinary creature that Rochester is! What can possibly detain him so long away? If it were any other person I should certainly feel annoyed at the host's absence.

Lord Ing: For my part, cher mama, I think it's all the better, he is such a half-savage, whole-riddle of a fellow, one never can feel at home with him.

Col Dent: Yes, and so long as he leaves such glorious wine to be drunk, noble horses to be ridden, and splendid game to pop at, what the deuce is it to us.

Lord Ing: He certainly is a most eccentric animal.

Lady Blanche: I love eccentricity.

Lord Ing: Especially when said eccentricity is mated with enormous riches, and both look sideways towards you; if I were in your place I should love it prodigiously.

Dow: Now, Ingram, don't be so impertinent; poor Blanche is absolutely blushing.

Lord Ing: What Arcadian simplicity! For Heaven's sake, Blanche, let me see it; natural color upon a fashionable cheek – preposterous!

Col Dent: Decidedly out of place.

Lord Ing: Vulgar in the extreme!

Col Dent: Absurd!

Lord Ing: And utterly dairymaidish.

Blanche: Brother, you have no heart.

Lord Ing: Haven't I, by Jove! ask Dent.

Col Dent: Don't ask me; I never saw any indication of the article, except you held it in your hand when you were playing écarte.

Lord Ing: And, by Jupiter, it's the only way you'll ever see mine, unless associated with diamonds. By-the-bye your heart, sister, has the benefit of such brilliant companionship.

Dow: Ingram, I command you to be silent on that subject; the establishment of a daughter is not so frivolous a matter as you may imagine.

Lord Ing: I know, amiable maternity, and hearts have nothing whatever to do with it.

Dow: Nothing in the world!

Lord Ing: But goes to the purchaser like the fixtures in leasing a house.

Dow: Precisely. I wonder if it was Rochester who came in that carriage a short time since. Dent, oblige me by touching the bell. (*Dent rings.*) Blanche, my love, brighten your eyes with a little of this *boquet*. (*Gives small phial.*) If it should be Rochester, don't let him find us moping.

Enter John, L.

John: That's a bright lot, the old tabby and the young kittens; the characters of all their female acquaintance are just like so many mice to them. Oh! what delight it is to seize hold of them one by one, and purr, and scratch, and worry.

Dow:	John!
John:	Yes, my lady (*aside*) Mouser.
Dow:	Was that Mr Rochester who arrived just now?
John:	No, my lady. Now I'll tease her a bit; she won't like to ask me who it is. I know she'll have to though.
Dow:	Not Mr Rochester?
John:	No; my lady.
Dow:	More friends, I presume.
John:	No, my lady.
Dow:	I certainly heard a carriage stop.
John:	Yes! my lady.
Dow:	I thought I couldn't be mistaken.
John:	No, my lady.
Dow:	A stranger?
John:	Yes, my lady.
Dow:	Indeed – a gentleman?
John:	No, my lady.
Dow:	A lady?
John:	No, my lady.
Dow:	Neither a gentleman or a lady? How stupid you are; who can it be?
John:	Only the new Governess, my lady.
Dow:	Governess! pshaw! how very provoking.
Lord Ing:	Frightful waste of sympathy, eh, Dent?
Col. Dent:	Excruciating my Lord.
Lord Ing:	All about some poor devil of a teacher. Do you recollect, Blanche, how we used to quiz your round of governesses?
Blanche:	Oh, yes, Theodore, what fun we used to have with them. Mary was always too sleepy to join in our plots.
Dow:	Now my darling pets, don't mention governesses; the very word make me nervous.
Blanche:	And do you remember, Theodore, how we helped you to persecute your tutor?
Lord Ing:	Yes, the poor, pale-faced wretch, he was positively ignorant of the commonest rudiments of education – didn't know a terrier from a bull-dog, and never saw a badger in the whole course of his life.
Col Dent:	The Hottentot.
Lord Ing (*To Blanche*):	I say, Blanche, wouldn't it be a prime lark to have up this new governess and see what she's like.
Blanche:	Famous, Theodore. I do love to see them blush and tremble when they first find themselves in an aristocratic element. Ma won't like it, though.
Lord Ing:	That don't signify, we shall have better fun. John?
John:	My Lord.
Lord Ing:	Bring some liqueur, and trot out the new governess.

John:	Yes, my lord.	(*Exit, L.*)

Lord Ing: I say Dent, I've just been laying the train for a grand explosion of fun.

Col Dent: What, sacking the cellar?

Lord Ing: No. I'm going to introduce a lamb amongst those old Dowager Lionesses. My dear, so you have a prejudice against governesses?

Dow: Don't mention the horrid name or I shall certainly faint.

Enter John, L.

John: The new Governess. (*Dowager screams.*)

Lord Ing: Bravo, John; consider yourself a sovereign richer for that.

Enter Jane, L. Recoils timidly at first but rapidly collects herself

Lord Ing: Dent, you ruffian, is not that a master stroke of comedy? See the poor timid fawn. How she shrinks from those high-blooded gruffins.

Jane (*advancing firmly*): I am either constrained to apologize for the *ignorance* of a servant, or I am obliged to suffer for his *malice*. It was not of my own will that I intruded here, for I was not aware there was so distinguished an assembly.

Lord Ing: Dem good, by Jupiter. Eh, Dent?

Col Dent: Admirable!

Jane: You will excuse me if I retire.

Lord Ing: Oh, dem it, no; 'twould be ending the comedy in the first scene. Don't tear yourself away.

Jane: Am I to understand that I was sent for?

Lord Ing: Yes, certainly. I did myself that honor.

Jane: Indeed! that makes an essential difference. It allows me at least the condition of equality. John, will you oblige me with a seat? (*John places seat.*) Request Mrs Fairfax, the housekeeper, to send for me here, if my services are required. (*John laughs, aside, but very respectful to her.*)

John: Yes, my lady – I mean Madam. Bravo! jolly good by jingo!

Lord Ing: Delicious! John, you brigand, you'll ruin me. I owe you another sovereign.

John:	Yes, and that's all I'm likely to get of it.	(*Exit, L.*)

Dow (*aside to guests*): Did you ever see more consummate boldness? And I declare, there's that foolish Mary going to speak to her.

Lord Ing: She's a magnificent creature, Dent, by Jove! Let's have a close look at her. (*Dent and Ingram walk round Jane with quizzing glasses.*)

Lord Ing: Bears close inspection too, by Jove.

Col Dent: Yes, as close as you can get – those eyes are dangerous, too near.

Jane (*to Mary, who has been trying to make her feel at home*): The thanks, deep and sincere, of a lonely heart are yours, my dear young lady; one touch of sympathy can obliterate volumes of looked and spoken insolence; but fear not for me. The mind that's conscious of its own superiority stands on too high an eminence to be reached by the petty shafts of pride and ignorance.

Lord Dent: Does she mean anything – eh, Dent?

Col Dent: Hang me if I know. I wish I had some of Rochester's burgundy.

Dow: Does the creature intend to stay here, I wonder.

Blanche: She has confidence enough, I do believe.

Lord Ing: Demme if she hasn't put a wet blanket on the party – eh, Dent?

Col Dent: A regular soaker.

Lord Ing: The Dowagers are shut up famously – confound me if I don't feel somehow demmed awkward myself. Dent, stir up the people, or this dem governess will think she has cowed us all.

Col Dent: Why don't you go and talk to her?

Lord Ing: I would if I knew what to say.

Col Dent: Don't be a fool; nonplussed by a governess!

Lord Ing: Demmit, that'll never do – (*stalks across dandified*) – aw – Miss: aw – I haven't the honor of your name.

Jane: Jane Eyre – you are? –

Lord Ing: Theodore, commonly called Lord Ingram – and so you are – aw – Jane Eyre. Yes, delighted – do you know, Jane, that you're devilish pretty?

Jane: My Lord!

Lord Ing: Upon my life you are – eh, Dent?

Col Dent: Undoubtedly.

Jane: Sir, your sisters, I believe, are in the room – were any one to address either of them as you have now addressed me, what would be the result?

Lord Ing: Positively I don't know, I can't imagine; it's a very different thing – they are –

Jane: Made of different clay: their hearts are more sensitive, their feelings more refined, perhaps. Reverse the picture, my Lord, and you will be nearer to the truth. In the school of poverty is oftener found that intuitive delicacy which fears to wound – inured to suffering themselves, they know and feel for that in others.

Lord Ing: A regular sermon, by Jupiter; quite Addisonian. Did you get that out of the Spectator?

Jane: My Lord, ignorant assumption, much as it may be involuntary, is simply pitiable; but insolence, where you know it cannot be averted, is cowardly!

Lord Ing: Dent, damme, did you hear that?

Col Dent: Distinctly!

Lord Ing: And must I swallow it? Oh, I wish you were a man.

Jane: Pray calm yourself, my Lord. I shall retire, not out of dread of your contumely, but from very pity of your infirmities: and it may be, that the poor, lowly-nurtured drudge, whom you sent for to bring you unworthy amusement, will have given you a wholesome, though unwelcome lesson.   (*Exit Jane, L.*)

Lord Ing: Snubbed, by Jove!
Col Dent: Prodigiously.

Tableaux of astonishment
End of Act I

Act II

Scene 1

Apartment in Mr Rochester's House

Enter Grace Poole, with a piece of cake and a pint of porter, followed by John, R.

John: Come now, Mrs Grace, I'll tell you what it is. I ain't agoing to stand your capers. I never was in a family yet that I wasn't made acquainted with the secrets thereof; here have I been three livelong weeks, and I don't know nothing yet; it's disgraceful.

Grace: Very!

John: There's a mysterious mystery hanging about the place somewhere and I'm blessed if I don't find it out.

Grace: Do!

John: I will, you may take your davy. Won't you tell me?

Grace: No!

John: Then I must depend upon my natural genius to find it out. – There was a jolly rumpus last night; who is it laughs in that awful manner every now and then?

Grace: Me.

John: You! pooh! don't tell me.

Grace: I won't.

John: There's something a going on in this house, that isn't right, and a fellow servant as won't confide in a fellow servant, don't deserve to belong to our honorable profession. How can we stand up for our masters or missises unless we knows their little imperfections; it keeps them in order, and makes wages a deal more reg'lar. I know a thing or two. You don't know what I am.

Grace: I do!

John: What am I, now let's know?

Grace: A fool.

John:	Am I! then there's a pair of us; but never mind. I won't be beholden to you. The master will be home soon, and while there's key-holes in the world, and ears ain't scarce, there ain't a master in the world can keep a secret from a servant as is determined to find it out; that you may take your oath of. Don't keep on a munching of that cake as if you really thought you were hurting it, and it did you good to bite so savagely. The new Governess will be here to-day, then your nose will be out of joint, thank fortune.
Grace:	Will it?
John:	Won't it?
Grace:	No!
John:	Then you're pretty certain of *your* situation whatever may come into the house?
Grace:	Yes!
John:	Now then, I know there's a something.
Grace:	Indeed!
Joh:	Yes! and if I don't come at it I'm a Dutchman.
Grace:	Don't try.
John:	None of your gammon. You want to frighten me. Why do you always eat in your own room? or walking about like a hungry ghost, and not amongst us as you ought to? But I know a way to penetrate the mystery.
Grac:	How?
John:	This way. (*Opens door, scream heard*)
Grace:	Stop!
John (frightened):	I saw it! oh lord! it's true! I heard so.
Grace:	What?
John:	That the house was haunted. Grace, what was that fearful looking thing.
Grace:	Nothing!
John:	Didn't you hear a scream?
Grace:	No!
John:	I'll take my oath I saw something.
Grace:	Fool!
John:	You're not a going in?
Grace:	Yes!
John:	Don't! don't!
Grace:	Go! (*Exit through door in flat, L.*)
John:	I will: my eyes could not have deceived me, and my ears too. Here's a beautifully awful mystery, a ghost in the house; there's something delightfully frightful, in having one's feelings harrowed up and agitated all ways at once. I've a great mind to peep, just to see if I was right. Pooh! don't be a coward, heart. I declare I'm goose-fleshing all over; my hair is getting wirey, and my knees wretchedly rheumatic. Pooh!

here goes. (*Approaches door; a wild laugh heard; he bolts precipitately, falls on his knees.*)
Grace enters with dress, touches him on the shoulder

John: Oh! don't; have pity, good ghost. I'll never be curious again. I won't, I won't.
Grace: Don't!
John: Is it you! oh good gracious what a coward I am. Oh! there's a good soul, tell me what I saw in the room.
Grace (holding up dress): Look!
John: Nothing but a white dress. Hurrah! Pleasant as it is to be mysteriously terrified, it's much more agreeable to be not. Oh! I could, I really could, very nearly, be induced to embrace you. Indeed my own feelings have undergone such a complete upsetting, that I do believe I could almost kiss you.
Grace: Fool!
John: You're right, of the long eardest description, but I'm cured. I'll never dive into secret mysteries again.   (*Exit Grace, R. through door*)

Scene 2

Garden; bright Moonlight

Enter Jane, L. Despondingly, leans against balcony

Jane: Shame, shame upon their cruelty; the pride that blazed within me is quenched in the flood of my great disappointment. Is this the pleasant change which I had pictured? This is the hard sterile rock my distant hope had tinted over with the softest moonlight. Better, a thousand times better, my solitary cell once more, than be gibed and mocked at by the vulgar-wealthy; to have the badge of servitude engraved upon my very heart, and know that tyrant circumstance has placed me in a world all prison, where every human being is a watchful jailor, and where you must endure the unceasing lash of insolence, the certain punishment of that statuteless but unforgiven crime, poverty. But why should I weep; it is my destiny – my stark and joyless destiny, and I must school myself, if not to be content therewith, at least to endure without a murmur. (*Noise outside*)
Roch (supposed to have fallen from his horse): How, Mesrour, what's to do now? you've hurt me, you ungrateful beast.
Jane: It is a traveller, who has fallen from his horse.
Roch (outside): Hallo! you hedge phantom, since you have frightened my horse away, the least you can do will be to help me up.
Jane: With pleasure, sir.   (*Exit, R.*)

Roch (outside): Pleasure, indeed; it ain't much pleasure to break a limb, is it?
Jane: Lean on me, sir; you are not injured, I hope?
Enter Jane and Rochester, U.D.R.

Roch:	Not injured! what a fool you must be; to be tumbled upon a hard rocky road doesn't necessarily give a man the most pleasurable sensations.
Jane:	I am sorry, sir, indeed I am.
Roch:	Pooh!, don't talk nonsense; why should you be sorry?
Jane:	If it was through my being here that your horse was startled, sir, I must feel sorrow for your accident.
Roch:	I'd advise you not to waste any sympathy on my account, it will be a bad investment of valueless capital.
Jane:	I may at least inquire if you are seriously hurt.
Roch:	I don't recognize your right! Who are you? and what brings you here at this time of the night? Go away home, if you have any.
Jane:	I cannot think of leaving you, sir, until I see that you can assist yourself.
Roch:	Can't you, indeed; you are rather a peremptory apparition, – where do you come from? Have you descended from a moonbeam, or are you a discontented Hamadryad, escaped from your oakey prison? Are you quite sure that you haven't bewitch'd my horse?
Jane:	I live at yonder house, sir; shall I run and obtain some assistance? for I know that you are suffering much pain, notwithstanding your apparent carelessness.
Roch:	Hold your tongue; you live there, do you?
Jane:	Yes, sir.
Roch:	Whose house is it?
Jane:	Mr Rochester's.
Roch:	Indeed! do you know him?
Jane:	No; I have never seen him; and if he resembles the majority of his visitors, I have no wish.
Roch:	You are not a servant, of course; I see you are not. Forgive me. You'll find me rough, but not rude; though what is it to you whether I am or not? May I inquire who you are?
Jane:	The governess, sir.
Roch	Ah! the governess! where do you come from?
Jane:	From Lowood school.
Roch:	That charitable concern over the way; how long were you there?
Jane:	Eight years.
Roch:	Eight years! you must be tenacious of life; I thought half the time in such a place would have done up any constitution. Who are your parents?
Jane:	I have none.
Roch:	But you had, I suppose; do you remember them? You think me impertinent, I perceive; never mind, it doesn't signify. Who were you waiting for here? did you know I was returning? but how could

you? – there, I think I can walk now. Lend me your arm. Have you an umbrella? No matter, I can hobble along pretty well.

Jane: You are suffering, sir – I know you are.

Roch: Well, what's that to you; confound it, can't you let me suffer quietly; don't for pity's sake fall into the common error of worldly friends, who think that condoling with you on your misfortunes, ameliorates them – the fools, when forgetfulness would be mercy, their tongues are never quiet; but where's your curiosity – are you not dying to know who I am?

Jane: I have no such unwarrantable desire, sir.

Roch: Ah, that's a famous sting for me; but I may as well tell you at once; that then is my home, ah! (*expression of disgust*) the casket of my treasure – look at those brilliant casements, those ivy-covered battlements, those old ancestral trees, that smoothly shaven lawn, that richly variegated garden, is it not an earthly paradise?

Jane: It is indeed, externally a –

Roch: What do you mean, do you know? Externally – why not internally; ah, your eye is placid – pshaw! it is a large pest-house, there is a memento written in the air in lurid characters, which – but is it not an enviable retreat?

Jane: Most enviable.

Roch: Aye – even to the arch fiend himself, so full of delicious memories, that I cannot but dally with my happiness, even within its very sight – but come, the threshold must be passed.

John (outside, L.): He's here – I see him.

Enter servants with torches, then Lord Ingram furred, Col Dent, &c. &c. U.D.L.

Lord Ing: Rochester, my dear boy, you gave us a deuce of a fright, made me feel remarkably queer. Your horse rushed into the stable, all in a foam, without you.

Roch: That will do; you see it is accounted for.

Lord Ing: But my sister Blanche, you know the tender interest she takes in you.

Roch: Is she here?

Lord Ing: No, she's fainting most grammatically in the drawing-room.

Roch: Silence, puppy – (*to servants*) home! come, my Samaritan. (*Rochester and Jane towards entrance to house – servants range at each side with torches*)

Col. Dent: How do you feel, Ingram?

Lord Ing: Snubbed again, by Jove! The dem Rhinoceros!

Music
Curtain

Act III

Scene 1

Temporary Stage with curtains in drawing room – preparation for the Charade

John fastening curtains, &c. Robert assists

Rob: What be these crincums for, John?

John: Bless your unsophisticated ignorance, these are the games that shuts up theatres; this is for domestic play acting – what with charades, as they call them, tableauxes, and fancy performances, in drawing rooms, the bread is fairly taken out of the poor people's mouths as makes it a purfession. I once had some hambition to be a player myself, but since the quality has taken it up, I've altered my mind.

Rob: I say, John, when do you think the wedding will take place; I likes weddings – housekeepers don't limit a chap's ale.

John: Whose wedding?

Rob: Why, Mr Rochester's, with that there highflyer, Miss Ingram.

John: Permit me, sir, as your superior in office, to give you a word of advice. Never you inquire about nothing, nor never you wonder at nothing. Specially in this enchanted castle.

Rob: Well I won't; but you'll tell us what these charades is.

John: The servants can come to the door and see them, then you'll be likely to know.

Rob: You're very kin[d.]

John: I tell you what it is, I can't get no satisfaction from anybody, and I'm resolved not to give no satisfaction to nobody; see if that there curtain will work.

Curtain drawn discovers Grace Pool with her cake and pint of beer

John: Hillo, what brought you there? look, Bob. that's what the gentry calls a tabloo.

Rob: Why, that's half-witted Grace, with her everlasting pint of beer.

John: What are you doing there, Grace?

Grace: Eating.

Rob: Here Grace. She knows everything if she'd only let it out. (*Grace comes down*) Is there going to be a wedding in the house?

Grace: No!

Rob: When will there?

Grace: Never. (*Noise of company*)

John: Hillo, here they come. Bob, down with the curtain! Grace, bundle out.

Grace:	No!
John:	But don't you hear the company's coming from the drawing room? (*Sits down.*)
Grace:	Yes.
John:	Come, you must be off.
Grace:	Shan't.
John:	Here they are. Well I don't care, you old fool. Won't there be a rumpus.
Grace:	Brute!

Enter Dowager, Lady Ingram, and all the guests. All stare with astonishment at Grace

Lord Ing:	By Jove, what a character! it's Rochester dressed up; no it isn't.
Grace:	Beer? (*Offering pint*)
Dow:	It must be one of the visitors in a fancy dress. Whoever you are, disclose yourself.
Grace:	Cake? (*Offering cake*)
Lord Ing:	Capital, by Jupiter.

Grace offers her beer all around, then stalks across, mysteriously, and exit

Col Dent:	Who the deuce can it be?
Lord Ing:	I have it! you remember on the occasion of our last visit here, we heard sundry mysterious noises, at strange times, putting one's nerves in an inelegant state of agitation. This must be the cause, depend upon it. It's a lunatic servant that Rochester don't like to get rid of.
Dow:	Dear me, suppose she had hurt somebody? Ah, here comes that odious governess; six months hasn't made her a whit more humble. I wonder Rochester keeps her here.
Lord Ing:	Because he's a dem'd original, and does nothing like anybody else: with his countless mine of money, it's astonishing how barbarous he is. I'm sure when we were in town last season, I used all my endeavors to transmute his rugged iron into smooth, fashionable gold, but all my efforts were of no avail. One might as well try to civilize a polar bear or teach an alligator the polka.

Enter Rochester

Lord Ing:	Ah, my dear Rochester, the sound of your praise has scarcely done echoing through the apartment. We are all dying with anxiety to see what Charade is about to be presented.
Roch:	Where is Miss Eyre? John, tell Miss Eyre to come here.

Lord Ing:	Demmit, Rochester, have a little feeling for the Dowager. You know how she dislikes the atmosphere of a domestic.
Roch:	The instructress of my child, my lord, ranks amongst the foremost of my friends; my acquaintances surely need not blush to be in such society.

Enter Jane

Jane:	You sent for me, sir!
Roch:	I did, Miss Eyre. Sit down; I presume you care as little as myself for those frivolous pastimes, and yet they may amuse you. (*Aside*) I cannot struggle against the heart spell she has thrown around me. Spite of the dark chasm of the future, my soul is hurried onward with the very speed of destiny. Could she but love me sufficient to brave all – this day shall prove it.

Enter John with letter which he gives to Rochester

Roch:	Excuse me, friends; what's this? (*Reads*) '*Depart at once; a matter of grave importance.*' You hear, friends, how abruptly I am summoned; but let not my absence check your enjoyment; I shall return as quickly as I can. (*Exit Rochester*)
Lord Ing:	Ah, Miss Eyre. Pray, how do you find yourself? don't be under any apprehension! I have forgotten what passed between us during my last visit.
Jane:	Indeed! my lord I congratulate you upon the complaisance of your memory. I wish I had so obliging a recollection.
Lord Ing:	Why, have you not forgotten it?
Jane:	No, my lord, nor ever shall!
Lord Ing:	What an unforgiving creature!
Jane:	Pardon me, it is *forgiven* long since; *that* is my share of the transaction. To teach me to *forget* it, must be *yours*.
Lord Ing:	Ah! yes. You're too dem'd metaphysical for me! (*Small bell*)
Col Dent:	The signal to prepare for the Charade.

Servants appear at stage doors; crowding their heads amongst them, Grace, John, Bob, &c.

Col Dent:	Who are to be the representatives?
Lord Ing:	Mr Rochester.
Col Dent:	And your lovely sister, of course!
Lord Ing:	I suppose so. If he's going to marry her, I wish he'd make haste about it. I want to cut in for a slice of his ready –
Col Dent:	Silence! Here comes the first syllable.

Curtain rises to music, and discovers Lady Blanche dressed as bride, two bridesmaids attending; Tableau : Music

Lord Ing:	Superb, by Jove! Blanche is rehearsing for the Mrs Rochester role, evidently.
Col Dent:	But what is the syllable intended?
Lord Ing:	Don't ask me. I never fatigue my brain with thinking.
Dow:	It must be – *Bride*
All:	Certainly!
Col Dent:	Now for the second syllable.

Tableau of Rebecca at the well, after Victor Adam: Music

Lord Ing:	We all know what it is, – fountain!
Col Dent:	No; Bride, fountain, spells no word that I know of.
Dow:	I know it, – it must be WELL!
All:	So it is. (*They applaud*)
Col Dent:	Now for the Tableau of the whole word.

Curtain: Tableau of the Momentous question

Col Dent:	Capital, by Jove, – '*Bride-well*' ain't it, Miss Eyre?
Jane:	Pardon me, sir, but I was not attending to the exhibition.
Lord Ing:	Perhaps you object to such frivolous amusement?
Jane:	My objections, my lord, carry but little weight.
Lord Ing:	Modest creature!

Enter John

John:	If you please, my lady, there's an old gipsy has ensconced himself by the library fire, and nothing can induce him to go.
Dow:	The wretched person; what does he want?
John:	He wants to tell the gentry their fortunes, and swears he won't leave till he does.
Blanche:	Oh! ma! do let us see him, it is so deliciously romantic.
Lord Ing:	What is he like?
John:	As old as Methuselah, and as ugly as a scare-crow, my lord.
Lord Ing:	Then let's see him, it would be a thousand pities to lose such a chance of making fun of the old sorcerer.
John:	He says whoever wants him must go to him.
Col. Dent:	An independent wizard; suppose I lead the way.
Lord Ing:	No; let Blanche, propitiate the fellow.
Dow:	I cannot possibly countenance any such inconsistent proceeding!

Blanche:	Indeed, ma, but you can and will; I have a curiosity to have my fortune told; John, lead the way.
Dow:	Oh, my best – oh, my dearest, consider –
Blanche:	Ma, don't be foolish! (*Exit with John*)
Dow:	Oh, my beloved darling; if any thing should happen to her, I should never forgive myself. Theodore, why don't you rush to the protection of your precious sister.
Lord Ing:	Don't alarm yourself, perturbated maternity; Blanche can take a good care of her precious self.
Dow:	Oh, you have no sympathy for a mother's feelings.
Lord Ing:	No! never had; don't think I ever shall.
Dow:	A horrible presentiment of evil oppresses me! I do believe if she don't come instantly I shall be positively obliged to faint.
Lord Ing:	Don't throw away a scene, indiscreet woman; there are no strangers present.
Lady Mary:	Ma, I'm frightened.
Dow:	So am I, my timid dove.
Lady Mary:	This silence is inexpressively awful.
Dow:	Perfectly appalling.
Lord Ing:	Absolutely excruciating – ha! ha! Dent for gracious sake, look at the interesting old hen and her one little chick. Here she comes; calm your fluttering hearts.

Enter Blanche

Dow (rushes to her):	She's safe; my own is safe.
L. Mary:	Well, love, what did he say?
Lord Ing:	What did he do?
Col Dent:	How did he look?
Dow:	How do you feel, precious?
Blanche:	Now, good people, don't press on me; restrain your curiosity. I have seen a gipsy imposter, who endeavored to practise the usual cheating of his kind; and I treated the knavery as it deserved, with contempt.
Dow:	But tell me, love, did he say any thing about – you know what – Rochester, you know?

Jane expresses anxiety

Blanche:	It's perfectly laughable – he told me this marriage should never take place.
Dow:	How absurd. (*All go up laughing.*)
Lord Ing:	Very likely.
Jane:	Ha! why does that sentence thrill through my frame, sharp and stunning as a shock of electricity; what is it to me – oh, weak, weak, foolish

heart, strive not against thy betters; down to thy station, down!
(*Exit, R.*)

Scene 2

Enter John, L., meeting Jane Eyre

John: Please, Miss, the gipsy won't go without seeing you.
Jane: You mistake, John, it must be one of the visitors he wishes to see.
John: No, Miss, he must be something not right, for he described you
           wonderful. What shall I tell him?
Jane: That I will go by all means. He may be in want of something; it's only
           those who have felt privation themselves who ever think that there is
           such a thing in the world as want.
John: If you like, Miss, I'll wait in the hall, and if he frightens you, call out
           and I'll see if the ditch water agrees with his gipsy stomach.
Jane: No, John, return to the kitchen; I am not in the least afraid.
                                                                  (*Exit Jane, L.*)
John: Oh, Lord!, the mysteriousness gets thicker than ever. Not content with
           having a ghost in the house, we must have a gipsy now. I wish the
           fellow would tell me my fortune. No I don't; for I'd rather not know it,
           if it's at all shy; and in the natural course of events I don't see any other
           chance for poor me. I only wish I was married and settled out of this
           nest of hobgoblins. That there Grace would make a good sort of wife
           for a chap, she's so chary with her syllables, and that's a good point.
           I wonder where she is? It's nice and dark and romantic; just the time
           to whisper soft nonsenses. I've a great mind to find her. I will too. I'll
           just take a glass of strong beer, and open my heart to her like a house
           a-fire.

Grace appears at Door in F. with plate, &c.

Grace: That inquisitive fool here. I'll soon get rid of him. (*Re-enters door. A
           groan heard.*)
John: Good gracious, what's that? I'll swear I heard a groan in that room (*goes
           towards door*). Pshaw! the keyhole's stuffed up (*a crash of crockery
           and loud laugh.*) The ghost! the ghost! oh, lord!
           (*Exit hastily, R.*)
Enter Grace

Grace: It's well for us he's such a coward. Now to relieve his terror: John,
           what's the matter?   (*Exit, R.*)

Scene 3

The Library: Stage partially dark – wood fire blazing on hearth

Rochester as Gipsy, and Jane Eyre discovered – the red light from the fire falls on his face

Roch:	Here we shall be more quiet; for I have a good deal to say to you, and hate listeners – you see that I know the house well; aye, and all who are in it. Ah! you doubt me. I knew that, you see – but to the proof. Come, you want your fortune told!
Jane:	I don't care about it, you may please yourself; but you are right in your conjecture – I have no faith.
Roch:	My conjecture, silly mortal – my *knowledge*. I heard it in your step just now.
Jane:	Did you – you have a quick ear.
Roch:	I have, and a quick eye and a quick brain.
Jane:	You need them all in your trade.
Roch:	Especially when I have customers like you to deal with. Why don't you tremble?
Jane:	I'm not cold.
Roch:	Why don't you turn pale?
Jane:	I'm not sick.
Roch:	Why don't you consult my art?
Jane:	I'm not silly.
Roch:	Lies, lies, all – you are cold, you are sick, and you are silly.
Jane:	Prove it.
Roch:	In few words. You are cold, because you are alone; no contact strikes from you the fire that you possess. You are sick, because the lowliness of your position keeps from you the companionship of your equals in soul and intellect. You are silly, because suffer as you may, yet even to those who could and would sympathise with you, you disdain to reveal the heart-agony that wears away your life.
Jane:	You might say this to any one, placed in my circumstances.
Roch:	Find me another placed as you are; happiness is near you – within your very reach, and yet your obstinate but noble pride keeps you from putting forth your hand to grasp it.
Jane:	I don't understand enigmas.
Roch:	If you wish me to speak more plainly, let me see your hand.
Jane:	I know it's folly, all, but there – (*Holds hand*)
Roch:	You don't! there's a doubt in your look. You are not quite certain that it is folly; pshaw! I can make nothing of the hand, 'tis too fine; besides, destiny is not written there; no, 'tis in the eyes, the forehead, mouth, the expression of the face: let me look in your eyes.

Jane: Now you are coming to reality; I shall begin to have some faith in you
             presently.

Roch: Um! good, very good. I wonder what thoughts are busy in your heart,
             for I can only read *them* now – I can! What thoughts, I say, pass within
             you, while you sit in yonder room, with all the fine people passing
             before you like shadows in a magic lantern?

Jane: I feel tired often, sleepy sometimes, but seldom sad.

Roch: Then you have some secret hope that pleases you with whispers of the
             future?

Jane: None!

Roch: None? no! not when you hear as you must do, tales of love and courtship,
             does not *your* heart yearn for a fitting mate? For instance, when Lady
             Blanche, and he, you know who I mean, when they converse in soft,
             silvery whispering together, their fervid looks and low murmuring
             syllables uttering the bliss of each, then –

Jane: Then! ah! spare me; then I dare not think.

Roch: You have looked forward, have you not, and seen them married, and
             beheld his bride happy?

Jane: No, I have not seen that; your witch's skill is at fault sometimes.

Roch: What in Heaven's name have you seen, then?

Jane: No matter. I came here to inquire, not to confess. I did not come to hear
             Mr Rochester's fortune, but to listen to my own, and you have told me
             nothing of it.

Roch: Because *your* fortune is yet doubtful. I can read upon your features,
             each passion of your heart, distinct as on a printed page. – That eye
             shining like dew, so soft and full of feeling, and yet in the cup of bliss,
             when offered, if there should be one dreg of shame, or one flavor of
             remorse, how firm its determined glance; it would foster, not blight, it
             would earn gratitude, not wring tears of blood. Ah! what tenderness,
             but what inflexibility! Leave me; I rave in exquisite delirium; so far I
             have governed myself thoroughly; leave me, Jane. – The play is played
             out.

Jane: That voice – do I wake or dream!

Roch: Don't you know me, Jane – there, then, off ye lendings! How do I play
             the Gipsy?

Jane: It was no Gipsy part you played with me.

Roch: Whose then, my own?

Jane: I don't know, sir; some unaccountable one. In short you have been
             talking nonsense to make me do the same. I have your permission to
             retire, sir?

Roch: Not yet: I want to ask your advice. Now, Jane, call your fancy to your
             aid; suppose instead of the bright incarnation of woman-hood, which
             you are, you had been a wild boy, indulged from childhood upward;
             imagine yourself in a remote foreign land, conceive that you commit a

capital error, no matter what, but one whose consequences must follow you through life, and taint all your existence; mind I don't say a *crime*, my word is *error*. Well, heart-weary and soul-withered, you come home after years of voluntary banishment, you make a new acquaintance, you find in this stranger much of the bright and good qualities which you have sought for all your life, and but just encountered; such society brings higher wishes, purer feelings, and you desire to recommence your life, and pass the remnant of your days in a manner more worthy of a human being; to attain this end, are you justified in overleaping an obstacle of custom?

Jane: Sir, if any one you know has erred and suffered, let him look higher than his equals for strength to amend, and solace to heal!

Roch: But the instrument! the instrument! I tell you without parable, that *I* have been a worldly, dissipated, restless man. Oh! dare I to hope that I have found a comforting spirit? Jane, if the finger of scorn were pointed at me, what would you do?

Jane: If it were deserved, my tears would attest my sorrow; if not, I would dash the mocker to the earth, if strength of indignation could effect it.

Roch: Bold, brave girl. You know my strange temperament, and won't wonder if I make sudden resolutions. You must go.

Jane: Go, sir?

Roch: Yes, go. What business have you here; you know I am about to be married.

Jane: Soon, sir?

Roch: Very soon.

Jane: Well, sir, I shall be ready when the order to march comes.

Roch: It is come now, Miss Eyre – you must get a new situation.

Jane: The blow is greater, severer than I expected.

Roch: But your pride will master it.

Jane: It will – it does; it – oh, this is torture –

Roch: No it don't. You are sorry to leave Thornfield.

Jane: I grieve to leave it. I love Thornfield. I love it, because I have lived in it a full and delightful life. I have not been trampled on – I have not been buried with inferior minds, and excluded from every glimpse of communion with what is bright and high, and energetic. I have talked face to face with what I reverenced, but I see the necessity for departure, and it is like looking on the necessity of death.

Roch: Where do you see the necessity?

Jane: *You* have placed it before me. Do you think I can stay to become nothing to you? Do you suppose I am a mere machine, without one spark of sense or feeling, and can bear to have my drop of living water dashed from my cup? Do you think, because I am lowly and obscure, that I have neither soul nor heart? You think wrongly if you do; and if heaven had gifted me with wealth, I should have made it as hard for you to leave me, as it is for me to leave you. I am not talking to you now, through the medium of custom; or even of mortal flesh; it is my spirit which addresses you, just as if both had passed through the grave, and we stood within the precincts of eternity equal, as we are.

Roch: As we are, and ever shall remain. I offer you my hand, my heart, and a share of all my possessions. Jane, decide my destiny!

Jane: You play a farce at which I merely laugh.

Roch: Unbelieving skeptic, you shall be convinced; the irresistible waves of destiny hurry me along; you strange – you almost unearthly thing – I love you as my own flesh, and I must have you for my own. Will you be mine? – at once, within the hour – say yes, and quickly.

Jane: Mr Rochester!

Roch: Yes.

Jane: Let me look in your face.

Roch: Why?

Jane: Because I want to read your countenance!

Roch: There you will find it scarcely more legible than a crumpled page. Read on – only make haste, for I suffer. Jane, you torture me with that searching but yet generous look; you torture me.

Jane: How can I do that, if your offer be real; my only feelings must be gratitude and devotion.

Roch: Gratitude! Jane, accept me quickly.

Jane: Are you in earnest? do you sincerely wish me to become your wife?

Roch: I swear it.

Jane: Then I am yours.

Roch: Come, come to me – my happiness is complete. Away! I will not give you time to change your mind. Prepare yourself at once – in my oratory we shall be wedded. Haste, haste, my own, own bride! (*Exit Jane*) God pardon me; and man meddle not with me; she is mine. and I *will* hold her in the teeth of fate; it will atone – it will atone. Have I not found her friendless! and will I not guard and cherish, and solace her? Is there not love in my heart, and constancy in my resolves! I know heaven sanctions what I do: for the world's judgment I wash my hands thereof – for man's opinion, I defy it. Hold! what am I about to do? Down, down thought! – sleep conscience; for in spite of all the powers of earth and hell combined, she must be mine. And then! for remorse and wretchedness. Well, let them come – heaven pardon and pity me – my heart and brain are burning!

End of Act III

Act IV

Scene 1

The Drawing-room at Rochester's. Dowager, Lady Blanche, Mary, Lord Ingram, Col Dent, discovered

Dow: Come here, Blanche, my love; remember the importance of the crisis which is evidently approaching: and don't shake your hair too much out of curl.

John: A note for you, my lady.   (*Exit*)

Dow: It is from Rochester, and marked private. The long expected declaration, no doubt. Blanche, calm your agitation, dear, while we see what he proposes in the way of dowry.

Lord Ing: Something enormous, I trust, to gild the fellow's atrocious vulgarity!

Dow (reads): Good Heavens!

Col Dent: No bad news, I hope.

Lord Ing: Surely nothing could have occurred to break off the match.

Blanche: Nothing, oh, nothing!

Col Dent: But death!

Lord Ing: Or Bankruptcy. (*Dow sinks into a chair*)

Blanche: You seriously alarm me, ma, has any accident occurred?

Dow: Accident! a frightful and unexpected one.

Lord Ing: What can it possibly be?

Col Dent: Is he sick?

Lord Ing: Hurt?

Lady Blanche: Dead?

Dow: Worse.

All: What? what?

Dow: He's poor!

Lord Ing: Inconceivable calamity!

Dow: Here, Ingram, read this, and wonder at the fellow's presumption; my own one. (*To Blanche*) I know in this, the most trying scene of your existence, you will comfort yourself as befits an Ingram – take my flacon, darling, and be heroic. Go on, Theodore.

Lord Ing (reads): 'I am ready to fulfill my contract, but honor, and a sincere desire for the happiness of her whom I love more than existence, prompt me to the avowal that the reputation of my wealth is far, very far, more than its reality; frankly, I am a poor man.' Disgusting wretch!

Col Dent: Terrible reprobate!

Dow: Impudent monster!

Lady Blanche: Ugly creature!

Lord Ing: What's this, why, this is simply laughable. (*Reads*) 'However, if love for myself and not for my possessions, animates your beautiful daughter,

I shall await her coming in the Oratory; and my Chaplain shall join us in the silken fetters of wedlock.' (*All laugh*)

Lord Ing: Well, upon my soul: that is about the coolest piece of effrontery ever attempted within the annals of Jeremy Diddlerism!

Dow: Don't weep for such an imposter, my precious –

Lady Blanche: It's not for him, ma; I don't care a pin for the creature itself; but this lovely house, those delicious grounds, ma, where I had absolutely planned all my alterations.

Lord Ing: And I had selected my suit of bachelor rooms, and actually named my favorite hunters; why, the fellow's a huge swindler.

Mary: I'm sorry you've lost such a nice fortune, Blanche, dear.

Dow: Don't be envious, child; come, darling, dry your sweet eyes, control your dear little feelings, your poor heart must suffer from this dreadful shock, I know, but it might have been worse; suppose this blow had come after the ceremony. We must leave, of course, as soon as possible.

Lord Ing: I vote we all go in a body to the fellow's oratory first, and take an affectionate leave; now I insist, mother; hang it, ain't I the head of the house; come Dent, take Blanche; now, Dowager, dignity; prepare to frown the creature into oblivion. (*Go up, closed in.*)

Scene 2

A passage or corridor, dark. Enter John frightened, L.

John: Oh! lord. I've seen it again; there can't be no sort of mistake this time, a wild looking ghost-like thing, with heavy hair, rushed by me at the end of the corridor. Ugh! what's that, – my heart beats like the fastest sort of a clock. There's something mysterious in the house, I knew there was in spite of Grace's denial. Ugh! I can't look round often enough to be sure there's nobody behind me; glaring with glassy eyes; there it is again, oh! lord! coming right through at me; mercy! mercy! your ghostship.

Grace rushes on L. and shakes him, she is frightened, but with a different expression

Grace: Up, fool!

John: Is it you! phew! it's like a reprieve on the very gallows.

Grace: What have you seen?

John: A ghost! the ghost!

Grace: Nonsense; what way did she, I mean did *it* go?

John: Whatever it was, she or it, flew right up the grand staircase like a puff of tobacco smoke. Mercy on us, Grace, what can it be?

Grace: Away, and be silent.

John:	Wasn't it a ghost, then, tell me that?
Grace:	Yes; and a mischievous one; see, it's coming back, run!
John:	Oh, lord! (*Bolts off*)
Grace:	Mischief! mischief! where will it end? (*Exit, R.*)

Scene 3

The Oratory. Octagonal recess with large stained windows, practicable, beyond which a portion of the house may be seen, consisting of turrets, to show effect of fire at the end of Act; low railing at opening of recess. Organ music.

Rochester discovered

Roch (*impatiently*): Why comes she not? my bounding soul would fain outstrip both time and thought and reach the consummation of my hope 'ere stern reflection, reason's officer, should cry, beware! Why will they leave me thus alone with conscience nicely scrupulous – Away! away! I will not think; in that direction madness lies; what, ho! (*Noise without*) Ah! here at last; be calm, my soul. (*Again noise*) 'Tis Ingram's voice; yes, as I live 'tis he and his proud sister. Have I wrongfully judged her, and my touchstone proven her to be right ringing metal? if so, I'm trebly cursed. They're here.

Enter Dowager, Ingram, Blanche, Dent, and Lady Mary, R.

Roch:	Suspense were more than agony, I must be resolved at once. How shall I welcome thee, lady; as my disinterested love, bride of my heart and not of my wealth? You are silent! be thanked for it, ye immortal powers. Speak, Blanche.
Dow:	Hold, sir; 'tis time this insolent mockery should have a termination; can you smile, deceiver, and behold the victim of your wicked perfidy?
Roch:	Perfidy! to whom, then, was your daughter betrothed, to me, or to my money-chest?
Dow:	Pshaw! what romantic nonsense is this; speak to him, Ingram, I can have no patience with the poor imposter.
Lord Ing:	'Pon my life it's a little awkward, lady mother; but as I'm the head of the house, I suppose I must.
Roch:	Let me look at you, Blanche. By heaven, her features are as calm as marble. What are promises and protestations, gentle looks and whispered sentences – all hollowness, pretence, and lies.
Lord Ing:	Come, come, Rochester, this is a most unimaginative age; that sort of talk reads tolerably well in novels, but sounds somewhat impertinent in real life. Your paper heroes are privileged individuals, but flesh and blood people don't feel inclined to listen to such improbable mouthing.

Roch: Miserable idiot!
Lord Ing (to Dent): Did you hear that?
Col Dent: Distinctly.
Lord Ing: What ought I to do?
Col Dent: Nothing!
Roch: I have no time to waste – be explicit. Do you wish this match to be broken off?
Lord Ing: Most undoubtedly. Do you suppose that I would suffer my sister to be sacrificed to a man –
Roch: Whose heart outweighs his wealth. I thought so, and am not disappointed; still I must have confirmation from the Lady Blanche, herself. Speak, lady; would you have me release you from your promise?
Blanche: Mr Rochester, I –
Dow: She would –
Roch: Hush! let *her* speak, I'll hear none other.
Blanche: I like you very much –
Dow: As a friend.
Roch: Silence! Proceed, Lady Blanche.
Blanche: My mother answers for me, sir.
Dow: Affectionate creature!
Roch: Am *I* released?

Motions Dowager to silence – a pause – he watches Blanche, as she quietly exclaims

Blanche: Yes! (*Rochester walks about quietly triumphant*)
Dow: Unconditionally; but we shall always be most happy to receive your visits in a friendly way, Mr Rochester. Shall we not, Ingram!
Lord Ing: To be sure, and I shall visit him in the shooting season. (*Aside*) Don't be disconsolate; there's a good fellow, we're all devilish sorry, you know. Keep up your spirits.
Roch: I mean to do so. My kind considerate friends, now listen to me all of ye. Had there been one touch of heart – one spark of noble feeling in that woman's nature – I should deeply regret the *stratagem* which I have used. (*All start*)
Lord Ing: *Stratagem!* I'm afraid we're sold!
Roch: But as it is, her unworthiness has, like a dull foil, made lighter still the starlike radiance of her, for whose beloved sake, I fling aside the gauds of title and of name. Come forth, sole mistress of this heart and home. (*Leads forward Jane Eyre – all start*)
Dow:
Blanche: } The governess!
Lord Ing: Lady mother, you are checkmated.
All the servants cluster round – the chaplain enters the enclosure

Dow: Marry the governess? revolting!

Roch: Yes, *the governess*! one pure instant of whose companionship were worth a whole eternity with such as ye. Come, be witnesses of the fulfilment of my soul's uttermost desire. Look up, sweet love – look up – a few moments nerve. (*Leads her towards enclosure – large bell, hastily rung – noise without*) What interruption's this?

Grace (*heard outside*): She has escaped!

Roch: Horror! what do I hear; must my cup of joy be dashed from me, even in the moment of my greatest bliss? Never. Proceed with the ceremony. (*Noise increases – bell louder*)

Enter John

John: The house is in flames.

Confusion – the oratory window is thrust open with terrible crash, and the maniac wife appears in the opening, a torch in her hand

Roch: My wife!

Jane: His wife! (*Faints – portion of the house beyond seen in flames*)

Curtain

Act V

Scene 1

Plain chamber

Jane discovered

Jane: Twelve months have passed since that fearful day. Oh, too faithful memory, why didst thou call up the loathsome picture in its terrible reality. I see it now before my eyes, as vividly as when stricken by the bolt of destiny, even at the very theshold of my joy; now almost a bride, and in an instant alone – alone; the Christmas frost had come at midsummer, and the smiling way of life that seemed to blu[sh so] full of flowers, became in a moment pathless with untrodden snow, and yet it was not for myself this bitterness of anguish – it was for him – that I dare not deem him worthy; that the pure and bright ideal that I had thought was found in him, should be so blurred and blackened. I have worshipped a false image, and I must tear it from the altar I myself have raised. Alas! alas! 'tis not a vapor sunshine can disperse – 'tis not a sand-traced effigy storms can wash away; it is a name engraved upon a tablet, which must last as long as the marble upon which it is inscribed. Oh! for some friendly hand to point my proper road. I fear myself there is a sweet, strange, dreamy spell pervades this solemn eventime my failing sense cannot resist. I'm powerless beneath its influence. Oh, if in dreams, good angels ere suggest the better course, may such welcome visitors be mine.

Sleeps – Music. The scene becomes luminous, and Rochester is seen stretching his hand towards her – he exclaims – 'Jane! Jane! where art thou?' – vision vanishes – Jane starts up.

Jane:　　　　I am here, Rochester, my still beloved: this is no deception of the mind – no witchcraft: I heard him distinctly – the music of his words yet rings in my ears. Again he speaks – he calls me, in tones of suffering. He may be dying, and I not near to look at my last of love and life. Rochester, wait for me – I come, I come.　　　　　　　　　　　　　*(Exit)*

Scene 2

Interior of a Cottage

Enter John, R.

John:　　　　Well, I never did see any one take on for any body in such an outrageous way as my poor master does for that there governess. One would naterally suppose that the whole race of soft sexes was abolished from the face of the inhabitable globe, which every body knows and we in perticular, they are not.

Enter Mrs John [Downey], Late Grace, L.

Mrs D:　　　Now, turnip skull, what are you wasting your time there for?
John:　　　　None of your vegetable allusions if you please, or else I might insinuate something respecting *Carrots*, Mrs Downey.
Mrs D:　　　Alluding to my hair, I presume, Mr D.
John:　　　　Precisely, Mrs D.
Mrs D:　　　Before we were married you used to call it auburn.
John:　　　　That's the poetical for red, you know; only an allowable ante-nuptial fiction, as my old master, the lawyer, used to say.
Mrs D:　　　I'll fiction your thick head with the broom-handle if you don't mind.
John:　　　　Ah, you let the devil's hoof peep out now. I suppose we'll have the horns soon. You were a different sort of an individual when you went

sneaking about Thornfield with your bit of bread and cheese, awaiting on that she-devil as was shut up there; you couldn't say boo to a goose then.

Mrs D:	I've often had a chance since.
John:	Mrs D., respect the head of your family.
Mrs D:	There's nothing in it.
John:	Honor the provider of your wittles. Oh why did I ever marry?
Mrs D:	That's a question that always comes too late, and moreover is never asked except by a good-for-nothing husband; see, who is that lady beckoning to you. Stupid, go and see what she wants – while I get master's dinner on the do. (*Exit into house*)

Enter Jane slightly concealing her face, L.

Jane:	Is this Ferndean farm?
John:	It is, marm.
Jane:	Your name is John Downey.
John:	I never had no other as I knows on, marm. (*Aside*) Exceptin' now and then, turnip skull and such like.
Jane:	They told me at the inn that you could give me the information that I require. You know Thornfield Hall?
John:	Yes, marm; I lived there once; I was the late Mr Rochester's own man.
Jane:	The late – I –
John:	Dear me, marm, anything the matter?
Jane:	A spasm – 'twll soon be over. Have I then lived and hoped for this? With one simple word to be forever crushed, destroyed.
Jane:	When did Mr Rochester die?
John:	I don't mean the present gentleman.
Jane:	Present? *he* is alive then.
John:	Oh, yes, marm, he's *alive*!
Jane:	Thank Heaven! I can bear anything now! the light of hope and joy rekindled! Does he live at Thornfield Hall now?
John:	No marm; no one is living there. You must be a stranger here or you would have known that the Hall was burnt down last harvest time.
Jane:	Burnt? the Hall?
John:	Yes marm. The fire broke out at dead of night. It was a terrible sight. It nearly caught fire once before, at a strange time – there was a wedding about to take place.
Jane:	But the last fire; how did it originate?
John:	The same way. A raving lunatic, that turned out to be Mr Rochester's wife, after having made several attempts, succeeded at last.
Jane:	And was *he*! Mr Rochester in the house?

John:	Oh, yes marm, and never left it until everybody else was safe. Then he tried to get his mad wife out of the place, but she fled to the roof, where she yelled and gave a spring and in the next moment she lay upon the pavement.
Jane:	Great Heaven! Dead?
John:	Yes, marm, as dead as the very stones she lay on.
Jane:	One question more. My laboring heart throbs painfully at each pulsation. I scarcely dare to ask him from fear. While there's delay there still is hope, and yet, suspense is anguish. What of the master of the Hall – is he in the country?
John:	Yes, marm. He can't get out of it well, now. He's a fixture.
Jane:	There is an awful meaning in your words.
John:	He's blind, marm, stone blind.
Jane:	Thank heaven! I had feared a worse calamity; the loss of reason – but where? do you know where he now is?
John:	He ain't far off, marm; he's in the garden yonder.
Jane:	So near. I was not prepared for this, John. Do you not know me?
John:	Dear heart – why it's the governess. Oh, but this will be a nappy meeting for us all.
Jane:	Let us retire from observation.
John:	You forget, Miss, he can't see a mite.
Jane:	Oh, terrible affliction – and I to be so long estranged from him, when words of solace were so needed. My very soul yearns to bring him comfort; it is not now a crime – it is a duty.
John:	You'll see him, Miss, won't you?
Jane:	See him, John! his very shadow in the sun shall not be nearer or more constant than I, while life remains.
John:	This is indeed a joyful return. I shouldn't wonder but it will even smooth Mrs D's wrinkles. I'm married, Miss; don't you recollect Grace Pool, she's what folks call a good woman in the *main*: I wish she *was* in it, just to try the experiment.
Jane:	Quick! let me see her; I must consult with her the means of introducing myself to Rochester. (*Exit John*) Be firm, be firm, my heart – no shrinking now; this is thy duty; perform it well, even though neglect and coldness be the recompense.

Re-enter John, with water

John:	He has just called for a glass of water.
Jane:	His kind fate points out a means for me to see him without danger of too sudden a recognition. Give me the water, John; I'll take it to him. Now, courage, courage. (*Exit, R.*)

Scene 3

Exterior of Farm House – Rochester discovered – his arms stretched out – he is blind – his hair streaming in the breeze. – The picture as before in the vision.

Roch:	Jane! Jane! ah, if you but knew that sky and mountain, field and flower, are shut out from me for ever, you would not desert the proud, strong man in the day of his affliction. In the wickedness of my heart I spurned all control, and would have done thee wrong, angel of brightness and purity; but I am punished, sorely punished. In vain for me the day dawns and breaks, the sun rises and the seasons change. All is to me a blank; my existence shrouded in unending night. Twelve months – twelve long, leaden, fearful months have passed since that bright earthly vision fled from me – even as the pure and good will ever flee from the assassin of the soul; yet how often has the cruel delusion seized me that she was in my very presence, though unseen, just as I feel this fire's genial glow, but cannot see the flame which causes it.

Enter Jane, L. with tray, tumbler of water on it

Roch:	Even now my mocking sense would almost persuade me that I heard her breathe; out upon this heart-consuming deception – it almost drives me to despair. (*Sits*)
Jane:	Ah, what a sight – what a sight! (*very quietly*)
Roch:	There is some one near me. Grace, have you brought the water. (*Jane hands it to him – he drinks*) Thanks. No news, I suppose; silent – ah, I knew it! I knew it. Thus for ever must I stretch the chord of expectation and of life until they snap together. Hush! did you not hear something – a small quiet murmuring sound like hers, so like Jane's. I heard it but a short time since; it said, '*Rochester, I come! I come!*' as distinctly as ever sound reached my ear. Ah! malicious spirits that sport with human hearts, this is the cruelest pastime. I hear nothing. Oh! for one week's eyesight. I would find her or a grave. (*Jane sighs*) Who is that? that wasn't you, Grace? Is there any one with you? answer me. Is that you, Grace
Jane:	Grace is in the kitchen, sir.
Roch (starts up in violent agitation):	I know that voice, if the cheating demon is not practising on my sense once more. Who is this? What is it? Speak again, whoever your are.
Jane:	Will you have a little more water, sir?
Roch:	Again – great heaven! this is distraction. Why don't you tell me whether you are a living thing or another of those tantalizing fiends that worry me to the verge of madness. Who or what are you?
Jane:	I come to wait on you.

Roch:	Delusion, nothing but delusion. What sweet madness has seized me?
Jane:	No delusion, sir, no madness; your mind is too strong for delusion, your health too sound for frenzy.
Roch:	And where is this speaker? is it only a voice? Oh! I cannot see, but I must touch you or my heart will stop and my brain burst.

Jane approaches him – he takes her hand

Roch:	Her very fingers, her small slight fingers; if so, there must be more. (*Touches, and finally clasps her in his arms*) Is it Jane? What is it? it has her shape and feature.
Jane:	Yes, Rochester, and her voice and heart. Jane is here – here with you.
Roch:	In truth and in flesh! my living Jane!
Jane:	You hold me in your arms. I am not vacant like the air.
Roch:	But if I let you go will you not fade away, vanish as all the rest have done?
Jane:	Never! never! from this day.
Roch:	Never, says the vision; but don't you know, unearthly thing, that bright as are these delicious moments, they must have an end. I know that in a moment this hand, which I foolishly deem real, will elude my grasp, and that voice which sounded to my enraptured sense like heavenly music, will die away upon the echoes and be heard no more. Gentle, soft dream, you will fly me like those who came before, many, oh, many a time.
Jane:	Is it a dream to grasp your kind hand with the warm truthfulness of love; to tell you that I am here – I, Jane, your own Jane; to avow that love and glory in that avowal; to say that my life, hitherto dark and hopeless, is once more bathed in the brilliancy of an enduring joy; that my heart which famished for your presence, is sated from the very fulness of its banquet.
Roch:	It *is* you, Jane – my living, breathing, loving, constant Jane. Come near me, and let me fancy that I see you with these rayless orbs. I cannot! I cannot! but I feel your presence like a shower of sunlight on my heart; and you've come back to me again, and will you stay with me?
Jane:	Unless you object! I will be your neighbor, your nurse, your housekeeper, your companion; to read to you, to walk with you, to sit with you, to be eyes and hands to you, – that is, if you wish it, not otherwise. (*Disengaging herself a little*)
Roch:	No, no Jane. You must not go. I have touched you, heard you, felt the comfort of your presence, the sweetness of your consolation, and I cannot give up these joys; my very soul demands you, Jane. There are other thoughts within my brain which I dare not utter. What right has such a ruin as I to bid a budding woodbine cover its decay with freshness?

Jane:	You are not a ruin, sir. Friends, troops of friends will cluster around you.
Roch:	Friend! I want a nearer tie, Jane, my Jane; do you not comprehend me? you do, and I may speak the wish of my soul. Jane, will you be my wife?
Jane:	I will.
Roch:	What! wife to the poor blind man whom you will have to lead by the hand?
Jane:	Yes!
Roch:	Truly, Jane?
Jane:	Most truly, sir!
Roc:	Oh, my darling! Heaven will bless and reward you for the sacrifice.
Jane:	Sacrifice? if ever I did a good deed in my life, if ever I thought a good thought, if ever I prayed a sincere and blameless prayer, if ever I wished a sacred wish, I am rewarded now. To be your wife is to be as happy as I can be on earth. (*Shout outside*)
Roch:	What is that? John?

Enter John

Roch:	What means that shout?
John:	Have you forgotten, sir, that this is your birth-day?
Roch:	Truly, I had, John. But now I accept the omen as a good one, for my life is again renewed through the heaven-gift of thy pure and true love, my earth-angel.
John:	Your tenants who love and respect you, sir, have brought their poor but honest gifts; it would make them and all of us so happy sir, if you would accept them.
Roch:	Let them approach. My wife, John, that is to be shortly, will accept them for me.
John:	Hurrah! there will be another shout for that. Come friends!
Roch:	I cannot see their merriment, my love; but what will the sum of all their joy be, compared with mine?

Enter Peasants; Jane and Rochester advance

John:	Don't spare your lungs. A cheer for our kind master and his intended bride. (*Hurrah all. Present bouquets to Jane.*)
Roch:	My good fellows – I – speak to them for me, Jane, the fullness of my joy chokes my very utterance.
Jane:	I am myself too happy for many words. My friends, he whose ambition is to be the kind landlord, and the good adviser, cannot, alas! behold your kindly glances, but he thanks you for your generous sympathy, as I do from my heart.

Jane leads Rochester to seat, a device is fixed by the peasants having printed thereon in flowers 'The Farmer's Friend.' Garlands depend from the center, which are held up by Peasants, forming a canopy for Jane and Rochester: Music

Curtain

Jane Eyre

A Drama in Two Acts

Anon.

1867

Editor's Notes

The Text

The play exists in a single hand-written copy in the Lord Chamerberlain's Collection of Plays in the Manuscript Room of the British Library (Add. MS 53063.F). The manuscript is written on plain blue foolscap, using both sides of the paper, in large, regular, legible script (the same hand throughout), which becomes more compressed towards the end. The play is bound with other plays in a large volume whose spine is broken, but the pages are in good condition. The *recto* pages are numbered 1–17; the *verso* pages are not numbered. The title page includes the following note:

Received November 14
Licence sent " 15.

W.B. Donne.

From Messrs Shepherd & Creswick
New Surrey Theatre
Blackfriars Road

The Licence No. attached to the manuscript is 15. The Lord Chamberlain's Day Book has no further information except 'Date of Licence November 15. Date of Entry November 20'.

The play is a much shortened version of Charlotte Birch-Pfeiffer's (first performed in Germany in 1853), and where Birch-Pfeiffer's version is in a Prologue and Three Acts, this play has only two acts, Act I corresponding to Birch-Pfeiffer's Prologue, and Act II compressing the remaining action. I have substituted 'Act I' for 'Scene 1', since the 'scene' ends with the words 'end of Act I' and is followed by Act II.

The text relies heavily on dashes for punctuation and some speeches lack final punctuation. I have retained dashes wherever the sense is clear, but have removed capital letters when these follow a dash rather than a full stop or question mark, and have removed dashes which follow other punctuation such as a question mark or comma. I have supplied some commas, question marks and full stops where these aid clarity, and have supplied apostrophes for possessives such as *Jane's* and for abbreviations such as *don't* and *can't*. I have removed capital letters from the middles of sentences (for example, 'It is so long since I have even seen a Book') and have corrected spelling errors (such as *grevious* for *grievous*) where this is not in character.

The Playwright

Nothing is known of the author of this play. Neither the manuscript nor either of the playbills has an author's name. The play is clearly a shortened and translated version of Charlotte Birch-Pfeiffer's play. It must have been pirated, since although the play was first performed in Vienna in 1853, it was not printed until 1870, when a dual-language version was published in New York.[1] In Act II, however, Jane's two speeches beginning, 'Made of different clay' and 'My Lord, ignorant assumption', are taken *verbatim* from John Brougham's play, first performed in New York in 1849 and published there in 1856.

Plagiarism, or 'piracy', was extremely common in the nineteenth century and Catherine Evans describes how Heinrich Laube, the manager of the Viennese Hofburgtheater where Birch-Pfeiffer's German play was first performed,

> moved swiftly to produce the piece so that its success would not be spoiled by the prior appearance at one of the suburban theaters by [sic] a copy of Birch-Pfeiffer's play bearing the same title which had appeared at several other theaters.[2]

John Russell Stephens claims that in England, despite the Dramatic Copyright Act of 1833, 'dramatised versions of novels […] were in effect immune from the law on copyright',[3] and in this case there was the added immunity of copying from a foreign source. At some point a translator must have been involved, but we have no information about this. We should not be surprised at this dearth; Stephens confirms that:

> Given the unprecedented number of dramatists writing in the nineteenth century, many of whom wrote perhaps only one play and had no other claim to fame, […] it is safe to assert that the vast majority do not appear in any of the biographical dictionaries. And there is a whole host of very active minor theatre melodramatists […] who are biographical blanks.[4]

The Theatre and Performances

The play was licensed for performance at the New Surrey Theatre, on the south bank of the Thames, on 15 November 1867, and was advertised in *The Times* the following day as companion piece to a more important play called *Nobody's Child*.[5] The part of Jane was played by Georgiana Pauncefort, who is described in a much later article as 'then leading lady at the Surrey, and afterwards for so many years associated with

---

1   *Die Waise von Lowood* was not printed in Germany until 1876, when it appeared in Vol. 14 of Birch-Pfeiffer's complete dramatic works (*Gesammelte dramatische Werke*) published by the Reclam Publishing House, Leipzig. I am grateful to Barbara Jean Frick for this information.

2   Evans, p. 235.

3   Stephens, *Profession*, pp. 91, 97.

4   Stephens, *Profession*, p. 192.

5   *Times* 16 November 1867, p. 8; see also *ILN* 16 November, 1867. Pascoe (p. 127) gives Watts Phillips as the author of *Nobody's Child*: the MS in the Lord Chamberlain's Plays (Add. MS 53061. P) is anonymous.

the epoch-making Irving held sway at the Lyceum'.[6] Several commentators note her performance as Gertrude to Irving's Hamlet, which Joseph Knight describes in emotional detail.[7] E.F. Edgar, who played Rochester, was also a notable actor who performed at all the West End Theatres, and was for a time joint lessee of the Surrey with Shepherd.[8]

The Surrey Theatre was originally built in 1782. It was situated at 124, Blackfriar's Road, in Lambeth, not far from the Victoria, and was often linked with its 'transpontine' neighbour.[9] During a brief closure of the Victoria in 1846, in fact, David Osbaldiston and Eliza Vincent appeared at the Surrey Theatre 'in Double Dramatic Company of the Victoria and Surrey Players'.[10] Thornbury and Walford report that 'St George's Circus, at the south end of Blackfriars Road, was so thickly peopled by second-rate actors belonging to the Surrey and the Coburg, that it was called the Theatrical Barracks'.[11] The two theatres openly competed for the same audience, sometimes showing the same plays,[12] although the Surrey specialized in nautical plays with impressive water scenes. Unlike the Victoria, however, the Surrey was repeatedly destroyed by fire (in 1799, 1805 and 1865) and was rebuilt for the third time in December, 1865, little more than a year before its production of *Jane Eyre*.[13] The new interior, with a seating capacity of over 2,000,[14] attracted a great deal of attention, and the *Illustrated London News* gives considerable details in addition to the engraving shown in Figure 7, including its overall dimensions (200 × 100 feet), the size of the auditorium (68 × 62 feet), and details of the seating (two rows of stalls, a dress-tier and gallery). The stage area (60 × 70 feet) and 'the various rooms appropriated to the actors, &c., are all lofty and spacious'.[15]

---

6 *Sketch* 5 May 1897, p. 58. *Daily News* lists 'Messrs Edgar, Terry, & Nelson; Miss Webster' as actors in *Jane Eyre* (16 November 1867) and carries intermittent advertisements until 8 February 1868. *Era* advertises the play as 'A New and Highly Interesting Drama', 17 November 1867 (p. 8) and weekly until 2 February 1868.

7 Knight, p. 5. Pascoe (p. 279) also mentions this role and Taylor (p. 5) gives 1874 as its date.

8 Edgar also acted in *Nobody's Child* (Pascoe, p. 127).

9 Howard, p. 233.

10 SLSL list of playbills for the Surrey Theatre, 1846 (No. 107).

11 Thornbury and Walford, Vol. 6, p. 371.

12 Davis and Emeljanow, p. 24.

13 Howard, p. 234. The theatre was demolished in 1934.

14 Howard gives 2,161 (p. 234); Davis and Emeljanow 3,000 (p. 24).

15 *ILN*, 20 January 1866, Vol. 48 p. 73. See also *ILN*, 4 February 1865, *Builder*, 1865 (4 February, p. 79; 10 February, p. 93; 1 April, p. 231; 16 December, pp. 889–90; 30 December, pp. 917–18) and *Building News*, 29 December 1865, p. 923. SLSL has a useful collection of clippings.

Figure 7   Interior of the Surrey Theatre, rebuilt after fire shortly before the 1867 performance of *Jane Eyre*: *Illustrated London News*, 20 January 1866. Image supplied by Hull University Photographic Service

On 18 December, when *Jane Eyre* was still running with *Nobody's Child*, the viewing figures claimed to be over 200,000.[16] *Nobody's Child* was typical of the sensational melodramas favoured at the Surrey Theatre, exploiting the theatre's resources for dramatic scene-setting, machinery and special effects. Figure 8 shows a scene in which the heroine, against a terrific backdrop, stands on the edge of a ravine holding a rope on which hangs her lover. During the following week, *Nobody's Child* was replaced by the Christmas pantomime, but *Jane Eyre* was still going strong. The playbill in Figure 9 shows *Jane Eyre* advertised 'on BOXING NIGHT, at Seven o'clock', followed by 'Surrey's Grand Allegorical & Nautical Pantomime, entitled The Fair One with the Golden Locks or Harlequin and DAVY JONES'S LOCKER'.[17] The style of the playbill and the programme shows the influence of David Osbaldiston, who was briefly manager of the Surrey Theatre in the 1830s and 1840s.[18] The pantomime scenery is clearly of great importance: three scene painters are named, and even more prominence is given to 'The GRAND TRANSFORMATION SCENE invented and painted by that eminent artist Mr F. Lloyds' and 'The Stupendous Machinery by Mr. T. LOWE'.

The *Daily Telegraph* gives a vivid description of the theatre atmosphere on this occasion, and since no Dickens or Mayhew has described the Surrey audience as they did the Victoria, I feel it worth recording this at some length:

> Transpontine theatres have always been famous for their boxing-night novelties, and above all for their unannounced attraction, a boxing-night audience. It was curious to notice last evening the patience of the hundreds of people who from an early period of the afternoon had waited in the dank fog for the opening of the doors of the Surrey Theatre, which has an ancient reputation for genuine pantomime. Physiognomists and students of character would have found ample scope for observation if they had carefully noted the various types of head and expression which were blocked under the portico at about six o'clock. Nothing, however, could exceed the good humour and forbearance of the mob of holiday-makers, and when at last the bolts rattled and the pit and gallery portals were thrown open there was a roar of satisfaction, and the usual scamper for the front seats. It was particularly amusing to notice the demeanour of the fortunate 'gods' who, by much patience and some hard fighting, had secured the first row in the gallery. After formally

---

16 *Times,* 18 December 1867, p. 8. *Daily News* shows that on 19 December *Jane Eyre* appeared together with *The Lady of Lyons* and *Julius Caesar*, and on 20 December with *Nobody's Child*.

17 Although *Daily News* advertises the pantomime for 26 December, it does not mention *Jane Eyre* until 4 January, when it runs until 9 February except 20–24 January. *Daily Telegraph* reviews *The Fair one with the Golden Locks* (27 December 1867), as does *Penny Illustrated Paper* (28 December 1867), which advertises both plays until 8 February 1868.

18 SLSL bookseller's notes for the playbill collection give Osbaldiston as proprietor of the Surrey in 1832; Baker (p. 395) cites 1848 as the last date for Osbaldiston at the Surrey. Howard (p. 234) gives no information on management before 1843, and does not mention Osbaldiston in 1848.

Figure 8   Scene from *Nobody's Child*, the companion play for the 1867 *Jane Eyre*, showing the elaborate scenery for which the Surrey Theatre was famous: *Illustrated London News*, 28 September 1867. Image supplied by Hull University Photographic Service

depositing themselves in their places, they calmly surveyed the scene with something of the self-complacency of heroes or conquerors. We have already borne testimony to the excellent temper of the 'highest' class of the audience, and their bearing generally was excellent. Certainly, at intervals, there were a few obstreperous squabbles about the rights of possession, but as the evening wore on the greatest amity prevailed, and in the gallery the company comported themselves with as much hilarity and with as many marked manifestations of enjoyment as if they were participating in some huge indoor picnic party.

This good-humoured audience was, not, however, quick to settle down:

The drama of 'Jane Eyre' preceded the performance of the pantomime, and the first act of necessity was given in dumb show; but we must deprecate a system which is becoming common on Boxing-night among actors and actresses of simulating dialogue by mere movements of the mouth, instead of delivering the ordinary colloquy as intended by the author. Notwithstanding the excellent acting of Mr E.F. Edgar, and of the lady who impersonated Jane Eyre, the audience, uproarious and impatient, heard not a word of the opening piece.[19]

The playbill names Mr Shepherd, Kennington Park, and Mr Creswick, Bloomsbury Square, as 'Actual and Responsible Managers' of the Surrey Theatre. 'Dick' Shepherd had taken over the management in 1848, when he was very briefly in partnership with Osbaldiston:

Shepherd was afterwards joined by Creswick, the tragedian. A more ill-assorted pair never coalesced; Creswick was nothing if not legitimate; he had all the pompous grandiloquence of the old actor; while his partner, a famous representative of the Surrey sailor, swore by rough-and-tumble melodrama, was vulgar and slangy, and always spoke of Creswick as 'Mr Bill Shakespeare. Yet their partnership endured [...] from 1848 to 1869.[20]

Shepherd was clearly a pragmatic manager, who

developed a policy that mingled melodrama, farce, Shakespeare, the legitimate drama, and the opera and also attracted many visiting stars, who would not have been willing to appear at the Victoria. The intention was evidently to offer a diversity of attractions, presumably to draw and/or cater to a diversity of playgoers. [...] The Osbaldiston/Vincent management at the Victoria and the Shepherd/Creswick management at the Surrey had consequently established quite diverse policies: the Victoria's emphasis on domestic drama arguably catered to a local, popular audience; whereas the Surrey's combination

---

[19] *Daily Telegraph*, 27 December 1867, p. 3.
[20] Baker, p. 395. *Entr'Acte* for 25 November 1882 has an impressive, dignified cartoon portrait of 'Mr William Creswick: Fifty Years an Actor – and a Very Good Actor Too'; see also Pascoe, pp. 117–18.

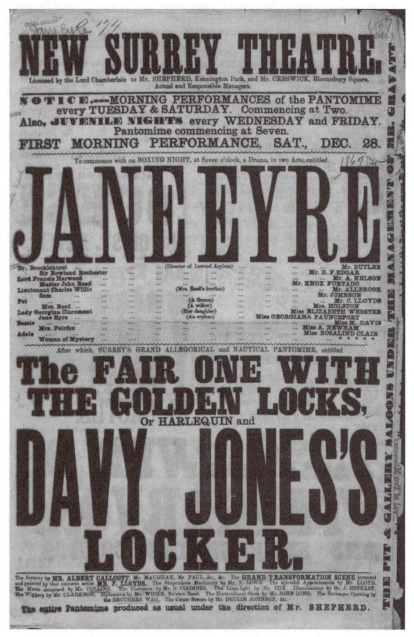

Figure 9   Playbill for the anonymous version of *Jane Eyre* performed at the
                  Surrey Theatre, London, in 1867. This unique copy is reproduced by
                  permission of Billy Rose Theatre Collection, The New York Public
                  Library for the Performing Arts, Lenox and Tilden Foundations

THE INTERIOR OF MRS. BROWN'S COTTAGE. A. CALLCOT

Mrs. Brown ... ... (late of the Egyptian Hall, but now of New York, U.S.) ... Mr. CLINGAN JON.
"The Fair One with the Golden Locks" (such a pretty little Lady with the Golden Hair) Miss AUGUST◁ THOMSON
(From the Royal Italian Opera, Covent Garden)

Baron Boguhee	(A Villain of the deepest Dye)	Mr. E. TERRY
Prince Hyacinth	(A Loud Swell of the First Water)	Miss ELIZABETH WEBSTER
Mopsey, Sig. MANGLETIZA	Scrubby, Sig. IRONH	Wringy, Sig. STARCHENI	Suddy, Sig. SODERINA
Topsy ,, BLUE BAGARELLI	Rubby ,, SOPEANI	Primmy ,, TURBERINI	Soapy ,, PALEINA
Handchopper, Mr. BATTLEAXE	Toothdrawer, Mr. TWO-HANDED CRACK	Thumbscrewer, Mr. POLEAXE	Corncutter, Mr. TOMAHAWK
Boss Slitter ,, LONGBOW	Eyegouger ,, FALCHION	Earlopper ,, SCIMATAR	Garotter ,, MACE
Fairy Pavonia	(Queen of the Peacocks)	Miss H. CLAYTON

GOLDEN GROVES OF LABURNAMS
AND GARDEN OF SWEET SCENTS. A. CALLCOTT.

CARLO - - (The original Howling Swell) Mr. KNOX FURTADO

THE FAIRY FLOWERS.

Rosebud	Lily	Verbena	Blue Bell	Pink	Heartsease	Marigold	Crocus
Geranium	Wallflower	Calceolaria	Forget-me-not	Poppy	Foxglove	Cactus	Primrose
Tulip	Narcissus	Violet	Carnation	Canterbury Bell	London Pride	Snowdrop	Thistle
Daisy	Buttercup	Fuschia	Convolvulus	Nasturtium	Lobelia

GRAND FAIRY BALLET BY THE WORLD OF FLOWERS.

EXTERIOR OF DAVY JONES'S LOCKER AND THE BED OF THE ATLANTIC CABLE. A. Callcott.
BRINY - (The original Horse Marine and Inventor of Salt Junk) - Mr. C. LLOYDS

DAVY JONES'S LOCKER
AT THE BOTTOM OF THE DEEP BLUE SEA. A. Callcott

DAVY JONES	-	(Managing Director of the Ocean Wreckers' Company, Unlimited)	-	Mr. W. HOLSTON
Leascupper...Mr Blue Peter	Mizenmast...Mr Six Water Grog	Binnacle...Mr Marling Spike	Gangway...Mr Quid
Jibboon ...Mr Saltjunk	Foresail ...Mr Captain Biscuit	Capstan ...Mr Box the Compass	Taffrail...Mr South-Wester

And a Large Family of the Breezes.
NILENUS (A Live Submarine Telegraph Boy, the only specimen in existence) Master WALLY JOHNSTONE

WHALE BAY ON THE SHORES OF GREENWICH A. CALLCOTT

THE WALRUS ... ... (The only one in England) ... ... Mr. NORTHSEA

THRONE ROOM IN PRINCE HYACINTH'S PALACE.

Masters SAMBO and JUMBO ... Masters BARNEY and PETE

TRANSCENDANTLY GRAND TRANSFORMATION SCENE.

REFULGENT TEMPLES OF BRIGHT WATERS
NEPTUNE'S HOMAGE
TO BRITANNIA.

Britannia ... ... ,, (the Pride of the Ocean) ... ... Miss DAVIS
Neptune ... ... ,, (King of the Ocean) ... ... Mr. ALLBROOK
Amphithrite ... ... (His Wife and Queen) ... ... Miss GRIFFITH

APOTHEOSIS OF EARTH, AIR, FIRE, AND WATER.
THE SCENE INVENTED AND PAINTED BY THAT EMINENT ARTIST
MR. F. LLOYDS.

CLOWN .... (By the Great Surrey Clown and Queen's Jester) ... HARRY CROUESTE
PANTALOON ... Mr. GELLINI SIR BOBBY Mr. CLINGAN JONES
HARLEQUIN ... ... Mr. A. SYLVAIN
COLUMBINE...Madlle. EMILIE COLONNA HARLEQUINA...Miss E. COLLINS

BENNETT'S, CHEAPSIDE. LICENSED VICTUALLERS AND TEA DEALERS. MAUGHAM.

FARMER'S COTTAGE & RURAL RETREAT
CITY CLERKS' DINING ROOMS. TAILORS' & CORPORATION DINING-HALL.

THE ISLAND'S JEWELS
THE PEEP SHOW MAN
IN PREPARATION, AN ORIGINAL DRAMA By T. J. WILLIAMS, Esq., ENTITLED

In which MR. SHEPHERD will make his first appearance this Season.

Doors open at HALF-PAST SIX, commence at SEVEN. Box Office open daily from 11 to 4. Private Boxes and Stalls at all the Libraries. STALLS, 2s.
DRESS CIRCLE, 2s. UPPER BOXES, 1s. 6d. PIT, 1s. GALLERY, 6d. SECOND PRICE TO BOXES AND STALLS ONLY at NINE o'clock.
Acting Manager and Treasurer, Mr. W. JAMES. Stage Manager, Mr. F. H. DALTON. The Auditorium under the Management of Mr. GAUNTLETT.
All Inspector, Mr. SPENCER, to whom all APPLICATIONS are to be ADDRESSED.

FEARES MORRISON, Printer, London, E.C.

of legitimate drama and opera with the more popular forms of melodrama, burletta, and farce, appealed to both a mixed local audience and to visitors from further afield.[21]

The fact that the Surrey advertised its *Jane Eyre* in *The Times* also suggests that its managers were hoping for a less local, and more cultivated, audience. Davis and Emeljanow comment that 'press reports of the Surrey from 1843 onwards are generally favorable', and expectations seem to be 'higher of this theatre than of the neighbouring Victoria,' but that in the 1860s this reputation was declining, and that the re-opened theatre of 1866 was struggling to regain popularity.[22] The 1867–1868 pantomime, however, was clearly a great success,[23] and a second Surrey playbill, still advertising *Jane Eyre* with the pantomime for 13–18 January 1868, gives prominence to the pantomime reviews. *Jane Eyre* continued to run, sometimes alternating with other plays, until the beginning of February.[24]

Reception of the Play

I have no information about the reception of this play beyond the general descriptions of the audience in the preceding section.

Distinctive Features of the Play

• Settings are confined to Gateshead and Thornfield.
• The treatment of orphans is a moral touchstone by which Mr Reed (in relation to Jane and her mother), Jane (in relation to Adèle) and Rochester (in relation to Adèle and Lady Rochester) are shown as worthy, in contrast to Mrs Reed.
• Rochester is 'Sir Rowland Rochester'; he has been 'in India'.
• The Reed family take the place of the Ingrams.
• Georgina Reed (Lady Claremont) is shown as a scheming widow.
• The dramaturgy is less melodramatic than in Brougham.
• The madwoman is the wife of Rochester's dead brother.
• Rochester presents Jane to his guests as his future wife at the end.

---

21   Davis and Emeljanow, pp. 25, 39. SLSL's large playbill collection confirms the range of productions.
22   Davis and Emeljanow, pp. 25, 31.
23   *Daily Telegraph* (27 December 1867, p. 3), *ILN*, 4 January 1868, Vol. 52, p. 19. *Examiner* (12 December 1867) is also positive, but is probably confusing the Surrey with the Standard, also newly rebuilt.
24   *Times*, 16 November 1867, p. 8; *Daily News* 16 November–18 December 1867; *Times*, 20 January 1868 (p. 6), 21 January 1868 (p. 8), 28 January 1868 (p. 6) and 31 January 1868 (p. 6).

Jane Eyre (Anon.)

[Act] I

Elegant Apartment

Christmas Carol without:

God bless the master of this house
And bless the mistress too
And all the little children
Who round the table go.

The lanes are frost and snow
Our shoes are very thin
But we've a little pocket
To put a penny in –

Enter Jane Eyre – kneels to portrait

Jane: Dear kind uncle Reed, do you see your poor Jane? You smile – all here call me wicked, ungrateful. Did I not love you as you loved me? but all now hate me. This, dear uncle, is your birthday. You gave all to them – and now thou art in the silent tomb – accept this day the only tribute I can offer to thy memory – my tears!

Enter Bessie

Bessie: Jane, what are you doing here? You are forbidden to enter this apartment.

Jane: I only came to look on Uncle Reed – this is his birthday – all here seem to have forgotten it.

Bessie: 'Tis now more than five years since your uncle's death – quite an eternity.

Jane: Eternity – true – true. How happy I was while my uncle lived – I knew not then what it was to be an orphan – to be wretched and alone.

Bessie: Come away, Jane. I am afraid lest missus should come and find you here – how angry she would be – come away – directly!

Jane: I will not.

Bessie: Do be good, Jane – don't get me into trouble.

Jane: Bessie, don't scold me, my heart is full.

Bessie: Why will you be so perverse?

Jane: It isn't my fault Bessie. You are so seldom kind to poor Jane – let me stay here to read the books – this is Christmastide – all are busy with

	joy and revelry – let me stay – it seems so long since I have even seen a book – Georgina has locked them all up.

Bessie: But if any one should know it!

Jane: Don't fear, Bessie. (*Takes book*) Hume's *History of England* – see, I've found it at once – now I'll hide myself behind these curtains – nobody will see me – here I can read the history of my native land.

Bessie: Don't move, Jane, for your life. Remember – in half an hour I shall come for you.

Jane: Fear not, I shall be as quiet as a mouse.

Bessie: Poor girl, Missus may scold as much as she likes, but I can't find it in my heart to deny her – (*going*)

Enter John Reed

John Reed: Hallo! Bessie! What are you up to – come here!

Bessie: I can't waste my time with you, Master John.

John: Stay here when I bid you. I want you to tell me a funny story – there's uncle Willis just returned from Spain and Mamma talking such twaddle – no fellar of sense can understand it, and there sits sister Georgina as stately as a queen listening to them. I kept pelting her with biscuit, just as if she was anybody.

Bessie: It doesn't become you, Sir, to treat your sister in that way – she is your elder, therefore you should be respectful to her.

John: Respectful to her! I have no respect for anyone. I don't care for Mamma – they will all one day be dependent on my charity. When I'm twenty-one the estate will be mine – and all those who offend me now will suffer for it.

Bessie: It won't grieve me.

John: What a pity Mamma has forbidden Jane to leave her room.

Bessie: Because you can't vent your spleen on her. You ought to be ashamed of yourself. How often have you struck her!

John: I beat her because I hate her! Didn't she scratch and bite me?

Bessie: Because you struck her on the head with a hammer.

John: She has no right to defend herself when I choose to beat her – she is a dependent on our charity. Dependent that – the curtains are shaking.

Bessie: It's only the wind – go to your Mamma, Sir – you've no business here.

John: I shan't. There is someone behind those curtains. (*Sees her*) It's Jane Eyre – I knew it. What do you want there, shameless hussy? Don't stare like that – can't you speak? I'll fetch you down quickly if you don't instantly tell me.

Jane: Don't come near me – remember I scratched and bit you.

John: I ain't afraid of you!

Jane: Touch me and I will kill you!

John:	Then stay where you are.
Bessie:	Come away, Jane!
Jane:	If he goes first.

Enter Mrs Reed and Willis

Mrs R:	What is the meaning of this disturbance? Ah, that creature here – how dared she?
John:	She hid herself behind these curtains, and threatened to kill me.
Mrs R:	My pet! – What brings you here?
Jane:	Only reading, Aunt.
Mrs R:	You were forbidden to enter this apartment – were you not?
Jane:	Yes aunt.
Mrs R:	How dared you then disobey?
Jane:	Georgina and John have taken all my books away – I am so cold upstairs!
Willis:	Let the poor girl remain.
Mrs R:	You could have asked me for a book.
Jane:	I did not come here to read only.
Mrs R:	For what then – to play the spy?
Jane:	No – to see dear uncle Reed – this is his birthday – I have no flowers to hang around his loved picture so I brought him the poor orphan's tears.
Mrs R:	My late husband spoiled this stubborn vixen by his blindness – did I not also forbid you to dress your hair in curls?
Jane:	It comes so naturally. I can't help it.
Mrs R:	Like your wicked nature. Did you threaten John?
Jane:	Yes, if he beat me.
Mrs R:	Ask his pardon instantly.
John:	Yes, ask my pardon!
Mrs R:	Will you not?
Jane:	No.
Mrs R:	You dare –
Jane:	Unless he first asks forgiveness of me.
Mrs R:	You hear, brother! – quit my presence. But once again will you enter here. Quit the Room – *(Jane Exits)*
John:	Bravo! I'll go and tell Georgina – won't she enjoy it. *(Exit with Bessie)*
Mrs R:	Now, brother, you can understand what I have endured in fulfilling the duty my inflexible husband imposed upon me.
Willis:	I can comprehend that the leaving this orphan girl an inmate here was a grievous error on my late brother in law's part since your hatred is so obvious.
Mrs R:	Yes I hate her. She must quit this roof.

Willis:	You had the same hatred towards her mother.
Mr R:	She brought shame on our house. Eloped with a poor officer – married him – she returned here a beggared widow – her brother, the weak minded Reed, received her with open arms – she died bequeathing her orphan brat – Reed in his last hours made me vow to tend and educate her but now my resolve is taken.
Willis:	What is your intention?
Mrs R:	To send her to Lowood Asylum – I momentarily expect the Director, Dr Brocklehurst, here.
Willis:	Lowood Asylum – is it not a Charitable Institution?
Mrs R:	I only know that young girls are there trained to labour and humility.
Willis:	Is not this resolve too late? – Jane Eyre is no longer a girl, sister – in the way you propose, are you acting up to the solemn promise you made to your husband?
Mrs R:	If you regard my plan as unjust, and desire to provide for the future of Jane, I will resign the charge with pleasure into your hands.
Willis:	You know that my profession and means render such a course impracticable.

Enter Dr Brocklehurst

Dr B:	Your servant, Madam.
Mrs R:	You are welcome, Sir – I have awaited you with anxiety, for in you behold an instrument to cleanse unruly hearts.
Dr B:	Yes, Madam, such an instrument am I, and this wayward girl you would confide to my care –
Mrs R:	Come hither, Jane. In truth I can say that I have acted consistently towards this orphan, but the seeds of my bounty fell on stony ground. She is devoid of heart – unthankful – dissembles –
Dr B:	Horrible! – Fear not, madam – I have subdued many stubborn natures and trust that even here I shall be successful.
Mrs R:	Jane – in this worthy gentleman's hands I place your future destiny
Jane:	Am I to leave this house and go to school?
Mrs R:	Yes, to a school where all perversity will be effectually eradicated.
Jane:	That task was performed by my dear uncle. What else shall I learn?
Dr B:	First you will be taught humility – for humility alone is acceptable in Lowood Orphan Asylum.
Jane:	Uncle Reed – you hear! Your foster child – your darling Jane – henceforth the orphan's home is hers – they call me wicked – oppress and hate me – as their hate, so will strangers' be.
Dr B:	Oh, horrid! This to her benefactress! Madam, allow me to withdraw – too much have I seen and heard – you have been too sparing – wayward, stony heart.

Jane: Stay, Sir – before I quit this roof for ever you shall hear the truth – Aunt Reed has told you I am ungrateful – 'tis false – the smallest kindness is for ever indelibly engraven on my heart! She has told you I dissemble – 'tis false, for could I lie I would say I love aunt Reed – were I a hypocrite I should mourn that I am thrust forth from this threshold – never again will I return – never more call her Aunt!

Mrs R: Dare you thus address me?

Jane: Yes. I dare because it is truth. You said my heart was stony: it needed love – to make me good and gentle – you knew not mercy – never shall I forget your treatment. You ordered me to be locked up in the death chamber of my uncle – there in suffering and darkness did I languish – in vain I implored mercy – you were deaf to my cries – if I am wicked 'tis you are the cause – 'tis you are the hypocrite – the perjurer – yes, perjuror to the dead and the living – did you not whilst grasping the death hand of my uncle swear to use me as though I were your own child – never to forsake me? How have you kept that oath? At another tribunal you will meet my uncle again – he will say, 'Where is the orphan girl I confided to your care? What have you made of her – how fulfilled thy vow?' Answer – 'I have persecuted – beaten her, banished her from my roof – to the stranger bequeathed her as a pauper homeless and friendless' – now Sir, I am yours!

Picture
End of Act 1

Act II

Eight years have elapsed

Drawing Room

Sam discovered

Sam: There, all is ready. I flatter myself Sir Rowland won't have much to complain of when he returns to Thornfield. I can't make out why he is so often away.

Enter Mrs Fairfax

Mrs Fairfax: What can't you make out?

Sam: Why Sir Rowland is so often from home.

Mrs F: Sir Rowland is Master here, and can do as he pleases.

Sam:	Ah! there was a time when I was everything, but since this pale-faced Miss Eyre made her appearance I am nobody.
Mrs F:	You are a ninny. This young girl has restored us to life, spared us all the trouble we used to have with Adèle – Within a few months Miss Eyre has quite mastered her.
Sam:	I only hope Sir Rowland may discover such a treasure in her as you do.
Mrs F:	I am sure by his manner that he is delighted with her appearance and accomplishments.
Sam:	She won't reign long at the Hall – and the child too, no-one knows her history.
Mrs F:	Being no business of mine, I have not enquired.
Sam:	Nothing to be got out of her, but I'll ferret it out – I am determined!
Mrs F:	Where can Jane be, I wonder.

Enter Jane

Jane:	Any news of Sir Rowland's return?
Mrs F:	None.
Jane:	Always mystery – do you know I have not found him the terrible being I at first imagined. Do you remember how he questioned me, how strange and mysterious he seemed as he examined one by one my poor sketches? He took my portfolio with him. I have never been able to get a glimpse of it since.
Mrs F:	Jane, have you not often remarked a strange and singular laugh ringing through the old mansion?
Jane:	Yes, a terrible ghostly laugh which in the stillness of the night has made my very blood curdle.
Mrs F:	Be cautious, Jane, never to speak of those sounds in Sir Rowland's presence.
Jane:	I thank you, Madam, for all your kindness to the poor orphan, who after passing eight years of my life in Lowood Asylum, through your goodness has found a home at Thornfield.
Mrs F:	Bless you, Jane – (*Exit*)
Jane:	To me all appears a dream – without, all is life – within, all quiet and gloom – 'tis now a fortnight since Sir Rowland left Thornfield. He seems not displeased with me – yet rarely exchanges a word. He is a riddle I should like to unravel yet I dare not attempt the task.
Mrs F (without):	Sam! Quick, get the visitors' chambers in order directly.
Jane:	Visitors at Thornfield.

Enter Mrs Fairfax and Pat

Mrs F:	Sam! Sam! Within an hour, Pat?

Pat:	Faix, ma'am, it can't be much longer for the masther is following at my heels; and the grand folks are coming behind the masther in a carriage.
Mrs F:	Now Jane, prepare yourself – you'll find a parcel for you in your room – there's not a moment to lose. Oh, dear me! I had almost forgotten – read that letter and then you will understand – Sam! Sam! *(Exit)*
Jane (reads):	'One hour from receipt of this I shall reach Thornfield. You will prepare the visitors' chambers – ladies are among the company – a parcel accompanying this contains a silk dress for the governess – she will do the honors of the tea table.' The governess – is my name so difficult to remember? So, Patrick we are to have lady visitors at the Hall?
Pat:	Yes, indeed, Miss, and beautiful creatures they are – that is to say – the young lady – as to the ould 'un I can only say she wouldn't suit my taste in the laste.
Jane:	But the young lady, Patrick?
Pat:	Faix, ma'am, she's as fresh as a rose in June.

Enter Mrs Fairfax

Mrs F:	Now, Jane – make haste – put on Sir Rowland's present.
Jane:	Thanks, Madam – but I must decline.
Mrs F:	Not wear it! Sir Rowland will be displeased. Pat tells me he had it made in town expressly.
Pat:	I'll swear to that – it's made from the pattern of one of Lady Claremont's who is as much like Miss there in figure as two peas.
Jane:	Indeed! Who is Lady Claremont?
Mrs F:	A very handsome, proud, yet poor young widow.
Jane:	I presume, then a marriage is on the tapis.
Mrs F:	Ever since Sir Rowland returned from France she has set her cap at him, but he is not smitten.
Pat:	Faix, ma'am, I rather think that this time she has set her cap to some purpose. He's coming with mother and daughter and a whole tribe of relations – and if that isn't quite enough Pat knows nothing at all about it.
Mrs F:	I can't believe it.
Pat:	Why not – because master happens to have reached the middle of his age – faix that's just the time we men get a bit maddish, and once caught with a pair of bright sparkling eyes – the devil himself couldn't relase you.
Mrs F:	Now you be off Pat – get ready to receive the company.
	(Exit Mrs F)
Pat:	All right, ma'am, but if this doesn't mane a matrimonial marriage – Pat knows nothing about it. *(Exit)*

Jane: A marriage! Why should he not marry? What is it to me? Hark! Sir
               Rowland himself – I know his proud step.

Enter Sir Rowland

Sir R: See to the horse – now then, where are you all? Ah, good evening, Miss
               Eyre!
Jane: Good evening, Sir Rowland!
Sir R: Running away from me? – afraid?
Jane: I fear no one.
Sir R: Then stay. I have something to say to you – you approve my choice in
               dress I hope?
Jane: Yes – thank you.
Sir R: I trust to see you wear it this evening.
Jane: I must decline.
Sir R: Why?
Jane: Because I prefer a costume befitting my position – I equally appreciate
               your kindness.
Sir R: Humph! I thought so – singular girl! Doubtless my way may appear
               somewhat rough, the result of my Indian associations – of what are you
               thinking now?
Jane: Whether there existed many employers who trouble themselves about
               the sensibilities of their *paid servants*.
Sir R: Paid servants. I think, Miss Eyre, you do not rank yourself as such – you
               are Adèle's governess – you believe her to be my child – (I ought to
               have been more communicative ere this). It is your prerogative to ask,
               'whose child am I educating?' She is an orphan. I brought her from Paris
               – have tended her as though she were my own, in fulfillment of a sacred
               promise made to one who is now no more. I feel myself bound to make
               this explanation – you possess intellect, talents, accomplishments and
               will one day realize a position in the families of the rich and noble.
Jane: Think not, Sir Rowland, the dazzling fortune you would picture can
               either charm or delude me. My post is far more glorious. Adèle, you
               say, is an orphan – let me then supply a mother's place. I am an orphan
               too, and know what it is to be parentless – with love will I tend and
               guide her – with love entwine myself around her heart – I will never
               leave, never forsake her unless you bid me hence.
Sir R: Miss Eyre, you are a noble girl – I take you at your word – you promise
               never to quit this house until I bid you?
Jane: I promise.
Sir R: Your hand to the bargain! You smile – until now I was not aware you
               could smile!
Jane: Sir Rowland!

Sir R:	You must often smile – 'tis as a bright ray of sunlight in this gloomy hall. (*Carriage heard*) Hey day! already arrived. You will receive my guests whilst I make some change in my toilette.
Jane:	With pleasure.
Sir R:	You will wear the dress I sent you.
Jane:	No, Sir Rowland.
Sir R:	Well, as you please – self-willed gipsy! (*Exit*)
Jane:	Strange unaccountable man! (*Sam places candles*)

Enter Mrs Fairfax, Georgina, Lord Harwood and Mrs Reed

Mrs F.	This way, ladies, if you please.
Mrs R:	Thank you, my Lord.
Georg:	Very kind of you, madam, to receive Sir Rowland's guests – I presume he is occupied?
Mrs F:	Sir Rowland did not anticipate so early an arrival.
Jane:	Georgina Reed!
Lord H:	Probably the extra care Sir Rowland devotes to his toilette.
Georg:	The first time in his life Sir Rowland has submitted to the tyranny of fashion. His example will never lead the fickle goddess.
Lord H:	Lady Claremont must have devoted much time to the study of the character of her admirer.
Georg:	No, only one experiences some pleasure in seeking to solve problems – Madam will you kindly ascertain whether we can retire to our apartments – the drive has fatigued us.
Mrs F:	I will see to the arrangements at once, your ladyship. (*Exit*)
Mrs R:	It is excessively oppressive and gloomy here.
Georg:	Intolerably warm.
Lord H:	Possibly the effect of conscience.
Georg:	Conscience! Ha! ha! ha!
Lord H:	That smile, Georgina, doesn't become you in the least – remember you once gave me hope, before this Creosus crossed your path.
Georg:	We are often subjects of delusion.
Lord H:	Although I possess no Thornfield, yet I have competence and an unblemished name – do you know what people say of Rochester?
Georg:	The vulgar generally ascribe something to singularity.
Lord H:	There is a secret and I will fathom it.
Mrs R:	What feeling is this?
Georg:	Mamma! What ails you?
Mrs R:	An oppression has stolen over me as though some calamity lurked in the very atmosphere of this dwelling. Let us return.
Georg:	Dear Mamma – how ridiculous – superstitious I declare.
Mrs R:	No, no, 'tis not superstition, but reality –
Georg:	Call Bessie here, my Lord.

Lord H (sees Jane): Oh, here is a person – what a magnificent creature – Miss – aw
        – I haven't the honor of your name –
Jane: Jane Eyre – you are –
Lord H: Lord Francis Harwood – and so you are Jane Eyre? Do you know that
        you are very – aw – pretty?
Jane: My Lord.
Lord H: 'Pon my life you are!
Jane: May I ask, my Lord, if you have sisters?
Lord H: Yes – I have, two sisters and very fine girls they are.
Jane: Were any one to address either of them, as you have now addressed
        me, what would be the result?
Lord H: That's a very different thing – they are –
Jane: Made of different clay – Their hearts are more sensitive – their feelings
        more refined, perhaps – reverse the picture and you will be nearer to the
        truth. In the school of poverty is oftener found that intuitive delicacy
        which fears to wound – inured to suffering themselves, they know and
        feel for it in others.
Lord H: A regular sermon, by Jove! Did you get that out of the Spectator?
Jane: My Lord, assumption, much as it may be involuntary, is simply pitiable
        – but insolence where you know it cannot be averted is cowardly – can
        I do anything to serve you, Madam? Sir Rowland has deputed me to
        attend upon you during his absence.
Georg: Indeed, and pray what is your position here to be considered fitting for
        such an honor?
Jane: I am the Governess.
Mrs R (recognizing her): Ah! I knew it (*sinks on sofa*).
Lord H: Madam!
Georg: Mamma, compose yourself!
Mrs R: Are you blind? Do you not see her, Jane Eyre? She will claim kindred
        with us.
Georg: She will not, if I know Jane Eyre.
Lord H: You know these ladies Miss?
Jane: No.
Georg (to Mrs R): You are right, that is Jane Eyre.
Lord H: How very remarkable – ah – Sir Rowland – at last.

Enter Sir Rowland

Sir Rowland: Loveliest of Amazons – Madam – My Lord – welcome. You arrived
        earlier than anticipated – Lady Claremont – dismiss that cloud from
        your fair brow. It surely does not threaten me.
Georg: Well, I suppose we must grant our gracious pardon for your seeming
        neglect (*gives hand*).

Sir R (*kisses her hand*): I trust your reception at Thornfield was satisfactory. You had
    no cause to regret the absence of the host.

Georg: Who could possibly supply your place? (*Sir Rowland kisses her hand again*)

Lord H: There'll be none left for me if he goes on like that.

Georg: This young person – though quite unknown to us –

Sir R: Has she not introduced herself?

Jane: At present I have had no opportunity.

Sir R; Miss Jane Eyre – Adèle's governess.

Georg: Adèle – Oh yes, I remember – the little French puppet you brought from Paris some three years since – I presume then the little Parisienne still exists here.

Sir R: Yes, still exists here.

Mrs R: Pray what instruction does Miss Eyre import to Adèle?

Sir R: The general rudiments of an English education with music and drawing – in that, Miss Eyre is a proficient.

Georg: Indeed! This praise from you is indeed astonishing – you are so exacting – and pray – Miss – really I cannot remember the name –

Jane: Jane Eyre.

Georg: Jane Eyre – where did you acquire so much excellence?

Jane: At Lowood Asylum.

Mrs R: I was not aware that in Lowood Asylum for orphans worldly accomplishments were acquired – I always understood Dr Brocklehurst implanted only the precepts of labor and humility.

Georg: That Jane Eyre should be so accomplished an artist is really astonishing.

Sir R: Your ladyship shall judge for yourself.   (*Exit*)

Georg (*To Mrs R*): Is it not strange that he should be so marked in his praise of that girl?

Re-enter Sir Rowland with portfolio

Mrs R: I never doubted her talent.

Sir R: Lady Claremont, look at these beautiful drawings.

Georg: Permit me to postpone the inspection till the morning – Mamma feels unwell and needs repose.

Mrs R: You must excuse us, Sir Rowland – come Georgina.

Lord H: Allow me, Madam.

Mrs R: Thank you, my Lord – one of us must yield – she or I. (*Exit Mrs R. and Lord [H]*)

Sir R: Lady Claremont, permit me – you are not angry with me?

Georg: We will decide that question tomorrow.

Sir R: You trifler! Miss Eyre, you can retire.   (*Exit with Georgina*)

Jane:	He loves this woman – this Georgina who has worked the miracle – what evil power has conjured up these persecutors of my infancy? My sketches, now I can –

Enter Sir Rowland – with Sam

Sam:	Sam, be careful that all is quiet in the Hall tonight (*exit Sam*). Miss Eyre, why have you not retired –
Jane:	I did not feel fatigued – any further commands, Sir Rowland?
Sir R:	No, stay – how do you like Lady Claremont?
Jane:	Before I can judge of a person I must have time to know what she is, not what she appears. Good night. (*Exit*)
Sir R:	Woman-like, not one point will she yield – what are you doing, Sam? (*Sam listening*)
Sam:	I was waiting to see that all was safe. The night will be a stormy one. We can't be too careful.
Sir R:	A stormy night – probably. See that the household retire to rest – I will follow their example. (*Exit*)
Sam:	If I hadn't seen it I wouldn't have believed it. Sir Rowland to bemean himself to hold a conversation with this stuck-up orphan-Asylum product. Ah, it can't come to any good. (*Puts out lights*) How the wind grumbles – if Sir Rowland marries Lady Claremont she'll make short work of Jane Eyre. (*Exit*)

Re-enter Jane

Jane:	All silent – what a stillness reigns through the Hall – I – fancied I saw a dark shadow flit noiselessly past the Library door, possibly my own. I cannot rest until I've possession of my sketches – they are here! He has forgotten them – these creations of my waking dreams would he show to her? No, never shall her scornful eyes rest upon them! (*Thunder, wind*) What is that – something certainly hurried past yonder door – all again silent – it must have been the hurricane – how foolish – because a gust of wind extinguished my candle a shudder must needs pass through me chilling my very blood – for shame, Jane – for shame – I must reach my chamber! (*Laugh heard*) Merciful heaven! that fearful yell – all is still now. I hear nothing but the beating of my own heart – I dare not remain and yet I fear to move. What choking and suffocating feeling is this – ah, 'tis fire – a bright glare through crevices of yonder door! (*She throws it open*)

A maniac appears at door, laughs and exits

Jane:	Ah! 'tis Sir Rowland's chamber – awake, Sir Rowland! Awake! fire! fire! (*Rushes off – thunder, wind*)

Re-enter Sir Rowland and Jane

Jane:	This way, Sir Rowland, this way – the air will revive you. I have torn down the blazing curtains of your bed and all immediate danger is past – that terrible woman – 'tis her work – be seated – I will arouse the household.
Sir R:	No, no, remain. Would you rouse my guests, have me become the mock of the whole county?
Jane:	But the fire!
Sir R:	Pshaw, it only reached the curtain of my couch which you tore down.
Jane:	But that woman who laughed so terribly – she seemed to be a perfect fiend.
Sir R:	And you a perfect angel – but for your timely aid I should have been destroyed – breathe not a word of this night's work to living soul.
Jane:	You shall be obeyed.
Sir R:	I command it. Also promise never to enquire explanation of this event.
Jane:	I promise, but will not this woman herself betray –
Sir R:	That is my affair.
Jane:	And now I would ask a favor of you.
Sir R:	For the first time then. What is this favor?
Jane:	To dismiss me from Thornfield.
Sir R:	Why ask that which rests with yourself?
Jane:	Because I pledged my word that I would never quit Thornfield till you bade me depart.
Sir R;	True, I remember – if it is your wish – go.
Jane:	Thanks! Thanks.
Sir R:	One moment – what moves you to this sudden determination? You are silent – Mrs Fairfax has told you that I keep imprisoned beneath this roof an unhappy woman, and that woman my wife.
Jane:	Not Mrs Fairfax, but others say so.
Sir R:	And this report, added to the event that has just occurred, has confirmed your suspicions.
Jane:	No, I believe it to be false.
Sir R:	From whence do you infer this?
Jane:	From my knowledge of your character – you have sheltered and protected the poor orphan.
Sir R:	And never shall you be deprived of that protection. I will explain all. Listen – the fiend who in woman's shape would have destroyed me is a raving maniac. She who has tarnished the honor of our name is –
Jane:	Lady Rochester.
Sir R:	Lady Harriet Rochester, my brother's wife. She was my betrothed. I was the younger son. My father sent me to London, and I returned to find her married to my brother – the heir to our father's wealth. Stung by man's

perfidy and woman's faithlessness I fled the paternal roof – years past away. My father died. One day I received intelligence of my brother's death. I returned and took possession of my estates – on my arrival a letter was placed in my hands – it contained my dying brother's sad history. Shortly after their marriage they went on the continent – at Geneva his faithless wife fled with a foreigner. My brother tracked the fugitives and in a duel slew her seducer. His unhappy wife, tortured by the agonies of remorse, lost her reason for ever. He had satisfied his revenge but his health succumbed – he implored my forgiveness, beseeched me to tend and rear his orphaned child (Adèle) – also to remove his guilty wife to this mansion – Miss Eyre have I fulfilled my duty?

Jane:	Nobly have you become the protector of the woman who deceived you – a father to her helpless child.
Sir R:	Are you still resolved to depart?
Jane:	Yes, it is my duty.
Sir R:	Your duty.
Jane:	You meditate marriage? Adèle will then be sent to school and my services no longer required – when you are married I could not remain beneath this roof.
Sir R:	But whither will you go?
Jane:	To my uncle at Madeira.
Sir R:	'Tis a great distance, Jane – the broad sea would be between you and your native land.
Jane:	The broad sea – yes! yes.
Sir R:	Also between us, Jane – we may never see or hear of each other more.
Jane:	Never more – no, no.
Sir R:	Why do you weep?
Jane:	Because I love Thornfield, and grieve to quit it. It has been the orphan's refuge – here I have not been spurned – here I have learned to know myself – to understand you, Sir Rowland, and now I must separate from all I hold dear.
Sir R;	Then stay.
Jane:	No, I will endure this separation. I am no automaton, no machine to be moved at pleasure without sense or feeling. Think you because I am simple, poor, forlorn I have no heart? I am a woman – I know and understand better than any other. In heart and mind I am your equal if not in wealth. Soul speaks to soul as though we had already crossed death's barrier and stood equal. Unloose me Sir Rowland, you are betrothed – unloose me!
Sir R:	No, Jane, the net encompasses you.
Jane;	I can break it asunder – I am free to go where I will!

Sir R:	At last you have spoken. From the first moment I beheld you, you have been part and parcel of my being. With all a man's might have I battled with you. Thy magic influence enthralled my very soul – Jane Eyre, this heart, this hand is yours.
Jane:	No, no. Your promised bride stands between us.
Sir R:	I have no promised bride.
Jane:	Have you deceived Georgina?
Sir R:	No.
Jane:	What does she here then?
Sir R:	To serve me as the key of thy fast-locked soul. Never have I breathed a word of love or marriage to any save you. I again offer you my hand and my heart – wilt take the offer? Answer quickly, 'Rowland Rochester, I will be thy wife, will love thee evermore' – speak ere this heart burst its bonds!
Jane:	Rowland Rochester, I will be thy wife. (*Embrace*)

Enter Georgina, Mrs Reed, Lord Harwood etc.

Lord H:	Delightful tableau – really, Sir Rowland, had we known we would not have intruded at this interesting moment.
Sir R:	Allow me to present you my future wife, Lady Rochester.
Omnes:	His wife!
Mrs R:	I knew it.
Sir R:	Yes, my wife, protected by this strong arm and heart from all persecuting and envious foes. We now only seek to complete their happiness by the approbation of all true friends –

Curtain
End of Drama

Jane Eyre

or

The Orphan of Lowood

A Drama in Two Parts and Four Acts

by

Charlotte Birch-Pfeiffer

1870

as performed by

Mme Marie Seebach

and her dramatic company in

New York

and

all the principal cities of the United States

under the direction of J. Grau.

New York

Fourteenth Street Theatre.

Editor's Notes

The Text

The copy-text for this edition is the English text from the dual-language German-English version printed in New York in 1870; the imprint is 'Fourteenth Street Theatre'. Despite being a published work, it is extremely rare, and I have identified only three copies in the world. One of these (at the University of Missouri at Kansas City) is seriously defective, since Act II Scene VII runs into Act III Scene VII, thus missing out Act II Scenes VIII–XII and Act III Scenes I–VI. I have not seen the copy at Trinity College, Hartford Connecticut. The copy at Harvard is complete and is now held in the Houghton Rare Books Collection.

I took my text from a photocopy held by the British Library Document Supply Centre, which is stamped 'Harvard College Library', but differs in minor ways from the copy now in the Houghton Collection. In all copies, page 29 seems to have been misnumbered 39, but the British Library copy has no page numbers after 35, whereas numbering continues in the present Harvard copy. The British Library copy also lacked pp. 32–3 (containing Act II Scenes VIII–X) and pp. 36–7 (containing the end of Act II Scene XII), but with the generous co-operation of Harvard College Library, I have now arranged for these pages to be supplied from their copy. The text shown here is, therefore, complete.

The published text has German on left-hand and English on right-hand pages; all pages are printed in double columns. Entrances and exits prompt a new scene heading, so some scenes are very short. Punctuation and presentation are fairly consistent, and editing has mostly consisted of correcting obvious misprints and adopting a single version of abbreviated names.

The Playwright

Charlotte Birch-Pfeiffer was born in Stuttgart in 1800 and died in Berlin in 1868 (see Figure 10). Born Charlotte Pfeiffer, she became an actress at the age of 13 and in 1825 married the Danish critic, historian and writer Christian Andreas Birch. She became a celebrated actress, performing in Vienna as well as all over Germany, and was also manager of the Stadttheater in Zurich for six years. In addition, she wrote about a hundred stage plays, predominantly adaptations of novels by Victor Hugo, Alexandre Dumas, George Sand and Charles Dickens.[1] Catherine Evans notes that although almost completely forgotten now, in the nineteenth century she dominated the German stage[2] in an unprecedented way, especially for a woman; she was by far the most

---

[1] 'Charlotte Birch-Pfeiffer', Gutenberg-DE Project (accessed 12 February 2005); 'Charlotte Birch-Pfeiffer', *Encyclopedia Britannica*, p. 959; Evans claims that she wrote far more plays than the 74 published in her collected works (p. 44).

[2] Evans, p. 3.

Figure 10   Portrait of Charlotte Birch-Pfeiffer. Reproduced by courtesy of the
Gutenberg-DE Project

successful dramatist of the time in financial terms.[3] According to Max Martersteig,
'in every season between 1830 and 1860 a new Birch-Pfeiffer play appeared which
then became the repertory play of the season at every single German theatre'.[4]

Since many of her plays were adaptations, critics have disparaged her originality,
but Evans points out that 'she often deviated drastically from the plot and motivation
of the source for the purpose of creating a tightly structured and well-motivated
drama'.[5] The *Encyclopedia Britannica* confirms that 'her intimate knowledge of the
technical necessities of the stage fitted her for the successful dramatization of many
popular novels, and her plays, adapted and original, make twenty-three volumes'.[6]
Die Waise von Lowood, which was among 'her biggest successes',[7] appears in Volume
14 of these works, published in 1876.[8]

---

3   Dauer. I am grateful to Barbara Jean Frick for finding and translating this essay.
4   Martersteig, p. 445. I am grateful to Barbara Jean Frick for finding and translating this
      extract.
5   Evans, p. 4.
6   *Gesammelte dramatische Werke* (Leipzig: Reclam, 1863–1880) (*Encyclopedia Britannica*
      p. 959).
7   Yates, p. 112.
8   Three later editions appeared in 1900 (Leipzig) and 1913 (Halle); I am grateful to Barbara
      Jean Frick for the information.

Although Birch-Pfeiffer is regarded as politically conservative, Catherine Evans makes a case for her as a champion of underdogs and women, and *Die Waise* is in this respect characteristic of her plays, which often focus on 'young women whose stations in life are inferior to those with whom they are in contact', in plots where they 'maintain their personal integrity and individuality, thereby demonstrating their superiority, in order that they be treated as equals.' Birch-Pfeiffer took a moral view of the stage, defining 'the province of art as to elevate, to amuse, to enlighten, and to cheer', and Evans reads her adaptation of *Jane Eyre* as part of her contribution to an emerging theatre of Realism in Germany:

> She at first wanted to delete some of the more melodramatic aspects of the novel, *Jane Eyre*, from her play. She endeavored to take both Rochester's secret (in the novel it is the presence of a mad wife in his house, in the play she is his sister-in-law) and the fire which this woman sets in Rochester's bedroom through which he has the opportunity to see Jane's strength of character, out of the play. She soon realized, however, that to do so [...] would destroy the essential intrigue of the material. While Birch-Pfeiffer was aware that she had created a very effective drama with a splendid role for the female lead, she did not regard it as one of her better plays.

Birch-Pfeiffer herself writes: 'I was taken aback by the huge success of this drama – I'm sure that now the next *good* play I manage will be a failure!'[9]

Although no translator is named in the 1870 dual-language edition, Donna Marie Nudd identifies him as Clifton W. Tayleure, who copyrighted the English version under his own name in 1871. There appears to be no copy of Tayleure's text independent of the 1870 edition.[10]

Theatres and Performances

The play was first performed at the Hofburgtheater in Vienna in 1853. It was one of Birch-Pfeiffer's 'most phenomenal successes overall: it remained in the repertoire of the theater until 1895, and played repeatedly in all German theaters'.[11] The German-language play was also performed in America on numerous occasions between 1854 and 1898.[12]

---

[9]   Evans, pp. 5–6, 125, 223 and 234 (translation of Birch-Pfeiffer quotation by Barbara Jean Frick).

[10]   Nudd, *Jane Eyre*, p. 73. Nudd lists Tayleure's play as 'not found', but she cites its copyright entry ('*Dramatic Compositions Copyrighted in the United States, 1870–1916*, US Copyright Office, Entry 22457') and defines it as 'a translation of Charlotte Birch-Pfeiffer's German dramatization of the novel' (p. 221).

[11]   Evans, pp. 235–6.

[12]   Leonard (p. 766) cites performances in 1854 and 1856, with cast lists. For other performance, see below.

Marie Seebach and Other German Performances

The first well-documented German-language performance in America is that at Fourteenth Street Theatre in October, 1870, with Marie Seebach in the title role.[13] Fourteenth Street Theatre (105–109 West 14th Street) had opened in 1866 as the Théâtre Francais but soon settled to its later title.[14] Marie Seebach (1830–1897) was an established actress in Germany, where Birch-Pfeiffer's Jane Eyre became one of her major roles, and in 1870–1871 she was on a tour of the United States. Travelling with her own dramatic company, she visited 17 cities in little more than a year, playing roles such as Schiller's Maria Stuart and Goethe's Gretchen.[15] It is almost certain, therefore, that although advertisements for the Fourteenth Street production of Birch-Pfeiffer's play give the title in English, the performance was in German. The *New York Times* is ambiguous on this point,[16] but the *New York Herald* focuses on the language, pointing out that 'the language of Goethe and Schiller is hardly a foreign tongue in New York. It is the language almost as much of our drawing room literature as of the student's closet'.[17] The dual-language edition printed in this year includes a portrait of Marie Seebach and a predominantly German cast-list. A review of Seebach in the part at the Stadt Theatre, Bowery, in January 1871, notes that Seebach's 'own country people' preferred this theatre to Fourteenth Street, and flocked to see her there.[18]

The *New York Times* reviewer felt that Seebach failed to identify herself sufficiently with the character of Jane, but *The Spirit of the Times* disagreed, arguing that

> She grasps the author's conception, developes, colors, vivifies it. […] Those who have seen her play the part of *Jane Eyre* will not soon forget her touching appeal addressed to the uncle's portrait, nor the little, strange, fierce, half-wild girl, as she threatens her tyrannical cousin, or stands rebellious and fearless in the presence of her aunt […] The whole impersonation, indeed, dwells in the memory.[19]

The *New York Herald* was simply ecstatic on four separate occasions, calling the performance 'a perfect and absolute triumph'.[20]

An 1874 review comparing Charlotte Thompson's English performance with Marie Seebach in German suggests that there were at least some audience members

---

13   *NYT* review 6 October 1870 (p. 4); 'final performances' announced 1 January 1871 (p. 4). Act I performed Fourteenth Street Theatre 27 and 28 March 1871 (*NYT*, p. 4).
14   Wilmeth, p. 189.
15   'Marie Seebach'. *LoveToKnow* (accessed 13 June 2005); *NYT*, 6 October 1870, p. 7.
16   *NYT*, 6 October 1870, pp 7, 4.
17   *New York Herald* preview, 17 August 1870. I am grateful to Judith Smith for this information.
18   *NYT*, 10 January 1871, p. 4; 14 January 1871, p. 5.
19   *NYST*, 15 October 1870.
20   *New York Herald*, 6 October 1870; 8 October 1870; 10 October 1870; 28 March 1871. I am grateful to Judith Smith for this information.

who could appreciate both languages,[21] and in 1883 the (London) *Saturday Review* commented on 'the extraordinarily cosmopolitan nature of the drama in America'. The 'German population of New York' was 'large enough to support a permanent company for now nearly twenty years' so that 'a constant succession of the best German actors and actresses has appeared before American audiences'.[22] The Thalia Theater, which had previously been The Bowery Theatre,[23] opened as a German theatre in 1879; Birch-Pfeiffer's 'The Orphan of Lowood' was performed in German there and elsewhere at least nine times between 1882 and 1898.[24] In 1894, *Jane Eyre* appeared as part of the 'Professional Success' of a young German actress called Ellen Vockey, whose elaborately decorated portrait figures large in the *New York Times*.[25]

Maggie Mitchell

The publication of a dual-language edition in 1870 suggests that the play was also performed in English in that year,[26] but the earliest English-language performance I have found was in 1872. After this, however, two different English versions were taken up by two rival actresses, who toured the States with them for more than twenty years. Maggie Mitchell (1832/37–1918) was described as a 'comedienne and soubrette' or a 'personality actress'; photographs show her as having a plain, sensible face,[27] and in 1870 she was already fairly old for the part, since Jane is supposed to be sixteen in the Prologue to Birch-Pfeiffer's play. An 1874 review claims that she was using Brougham's adaptation,[28] but most of her programmes specify that she is using Clifton Tayleure's version.[29] Her tours included Utica (1872), Boston (1874, 1875), Chicago (1875), St Louis (1875), New York (1874, 1881, 1882, 1883), Harlem (1886) and Washington (nd).[30] Mitchell's 1894 'farewell tour' of 'her old repertory'

---

21 *Graphic*, 20 August 1874.

22 *Saturday Review*, 20 October 1883, p. 501.

23 Connor, p. 8.

24 *NYT*, 9 January 1883, p. 5; 19 October 1889, p. 5; 6 January 1892, p. 5; 26 February 1892, p. 5; 10 April 1892, p. 13; 24 March 1895, p. 13; 10 October 1897; 8 May 1898, p. 9. Leonard lists performances in 1882 and 1884 (pp. 767–8).

25 *NYT*, 3 October 1894, p. 2.

26 Nudd states this to be the case (*Jane Eyre*, p. 73).

27 *Theatre Ephemera* (accessed 17 August 2005).

28 *NYT*, 16 November 1874, p. 4.

29 Copyrighted in 1871 (Nudd, *Jane Eyre*, p. 221).

30 NYPLPA: BRTC has programmes for McVicker's Theatre (Utica), 1872; the Boston Theatre, 1874 and 1875; Park Theatre (Boston), McVicker's Theatre (Chicago) and DeBar's Grand Opera House (St Louis), 1875; Grand Opera House (New York), 1881; Park Theatre (Boston), 1881 and 1885; Olympic Theatre (St Louis), nd and the Gaiety Theatre (Washington), nd. *New York Dramatic Mirror* reviews Park Theatre (New York) 16 September 1882, p. 2. Leonard (p. 767) lists Grand Opera House (New York), 1882. NYT reviews Grand Opera House (New York) 16 November 1874, p. 4; 2 and 3 March 1882, p. 5; 6 May 1883 and Theatre Comique (Harlem), 9 May 1886, p. 9. Two of these

included *Jane Eyre*.[31]

Maggie Mitchell received adulatory reviews. The *Utica Observer* (1872) speaks of 'her absolutely faultless acting' and 'her whole-souled rendition of her character' which 'goes at once to the heart' and

> commanded throughout the most absorbing attention. Now her abandon to overpowering, uncontrollable grief was affecting in the extreme, and tears were furtively wiped away from many eyes in the audience. Again her burst of indignation at her wrongs enlisted the highest sympathy of the assemblage.[32]

Another review claims that Miss Mitchell's acting 'approaches as near perfection as it would seem possible to reach'.[33]

Charlotte Thompson
Charlotte Thompson (1843–1898) achieved even more personal fame in the part. She was born in England, came to the United States in 1852 with her father, Lysander Thompson, a 'distinguished actor', and first appeared in the English version of Birch-Pfeiffer's play at Union Square Theatre (New York) from 18 June to 9 July 1873.[34] Her brother, also called Lysander, was also in the company.[35] Photographs of her as Jane Eyre show her both as an adult and in pigtails,

---

> programmes specify the music to accompany the performance: for the Olympic Theatre: Balfe's 'Bohemian Girl' overture, Gungl's 'Improvisationen, waltzer', Lecoeg's 'Prinz Canti, medly' [sic], Herfurth's 'Taendelei Tyeolien' [sic] and Neibig's 'Bunte Blaetter Potpauri' [sic]; for the Park Theatre, Boston, 1881: Bela's 'Romantic' overture, Catlin's medley 'I'll meet you dar' [sic], Waltenfel's 'Golden Shower Waltz', A. Thomas' 'Le Caid' selection and D. Muller's 'Juno March'.

31 *NYT*, 19 March 1894, p. 6.
32 Review inside programme, 31 October 1872 (NYPLPA: BRTC).
33 In programme for Park Theatre (Boston), 1881 (NYPLPA: BRTC).
34 NYPLPA: BRTC has programme for Union Square Theatre, Wednesday, 18 June 1873. Music is specified: Giachetti's overture, 'Orion', Bela's Walzer 'Berliner Vinder', Flotow's 'Marta' (operatic selection) and Lumbye's Galop, 'Champagne' with 'Clarionet Solo'. There is a *NYT* review, 19 June 1873, p. 5; and a *NYST* review (which I have not seen), 21 June 1873 (NS 3 Vol. 28, p. 314). Leonard gives a complete cast list (p. 766). She was playing again at Union Square Theatre August to December 1874; Leonard gives 21 September as the finishing date (p. 766), but there are references to a 'revival' in November. See *NYT* reviews, 20 August 1874, p. 5; 29 August 1874, p. 5; 13 September 1874, p. 5; 17 November 1874, p. 4; unidentified reviews in HTC: 22 August 1874 and 25 December 1874. Programme for 3 September in NYPLPA: BRTC.
35 Obituary, *NYT*, 15 May 1898, p. 9.

supposedly aged 16 (see Figure 11).[36] Jane Eyre became one of Thompson's major roles and as well as New York performances in 1874, 1882, 1883, 1884 and 1885,[37] she toured in the part, visiting Boston (1875),[38] Buffalo, NY (1876),[39] Fort Madison, Iowa (1885),[40] Philadelphia (1887),[41] Detroit and Louisville (nd).[42]

Thompson was widely reviewed, and even the *New York Times* critic who claimed in 1873 that 'Miss Thompson is not a great actress' also concedes that 'her efforts bear the impress of abundant stage experience; and a sweet though somewhat unchanging face, and a winning manner, do the more difficult work of captivating and holding the sympathies of an audience'.[43] The general response, however, was adulatory. The American correspondent of the London *Era* finds her 'picturesque in appearance and fascinating in temperament, and precisely the sort of governess that might charm the murkiest of Rochesters'.[44] The *Graphic* claims that she is 'even more successful' than 'that exquisite artiste, Mme. Seebach', and the *Post* expatiates:

---

[36]   Annotation on the photograph gives her private name as Mrs Loraine Rogers; it is dated 1874 on the front, and 'about 1873' on the back (NYPLPA: BRTC (John. H. James Collection): MWEZ + n c 8196). There is a different photograph of Thompson on the *Theatre Ephemera* website (accessed 17 August 2005).

[37]   *NYT*, 9 August 1882, p. 4. (Leonard [p. 767] lists this as Brougham's play but it is more likely that Thompson was developing an amalgam of Brougham and Birch-Pfeiffer); *NYT*, 29 September 1883, p. 4; 16 November 1884; 9 December 1884. NYPLPA: BRTC has programmes for [Mount Morris Theatre], 1883; 8 December 1884 and 2 April 1885; programme for 23rd St Theatre, 1883, specifies music: Hartman's Overture, 'Volmar'; Reiff's aria, 'Chimes of Normandy', Risch's waltz, 'Fleurs de St Petersbourg' and A. Reiff Senior's Grand March, 'Alexis'. *NYT* has notice for 'next week', 16 November 1885, p. 5.

[38]   Playbill in BPM; also in NYPLPA: BRTC. Music is specified: Rossini's Overture to 'La Gazza Ladra', Balfe's 'Bohemian Girl' (selection), Lecoq's Valse, 'La Fille de Madame Angot' and Potpourri – 'Happy Thoughts' 'with Solo for the Wood Harmonicon'.

[39]   NYPLPA: BRTC has programmes for 8 April 1876; [Mount Morris Theatre] and 23rd St Theatre, 1883, which specifies music: Hartman's Overture, 'Volmar'; Reiff's aria, 'Chimes of Normandy', Risch's waltz, 'Fleurs de St Petersbourg' and A. Reiff Senior's Grand March, 'Alexis'.

[40]   NYPLPA: BRTC programme for 2 April 1885.

[41]   NYPLPA: BRTC programme for week commencing 31 October 1887. Music is specified: D.F.E. Auber's Overture, 'Les Diamants de la Couronne', Planquette, selection from 'Chimes of Normandy', E. Waldteufel's walz, 'Sentiers Fleuris', D. Braham's request medley 'Surprise', Introducing 'Whist, the Bogie Man', 'Dat Citron Wedding Cake', Walz 'Walk Around', 'Never take the horseshoe from the door', 'Hark, Baby Hark', 'I'll Wear the Trousers. Oh', 'The Secret Order of Full Moons'; Bonnisseau's polka, 'Infernal' and Louis Wallis's gallop, 'Pearls of the Orient'.

[42]   HTC, unidentified clippings.

[43]   *NYT*, 19 June 1873, p. 5.

[44]   HTC: unidentified clipping.

Figure 11   Photograph of Charlotte Thompson as Jane (supposedly aged sixteen)
in an American touring production of Birch-Pfeiffer's play, 1874.
Reproduced by permission of Billy Rose Theatre Collection, The
New York Public Library for the Performing Arts, Lenox and Tilden
Foundations

her fear for *Rochester*, her dread of the flames and her determination to brave them; the reaction when the danger was over, and her first perception of *Rochester's* love for her – all the different hopes, doubts and fears by which an excited woman can be affected – were portrayed with something very like genius.[45]

A Louisville review states that 'the charm of Miss Thompson's acting is that she is unconventional and real, thinks for herself, forms a clear conception of the character which she has to impersonate, and then embodies that conception'.[46] Another review calls her 'the very *Jane Eyre* of Charlotte Brontë's imagination [...] The intense inner life of the helpless orphan, her fervent nature, her womanly pride, all are vividly presented in Miss Thompson's portraiture'.[47] Yet another reviewer points out that *Jane Eyre* 'is one of the most difficult of plays', in that its effects depend on dialogue rather than plot or sensation. 'To kindle in the audience the spark of sympathy and fan it into a vigorous flame, is, therefore, a work of consummate art [and] Miss Thompson's success was therefore in the nature of a triumph.' For this reviewer, it was above all 'an intellectual interpretation'.[48]

It is difficult to reconcile this praise with the evident emphasis on comedy in Thompson's performances. Even in 1873, she seems to have taken some liberties with her text. The earliest *New York Times* review noted that 'the most conspicuous personation of the evening [...] was that of *Jacob Buttercup*, by Mr Montgomery, whose appearance and acting were original and comical in no ordinary degree'.[49] No such character appears in Birch-Pfeiffer's or any other recorded version of the play, but he is there ('h'is h'always snubbed') in the cast list for the *Boston Globe* in 1875.

Another innovation is suggested by a full-page engraving of a scene from *Jane Eyre* with a caption reading 'Lord Rochester presenting Jane Eyre to his guests as the future Lady Rochester: [Last Scene in the Play of "Jane Eyre"]' (Figure 12). The unidentified clipping is annotated in ink 'July 21, 1873, Union Square Theatre', which defines it as one of Charlotte Thompson's earliest performances. The scene is reminiscent of the last scene in Act IV of Brougham's play, when the Dowager Lady Ingram exclaims 'Marry the governess? revolting!' Birch-Pfeiffer's play, however, does not include such a scene, ending instead with a private scene of reconciliation between Jane and Rochester. The picture, however, does not fit Brougham in other ways: the caption names Rochester as 'Lord', where he is 'Mr' in Brougham's play, and Brougham's scene ends Act IV, not the whole play. It seems probable, therefore, that Charlotte Thompson has written (or stolen from Brougham) an extra scene for Birch-Pfeiffer's play.[50] Both the 1867 and 1877 British versions of Birch-Pfeiffer also

---

[45] HTC clippings: *Graphic*, 20 August 1874; *Post* (undated).
[46] HTC: unidentified clipping.
[47] *NYT*, 20 August 1874, p. 5.
[48] HTC: unidentified clipping headed 'Chestnut Street Theatre' and dated in ink 'Dec 25th 1874. Page 7th'.
[49] *NYT*, 19 June 1873, p. 5.
[50] The text of Thompson's play has not survived.

Figure 12   Etched scene entitled 'Lord Rochester presenting Jane Eyre to his guests as the future Lady Rochester. [Last scene in the play of "Jane Eyre"]': Charlotte Thompson's version of Birch-Pfeiffer's *Jane Eyre* as performed at Union Square Theatre, New York, 1873. Reproduced by permission of The Harvard Theatre Collection, The Houghton Library

include such a final scene, theatrically desirable in bringing the whole cast together for a final tableau.

Thompson's naming of Jane's rival also suggests some assimilation from Brougham. One of the distinctive features of Birch-Pfeiffer's play is that the Reed family take the parts played by the Ingrams in the novel, Georgina Reed taking the place of Blanche Ingram, but from 1874 onwards, Thompson substitutes 'Georgiana Ingram' for Birch-Pfeiffer's 'Georgina Clarens' (née Reed). Georgiana Ingram appears, however, together with Mrs Reed (as in Birch-Pfeiffer), not the dowager Lady Ingram (as in Brougham).[51]

By 1882, Thompson is advertising the fact that she is using her own version of *Jane Eyre*. A *New York Times* review states that 'her old play on this subject, which was merely a translation from the German of Charlotte Birch-Pfeiffer's "Orphan of Lowood", has been discarded for a new dramatization of Miss Brontë's novel', and in 1883 she 'has modified her usual arrangement of the play'.[52] The 1884 programme for the Star Theatre, New York, plays down any link even with the novel and places its emphasis on comedy:

> The play is not a dramatization of the book of the gifted Charlotte Brontë, but it was suggested by several dramatic passages in her famous work. Miss Thompson's comedy drama, 'Jane Eyre', abounds in sparkling fun and eccentric character. Its performance affords an entertainment of unalloyed amusement, causing an almost continuous peal of laughter, replete with thrilling climaxes, and telling an intense dramatic story.

Like several of the later programmes, this one includes a character called Achille de Leon, who in the programme in 1883 is described as 'Idiomatically astray'.[53] Another review confirms that 'the comedy features of the play are intrusted to a Frenchman idiomatically astray, a watchful housekeeper and two fun-making servants'.[54]

The New York Times in 1883 shows some weariness with Miss Thompson's tenacity in this role,[55] and in 1884 damns with faint praise:

> Miss Thompson has frequently been seen in the same character in this city, where her acting was formerly much admired. [...] She is pathetic and impassioned; she depicts grief, love, terror, jealousy, and joy, but is never hysterical, and in the lighter passages she

51 NYPLPA: BRTC: 1874 programme. Lady Georgina Ingram also appears Boston Globe, 1875 (BPM; also NYPLPA: BRTC); Jacob Buttercup and Lady Georgina Ingram also appear Buffalo, NY, 1876 (NYPLPA: BRTC).

52 *NYT*, 9 August 1882, p. 4; 29 September 1883, p. 4. Leonard (pp. 767–8) claims that the 1882 performance and 1887 road tour used Brougham's dramatization, but a piecemeal adaptation is more likely (see above).

53 NYPLPA: BRTC: programme for [Mount Morris Theatre] includes a review stating that 'the version used by Miss Thompson is better than the dramatization of Miss Brontë's novel generally seen' (*New York Dramatic Mirror*, 13 December 1884, p. 2).

54 HTC: undated review for 'Grand Opera House'.

55 *NYT*, 29 September 1883, p. 4.

is demure and vivacious by turns, and always pleasing. In other words, Miss Thompson is an efficient actress.[56]

Several of the programmes specify the music to be performed during the play (see footnotes for details), but it is difficult to imagine how the 1887 Philadelphia performance would have integrated the 'surprise request medley' including 'Whist, the Bogie Man', 'Dat Citron Wedding Cake', 'Never take the horseshoe from the door', 'Hark, Baby Hark' and 'I'll Wear the Trousers. Oh'.[57]

It would be interesting to know whether Maggie Mitchell continued to use the unchanged 1870 English version by Clifton Tayleure, especially in view of Thompson's *New York Times* obituary, which singled out Jane Eyre as her most memorable part:

> Miss Thompson's large pathetic eyes, plain but agreeable features, slender figure, unaffected simplicity of manner and clear, honest dramatic art made this role very attractive, long after Maggie Mitchell and other popular actresses had failed in well-meant dramatizations of the book.[58]

Reception of the Play

In German-speaking countries, Birch-Pfeiffer's play was valued for its morality. In a survey of German reception of English-language literature in the nineteenth century, Susanne Stark summarizes an essay by Inga-Stina Ewbank:

> The author explains how the very literal German translation [of *Jane Eyre*] by Christoph Grieb in 1850 was adapted in 1862 by the Viennese pedagogue Jakob Spitzer for the use of Austrian schoolgirls. Spitzer, who at this point of time was teaching at a school for young ladies, was well-known for his pedagogical works for teachers and pupils. 'Die Waise aus Lowood', however, remained his only attempt at portraying educative ideas in the form of a novel. The title of his adaptation points clearly to his having known Birch-Pfeiffer's drama adaptation, which was performed 102 times at the Burgtheater in Vienna between the years 1853 and 1895. It is also very probable that his pupils knew the play, and his reworking of the novel can be seen as a reaction to both the translator Grieb and to Birch-Pfeiffer.
>
> While Birch-Pfeiffer had restructured Brontë's material by giving it a much simpler, morally and emotionally much less complex plot, Spitzer removed all the imaginative, gothic and psychological elements in the novel. He described Jane Eyre's education in much more detail than Brontë ever did, portraying his heroine as an exemplary figure for his own pupils.[59]

---

56 *NYT*, 9 December 1884, p. 4.
57 NYPLPA: BRTC programme, week commencing 31 October 1887.
58 *NYT*, 15 May 1898, p. 9.
59 Stark (accessed 8 March 2005). I am extremely grateful to Barbara Jean Frick for her research into and translation of various German-language sources.

It is likely that Spitzer developed Birch-Pfeiffer's emphasis on Jane's ability to conceal her feelings for Rochester. Even under his provocation, she is inscrutable – 'No word, no look betrays her thoughts!' (III ii).

The novelist Theodor Fontane wrote reviews of the German stage play on 24 October 1876 and 19 May 1878.[60] The influence of Birch-Pfeiffer's play went well beyond Germany, however. It was translated into Spanish in 1869,[61] and *The Times*, reviewing Willing's *Jane Eyre* in 1879,[62] mentions not only Jacob Spitzer's adaptation but also an Italian stage version called *L'Orfanella di Lowood*[63] and a Danish version – 'a true melodrama with incidental songs' – called *Et Vaisenhuusbarn*.[64] A German film entitled *Die Waise von Lowood* was made in 1926 with the Danish actor, Olaf Fönss, as Rochester,[65] and a Hungarian film with the same title was made in 1920;[66] a child's version of *Jane Eyre* with this title was available in Hungary in 1993.[67]

In America, responses to the German play changed significantly during the twenty years of its popularity. Some of the early American reviews showed a hazy knowledge of Charlotte Brontë's novel. An 1874 review claims that Charlotte Birch-Pfeiffer's version 'not only conforms […] to Miss Brontë's novel, but preserves in a remarkable degree the spirit of that wonderful story' and wonders 'if any but a German dramatist could have entered so fully into the mystic and psychologic peculiarities of the leading characters of the novel'.[68] Other reviewers praise its 'wholesome' quality which 'affects one as gratefully as basking in the early rays of the morning sun', so that 'when we leave the theatre we feel a hundred nobler impulses manifesting themselves',[69] especially in contrast with such a 'repulsive element in the novel' as Rochester's attempt at bigamy.[70]

Other reviews were more concerned with dramaturgy. The London *Era*'s correspondent prefers 'Miss Thompson's Jane Eyre' to Charlotte Brontë's because 'Jane Eyre in the book is not a dramatic personage'.[71] The *New York Times* reviewer, discussing the very first performances in New York, by Marie Seebach, disagrees: 'Charlotte Brontë's famous novel has plenty of dramatic interest, and yet, paradoxical as it seems, that which is most dramatic about it can but imperfectly be represented

---

60   See Agerer.
61   Morera y Valls.
62   *Times*, 1 September 1879, p. 6, col. B.
63   Michély; the text follows Birch-Pfeiffer closely.
64   See head-note to Hering's play for possible Danish links.
65   *Die Waise von Lowood*, dir. Curtis [Kurt] Bernhardt; see Staedeli (accessed 8 March 2005).
66   BPM exhibition, 1991–1992.
67   I am grateful to Marta Minier for this information.
68   *Graphic*, 20 August 1874.
69   HTC: unidentified clipping headed 'Union Square Theatre', dated in ink '22 Aug 1874'.
70   HTC clipping headed 'Union Square Theatre': *Post*.
71   HTC: unidentified clipping.

on the stage' because 'the attempted visible picture of spiritual vicissitudes like theirs will appear crude, insufficient, and unsatisfactory'.[72] By 1884, however, a weary *New York Times* reviewer (referring to Charlotte Thompson's version) complains about the plot changes ('Rochester is made a nobleman for some unexplained reason'), which are still bothering the paper in 1889:

> In the novel the nobles are decidedly of the wax-work order, though Rochester is human enough in some ways, albeit of the Byronic kind – wicked, cynical, but not entirely perverted by circumstances and his own wild life. In the play Rochester is a lord indeed, that is to say a lord of the footlights tempered by Teutonic imaginings of what a live lord really is. If the French cherish the belief that all Englishwomen have teeth like rabbits, the Germans are prone to the view that opulence is a characteristic of the English lord.

This reviewer definitely prefers Charlotte Brontë, not just because the play 'suppresses the plot against the virtue of Jane Eyre, her flight, the blinding of Rochester, and the return of Jane to her maimed lion', but because the novel has 'a sobriety of touch which is appreciated by those who enjoy the finer shades in literature, a reserve that is not so much maidenly as in sturdy good taste' and 'this atmosphere is of necessity lost on the stage.[73]

In 1898, the *New York Times* obituary for Charlotte Thompson includes ambiguous praise for 'that estimable German manufacturer of stage plays, Frau Börch-Pfeiffer', whose 'Waise von Lowood' was 'as little like Charlotte Brontë's novel as a dramatization could be'.[74]

Distinctive Features of the Play

- The action is restricted to Gateshead (Part 1) and Thornfield (Part 2).
- There is much emphasis on the humane treatment of orphans, with Uncle Reed (in relation to Jane), Jane (in relation to Adèle) and Rochester (in relation to Adèle and Lady Rochester) shown as worthy by contrast with Mrs Reed.
- Jane is virtuous and able to conceal her feelings for Rochester.
- Rochester is Lord Rowland Rochester.
- Rochester greatly admires Jane's paintings.
- The Reed family take the place of the Ingrams, with Lady Georgina Clarens (née Reed) in the place of Blanche Ingram.
- Jane refuses the gift of a dress from Rochester.
- The madwoman is the wife of Rochester's dead brother, and Adèle's mother
- The play ends with Jane and Rochester alone.

---

72 *NYT*, 6 October 1870, p. 4.
73 *NYT*, 9 December 1884, p. 4; 19 October 1889, p. 5.
74 *NYT*, 15 May 1898.

Jane Eyre or the Orphan of Lowood by **Charlotte Birch-Pfeiffer**

Dramatis Personae.
First Part – One Act

Jane Eyre	**Mme Marie Seebach**
Mistress Sarah Reed	Mme Mathilde Veneta
Capt. Henry Whitfield	Mr Paetsch
Dr Blackhorst	Mr Harry
Bessie	Mlle Bissinger

Second Part – Three Acts.

Jane Eyre	**Mme Marie Seebach**
Lord Rowland Rochester	Mr Drombrowski
[Lord] Clawdon	Mr Becker
Lady Clawdon	Mme Schroeter
Francis Stienworth	Mr Brinkmann
Edward Harder	
Mistress Reed	Mlle Veneta
Lady Georgin[a] Clarens	Mll[e] Bardenhauer
Capt. Henry W[h]itfield,	Mr Paetsch
Mistress Judith Harleigh	Mme Grahn
Adèle, a child eight years old	-----------------
Gratia Poole	Mme Meier
Sam, a servant	Mr Muller
Patrick, coachman	Mr Koppe

The second part is supposed to take place eight years later than the first part, at Thornfield Hall, an estate of Lord Rochester.

Entered according to Act of Congress, in the year 1870, by Maurice Grau, in the office of the Librarian of Congress, Washington, D.C.

Prologue

A room with bookcases and statues. Middle and side doors. Left, a high window, with red curtains, which are drawn back; before it stands a chair. Right, a chimney, over which hangs the portrait of a man between forty and fifty years old. Near chimney stand a sofa and an arm-chair. – General appearance of wealth.

Scene 1

Mrs Reed, Henry Whitfield

Henry: I have been too long absent to comprehend at a glance just how matters stand here. It is easy, however, to see that the position of this orphan in your family is a false one, for she suffers severely from your hatred.

Mrs R: You are right – I do hate her. It is possible I have not understood her, and that I have not tried to understand her. I have done everything in my power, have indeed used every means to make her obedient, but all has been in vain. She hates my children, defies my authority, and now I am determined to send her away. This is the only way to establish peace under this roof. She is the very counterpart of her mother – as wilful and obstinate as she was.

Henry (shakes his head): If I remember rightly, you always had a great dislike for her mother.

Mrs R: And not without good cause. She covered our name with disgrace; she eloped with a miserable wretch of a naval officer, who soon squandered her little fortune, and then in a few years died, leaving his widow a beggar. I was compelled to endure her presence, and nurse her until death came to relieve me. Then I breathed freely once more; I thought the cup was drained to the dregs, but I was in error, the bitterest was yet to come. She had implored Reed to be a father to her orphan. He was a severe, obstinate man. I dared not let him see how I hated this little creature, who was the idol of his heart. He would sit by the hour with the child on his knee, playing with her blonde locks, and listening to her silly prattle. Yes, when he was suddenly overtaken by death, his last thoughts were busy with the girl, for he exacted from me a solemn promise that I would bring her up with my children, according to her equal rights and privileges.

Henry (astonished): Well, and what do you propose to do with her now?

Mrs R: I am going to put her into Lowood Institute. I have arranged everything with the director, who arrived here yesterday, and I expect him to come for her every moment.

Henry: Lowood Institute! Is not that an orphan asylum – a sort of charity school for poor orphan girls, some eighty miles from here, in an unhealthy district, supported by voluntary contributions?

Mrs R: Yes, it is an orphan asylum. As for the part of the country where it is located, I know nothing about it, but I *do* know that it is a Christian institution, in which young girls are taught to be industrious and humble. By taking this step, I feel that I fully discharge my duty towards her.

Henry: At all events, Sarah, you take this step too late. A few years ago she might have become accustomed to this terrible change in her situation – now she has arrived at an age when it is impossible. It was certainly not your husband's intention that his little favourite should be educated in a charity school.

Mrs R: Oh no, that is very certain! He would not have thought the most fashionable school in London good enough for her. (*Turning quickly*) Since, as it seems, you do not approve of my course, you are at liberty to provide for the girl as you think proper. I will resign my authority into your hands with pleasure.

Henry: You mock me Sarah. My circumstances do not, like yours, admit of my providing for her.

Mrs R: Then you would do well to allow me to pursue the course I deem advisable, which I have the satisfaction of knowing receives the approval of the whole neighbourhood.   (*Exit*)

Henry: But not of your own conscience, Sarah.   (*Follows her*)

Mrs R (*will answer indignantly*).

Scene 2

Jane enters alone L. She shows her head at door L. enters carefully, treading on her toes, looking about and listening, then she glides across the stage towards the chimney. She is pale; wears a calico dress and dark apron; a white handkerchief around her neck. She stops before the picture, clasps her hands and looks at it earnestly. After a pause:

Jane: Uncle Reed, dear Uncle Reed! Do you see me? You smile, You *do* see me! Why do you smile? No, weep, weep! They all say that I am an ugly, spoiled, ungrateful child – it must be so! Oh, why did you leave me! I loved you so dearly, and you, too, loved me, did you not, Uncle? But they all hate me – should I, *can* I be grateful for their *hate*? Yesterday was Christmas; they are still feasting and making merry, but they don't think of you, Uncle Reed, to whom they owe everything, although it is your birthday. (*Sinks on one knee.*) Oh, Uncle, I can bring you nothing but my tears, they are all I have, they deny me everything else – take them; they are tears of love and gratitude, and yet they say I am ungrateful. Do you believe it, Uncle? No, no, you do not believe it. You know I am not ungrateful.

Scene 3

Bessie (Enters L.), Jane

Bessie: Good heavens! Just as I thought! Jane, what are you doing here? You
know if your Aunt Reed was to find you here, she would be very angry.
I must watch you every minute. What are you doing?

Jane: This is Uncle Reed's birthday, Bessie; I came to visit him. All the rest
seem to have forgotten it.

Bessie: How? – is today really –

Jane: The day after Christmas. When he lived his parents used to make this
[the) happiest day of the year for us all.

Bessie: But, Jane, it is five years since he died – a little eternity!

Jane: Five years! Yes, yes, a little eternity, indeed! What a happy child I was
then! Before Uncle Reed's death, I did not know that good people ever
died, or that poor orphans could be unhappy!

Bessie: But you had lost your father and mother.

Jane: I never knew them; Uncle Reed was both father and mother to me.
While he lived I did not know what it was to be an orphan! (*Wildly*)
Oh, Uncle Reed, where are you now? Will you not come and take me
with you?

Bessie: Come away with me, Jane; you begin to talk wildly as you did last
summer, after you had the fever. (*Gently*) Come, come, don't be
obstinate.

Jane: Why do you scold me no more, as you used to do, Bessie; why don't
you drag me away by force; why don't you beat me? You know Mrs
Reed allows you to.

Bessie: Because you are no longer a child; because you are now a young
woman.

Jane: Oh, that is not the reason. If I am almost a young woman in years, I
am still as helpless and ignorant as a child. You do not strike me any
more, because you still remember picking me up for dead, after they
had locked me up all night in the garret.

Bessie: I am afraid of making Missis hate you worse than she does already, and
– and then I don't want you to get sick again. Come now Jane, dear;
you know if any of the family should find you here –

Jane: No, I am not going!

Bessie: Jane! Be good! Don't get me into trouble.

Jane (*throws her arms round Bessie's neck*): Oh, Bessie, do not scold me! My heart
is so full!

Bessie: What a strange child. Now you are so gentle, and just now –

Jane: I can't help it, Bessie! You are so often cross with me and so seldom
kind! Please let me remain – nobody will know it. I want to read for a
little while. It's all the pleasure I have, and Georgina has taken all my
books away from me.

Bessie: I should like to let you remain, but if they should find you out –

Jane (springs to the book-case and takes a book): No one will see me. Here it is! Hume's History of England. (*Comes down breathless with joy.*) Do you see? I found it instantly and I remember where I left off, too. (*She hurries to the window, the lower casement of which is aside. Places a chair before it, springs up on the chair and sits on casement. Her face is radiant with joy.*) Now, Bessie, I will close the curtains and no one will see me – so nobody can see me and I can go on reading Hume. I am determined to know something in spite of them all!

Bessie: Stay then, if you are determined to; I will come for you in an hour. Mind you do not stir. Think of me if you do not think of yourself. You know Mrs Reed!

Jane (closes the curtains): Never fear, Bessie. I will be still as a mouse.

Bessie (aside): Let Missis scold as much as she likes! I can't rob the poor girl of the only pleasure she has.   (*Going*)

Scene 4

The former, John, M.D.

John: Bessie, what are you doing here? Stop, I want you!

Bessie (frightened): I have no time, Master John.

John: I don't care whether you have time or not. I want you to remain here and amuse me. Uncle Henry, who has just returned from Spain, and Mama are talking about – I don't know what – some nonsense or other. Georgina sits at the table as stiff as a post and makes faces when I throw bread crumbs at her, as though she were a great lady.

Bessie: You shouldn't throw bread crumbs at your sister, Miss Georgina is older than you and you ought to show her more respect.

John (throws himself on the sofa): Respect! Show *her* respect? I have no respect for anybody – not even Mama. They will all have to look to me for their bread and butter some day. They will be no better off than this beggarly Jane Eyre. Just wait till I come of age! I will show them who is master here! Mind that, Bessie!

Bessie: It will be some time before that.

John (springs to his feet): I have heard that often enough. What a pity Mama won't let Jane Eyre come into the parlor and library any more!

Bessie: Certainly! now you have no one to abuse and quarrel with. Fie! Are you not ashamed of yourself for beating that poor girl as you sometimes did.?

John: I gave her that blow with the hammer because I hated her. That was a long time ago, but I have always been glad of it. I only wish I had struck her harder. But didn't she bite and scratch me though!

Bessie: She had nothing but her hands and teeth to defend herself with.

John: She has no right to defend herself when I strike her. I am the head of the
                 family and she is a beggar, living on our bounty. (*Looks at the curtains.*)
                 What is that? See the curtains move!
Bessie: Yes, indeed! Come, let me go – I am afraid.
John: I am not! There's some one behind that curtain; I'll bet it's that little
                 vixen! (*Springs forward and opens the curtains.*) Ha, ha, I knew it.
                 What are you doing here, you beggar?
Bessie (aside): Good heavens! Just as I feared!
*Jane (sits on the casement, her feet on the chair, both hands with the book on her
knees. She trembles with anger and fixes her eyes on John.)*
John (starts back somewhat frightened): Well, what are you staring at? Can't you
                 answer? What do you hide in that way for? To frighten people? Answer
                 me, or I will make you answer! (*Approaches her.*)
Jane: Touch me if you dare, John Reed!
John (laughing scornfully): Perhaps you think I am afraid of you. I'll show you
                 whether I am or not. (*Goes toward her.*)
Jane (remains sitting): If you dare to touch me, I'll not scratch you again, (*Springs
                 suddenly to her feet and stands before him.*) I'll kill you!
John (starts back): Bah, you'd better not!
Jane: Then do not dare to touch me!
Bessie (takes her hand gently): Come, Jane; come away.
Jane (keeps her eye on John): Not till he goes!

Scene 5

Mrs Sarah Reed, Henry Whitfield, the former

Mrs R: What is this (*She sees Jane and turns away with an expression of
                 disgust*). Ah, is that creature here?
John: Mama, Jane hid behind the curtains there and threatened to kill me if
                 I came near her.
Mrs R: Why did you have any thing to say to her? It is your fault. You should
                 obey me. (*To Jane*) What were you doing here, Jane?
*Jane (who, from the moment Mrs Reed entered has been trembling with fear and
looking down)*: I was reading, Aunt.
Mrs R: Have I not forbidden you entering any of the rooms on the first and
                 second floors?
Jane: Yes, ma'am!
Mrs R: Well, how dare you come in here, contrary to my orders?
Jane: Georgina and John have taken all my books away from me, even those
                 Uncle Reed gave me for my own. Up in my room it is cold and dreary,
                 and then I wanted something to read.
Henry: Let her remain, Sarah.

Mrs R (looks at him with a threatening glance): You should have asked for a book, instead of disobeying my orders.

Jane (fixes her eyes on Mrs Reed for a moment): It was not alone for the book I came.

Mrs R: Well what did you come for? To hear what we were saying in the next room, I suppose.

Jane: No; I came to visit Uncle Reed. (*Points to the portrait.*) This is his birthday.

Mrs R (starts suddenly aside): The viper!

Henry (looks at Mrs R. astonished): True, the 26th of December. When my brother-in-law was living, this was a great day with you here at Gateshead. It seems you have quite forgotten it.

John: But it's so long since papa died. No wonder we didn't think of its being his birthday.

Mrs R: Be silent John! (*To Henry*) It is not strange that Jane Eyre should remember the day. It is to her uncle's indulgence that she is indebted for her haughty obstinacy and wilfullness, which makes her the evil spirit of what would otherwise be a quiet house. (*Looks at her reproachfully*) Have I not forbidden your wearing curls? Don't you know it displeases Georgina? This style of dressing the hair is only suitable to the daughters of the better families, for Georgina for example, who are born to command and not for those like you. Answer, why do you do it?

Jane (runs her hand slowly through her curls): My hair curls naturally, Aunt Reed – it don't take any pains to curl it – I can't help it.

Mrs R: The obstinacy of your hair is a symbol of your character. Is it true that you threatened John?

Jane (calmly): If he dared to strike me again, yes!

Mrs R: Indeed! Then beg his pardon.

Jane (looks down and does not reply)

Mrs R: Are you going to obey?

Jane (calmly): No!

Mrs R: You will not beg his pardon?

Jane: Not till he has begged mine for the abuse he has heaped upon 'the little beggar,' as he calls me.

Mrs R (to Whitfield): Do you hear, Henry? Do you hear? (*To Jane.*) Leave the room!

Jane (Bows and turns to go)

Mrs R: Lay that book down.

Jane (returns and lays down the book)

Mrs R: You will enter here just once more, but not till I send for you.

Jane (fixes her eyes on Mrs R)

Mrs R: Now go, you obstinate, ungrateful creature!

Jane (goes off left)

John (to Bessie triumphantly): I must go and tell Georgina of this, she will be
   delighted.   *(Exit, M.E.)*
Bessie (follows him shaking her head)

Scene 6

Mrs Reed, Henry

Mrs R: Now you have seen and heard the creature that for years has destroyed
    the peace and quiet of this household! Now you can understand what I
    must have suffered in the discharge of the duties my husband imposed
    upon me. Thank heaven, it will soon have an end.

Scene 7

The former, Bessie, Blackhorst, then Jane

Bessie: Mr Blackhorst, ma'am!
Mrs R: Ah! He is very welcome. Call Jane Eyre.
Bessie: I have sent James up for her. She will be here in a minute. *(Opens the
    door for Blackhorst and exits.)*
Black: Madam, your servant!
Mrs R: I am glad to see you, sir. *(They sit.)* I have longed for your arrival.
Black: You are very kind, madam.
Mrs R: I can indeed say that I have longed for your arrival, for I see in you an
    instrument in the hands of Providence by which many shall be turned
    from the error of their ways.
Black: Providence has been pleased to make of your humble servant such an
    instrument, and I trust that with His aid I shall be able to lead back into
    the right path this lamb which, in spite of all your endeavors – as your
    letters tell me – has strayed so far from His flock.
Mrs R: It was my painful duty, Mr Blackhorst, to acquaint you of these facts,
    in order that you might be better able to effect a reform.

Jane enters L. and remains at door

Mrs R: Come here, Jane. You shall not be able to say I spoke ill of you behind
    your back.

Jane comes forward astonished

Mrs R: I have done everything for Jane Eyre that heaven commands us to do
    for the orphan. She has lived since her second year under my roof. I
    have treated her as my own child; endeavored to educate her as I have

educated my own daughter, but she has proven insensible to all my kindness. (*Sighs.*) She has no heart, she is ungrateful, false and deceitful! And having in vain tried everything to correct her disposition, I feel it a duty incumbent on me as her guardian to resign my authority into severer and more competent hands.

Black: What you tell me, madam, is shocking, truly shocking! But I think I may venture to assure you that you have nothing to fear. I have been the unworthy instrument of humbling many a haughty, obstinate spirit, and trust that I shall succeed in this instance, although it is somewhat late to turn this soul from the enormous wickedness of its ways!

Mrs R: Jane Eyre, you see before you the estimable man to whose guidance and direction I resign you. In a few days you will go to Lowood Institute, where I have arranged for you to remain for four years.

Jane (overjoyed): How! I am to go away from here?

Mrs R: You are.

Jane: You are going to send me to school?

Black: Where the wicked are taught to love and fear God.

Jane (measures him with an earnest glance): That, sir, I learned from Uncle Reed. Tell me what else I shall learn at your school?

Black (greatly astonished): A great deal, Miss, if you have a desire to learn.

Jane: Oh, I desire to learn! I will be studious! I will do everything – everything that will tend to make me independent of others.

Black: First of all, Miss, you shall learn humility, for only an humble heart should be tolerated in an orphan asylum like that at Lowood, which owes its existence to private charities.

Jane: An orphan asylum! Are you sending me to an orphan asylum, aunt?

Mrs R: It is the proper place for you. There you will be brought up in a manner suited to your prospects, made useful, and kept humble.

Jane (looking at picture): Do you hear that, Uncle Reed? They disown your little favorite – your Jane – an orphan asylum is to be her home. But, so be it! For if I am still hated and persecuted, it will be by strangers, and not by those to whom I am related.

Black: Merciful heavens! such language in the presence of her benefactress!

Jane: Benefactress (*To portrait)* Do you hear that, Uncle Reed?

Black: Allow me, Madam, to retire. I have seen and heard enough to inspire me with the deepest regret, that you did not, year[s] ago, confide your ward to the christianizing influences of our institution. You have been too indulgent. The goodness of your heart has blinded your judgment. You have not told me the whole truth.   (*Going*)

Jane (steps before Blackhorst. She is highly excited. Her lips tremble, but her movements are calm and decided): You are right, sir; she has not told you the whole truth; that you shall learn from me! I should die if I were not to relieve my bosom of what I have smothered within it for years. Mrs Reed tells you that I am ungrateful: it is not true! I never forget a favor. Those who are kind to me always have a place in my heart. (*To portrait*) You know I speak truly, Uncle. (*To B.*) Mrs Reed says that I tell lies, and am deceitful. That, too, is false. If I were a liar I might tell you that I loved Mrs Reed, that she has been kind to me, has been a mother to me; if I were deceitful I would weep and lament because I am turned out of the home of my childhood. But I tell you there is nothing in the world I so abhor as this woman, whose glances have been thorns to me, whose words daggers, since I could think and feel! For five long years she and her heartless children have treated me with unrelenting cruelty. I hope that I part from them forever! Never again will I call her 'aunt', never! never!

Mrs R (terrified): Jane, how dare you talk to me thus?

Jane (passionately; almost in tears): How dare I, Mrs Reed, how dare I talk to you thus? Because I tell you the truth! You say that I have no heart, that I am insensible to love and kindness. A little love would have made me good and gentle; for a little love I would have worshipped you, as I did Uncle Reed. But love and pity are strangers to your bosom. Oh, to the day of my death I shall remember how, because I defended myself when your wicked son knocked me down with the hammer, you locked me up all night in the garret, although I cried out, half dead with pain, 'Have mercy! Be compassionate, Aunt Reed!' Oh I will tell the whole world how merciful, how compassionate you are! If I am bad, it is you who have made me so – yes, you, who are what you say I am, deceitful; yes, you are more than deceitful – you are a perjured woman.

Mrs R: Jane!

Jane: Yes, a perjured woman: for in my presence, holding the hands of my poor, dying uncle, you made a solemn promise to bring me up with your own children, according to my equal rights and privileges, and never to abandon me. How have you kept your promise? You have denied me admission to the rooms occupied by yourself and your children, have deprived me of the aid of their teachers, that I might remain ignorant, and to-day you consign me to the tender mercy of an orphan asylum. Thus you have kept the promise you made to my dying uncle! When he (*points to portrait*) asks you, in the other world, how you kept your word – what you did with your orphan niece – say that you ruined her disposition by your injustice and barbarous cruelties, and then thrust her into a charity school. (*To Blackhorst*) Come, sir, lead the way. I am ready to follow you!

                                                                        (*Exit*)

Mrs R (sinks on sofa, and covers her face with her hands).
Black (follows Jane greatly embarrassed).
Henry (shrugs his shoulders, and goes towards Mrs R.).

Curtain falls.

Act I

Salon at Thornfield Hall decorated to the style of the seventeenth century. The formation should appear somewhat more modern. The door is flat; the middle door is the general entrance, the door R. leads to Rochester's apartments, the door L. to the library. R. a window. L. a fire place over which the coat-of-arms of the Rochesters. On the mantle two candles lighted and vases of flowers. A fire burns brightly in fireplace. Near fireplace a sofa or lounge and table. R. another table, near it two arm-chairs. In background R. of middle door a tea table set with elegant service. L. of same door a chair. On the two tables are also candles.

Scene 1

Sam, Mrs Judith Harleigh

Sam (has just placed last vase on table): There, everything is in order. I think his lordship will be satisfied if he takes his tea here tonight.

Judith: Why shouldn't he be satisfied?

Sam: He was in an awful bad humor when he arrived, and went straight to his room without saying a word to any one except Grace Pool, although he has been away almost a year.

Judith: That is the way he always does since he returned from the Indies. But what has happened to put you so out of sorts to-day, Sam?

Sam: Oh, you know very well what puts me out of sorts, Mrs Harleigh. Formerly my wife Sarah and I were something to you, but since this wan-faced haughty Miss Eyre has been at the Hall, we are just nobody.

Judith (smiling): You and Sarah are both very silly, Sam. Have we not all of us good reason to be thankful to Miss Eyre? In three months has she not made quite a different child of Adèle, who used to give us so much trouble? I thank heaven daily for sending us Miss Eyre, such girls as she are not often met with.

Sam: I hope his lordship may discover such a treasure in her as you do; if he don't, she wont remain here long. (*A bell is heard, Sam starts.*) His lordship!

Judith (listening): Only once – that is for his valet. (*Bell.*) No, he wants you, Sam; be quick!

Sam: (*Exit quickly, R.*)

Judith (alone): So long as he does not ring three times it does not concern me; but he will not be very likely to take his tea here this evening. If he should, however, and he should ask to see the new governess – what did I let her go to Millcale for to carry my letter! It is already dark! (*Walks to and fro.*) But, who could think his lordship would come home this evening! The poor girl has a long walk – I hope nothing has happened to her.

Scene 2

Judith, Jane

Jane (speaking at M.D.): Ah, here you are?

Judith: Oh, I'm so glad you have returned! What kept you so long? I began to be worried about you.

Jane (she has a little more color than in the prologue, her carriage is more erect and she should appear fully developed and taller. She seems cheerful and contented, bus is somewhat serious and staid in her manner): Your letter is posted. I went to my room to lay off my things, then I looked for you in your room and learnt from Sarah, whom I met in the hall, that I should find you here. (*Looks about astonished.*) But what is the meaning of all this – so many candles, these flowers, and this blazing fire?

Judith: This means that during your absence his lordship has arrived.

Jane (calmly): Lord Rochester? indeed! But you were not expecting him.

Judith: No, we never expect him till he comes.

Jane: Oh, what an eventful day!

Judith: Eventful? How so?

Jane (smiling): Oh, I have had one of the strangest adventures! The air was cold and bracing: I walked fast and became tired – Coming home, I sat down to rest on the stone bench, by the roadside, on the hill beyond Hay Lane, and was surveying the surrounding country, thinking that Lord Rochester must be very rich, for I remembered your telling me that all the land to be seen from this elevated point was his, when suddenly I heard the tramp of a horse ascending the hill and a moment afterwards an immense Newfoundland dog stood before me. I was frightened at first and sprang to my feet just as a rider reached the summit of the hill. At sight of me his horse jumped to one side, stumbled and fell, half burying his master under him –

Judith: Good heavens! Well?

Jane: I heard a wild cry, then a muttered oath. And when I hurried to the spot and asked: 'Are you hurt, sir? Can I do anything to help you?' he answered, in a gruff voice: 'If you are not a sprite and are not afraid of my horse, you may assist me to extricate myself.' I reached him my hand and he was no sooner on his feet than taking the reins in one hand, he gave the animal a blow with the other crying: 'Get up, Mesrour, get up, you rascal!'

Judith: Mesrour, did he call his horse?

Jane: Yes, and he knew his name, too, for he lost no time in getting on to this feet. The first thing the ruffian did was to give his beautiful horse a blow, crying: 'You must be punished, sir! What did you throw me off for?'

Judith: Well, and what then?

Jane:	Then he tried to mount, but, having sprained his ankle, he was unable. 'Can I assist you, sir?' I asked again. He fixed his eyes on me a moment and then said, 'Necessity compels me to make you useful – hold the opposite stirrup; Mesrour will not hurt you.' I did as he bade me, and with a bound he was in the saddle. 'Thank you! Now hurry home!' said he in a commanding tone, and away he went like the wind. (*Humorously.*) Isn't that an adventure for a winter's evening?
Judith:	My child, don't you know who the traveller was? Lord Rochester and no other.
Jane:	Lord Rochester on horseback and alone?
Judith:	Yes, you must know that in some things he is very eccentric. He always leaves the coach in some of the neighboring villages, and we never know when to expect him or whence he comes. His ride to-day has been an unfortunate one.
Jane:	Oh me! And it is all my fault!
Judith:	Now I understand why he went directly to his room. It is one of his peculiarities to be alone when he suffers.
Jane:	Pecularities! But I understood you to say he has none.
Judith:	Oh, I meant it was easy enough to get along with him. One has only to do his bidding.

Jane (thoughtfully): It is very evident that his lordship is not over polite and gentle.

Judith:	Perhaps not, my child. I have never spoken to you of the family affairs of the Rochesters; it is a subject I usually avoid, but now it is perhaps better that I should do so. Lord Rochester is a younger son and was poor, his brother having inherited the estate. The brothers lived tolerably harmoniously together until some circumstances transpired, I never knew what, that made them the bitterest of enemies, and obliged their father to separate them. The present lord Rochester was sent to the West Indies, where he lived, almost forgotten, until a few years ago, when his brother suddenly died and he succeeded to the family estates and titles. Now Jamaica, it would seem, is not the best place in the world to learn good breeding, but Lord Rochester is at heart a thoroughly high-minded gentleman, a lover of justice and a friend to the poor and oppressed. (*Looks about mysteriously.*) One thing more, my child; you told me, the other day, that you had heard a strange noise in the third story.
Jane:	Yes, a strange demoniac laugh, that seemed to come from the tower. It fairly chilled my blood.
Judith:	Poor Grace! She often disturbs us at night in that way.

Jane (fixes her eyes intently on Judith): So you have told me before; but I met Grace on the stairs just now, and as I went through the hall, I heard the same horrid laugh again.

Judith (confused): How? Ah, so, she must have been coming down stairs to see his lordship.

Jane: What! She –

Judith (confused): I do not know – I think. But be on your guard, my child. I would
                 advise you never to mention this circumstance to his lordship and to
                 pay no attention to Grace Pool. It is for your good that I give you this
                 advice.

Jane: Thank you, Mrs Harleigh, I will be on my guard.

Scene 3

The former, Grace Pool

Jane: Here she comes now.

*Grace (she comes from R. An elderly woman. Her manner is serious and simple,
        her bearing dignified and decided, her tone masculine, she makes no
        gestures)*: Mrs Harleigh, his lordship will take his tea here.

Judith: I am glad of it. Who is with him?

Grace: Adèle and Dr Spanley; he met with an accident on the road.

Judith: I hope it is nothing serious.

Grace: I don't know. You know he never complains. Have you everything
                 ready for to-night?

Judith: Yes, everything prepared.

Grace: His lordship wishes to see the new governess when he comes to his tea.
                 (*Going*)

Judith: Very well – Grace!

Grace: Well?

Judith: Too much noise, too much noise!

Grace: I will see to it.   (*Exit M.D.*)

Scene 4

Judith, Jane

Jane (aside):   Very strange!

Judith: It is a good sign that he takes his tea here – the accident cannot be very
                 serious. – Listen, is that not Adèle's voice?

Jane: What, hasn't her nurse put her to bed yet?

Judith: It is hard getting her to bed when his lordship is at home. Ha, I think I
                 hear his step. Yes, he is coming. (*Goes to arrange the tea table*)

Jane: (*Aside*) How my heart beats! This accident of which I was the innocent
                 cause, has certainly prejudiced him against me. (*Goes up*)

Scene 5

The former, Rochester, Adèle followed by Sam

Adèle (has Rochester's hand. A child at most eight years old, nicely but simply clad.
    She is lively and joyous): That is Miss Eyre. (*Will go over to her*)
Roch (a man forty years old. He has marked features, serious almost stern expression,
    full dark hair, dark beard. He wears a dressing gown and smoking cap.
    His manner of speaking is abrupt and commanding. Sometimes there is
    something wild in his manner, but this is only momentary. As he enters
    he looks neither to the right or left. In a commanding tone to Adèle):
    Very well – be still! (*He limps toward the lounge.*) Sam!

Sam:	My lord!
Roch:	Move that chair nearer to the fire. I can never keep warm in this old rookery. The devil! Sam, your arm. (*Sam assists him to a chair.*) That will do! Move that table nearer. (*Sam obeys and Rochester leans his arm on the table.*) There – go!

Sam (aside to Mrs Harleigh as he goes off): Now is your pet's turn. (*Exit M.D.*)
Roch (still lost in thought)
Adèle (clambers on his knee): Are you angry with me, Uncle Rowland?

Roch:	No!
Adèle:	Have you brought me anything?
Roch:	I must first know whether you deserve anything. Do you?
Adèle:	Yes, indeed, I deserve a great deal. Don't I Miss Eyre?

Jane (puts her hand on Adèle's mouth and whispers to her)
Roch (glances at Jane as though he expected her answer. After a pause, as Jane does
    not reply, he turns towards Judith): Good evening, Cousin Judith!

Judith:	Good evening my lord – You met with an accident on the road?
Roch:	As usual, when I approach these walls!
Judith:	How did it happen?
Roch:	Mesrour shied at an ugly elf that sat by the roadside.
Jane:	That's frank, at least!
Judith:	But it was not her fault.

Roch (changing his position with difficulty): Perhaps not; but the consequences are
    all the same. Madam, I should like some tea.
Adèle (springing up): Me! Me! Let me carry it. (*Runs to Judith*)

Judith:	No, no, you would be sure to spill it. Miss Eyre, will you be so kind. (*Hands cup of tea and whispers to her*)

Roch (aside): At all events the new governess is not presuming. She is either very
    modest or very sharp.

Jane (puts the tea on a waiter, comes down and offers it to him, modestly but not
    timidly)

Roch:	On the table!

Jane (puts the cup on the table)

Roch (looks at her): Eh, the mischief! Good evening to your elfship! Have you
    bewitched my tea as you did my horse this evening?
Jane (looks at him calmly and earnestly, but modestly): I fear, my Lord, the fault
    was Mesrour's rather than mine. I am not conscious of presuming the
    power of witchcraft.
Roch (looks at her astonished): So! Hem! Find yourself a chair!
Jane (goes to arm-chair L)
Roch (aside): The 'elfship' has vexed her! – Full of vanity like the rest of them.
    (*Aloud*) Move your chair this way. (*Jane obeys, placing her chair at
    foot of the lounge. He says aside.*) Not easily frightened, at all events.
    (*Aloud*) You are the new governess.
Jane: Yes, my Lord.
Judith (who has stood at a distance, comes forward): And I thank heaven daily, my
    lord –
Roch: Has the young lady had her tea?
Jane: Thank you – I do not wish any.
Roch (to Judith): Then sit down there and take yours. (*Points to chair on the opposite
    side of the table*) and be quiet.
*Judith (without showing the least irritation, sits down in the chair designated. She
sips her tea, and knits, but follows the conversation attentively.)*
Adèle (crossing to him): But Uncle Rowland, tell me, did you bring me anything?
Roch (to Jane): Does she merit anything?
Jane: Yes, sir.
Roch: Then go to my valet, and tell him to give you that little box.
Adèle: (*Joyfully*) Oh, thank you, thank you! (*Goes towards centre, and stops
    suddenly*) Did you bring Miss Eyre something too?
Roch: (*Glances at Jane*) We shall see.
Adèle: If you haven't, I shall give her some of mine.   (*Exit M.D.*)

Scene 6

The former, without Adèle

Roch (looks at Jane sharply): Did you expect a present? Are you fond of presents?
Jane (modestly, but not timidly): I hardly know, sir. It is so long since I have received
    or expected any.
Roch: You are not so frank as Adèle; she demands a present clamorously, the
    moment she sees me – you beat about the bush.
Jane: Because I have less confidence in my deserts. She can prefer the claim
    of old acquaintance, and the right, too, of custom. If I had to make out a
    case, I should be puzzled, since I am a stranger, and have done nothing
    that entitles me to an acknowledgement.

Roch: Oh, don't be over-modest! I have already examined Adèle, and find
                 you have taken great pains with her; she has made good progress.

Jane (bows, and seems pleased): Thank you, I have my present.

Roch: Humph! Your name is?

Jane: Jane Eyre.

Roch: You have been in my house three months.

Jane: Yes, my Lord.

Roch: And come from – where?

Jane: From Lowood school.

Roch: From Lowood! Ah, a charitable concern! How long were you there?

Jane: Eight years.

Roch: Eight years! You must have a constitution of iron; for, so far as I know,
                 the children are half starved in this *benevolent* institution, and are shown
                 no mercy by the hypocritical Blackhorst. I thought half that time was
                 sufficient there to ruin the health of any child. But why did you remain
                 so long at Lowood?

Jane: The first four years I was a pupil; the rest of the time I was one of the
                 teachers, with a yearly salary of five pounds.

Roch: Humph! Who recommended you to come here?

Jane: I read in the newspaper that a governess was wanted at Thornfield Hall;
                 the conditions were very brilliant. I felt that I could give satisfaction, and
                 sent my recommendations. Mrs Harleigh sent for me immediately.

Judith: Yes, and I am sure I shall never regret I did, too.

Roch: Who knows?

Judith: How?

Roch: There, there, be quiet, Cousin Judith! (*To Jane.*) As you were at Lowood,
                 I suppose you are an orphan. Who were your parents?

Jane: I never knew them.

Roch: Well, you have relations – sisters, brothers?

Jane: No, I never had any.

Roch: But you have uncles, aunts?

Jane: I had one of the best of uncles, but he is dead; now I have no one.

Roch: No one – no one at all?

Jane: I have been told that one of my father's brothers went to America,
                 many years ago, but I have never heard from him. I am quite alone in
                 the world.

Roch: But not helpless!

Jane: Sir!

Roch (smiles, and points to his forehead): You have a wonderful protector here. Well,
                 Miss – Miss – what is your name?

Jane: Jane Eyre, sir.

Roch: True, true, Miss Eyre! What did you learn at Lowood? Do you play?

Jane: A little.

Roch: The stereotyped reply, 'a little,' as much as most school-girls, I suppose, but not well.

Jane: You are, doubtless, right, sir.

Roch: Are these sketches Adèle shows me yours?

Jane: Yes, sir.

Roch: Have you more of them?

Jane: I have several in my portfolio in the library.

Roch: Go bring it!

Jane (rises)

Roch: I mean if you please; you know I am lame.

Jane (goes)

Roch (calls after her): If your portfolio contains only copies, you need not take the trouble to fetch it. I can recognize patchwork.

Jane: Then you shall judge for yourself, my lord, when you see them. I have never been able to reproduce what did not find an echo in my heart. (*Exit L.*)

Roch: Hem! A proud Miss! Now we shall see some botchery.

Judith: I think not, my Lord; when Jane Eyre says she can, she will never disappoint you.

Roch: Eh, cousin! You have here a person who, with an outward show of modesty, has the confidence of a senator; I have never met such a girl before.

Judith: And you never will meet with another, if you drive her from Thornfield.

Roch: It would not be easy to drive her away; a salary of £30 instead of £5 is a consideration.

Judith: Be on your guard. You don't know the girl.

Roch: Nor ever shall, perhaps.

Jane returns with large portfolio of drawings, which she opens and lays before him.

Roch: Be seated.

Jane (sits)

Roch (looks over the sheets): These are in water colors – you paint?

Jane: Yes, sir – with the pencil I was only able to express the thought; in order to embody the feelings, the colors became necessary.

Roch (examines the sketches. He cannot conceal his astonishment): What strange ideas! Here nothing but clouds low and livid, rolling over a soulless sea – a half-submerged mast, on which sits a cormorant – his wings flecked with foam – holding in his beak a bracelet set with gems, which have been torn from a fair arm, that alone is visible above the waters. No living thing is to be seen but this king of the cliffs, and yet all is life. Where did you get your copies?

Jane: Out of my head.

Roch: Out of that little head I see on your shoulders?
Jane: Yes, sir!
Roch: Has it any more furniture of the same sort?
Jane: Better, I should hope.

Roch (takes up another sketch, rests his head on his hand, and examines it closely. Apparently lost in thought, he glances at Jane, takes off his cap, and lays it on the table)

Judith (aside): She has conquered! He takes off his cap.

Roch (turns quickly to Jane): Were you happy when you painted these pictures, Miss Eyre? Your imagination chose a dark and gloomy path.

Jane: I was absorbed sir; yes, I was happy so long as I painted, and yet it pained me to see how far short the execution fell of my conception.

Roch: You have, at least, secured the shadow of your thought, but no more, probably. For a school-girl your drawings are wonderful; as for the thoughts, they are elfish, but full of poetry. Who taught you to paint wind? What a storm sweeps over this plain! There, I have looked at them enough for to-night; they will keep me awake, or haunt me in my dreams! It must be late!

Judith: After 11 o'clock, my Lord!

Roch: So late! It is time to retire, Miss Eyre; we keep early hours here. The devil but my foot hurts me. For a few days at least, I shall not be likely to forget your elfship. Good night! (*Goes off R. taking the portfolio*)

Jane (rises when Rochester rises, and watches him calmly and attentively till he goes off)

Judith: There! You are in disgrace with him!

Jane: I think not. But did you not tell me there was nothing strikingly peculiar about his lordship?

Judith: Well, is there?

Jane: I think there is. To me he seems very changeable and abrupt.

Judith: You did not appear to be timid.

Jane: Perhaps not. I remembered that, to keep a lion at bay, we should face him resolutely.

Judith: You compare his Lordship to a beast of prey! Ah me! I fear you will not be pleased with him.

Jane: But I fear nothing of the kind. I would not have him other than he is, and I trust that when he becomes accustomed to her 'elfship', we shall get along very well together; but come, let us retire; I shall sleep well to-night, for now we have a severe but reliable protector – now we have a MAN in the house!   (*Exuent M.E.*)

Curtain Falls

Act II

Same room as in former act

Scene 1

Jane alone

Jane (stands at the window and looks out thoughtfully): Again the outer world is clothed with the verdure of budding spring – without all is life and animation; but how different it is in this gloomy old hall – here it is so monotonous, so quiet! Ten days ago, he went to take his morning ride – ten days! And yet no one inquires where he can remain so long. A strange man! Weeks have passed since that evening – he was not wholly displeased with me – no, no; I cannot be deceived – and yet since then his pride has not deigned to give me one friendly word. He seems angry with himself for having noticed the 'School-girl', and still I sometimes imagine that although he appears not to notice me, he would be glad if I would speak to him. Never! But why does he not give me back my portfolio? What can he want of it? I really wish I knew where he is and what keeps him so long! Fie! What is he to me? An enigma that I cannot – dare not explain.

Judith (behind the scenes): Quick now, Leah! Fires everywhere and see that the spare rooms are well aired.

Scene 2

Jane, Patrick, Judith

Judith (entering very hurriedly): Sam! Sam! Where are you. (*To Patrick*) In an hour did you say, Patrick?

Pat: It will not be longer than that. His lordship was not far behind me on Mesrour. The others are in carriages.

Judith: But why didn't you bring me word sooner?

Pat: They didn't think of coming till this morning.

Judith: Ah, Miss Eyre, I was just going to look for you. Go dress yourself quickly – make yourself handsome – quick, quick, to your room. I have already sent up the package. Come, come don't look so astonished! There is not a moment to be lost, my child. You hear they will be here in an hour.

Jane: Who will be here? For whom shall I make myself handsome?

Judith (gives her letter): Here see for yourself. I must see Sam, the old drone! Sam! Sam!   (*Exit L.*)

Jane (looks after her astonished, opens letter and reads): 'In an hour after the receipt of this, I shall arrive at Thornfield, accompanied by several guests, including two or three ladies. Mrs Harleigh will prepare to receive them. I send a silk dress by the bearer for – the governess: I wish her to be – presentible. Rochester.' 'The governess' Hum! He has even forgotten my name. *(To Patrick)* Then there are some ladies in the party?

Pat: Yes, miss, and beautiful ones, too – that is the young one, as for the other – if she wasn't a lady she wouldn't exactly suit me.

Jane: But the young lady, she pleases you, does she Patrick?

Pat: Oh, I'm not the only one she pleases.

Judith (returning): There that is arranged. Now, my child, wasn't that thoughtful in his lordship? You will see how the dress will become you.

Jane: I shall not wear it.

Judith: What – not wear it? His lordship ordered it expressly from London for you, didn't he Patrick?

Pat: Right direct, ma'am, and it was made after the measure of Lady Clarens' waiting maid; you are just one size.

Jane: Really! And who is Lady Clarens?

Judith: She is a beautiful young widow, whose husband left her a title but little to support it with. She has a small estate some twenty miles from here.

Pat: And will soon be mistress of a large one less than twenty miles from here.

Judith: Ha, no danger of that. If it only depends on the lady such a thing might be. Three years ago, when his lordship returned from France, she turned her eyes towards Thornfield, but he was blind to her glances.

Pat: Yes, but that was three years ago, Mrs Harleigh!

Judith: Patrick, don't talk nonsense. I tell you she will have her trouble for her pains.

Pat: Humph! We shall see. His lordship after making the usual visits in the neighbourhood, spent a whole week at Clarens-House. And oh, they made such an ado over him! Now the whole party are coming here, and then a good many more are invited. Heaven knows how long they will stay. You mark my words this will end up in a wedding, Mrs Harleigh!

Judith: I will not believe it.

Pat: Why not? On account of his forty years perhaps! Ah, then the men begin to be worse after the girls than ever. I know his lordship only a couple of years, its true, but I tell you that this time there will be a wedding. What will you wager?

Judith: Very well, I have heard enough about it. Go and make room for the strange horses.

Pat: They will not be strange very long in our stable. *(Exit M.D.)*

Judith: The simpleton, to talk such nonsense – marry Lady Clarens – no, that he never will!   *(Exit M.E.)*

Scene 3

Jane alone

Jane: And why should he not marry! I know not why, but I cannot imagine
                 Lord Rochester as a bridegroom. He always appears to me as though he
                 could devour whatever might belong to him with love or hate according
                 to his humor. Hark! I hear his imperious step. Now for another encounter
                 with the lion.

Scene 4

Rochester, Jane

Roch (enters quickly at M. E. in an elegant riding suit, hat on and whip in his hand):
                 What the devil! Nobody to be found! (*Sees Jane, changes his tone
                 somewhat*) Ah, good evening, Miss Eyre!
Jane (bows):   Good evening, my lord! (*Starts to go*)
Roch (throws hat and whip on the table, half angrily, half good naturally): Are you
                 about to run away from me again?
Jane (stops): I run away from no one, my lord.
Roch: Very well, then remain. I am glad to have met you first on entering the
                 house, for many things occurred to me on the way of which I should
                 have spoken to you before. I had almost forgotten you of late – other
                 ideas had driven you from my head – you have not put on your new
                 dress?
Jane: No, sir!
Roch: Why not?
Jane: Because I cannot forget my position. I am sensible to your kindness,
                 but without imposing upon it. I shall find means to make myself
                 'presentible'.
Roch: You have read my note note to Mrs Harleigh?
Jane: Yes, my Lord, at her request.
Roch: You are annoyed because I am not pleased at your plain attire.
Jane: No, not at all.
Roch: Yes you are, and then you will not understand that in this gloomy old
                 rookery the eye finds relief in looking on light, lively colors, but that
                 is not all. You are too proud and independent to accept presents.
Jane: My lord – I –
Roch: Oh, I understand your character, little conversation as I have had with
                 you. With all your meekness and simplicity you have your pretensions
                 and your own idea of things. You dislike my manner, you think me too
                 dictatorial, too abrupt. My life in the West Indies, and the injustice,
                 treachery and deceit of mankind have made me rough, somewhat
                 misanthropic perhaps! What is the meaning of that smile?

Jane: I was thinking, sir, that very few masters would trouble themselves to inquire whether or not their paid subordinates were piqued or hurt by their orders.

Roch: Paid subordinates? Oh, yes, I had forgotten the salary! But to return to what I have to say to you. If I have not been communicative before, it was because you have given me no opportunity. You doubtless judge me wrongfully, and I would be justified in your eyes before my guests arrive. I am in a confidential mood to-day. Heaven knows when I shall be again! So listen to me attentively.

Jane: But, my Lord! –

Roch: You are Adèle's governess. – What relation do you think exists between her and me?

Jane: That is a matter I have not thought of, sir, nor do I think it a matter that properly concerns me.

Roch: Miss Eyre, you have thought of it. You talk too little not to think a great deal. You suppose Adèle to be my child?

Jane: And if I have thought so, and if she is your child, whose business is it but your own?

Roch: Yours! You have a right to ask whose child you are educating. Adèle is an orphan, and I have good reason to believe is the offspring of an illicit union. A solemn promise made to the dying renders it my duty to provide for her education; but I am not her father.

Jane: Then your paternal care is all the more meritorious.

Roch: Bah! No matter about that! And you know, Miss Eyre, that your pupil was, probably, born out of the pale of wedlock. I thought it my duty to acquaint you with these facts, as I am about to receive several guests at Thornfield, through whom you might be offered a more honorable and brilliant position. In such an event, of course, you would be at liberty to consult your own interest and inclination.

Jane: Do you think, sir, that the offer of a more brilliant situation would induce me to forsake this unfortunate child, whom I have learned to love? What is more honorable than being a mother to the motherless? Oh, my Lord, I, too, am an orphan – I know what it is to be fatherless and motherless! I thank you for your generous confidence! Now I shall love Adèle more than ever, and never will I forsake her (*Stops suddenly, and fixes her eyes on Rochester*) unless you yourself send me away, sir.

Roch: You are a noble girl, Miss Eyre! I take you at your word! You promise to remain until I send you away. (*Offers hand*) Give me your hand.

Jane: Most willingly!

Roch: Ay, see that you smile! I thought you incapable of smiling.

Jane: My Lord!

Roch: Do you know that lights up your features like a gleam of sunshine? You must smile oftener, Miss Eyre. (*The cracking of a whip is heard without. It grows dark.*)

Roch: The deuce! There they are already; it is almost dark, and I am still in
           my riding-suit. Here I stand prating, and forget the time. Miss Eyre, you
           receive my guests and remain here until I return. That is: you would
           oblige me by remaining and doing what you have such an aversion to
           doing – entertaining my guests.
Jane: With pleasure, my Lord.
Roch: But those people see only the exterior. You will gratify me by putting
           on the pink silk, will you not?
Jane: No, sir; I must go as I am.
Roch: Well, have your own way. I will not force you to look pretty.

                                                                    (*Exit quickly R.*)

Jane (*alone looks after him thoughtfully*): What a strange man! Eccentric, upright,
           and misanthropic! (*She stands lost in thought.*)

                              Scene 5

The former, Sam, Judith, Georgina, Mrs Reed

Sam (opens M.D. and enters with candles, which he places on tables in foreground)
Judith: Please walk in here ladies, for a few moments. Your rooms are not quite
            ready.
Mrs R (enters leaning on Francis' arm): Thanks.
Jane (aside): Mrs Reed!
Georg: It is very kind of Madam (*To Judith*) to discharge a duty that properly
            belongs to his Lordship – that of receiving his guests. Lord Rochester
            is, doubtless, occupied.
Jane (aside): That is Georgina! Then 'tis she – she whom he has chosen!
Judith: He hardly expected your Ladyship so soon. He will, however, be here
            in a few moments.
Francis: His Lordship, doubtless, deems the occasion and the object of sufficient
            importance to justify him in bestowing by way of exception, some care
            upon his toilet.
Georg: It would be the first time in his life that Rochester aped the dandy, and
            did homage to the tyrant Fashion!
Francis: My beautiful cousin seems to study the characters of her admirers
            carefully.
Georg: Not all of them; they are not all worth the trouble. This one only – the
            others are too shallow.
Francis (turns toward Mrs Reed)
Georg: Mrs Harleigh, you will please see that our rooms are ready as soon as
            possible. – We are very much fatigued after our drive.
Judith: I will see to them, myself, Madam.   (*Exit*)

Scene 6

Georgina, Mrs Reed, Francis, Jane

Mrs R:	It is very warm and close here.
Georg:	It is not cold anywhere to-day, mama, and yet you will have us bundle up as if it were midwinter. How very absurd!
Mrs R:	But, my lily flower, you know how easily you take cold, and as for me, I can never get warm.
Georg:	That's because you are so cold-blooded, mama! It is intolerably hot here.
Francis (in a low tone to Georgina): Your blood is heated, Georgina, by the reproaches of your conscience.
Georg:	My conscience, Ha! ha!
Francis:	If I do possess no Thornfield, I have enough for us both, and if I have no title, I have, at least, an unsullied name. Do you know what this Rochester is accused of?
Georg:	No, and what is more, it is not a matter that interests me.
Francis (aside): But it does me, and I am determined to know the truth!
Mrs R:	How strangely I feel!
Georg:	What is the matter, mama?
Mrs R:	I hardly know – since I entered this room, I have felt a kind of depression – that indescribable anxiety that has always been the precursor of every great misfortune of my life.
Georg:	How foolish you are!
Mrs R (rises): I tell you, Georgina, that there is something hostile in the very air of this house. Let us return home!
Georg:	But, mama, how superstitious you are!
Mrs R:	It is not superstition. I am not well!
Georg (to Francis): Please call Bessie. She shall bring a *flacon* for mama.
Francis (turns towards M.E. – sees Jane): Ah! Here is some one. Will you be so kind, Miss –
Jane (comes down): If I can be of any service to you, Madam, pray command me. It is his Lordship's wish that I should attend to the wants of his guests – anticipate them, if possible.
Georg:	Really! That is very kind of his Lordship! And who are you, upon whom such an honor is conferred?
Jane:	The governess of his lordship's ward, madam.
Georg:	The governess!
Mrs R (as Jane began to speak, she starts suddenly, listens without having the courage to look round. Finally she turns and exclaims in a low tone): Ah! I knew it!
Francis (looks at her amazed)
Georg:	What?

Mrs R: That creature here!
Georg: Be calm, mama! What does this mean?
Mrs R: Are you blind? Don't you see Jane Eyre?
Georg: Heavens!
Mrs R: She will be revenged.
Georg: No, she will not, or I never knew Jane Eyre.
Francis (to Jane): Do you perhaps know these ladies, miss?
Jane (she looks coldly at Mrs R.): No, sir; they are strangers to me.
Mrs R (starts)
Georg: You are right, it is Jane Eyre!
Francis: Strange! They are deeply agitated!

Scene 7

The former, Rochester

Roch (in evening dress): Ah, ladies, you out-sped my expectations and have robbed
          me of the pleasure of discharging my duties as host. You are heartily
          welcome! But a cloud lowers over the brow of my beautiful amazon.
          It does not threaten me, I hope.
Georg: By no means, my lord. I only fear for the reputation of the renowned
          Mesrour, if it should be known in the neighbourhood, that we left
          Clarens House together and that our blacks kept pace with the fastest
          horse in all England.
Roch: Mesrour, I fear, is less at fault than his master, for arriving so little in
          advance of you.
Georg: How? Does Lord Rochester confess that –
Roch: I confess that on the way I fell into strange and to me new dreams and
          unconsciously compelled the noble animal to slacken his pace.
Jane: Indeed!
Georg: That sounds almost as though you could excuse yourself. You are
          forgiven.
Roch: Now you are your radiant self again. But I hope my absence has not
          been seriously felt.
Georg: Who could fill your place? This person perhaps? She is unknown to
          us.
Roch (glances at Jane): How, she has not introduced herself?
Jane: I have had no opportunity.
Roch: Miss Jane Eyre, Adèle's governess.
Georg: Adèle? Oh, yes, the little French girl you brought over from Paris three
          years ago. So the little Parisian is still here?
Roch: Certainly!
Georg: One might almost ask what you had not at Thornfield. But I thought
          Miss Ellen Warner was the governess of your little protégée.

Roch:	Miss Eyre has been here about five months.
Mrs R:	Indeed, and what does she teach her pupil?
Roch:	The modern languages, music – in short everything necessary to a liberal education. Miss Eyre even paints, and somewhat better, too, than most amateurs.
Georg:	Is it possible! The praise from you, who are so critical, surprises me. But Miss – I never could remember names – where did you acquire all your accomplishments?
Jane:	At Lowood school, madam.
Mrs R:	I was not aware that the ornamental branches were taught in orphan asylums. I have always understood that the pious Mr Blackhorst sought to teach his pupils above all things industry and humility.
Jane:	And so he does, Mrs – (*To Roch*) I beg[75]* your pardon, my lord, but you forgot to tell me the lady's name.
Roch:	Ah, true! Mrs Reed.
Jane:	I assure you, Mrs Reed, that I learned everything taught at Lowood School, and I shall be forever grateful to those who placed such advantages within my reach.
Roch:	You are easily contented, Miss Eyre. I am ignorant of your history and consequently know not why you were placed at Lowood; one thing, however, is certain, those who sent you there scarcely merit so much gratitude.
Jane:	Perhaps not. They bestowed a blessing without intending it.
Mrs R:	Ugh! The vampire!
Georg:	But that she should paint so well astonishes me. Perhaps your lordship is partial.
Roch:	To Miss Eyre? I scarcely have […] cause to be. You shall judge for yourself. (*Goes up*)
Jane:	Oh, my lord, I beg that you will not –
Roch:	Come, come, no affectation. (*Exit*)
Jane:	(*Remains on stage and looks down thoughtfully*)

Scene 8

Francis, Georgina, Mrs Reed, Jane, later Rochester

Georg (aside to Mrs R): Don't you think [it] very strange that Rochester should take such pains to convince us of this person's talent?

Mrs R: I never doubted her aptness.

---

75   * text from * to * missing from British Library photocopy and supplied by Harvard College Library.

Georg: Mama, you betray yourself.
Mrs R: Be on your guard, or we shall not escape the jaws of the crocodile.
Francis: What is there between them and this girl? They must have met
                  before.
Roch (returns with portfolio, goes to table and opens it): Now, Lady Clarens, look here
                  and tell me if they are not remarkable for a Lowood school-girl.
Jane: Oh, sir! –
Roch: Well! –
Jane (looks down abashed)
Georg: Allow me, my lord, to postpone my examination of these master-pieces
                  until to morrow. My mother is much fatigued, and I myself require
                  rest.
Roch (closes the portfolio and goes quickly to her): How? You will not accompany
                  me to the dining-room? The cloth is already laid.
Mrs R: Thank you, my lord; you will please excuse us for this evening. I am
                  old; it was a long drive; I need rest, and then there is an atmosphere in
                  this house – Come, Georgina.
Francis (offers his arm): Madam, allow me!
Mrs R: Thanks! Either she or I – one must give way to the other!
                                                              (*Exit slowly*)
Roch (to Georgina): Then I am not to have the pleasure of your society this evening
                  – I fear you are still angry with me.
Georg: For to-day I will be content with your arm, my lord, to lead me through
                  this enchanted castle; to-morrow, when sleep shall have interposed as
                  a mediator, we will see if one can be angry with you.
Roch (presses her arm to his heart): Ah, that smile, and the expression of those eyes
                  tells me that I am already forgiven. (*He turns carelessly to Jane*) Miss
                  Eyre, you can retire. For to-day you are released from your duties.
                  (*Exit with Georg. M.E.*)

                                          Scene 9

Jane (alone): For to-day only? Who knows, perhaps forever! Is that Lord Rochester
          – the same man whom, for two months, I have scarcely heard speak
          and never seen smile? The same gloomy spirit whose thoughts were
          unfathomable as the depths of the sea? No, it is not the same man; or
          – he loves! Ha, and it is Georgina who has effected this transformation?
          Again the evil genius of my youth stands before me – again all that
          is hateful and wicked in my nature is aroused from its long and deep
          slumber. (*Sees portfolio*) Ha, my sketches! Now I can – (*Is about to
          pick up portfolio, starts suddenly and listens, letting her hand fall*) I
          hear his step again in the hall.

Scene 10

The former, Rochester, Sam

Roch (to Sam entering): Sam, see that every-thing is quiet to-night; the ladies need rest. I saw Grace just now on the stairs.

Sam: I don't know indeed, sir.

Roch: I saw her quickly as she passed. What has she to do at this hour on the ground floor?

Sam: Perhaps some of the guests sent her down.

Roch: Curiosity rather! What is she doing away from her post at this time of night? Woe be unto her if I find her negligent! Tell her that! Go!

Sam: (*Exit M.E.*)

Roch (sees Jane): Eh! What is this? I told you, Miss Eyre, to retire. Why did you not obey?

Jane: I am not sleepy.

Roch: Not sleepy? So you remain here to watch me, I suppose?

Jane:- Has your lordship any further orders?

Roch: No!

Jane (bows and turns to go)

Roch: One moment! How are you pleased with Lady Clarens?

Jane: I hardly know yet.*

Roch: No? I think you have seen enough of her to form some opinion.

Sam (enters M.E. and remains listening)

Jane: True, I have seen her; but in order to tell how a lady pleases me, I must know what she is, and not how she looks. Good night, my lord! (*Exit quickly M.E.*)

Roch: She always has the last word. Not a hair's breadth will her accursed humility yield. There never was such another woman created. Who could divine her thoughts? She suffers abuse even and remains silent. (*Sees Sam*) Sam, what still keeps you here?

Sam: I was waiting till your lordship retired to put out the lights, sir; one cannot be too careful of a stormy night like this, sir!

Roch: Ay, a stormy night indeed! And my guests?

Sam: Have all retired, sir.

Roch: Very well, I will follow their example. (*Aside*) if I can.

Sam: Did anybody ever see anything like it! She contradicts him without drawing a muscle. And when he speaks to her in a tone that would make one of the rest of us tremble, goes her way and pays no attention to him. If this was one of us – ay, one of us that knows his secret he would throw us heels over head out of the window. Ugh! How the wind whistles! A bad night for poor Grace. They say he is going to marry this great lady. If he does, she will make short work with this Miss Eyre, but he won't do it. No, no, we shall never see him married! It's a pity! A great pity! (*Exit L.*)

Scene 11

Jane (*enters after a pause cautiously*): Thank heaven! nobody saw me. How frightened
I was as I came down the stairs! I thought I saw a dark object glide
noiselessly part the door of his cabinet. It must have been my shadow
that startled me. How childish! I can't sleep until I have rescued my
portfolio. Ah, here it is! He fortunately forgot it. Her eyes shall not rest
on my only treasure, her lips shall not curl in disdain at the off-spring
of my imagination – the products of my lonely and solitary hours at
Lowood. I will take them, since he will not give them to me. (*A gust of
wind is heard, and the light is extinguished*) Good Heavens! What is
that? And my light is out! How awkward! – Hark! There is surely some
one in the hall! No, all is still again! It must have been the wind. Fie!
If Adèle were to be so foolishly timid, how I should scold her. Now I
must feel my way back to my room in the dark. Heavens! There is that
demoniac laugh again! What a horrid creature that Grace Pool is! No
one seems to have heard her. (*Listens*) I hear no sound but the beating
of my heart. I dare not remain here, and the fear of meeting her makes
my blood run cold! Ugh! What is that! I am suffocating! It is smoke!
The house is on fire! (*Hurries off the stage*) But where! (*bursts open
the door at right – smoke pours into stage*) The door of his cabinet is
open, and the room is in a blaze! Merciful heavens! (*She disappears.
She calls without*) My lord! my lord! Lord Rochester! Awake! Awake!
Fire! Fire!

Roch (without): Wha – what is this?

Jane: Get up! get up! Fire! Fire!

Scene 12

Jane (*supporting Rochester*): There, sit down and I will call up the servants.

Roch: No, no, not a step! Remain where you are. Would you waken my guests?
                 Would you publish the affair in the whole neighborhood?

Jane: But, sir, the fire –

Roch: Ah, bah! the fire! 'Twas only the bed-curtains. If you had only smothered
                 the flames instead of deluging me with the contents of my water
                 pitcher!

Jane: You would have been burnt alive, sir – you slept so soundly!*

Roch: I carelessly threw myself on the bed with my clothes on, and read myself
                 to sleep, leaving the candle burning, and –

Jane: Oh, sir, it did not catch from the candle! The curtains caught at the foot
                 of the bed while the candle stood at the head – and do you know, the
                 door[s] leading through your cabinet were all open?

Roch: Open were they? Then I forgot to close them.

Jane:	Some criminal hand took advantage of this circumstance, to destroy you, sir.
Roch:	True, true, you may be right; but who could – who, think you, is guilty of the crime?
Jane:	Grace Pool, sir.
Roch:	Ay, ay, Grace Pool!
Jane:	This woman, who has such a fiendish laugh – I believe she must come from the infernal regions.
Roch:	While you come from the celestial regions to rescue me from being burned alive. But you must be discreet, and say nothing about the affair – that is, if you can be silent. Our guests must know nothing about it.
Jane:	I will be silent, sir, if it is your wish.
Roch:	It is my wish. You would further oblige me, Miss Eyre, by restraining your curiosity, by not being over inquisitive.
Jane:	I am not given to meddling with what does not concern me – but is this woman to go unpuni[s]hed?
Roch:	That is my affair.
Jane:	Good night, sir.
Roch:	One thing more – what were you doing at this late hour?
Jane:	I came down for my portfolio.
Roch:	Ah, so! Then you are going to take it away from me.
Jane:	Not from you, sir.
Roch:	But from Lady Clarens?
Jane:	Yes, sir.
Roch (aside):	What an enigma! (*Aloud*) And you are going without even offering me your hand. Have I then wounded you so deeply? Give me your hand, you – you obstinate girl!
Jane:	Here, sir.
Roch:	So! I thank you, Miss Eyre.
Jane:	You have no reason to thank me, my Lord. I am not quite such a barbarian as to stand and see my fellow-man burned alive, when a pitcher of water will save them, although I was the cause of Mes[rou]r's fall, for which you have never been able to forgive me.
Roch:	Oh, now *you* are unjust! You must have felt that that was long since forgiven and forgotten. (*Grasps her hand, and throws his arm around her. Jane starts, and then stands motionless.*)
Roch:	Was there ever such another school-girl! You have the courage of a man, and the tact of a woman. My heart beats furiously, while you were never more calm, so little does my escape interest you.

Jane (tries to draw away her hand)

Roch:	What! By heavens! no, the end[s] of your fingers throb. Ah! You blood is more honest than your face – it betrays you.

Jane (releasing herself forcibly): Good night, my Lord.

Roch (reaching his arms out towards her): You little school-girl! You are a dangerous

minx! Jane Eyre, I fear it would have been better for you had you
allowed me to be burned!   (*Exit R.*)

Curtain Falls*

Act III

A grand apartment, richly furnished. Right and left, in the foreground, small divans; near them small tables. Somewhat farther up the stage, other divans and arm-chairs. A glass door and two windows in flat lead to a terrace, ornamented with flowers; steps lead from terrace to a garden. The view shows but little green near by, but the distant landscape is very pleasing. The middle door is closed. Side-board with refreshments.

Scene 1

Rochester, Francis, Edward, Adèle, Georgina, Clawdon, Lady Clawdon, Sam, Mrs Reed, Jane (The ladies in elegant morning toilets)

Sam [and] a servant: (Go round among those present and serve coffee or collect the empty cups. They take the empty cups to Jane, who fills them. No one takes the second cup.)

Georg (turning over the leaves of a large album): I have often wondered how you
      could content yourself in our cold England, after having lived so long
      in the tropics; there the air is ever perfumed at once by the blossoms of
      Spring and the fruits of Autumn. True, I have heard that there serpents
      are as plenty as flowers.
Roch: And do you think there are no such creatures in England?
Georg: At all events they are not concealed under flowers. (*Goes to Edward
      and speaks to him*)
*Mrs R (who is busy with some fancy work, and now and then glances at Rochester
      and Georgina)*: But so much the oftener behind books!
Roch: How so?
Mrs R: There is a kind of serpent that crawls into great houses, where they
      silently watch their prey; and once they have gained a foot-hold, it is
      very difficult to exterminate them.
Roch: Ah! To what class do these reptiles belong?
Mrs R: To the class of tutors and governesses who instil their poison into the
      heads of their pupils.
Lady Clawdon: Mrs Reed is quite right. One cannot be too careful in the selection
      of governesses.

Adèle (who has sat and watched every movement of Georgina, and listened to the conversation): But I have a kind and good governess, hav[e]n't I, Uncle?

Roch: Yes, my child, that you have!

Adele (crosses to Georgina): You, too, had a governess like Miss Eyre, didn't you? And that is the reason you are so beautiful and amiable. I shall be like you, shall I not?

Georg (pushing Adèle away): Why, child, do you want to spoil my dress? Go away! – But tell me, my lord, I always thought you were not fond of children!

Roch (reaching out his hand to Adèle, who goes to him): Nor am I!

Georg: What induced you then, to take charge of such a little Parisian doll as that? Where did you pick her up?

Roch (mildly): Go to Miss Eyre! (*Adèle goes over to Jane, leans against her, and weeps.*)

Roch: I did not pick her up; I inherited her as I did this house, my gardens, and park – (*Glances at Jane, who is occupied with Adèle*) – and am well content with all!

Georg (bites her lips and seeks to change the topic of conversation): Your park, my lord, is charming; it must be a perfect paradise in summer! The week that we have been here has passed like a dream. What is your programme for the day, my lord?

Roch: Unfortunately, business of importance will occupy me for some hours this afternoon. Lord Clawdon, however, has kindly promised to conduct the ladies to the old abbey, an edifice now in ruins, said to have been built by Henry VIII.

Georg: Oh, that will be charming! And Lord Clawdon will accompany us?

Francis and Edward: Oh, all of us!

Lord Clawdon (who is playing chess with Francis – sarcastically): That is, if your lady-ship is content with our escort!

Georg: (*Smiling*) Oh, perfectly, my lord. I shall busy myself with the historical recollections of this gifted tyrant. You must know that I have the most profound respect for the memory of Henry VIII.

Francis (disdainfully, moving a figure as he speaks): Lady Clarens regrets that he is gathered to his fathers; she would have been capable of marrying him.

Georg: And why not? Indeed I would; for if Henry VIII was a tyrant, he was also a MAN.

Mrs R (has continued to observe Rochester very closely): Heaven protect you from a man, my darling!

Georg: Why, mama? To my mind a man is nothing unless he have a spice of the devil in him. (*Clawdon and Edward laugh*) Oh, I am heartily disgusted with the young men of the present day – poor puny things, not fit to stir a step beyond papa's park gates, nor to go even so far without mama's permission and guardianship; creatures so absorbed in the care of their pretty faces, their white hands and their small feet. As though a man had anything to do with beauty! As if loveliness were not the special prerogative of woman! I grant you an ugly woman (*glances at Jane*) is a blot on the fair face of creation; but as to the men, let them be solicitous to possess only strength, valor, and honor, the rest is not worth a fillip!

Roch (glances at Jane, who evinces no interest in the dialogue): Nobly said, upon my honor! You are quite right; but what woman beside yourself would be justified in making such demands?

Francis (aside): By heaven! She merits the humiliation that awaits her.

Sam (who has gone off, returns and whispers to Jane)

Jane (advancing): My lord, the carriages are waiting.

Roch: Come ladies, you have a long drive before you; you have much to see, and I shall expect you back to dinner.

Mrs R: You will please excuse me – I fear this cold wind.

Georg: Well, who is of the party?

Lord and Lady Clawdon, Francis, Edward: All of us!

Georg: Except our host, without whom we must try to be merry.

Roch: Oh, never fear; you are sure to succeed.

Georg (significantly – rises): Who knows? (*Turns to go*) Ah, me! My shoe is untied!

Francis (glancing at Rochester): And who shall be deemed worthy of performing the knightly office of tying it?

Georg (looks at Rochester, expecting him to tie it – after a pause – piqued): None of you, gentlemen – you are neither worthy to tie nor untie my shoes. (*To Adèle*) Come here, my little doll, and make yourself useful.

Adèle (looks at her annoyed): What shall I do?

Georg (impatiently): Come tie my shoe, child!

Adèle (shaking her head): I had rather not.

Roch: Adèle, do as you are told.

Adèle (decided): She is only beautiful, not good. I don't want to tie it.

Roch (greatly annoyed – glances at Jane): What is this?

Mrs R: The fruits of Miss Eyre's teaching!

Georg (looks disdainfully at Jane): From whom she has not learned humility.

Roch: So it would seem.

Jane (to Mrs R. modestly, but earnestly): Adèle has been my pupil only five months, and you know, Mrs Reed, that it often requires years to eradicate the results of pernicious influences. (*To Georg*) Pardon the child, madam, and allow me to expiate her fault. (*Kneels quickly and ties her shoe*)

Sam (gives expression to his delight)

Roch (makes a gesture as though he would hold her back; then folds his arms, and looks down as though the scene were painful to him)

Georg (surprised and disconcerted): Oh, thank you!

Jane (rises, bows, takes Adèle's hand and goes up the stage): Go upstairs, Adèle!

Adèle (goes off chagrined, R.)

Georg (aside to Rochester): There is no denying that you have your serpent well tutored. One might almost fear you, if one were less prejudiced in your favour.

Roch (controlling himself): Madam, spare my modesty.

Georg: Ah. Rochester!

Francis: The carriages are waiting. Let us be off. (*They go*)

Georg (as she turns to go, she accidentally touches Mrs R. who has just risen): Ah, mama, good bye! (*They go off, R.*)

Mrs R (follows slowly – as she passes Jane she suddenly stops before her, and says very coldly): Jane Eyre, I must speak with you!

Jane (surprised): With me?

Mrs R: When they are all gone and all is quiet, seek me here –

Jane: I will, madam.

Mrs R (goes off slowly, L.)

Jane (alone – looks after Mrs R.): With me? she will speak with me? Ah, have I not enough already to fever this poor brain? (*Passes her hand over her forehead*) No word, no look explains the strange event of that horrid night! Grace Pool goes about as before. There is still the same mysterious silence in all her movements. What right has she to his forbearance? Does he fear this woman? These walls enclose some dark, some dreadful secret – or perhaps – 'tis Rochester's breast! Oh, I was blind – he forgets all else in his love for Georgina! He calmly witnessed my humiliation – not a hand did he raise to hold me back! Be calm! be calm! my heart! You have not even the right to break.

Scene 2

Rochester, Jane.

Roch: Still here, Miss Eyre! Are you not going to the Abbey?

Jane (perfectly calm): You will please excuse me, sir, Adèle must remain at home as a punishment for her disobedience, and I dislike to leave her alone.

Roch (looks at her searchingly): And besides, you think that I have no right to ask you to make any sacrifices for my guests.

Jane: I know that they will not miss me, while Adèle would.

Roch: Adèle! Adèle! Do you think there is no one else, who would miss you?

Jane: Oh, yes, poor Mrs Harleigh, who is almost worn out – she has so much to look after and think of.

Roch: And no one else?

Jane (calmly): No, no one!

Roch (turns to go): And you have nothing to say to me?

Jane: Nothing, sir.

Roch: Nothing to ask me, Miss Eyre?

Jane: I shall never question you, sir; for I am sure that you will tell me, unasked, whatever you wish me to know, and that by asking I should not draw from you anything you wish to conceal –

Roch: So! And yet ever since the night you rescued me from the flames, there has been a question on your tongue's end, a question too, you had a right to ask. Why do you hesitate? Are you not a woman? – have you no curiosity? – no desire to know who sought to destroy me? – or have you, perchance, already forgotten that night?

Jane: If I were to say yes, I should lie to you, and I never lie.

Roch: Then you will not ask, and – have you nothing to say to me, nothing?

Jane: Nothing at present, sir – At another time perhaps.

Roch: Ah, another time! And if I – What would you say if I were suddenly to marry?

Jane (motionless): I would say, sir, that you were quite right to do so.

Roch: Then it is a matter of indifference to you.

Jane: No, sir, I should rejoice to see you happy.

Roch (looks at her with an expression of pain): Indeed? (*With emotion*) Miss Eyre – you – (*Recovers his selfpossession.*) You can go!

Jane (bows calmly and exits, R.)

Roch (enraged): She goes! No word, no look betrays her thoughts! The sphinx will drive me mad!

Scene 3

Rochester. Judith enters R.

Roch: Oh, madam, have my tenants come?

Judith (very much excited, but controlling herself): No my lord; but I have come to talk with you seriously.

Roch: That sounds as though you had something of real importance to discuss. I think, however, we will have to postpone it for the morning.

Judith: No, you must listen to me now. You know I have never shown any desire to pry into your secrets, or to give you advise, and that if I do so now, It is not without a reason. Soon after you came into possession of Thornfield, you ordered the rooms in the tower to be prepared for the reception of a guest, and there in the dead of night, you suddenly brought a closely veiled woman here, whose face no one has seen. As you desired, I have concealed the lady's presence from every one and have not sought to learn her history. I have obeyed silently – have kept your secret as though it had been my own – Have I, or have I not?

Roch: You but did your duty.

Judith: But now you yourself reveal the secret, that we have guarded so carefully – you bring a crowd of people into the house, and I have come to tell you, that, unless you soon get rid of them, what is now only a suspicion, will soon be known as a fact in the whole neighbourhood. Last night, Grace heard a noise in the tower, and as she opened her door, she caught one of the servants of your guests listening. Of course, he fled when he saw her. This morning Leah overheard these servants saying things among themselves that you would not find very edifying if I were to repeat them to you. I tell you this in order that you may not think it is owing to any indiscretion of mine should this secret become known –

Roch *(kindly)*:   Do not let that matter trouble you, Cousin. I know that you do your whole duty. My house is in good hands, and I am not ungrateful to you.

Judith: Yes, you are, my lord. You think to requite all with gold, as though gold alone were all we require to make us happy. – My joyless old age needed the sympathy of a youthful heart, the warmth of a light cheerful nature, that should dispel the gloom of this old antiquated mansion – I had found both in Jane Eyre. I lived again! But now you are about to drive her away, and I shall again be alone and forsaken. (*Struggles to keep back her tears*) This is unworthy of you, my lord; it is cruel!

Roch *(fixed his eye on her)*:   What tells you I would drive Miss Eyre away? I have never thought of such a thing.

Judith: Have you not? Well, she thinks of going.

Roch *(turns quickly)*: She dare not!

Judith: Dare not! I know her better than you do. – Heaven only knows what you are aiming at with the poor girl. You send for her daily, and when she comes, you take no more notice of her than if she did not exist. And then you suffer her in your presence to tie the shoe of the haughty Lady Clarens. I tried to console her as she passed me silent and determined – She would not even look at me, but I saw –

Roch: Well, well, what did you see?

Judith: I saw that she was deathly pale, that her eyes were filled with tears, that her self-love was deeply wounded, that her heart was broken. Oh, I saw enough! Jane Eyre may be crushed, but she can never be humbled. I understand her proud sensitive nature. She means to go! Prevent it, if you can on Adèle's account – or your own.

Roch *(looks at her sternly)*: Well, is that your entire errand?

Judith *(astonished)*: My errand! You suppose, then – Oh, how meanly you think of me and this poor girl! You are to be pitied! You are incapable of appreciating a soul like Jane Eyre's. Let her go, and if you are displeased with what I have said, send me with her. I will go willingly. – Thank heaven, I have in my power to do the noble girl a lasting service! She wept for you, whom she reveres as a superior being, but I, sir – if I do obey blindly, am not blind. I will do my duty and teach Jane Eyre that Lord Rochester is unworthy of her tears. This will lessen the pain of parting. (*Goes*)

Roch (following her): Judith, what are you going to do? (*Stops*) No!

Judith (stops at door and turns).

Roch (in a commanding tone): Go and do as you think proper!

Judith (goes off reluctantly)

Roch: Be it so. This farce must have an end. If it breaks her heart, it will teach her to not be so silent.   (*Exit M.E.*)

Scene 4

Mrs Reed (Alone)

Mrs R: Not yet here! (*Advances*) She lets me wait for her – Oh, this is a hard, hard step to take! But I must, aye, I must! What then is between the creature and Rochester, I cannot discover, but there is something, I feel it, and this something is the only obstacle that Georgina has to encounter. I must get the cunning viper out of the way, or she will frustrate our designs. With what an air she humbled herself before Georgina! Ah, she is to be feared – she is dangerous! Ugh! I hate her worse than ever; but I must tell her all!

Scene 5

Jane, Mrs Reed

Jane (pale, calm, quiet, and resolute): Madam, I am sorry if I have kept you waiting.

Mrs R (coldly): Come nearer. This is no time to be hypocritical – no time to practice deception. Dissimulation would be unworthy of us. Time has little influence on natures like ours. We have, do still, and always shall hate each other.

Jane (calmly): You hate me, Mrs Reed, and will always hate me; but you are wrong in supposing that I am equally implacable. When I left Gateshead, I was so young –

Mrs R (painfully affected by the sound of her voice – looks at her more attentively): Oh, you are unchanged! You are still the same pale, silent, obstinate creature you were then. These are the same dark eyes, whose wicked glances seemed ever to be on me and mine. Ah, what did I and my poor children not suffer! What a burden you were! How rejoiced I was when you were gone, and how I hoped it was forever! But now, here you stand before me again; you, who have made of a just and upright woman a criminal!

Jane (has listened patiently and quietly): I – I have made you a criminal?

Mrs R: Yes; you and you alone! For that reason I hate you, as you do me! Jane Eyre, the rich Mrs Reed is poor, is almost penniless. Are you not rejoiced?

Jane: Heaven forbid! You, poor? It cannot be!

Mrs R: I gave my dear son, John, everything. I have sold Gateshead, and am now dependent on Georgina for a home. I have nothing left; John has squandered all your uncle left us.

Jane (feelingly): Oh, the profligate!

Mrs R (incensed): I could not see my son want, and it is so expensive living in London. (*Recovering*) Now I have no one but Georgina and as she is about to marry Lord Rochester, my future home will be here. So you see, Jane Eyre, you must prepare to leave Thornfield, in order that I may remain. It would be impossible for us to live and breath under the same roof.

Jane: Oh, this is what I had already for[e]seen; but is it not hard, very hard, Mrs Reed, that you, after having condemned me to eight long years at Lowood, should now drive the poor orphan, helpless and alone, out into the wide world?

Mrs R: Not poor, not helpless –you are richer than I, if –

Jane: How, what! Richer than you?

Mrs R: You had been a long time at Lowood, when one day a letter came from Tybald Eyre, your father's brother, who is in Madeira. He wanted me to send you to him, and said he was rich, and would make you his heir if you would come.

Jane: And this letter! What have I never seen it?

Mrs R: Because I could not endure the thought of seeing you in affluence while my fortune was fast disappearing and Georgina possessed only a very modest income; because I could not forget what I experienced, when, in the presence of Mr Blackhorst, you swore you would never call me aunt again, and said there was nothing on earth you despised and abhorred so much as me and my children.

Jane: (*Gently*) I must have been a very bad child; but, though I was, I have been made better. You, too, will forgive and forget the past, as I have done, will you not?

Mrs R: If you go; Jane Eyre, yes!

Jane (drops her head and looks down thoughtfully)

Scene 6

The former, Henry, Whitfield, Rochester

Roch (comes directly after Whitfield from terrace, opens M.D. and looks in astonished)

Henry (entering in travelling suit): Ah, here you are, Sarah!

Mrs R (startled): Henry, you bring bad news.

Henry (looking at [Jane]). I fear so; but, we are not alone!

Jane (grasping his hand). Don't you know me, Uncle Henry? I am Jane Eyre!

Henry: Jane Eyre? You? Yes, indeed, as I live, and here? and with you Sarah? Ah, at last you are reconciled.

Mrs R (looks at him anxiously – she hardly hears what he says): Henry, you came from Clarens House – you have letters from John?

Henry (producing letter): Not from John, but from a London banker. I hastened to Thornfield as it may not yet be too late to –

Mrs R: Too late, too late for what?

Henry: Your obstinate blindness to John's excesses has, as I anticipated, resulted in impoverishing you and ruining him. There is no time to be lost. You must know the worst. John has suddenly disappeared, after having forged drafts to the amount of thousands of pounds, which must be immediately taken up, or we shall be forever disgraced.

Mrs R (faints in Jane's arms)

Jane: Good heavens!

Roch (is on the point of entering, but stops and steps back)

Henry (assists Jane to place Mrs Reed on the sofa)

Jane (rubs her hands and forehead): Aunt Reed, compose yourself! Aunt Reed, listen to me!

Henry: Ah, unfortunate woman! you have yet to learn the worst. It is fortunate that John has put an end to his miserable existence.

Jane (clasps her hands): May heaven have mercy on us!

Henry: She is at last severely, but justly, punished for her cruelty to you, my child.

Mrs R (moves and opens her eyes): Ah!

Jane: She is recovering. Aunt Reed, are you better?

Mrs R: What! You call me "aunt"! Have you forgotten that you once swore –?

Jane (in tears): I was a wayward, obstinate child, and I know now that I was unjust. You will forgive me, will you not, aunt?

Mrs R: I promised my husband to treat you as my own child; and yet I consigned you to Lowood. Twice I have done you a great wrong. I have, therefore, nothing to forgive. It is a misfortune that you were ever born!

Jane (covers her face with her hands): True, too true!

Mrs R: Something horrible has happened. I know it – I feel it here. (*Presses her hand to her heart*) I have loved no one in the world but John, and he is dead!

Jane: But you still have a daughter!

Mrs R: Yes, yes; and she must be happy, must be rich! For that reason you must leave here at once.

Roch (makes a gesture as though he understood the state of affairs)

Mrs R (taking letters from her pocket): Your uncle still lives, and wishes you to come
    to him. Here are both his letters. I have always kept them about me,
    thinking that some day the moment would come when I could relieve
    my conscience of this burden. Here, take them and go. Thank heaven,
    now I owe you nothing!

Jane (takes them): I will go, Aunt Reed, as you desire; but first give me your blessing.
    (Reaches out both hands to Mrs R)

Mrs R (recoils): My blessing! You have always hated me and mine. I cannot bless
    you; but as you go in order that Georgina may be rich and happy, and
    that I may have a home, I will always wish you well. Ask no more,
    ask no more!

Roch (looks up and retires)

Mrs R: Heaven alone is just. Let it judge between us! *(She leans on Henry's*
    arm and retires. Henry presses Jane's hand as he goes off.)

Jane (alone – filled with despair): Hate! hate! hate! And nowhere love for the poor
    orphan! *(Looks towards Mrs R)* Yes, I will go; alone and unprotected.
    I will seek, in another quarter of the globe, the only being who has one
    thought or care for Jane Eyre. *(In a tone of dark resolve)* I am his! *(As*
    she turns to go Rochester enters – she starts)

Scene 7

Jane, Rochester

Jane (aside): Ah, there he is!

Roch (coming down): Which way, Miss Eyre?

Jane (calmly): I was going to look for you, my lord.

Roch: An honor you have never deigned to do me before.

Jane: I have never before had a favor to ask of you.

Roch: A favor to ask – you! What is it, pray!

Jane (calmly): That you will send me away from Thornfield, sir.

Roch: Ah, but if I were to refuse, you would still be at liberty to go.

Jane: I gave you my word that I would remain unless you yourself should
    send me away.

Roch: True! I remember now. Well, if you are determined to go, I will comply
    with your request, and send you away.

Jane: I thank, you sir!

Roch: But may I not ask what prompted this sudden decision? *(Pause)* You are
    silent – no matter; I think I know without your telling me. Mrs Harleigh
    has told you that I am a monster – that I have a poor woman, my wife,
    imprisoned within these walls.

Jane: Not she, sir; but others have told me so.

Roch: And this report being corroborated by the strange attempt on my life,
    by some unknown hand, you think me guilty, do you not.

Jane (looks him full in the face): No, sir, I am sure it is all a gross falsehood!

Roch: Indeed! And whence comes this conviction?

Jane: From my faith in you, sir; which will be my consolation when I am far
               from here, alone and friendless in the wide world.

Roch: That is noble, that is generous, Miss [Eyre), and in order that nothing
               may rob you of this conviction, even though we part forever, I will
               confide to you a secret, which, till today, I have not breathed even to the
               dead, much less to the living. (*They sit*) Accident, or fate, has betrayed
               to you a secret, that you alone, together with the judge of the district
               and myself, are in the possession of. You will not question me, so I will
               confide in you voluntarily. The demon that would have destroyed me
               was not Grace Pool; it was a maniac for whom I am in duty bound to
               provide. I can entrust her to no asylum, nor to the care of another than
               Grace Pool, for she has dishonored our house. She is –

Jane (in a tremulous tone, expressing deep emotion): Lady – Rochester.

Roch: Lady Henrietta Rochester.

Jane (shudders, clasps her hands, looks down and remains silent)

Roch (observes her closely as though he expected a reply, then continues): She was
               my first and, until a few months ago, my only love. Life I have studied
               in all its phases; but I have loved not again. I was the younger son,
               and consequently poor; but we loved each other, and she became my
               affianced bride. I was sent for a year to London. On the day I returned,
               she was wedded to the wealthy heir of our house – she preferred Arthur
               to poor Edward, and became –

Jane (unable to control herself, cries out joyfully): Your brother's wife!

Roch (in a low measured tone): My brother's wife! I would have strangled him; but
               they bound me, declared me insane; I was dragged on board a ship, and
               in the West Indies I regained my reason, but not my faith in God and
               humanity. My father died, and my brother went, with his wife, to the
               Continent. Not long afterwards I heard of her death. Years passed, when
               suddenly came the news of my brother's decease. I returned to England,
               took possession of my inheritance, and with it received a paper, bearing
               my brother's seal, in which he humbly begged my pardon, and imposed
               on me a sacred trust. He robbed me of my faithless bride, but fearfully
               was I avenged, both on him and her. Her momentary infatuation for
               Arthur had given place to the most bitter hatred. During a short sojourn
               in Genoa, he was taken suddenly ill, and when he recovered she had
               eloped with a young Polish officer.

Jane (starts back, horrified, then looks down thoughtfully)

Roch: Rather than acknowledge his disgrace, Arthur caused his wife's
               death to be published in England, and then silently followed
               the fugitives. His untiring vigilance discovered their retreat in the
               environs of Paris. Her paramour he laid dead at her feet, and then,
               after confiding a babe she pressed to her bosom to the care of others,

he dragged her, with her nurse, Grace Pool, back to England. The loss of Adèle and the death of her lover deprived the unfortunate woman of her reason. She remembers nothing but her hatred for his murderer. Arthur's thirst for revenge was now satisfied; but grief, and perhaps remorse, soon threw him into a decline. His dying wish was that I should bring Adèle to England, remove the maniac mother to Thornfield Hall, and carefully conceal our disgrace. How I have thus far discharged this sacred duty is known to you, Miss Eyre.

Jane (her voice trembles): Also how your generosity is requited. This woman wanted to burn you alive.

Roch: Yes, supposing me to be another. She does not understand that her husband is dead. To her disordered mind, I am he, and with the instinct of hatred she always detects my presence here, then, with a maniac's cunning, she plans my destruction. So she improved Grace's momentary absence to set fire to my bed, but for which I had never known what a resolute spirit animates the delicate organization of Jane Eyre.

Jane (thoughtfully, without showing her inward emotion): So, then, you are the protector of the woman, who betrayed you, and the guardian of the child, whose mother destroyed your happiness. That, sir, is noble – magnanimous!

Roch (drily): I wished for no criticism on my conduct, Miss Eyre. I desire simply to save you from blushing, should you, when you are gone from here, have occasion to speak of the present Lord Rochester, or – perhaps you will now decide to remain?

Jane (starts): Oh, no, sir – I shall go. (*With energy*) Aye, and to-day, too!

Roch (looks at her sharply): Then that was not your reason for wanting to go?

Jane: No, that was not the reason – I never thought you guilty.

Roch: But why do you go, then? Is it because this woman, who hates you so bitterly, your aunt, wishes you to go?

Jane (astonished): Mrs Reed? No, I had already decided not to remain.

Roch: Indeed! And why?

Jane: You have told me, that you intend to marry.

Roch: That is true – I think of marrying, and soon, too.

Jane (calmly): Then Adèle will be sent to school, and you will no longer require my services.

Roch: Hem! That is quite possible. Georgina is not fond of children, and then you fear that she might prove too haughty and overbearing – is it not so?

Jane (in a low tone): It is not that. I feel that this will be no place for me, sir, when you are married.

Roch: You may be right. But when will you go? You have no situation.

Jane: I shall go to my uncle in [Madeira].

Roch: [Madeira]! That is a long way off, Miss Eyre.

Jane (very low): Yes, it is a long way off!

Roch: Yet, for a girl with your determined spirit, that is no obstacle. But then, the broad ocean will be between you and your native land.

Jane (deeply moved): True!

Roch (mildly): And between us, too!

Jane: Aye, and between us!

Roch: We shall hear nothing more of each other.

Jane: No, nothing!

Roch: And shall never see each other again.

Jane: No, never, never! (*Bursts suddenly into tears*)

Roch (calmly): Why do you weep, Miss Eyre?

Jane (dries her eyes, and then speaks): Because I love Thornfield, sir, a quiet and happy home. Here, I have not been trampled on – I have not been chilled by cold, unfeeling injustice – I have not been buried with inferior minds, and excluded from every glimpse of communion with what is bright and elevated. I have talked face to face with what I reverence, with what I admire – with an original, a vigorous, and independent mind – I have known you, my lord; and it strikes me with terror and anguish to feel the necessity of tearing myself from all this forever. It is like looking on the necessity of death. Tell me, have I not cause to weep? (*She covers her face with her hands, and sobs bitterly*)

Roch: True, you have; but if it costs you so much pain to go, why not remain?

Jane (lets her hand fall suddenly, turns to him and says, indignantly): Remain, sir, at Thornfield, when you are married?

Roch: Why not? You will not be able to endure the separation – You must remain!

Jane (trembling with emotion): I tell you I must not remain – I must go! I can endure the separation! Live here? No, never, never! Do you think I could stay to become nothing to you? Do you think I am an automaton – a machine without feeling? Do you think I could bear to see my morsel of bread snatched from my lips – my drop of water dashed from my cup? Do you think because I am poor and obscure, I have no soul, no heart? If you do, your pride misleads you. I have as much soul as you, and full as much heart, and if God had given me beauty and wealth, I should have made it as hard for you to leave me as now for me to leave you. I am not now speaking to you according to custom and social usage, nor even through the medium of mortal flesh; it is my spirit that speaks to your spirit, just as though we had passed through the grave and stood in the presence of the Creator, equal as we are!

Roch (throws his arms suddenly around her, and presses her to his bosom): Equal as we are. Indeed, my wayward little Jane!

Jane (surprised, but remains in his embrace, and continues): Yes, so, sir, and yet not so, for you are married, or as good as married – wedded to an inferior – to one with whom you have no sympathy – with one whom I do not believe you truly love, for I have heard you sneer at her. I would scorn such an union, therefore I am better than you. Let me go!

Roch (holding her): It is too late, the net has ensnared you, you are caught at last!

Jane: I am no bird, and no net can ensnare me. I am a free human being, with an independent will, which I now exert. (*Tears herself away*)

Roch: And do you think I will allow you to go, after what you have said. (*Throws both arms around her*) Do you know, little girl, that in my hands you are powerless, that unless I will, you cannot move?

Jane (stands motionless in his arms, and looks at him full and calmly in the face): True, for my body is weaker than yours, but my soul is stronger, and my soul is my own!

Roch: Oh, how well she knows me and herself! How truly she speaks! What would I then? (*Releases her*) And you will, shall decide your destiny. At last you have shown me your inner self. Now look you at mine – Since first we met, since in your nature I recognized a resemblance to my own, I have struggled manfully to resist the strange spell that drew me towards you, but all in vain! I am, and long have been, yours, heart and soul. Accept now what alone you have left me to offer you – my hand!

Jane: (*stares at him, and steps back some distance*): Oh, sir, how cruel thus to mock me!

Roch: Jane, come to me.

Jane: You bride stands between us.

Roch: I have no bride!

Jane: Then you have deceived Georgina, who loves you.

Roch: Georgina loves nothing but herself, and my fortune.

Jane: Then why is she here?

Roch: To unlock the casket of thy hidden thoughts, obstinate girl. Jealousy alone could disclose even to you the secrets of your own bosom. Never have I spoken to Georgina of love or marriage. No one, no one but you, has any claims to my heart. 'Tis you I would possess! I would have you, and you only! Jane, say that you will be mine!

Jane: Are you in earnest? truly in earnest?

Roch: I am, and if an oath be necessary to convince you, I swear it.

Jane: Oh, Rowland, my lord, my love, I am thine! (*Throws herself into his arms*)

Roch: And shall be forever!

(The End)

Jane Eyre

A Drama in Four [Two] Acts

by

Mme von Heringen Hering

(An Adaptation from a Danish Play)

1877

Editor's Notes

The Text

The play exists in a single hand-written copy in the Lord Chamberlain's Collection of Plays in the British Library (Add. MS 53182 N). The title page bears the words 'To be performed at the Theatre Royal Coventry. Mad^lle Leander' (Figure 13). The Licence No. attached to the manuscript is 45, dated 'Feb–March 1877'. The Lord Chamberlain's Day Book dates the licence 'March 2; Entered March 6. Theatre Royal Coventry'. The title page also has an annotation in a later hand, stating:

> This Manuscript is incorrectly described as a drama in two Acts – it is in four Acts – Act I comprising 29 – Act II 32 – Act III 43 and Act IV 48 pages. The end of each Act is sufficiently indicated by the fall of the curtain.

The statement is signed 'EP', presumably for Edward Pigott, the Lord Chamberlain's Examiner of Plays,[1] and the same hand has struck out 'two' and inserted 'Four' on the title page. The play is clearly a version of Charlotte Birch-Pfeiffer's play, and the confusion about the division into acts probably arises from the title-page of Birch-Pfeiffer's printed play, which defines it as 'a Drama in Two Parts and Four Acts', Part 1 being the Prologue, and Part 2 consisting of Acts I–III.[2] The original manuscript of the Hering play has headings for Act I (corresponding to Birch-Pfeiffer's Prologue) and Act II, but its division into scenes (with some minor differences) follows Birch-Pfeiffer's, producing the anomaly that the scenes in Act II are numbered 1–6, 2–12, 3 (very odd!) and 2–9. EP has attempted to introduce some order by striking out all the scene numbers (and since 'scenes' indicate entrances and exits rather than changes of scenery, this is not a damaging change) and inserting 'Act III' before the 2–12 group and 'Act IV' before the final group. He has in turn been confused by the fact that Birch-Pfeiffer's fourth act is labelled 'Act III' (since her first 'act' is a 'Prologue') and has thus written 'This appears really to be a Third Act' before the final group of Hering scenes which he then labels 'Act IV'. In representing this chaos, I have adopted EP's numbering in four acts, indicating the original Act and Scene numbers in square brackets.

Apart from EP's revisions, the hand appears the same throughout. The pages are written on both sides and are stitched and glued into a small coverless notebook of seventy-nine leaves in four gatherings. Some letters are lost in the binding and I have supplied these, where obvious, in square brackets. The top right-hand corners of all pages have been cut off, as if the original numbering has been removed, but the recto pages have been re-numbered throughout in one hand. Page 34 has been cut off two-thirds of the way down and a new section, numbered 35, has been stitched on to it;

---

1 Stephens, *Censorship*, pp. 32–3. The Lord Chamberlain's Day Book also records '4 Acts'.

2 The 1867 version of Birch-Pfeiffer is in two acts.

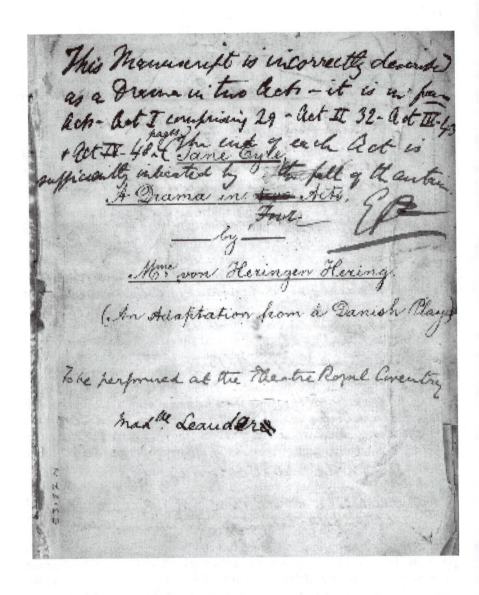

Figure 13   Facsimile of the title page of the manuscript of *Jane Eyre*, 'An Adaptation from a Danish Play', by Mme von Heringen Hering, 1877. Reproduced by permission of the British Library: Add. MS 53182 N

both are stitched into the binding as normal. Page 33 is loose and its edges tattered, though no words seem to have been lost; the hand is the same or similar, although the page contains some errors of punctuation (e.g., 'were'nt') which do not appear in the bound text. The sense of p. 32^V is, however, continued on p. 34; the material on pp. 33 and 33^V follows that of p. 34^V/35^V – the new numberer has, presumably, misplaced the loose page. I have restored the sequence but indicated the misplaced passage by asterisks.

The stage directions appear to have been written in blue ink as opposed to the black of the main text, and some of these seem to have been added later, though in the same hand. Many of these are concerned with the manner in which characters speak or receive speeches, and the extent of these directions is unusual, accounting for the play's extra length as compared with Birch-Pfeiffer's printed text. Compared with the other manuscript plays, this one also has relatively many alterations and insertions in the original hand, and where these seem to be the translator's second thoughts rather than copyist's errors, I have thought it worth while to include both \inserted material/ and {cancelled material}, indicated as here. The spelling, interestingly, is sometimes American (color, honor) and I have substituted English spelling. The punctuation (apart from p. 33, which I have corrected) is orthodox and the editing therefore relatively light; I have removed some capital letters from the middles of sentences, and have made minor changes to the presentation of characters' names and stage directions to conform with the usage of this volume.

The Playwright

The play is clearly a version of Charlotte Birch-Pfeiffer's (it was advertised as *Jane Eyre, or the Orphan of Lowood*),[3] but I have discovered nothing about Mme von Heringen Hering. The name Hering does exist, and a Danish translation is not unlikely, since Birch-Pfeiffer's husband, Christian Birch, was Danish. The Danish connection is confirmed by a short review of the Coventry performance in *The Era*, stating that the 'Mdlle. Leander' named on the title page of the manuscript is 'a Danish lady',[4] but she does not appear in any of the standard reference works.

There is, in addition, some direct evidence that Birch-Pfeiffer's play was translated from German into Danish and performed in 1879, since a review of Willing's 1879 play mentions a Danish translation called *Et Vaisenhuusbarn* (*The Orphanage Child*).[5] *Et Vaisenhuusbarn* is, it seems, a plausible Danish title, but I have only found one reference to a play of this name, on a Norwegian website listing the music used in various dramatic productions, which shows that the play was performed on 24 October 1879, in Kristiania (the nineteenth-century name for Oslo), and again, by Olaus Olsens' company, on 7 September 1882. It is described as a 'popular drama with Songs in 4

---

3   *Era*, 18 March 1877, p. 8.
4   *Era*, 18 March 1877, p. 8.
5   *Times*, 1 September 1879, p. 6 col. B.

acts by Charlotte Birch-Pfeiffer after Charlotte Brontë's novel'.[6]

Hering's play has very detailed stage directions, which make it the longest play in this collection. The actors are minutely directed about their motivation, gestures and facial expressions, as well as their movements on the stage. Catherine Evans confirms that this was characteristic of Birch-Pfeiffer herself, whose stage experience led her to be as helpful as possible to the performers. In all of Birch-Pfeiffer's plays,

> there are extensive scene descriptions, staging tips (for instance, the placement of characters on the stage during a particular scene), costume and character descriptions [...], and numerous instructions to the actor about the motivation for the words he is about to speak, and the tone and inflection most appropriate.[7]

This description fits Hering's play so well that it may be a more authentic translation of Birch-Pfeiffer's play than the 1870 version published in New York, which has much less detail of this kind.

The Theatre and Performance

The play was licensed for performance at the Theatre Royal Coventry, and both the *Coventry Herald* and the *Coventry Standard* advertised performances from Monday 12 to Saturday 17 March 1877.[8] *The Era* carried a short review of the play on 18 March:

> COVENTRY: THEATRE ROYAL,– Lessee, Mr Edward Bell.– Miss Errington's company commenced a six nights' engagement here on Monday last in <u>Jane Eyre; or the Orphan of Lowood</u>. The heroine of the piece, Jane Eyre, was ably represented by Mdlle. Leander, a Danish lady, who bids fair to become a favourite. She was supported by Mr Lester Herbert and company, who have been fairly patronized during the week.[9]

Coventry's Local Studies Librarian, however, was not able to find any other information about the play.

The Theatre Royal, Coventry, was built in Smithford Street in 1819 and closed in 1889. Ted Bottle's admirable book, *Coventry's Forgotten Theatre*, has a photograph showing it as having a modest, house-sized frontage only 23 feet across; its proscenium was probably only 16 ft wide and 36 ft deep, and the total dimensions of the theatre

---

6   'Kronologisk oversikt over Halvorsens konsertvirksomhet Del 1 (1864–1883)' (accessed 1 July 2005). I am grateful to Philip Holmes for his translation of the entry and for confirmation that the language used here is Norwegian. In the early nineteenth century, Norway was a colony of Denmark and it is not always easy to distinguish nineteenth-century Norwegian from written Danish.

7   Evans, p. 15.

8   I am grateful to James Salter, of Coventry City Libraries, for providing this information.

9   *Era*, 18 March 1877, p. 8.

34 × 96 ft. Bottle is cautious about the 'Royal' title, suggesting that it was one of many 'honorary Royals', so called 'because it was thought to elevate the venue in the mind of the public.[10] The theatre had very many changes of management, decoration and use during its lifetime, but nevertheless it housed visiting companies from London and America as well as the provinces, and offered all the fashionable excitements provided by 'machinery', including the famous play where the heroine is tied in front of an approaching train.[11] Edward Bell, the lessee in 1877, abandoned the old repertory system with its 'stock company' in favour of touring groups, 'often of a high standard'. I have found no other information about the performance of *Jane Eyre*.[12]

Reception of the Play

It seems that there are no reviews of the play apart from the short notice in *The Era* quoted above.[13]

Distinctive Features of the Play

- There are unusually full stage directions and instructions to the actors.
- The play largely follows the structure of Birch-Pfeiffer's play, and the action is confined to Gateshead and Thornfield.
- The Reed family take the place of the Ingrams in the novel, with Lady Georgine Clarence (nèe Reed) taking the place of Blanche Ingram.
- Rochester is Lord Rowland, as in Birch-Pfeiffer.
- Rochester admires Jane's paintings.
- Jane refuses his gift of a dress.
- Jane does not reveal her feelings even under provocation.
- The madwoman is the wife of Rochester's dead brother.
- Rochester presents Jane to his guests as his future wife at the end.

---

[10] Bottle, pp. 5, 8, 9, 11 and 55. *Coventry Standard*, 26 January 1923, gives 1818 as the date of building (p. 4). I am grateful to James Salter, of Coventry City Libraries, for providing this information.

[11] Bottle, pp. 61, 70–77, 84, 103 and 108.

[12] Bottle, pp. 122, 125. The play does not appear in *Era* for any provincial or London theatre during the ten weeks following the Coventry performance. Ted Bottle also searched his private records for me, but found nothing, confirming that the play was not recorded as having been performed at York, Wakefield or Northampton, theatres which might have figured in a touring circuit. Either the tour continued in cities which I have not searched, or it was abandoned. I am most grateful to Ted Bottle for his help.

[13] I am grateful to James Salter, of Coventry City Libraries, for searching local publications for me. The 'review' is in *Era*, 18 March 1877, p. 8.

Jane Eyre by Mme von Heringen Hering

Dramatis Personae

Mrs Sarah Reed, a rich Widow
John, her Son, 15 years of age
Capt. Henry Wytfield, her Brother
Jane Eyre, an Orphan, 16 years of age in 1st Act
Lord Rowland Rochester
Lady Georgine Clarence, a young widow, daughter of Mrs Reed
Mrs Judith Harleigh, a relation of Lord Roches[ter]
Dr Blackhorst, Superintendent of an education[al] establishm[ent]
Lady Clawdon
Lord Clawdon
Sir Francis Steenworth, Bart
Edw. Harder Esq.
Adèle, a child, 11 years of age ⎫
Grace Poole ⎪
Sam, Man-servant ⎬ in Lord Rochester's House
Patrick, Groom. ⎪
Tom, an old Valet at Mrs Reed's ⎭

Act 1 is at Mrs Reed's Landed Property; Act[s] II[–IV] at Thornfield Hall, Lord Rochester's Estate.

Act I

A room with book-cases and statues. Centre door in back scene, and side doors to right and left. In the first coulisse to left of actors, is a high window with damask curtains, before which a chair. To the right, a fire-place, and, above this, a life-size portrait of a handsome gentleman of upwards of 40 years of age; before this, a sofa, and, by the side of it, an arm chair and a table. Everything indicates wealth.

Music

[Scene 1]

Enter Jane from side door left. She first puts her head in, enters on tip-toe, and looks around her cautiously and listens; then she hastens lightly over the stage, to the fireplace; her face is pale and surrounded with dark, waving hair; she is clad in a dark cotton dress, over which she has on a black apron, and a small white handkerchief round her neck; she stops before the picture, clasps her hands, and looks at it in a melancholy way.

Jane (after a pause): Uncle Reed, my dear Uncle Reed! Do you see me? – You smile, you do see me! Why do you smile? No, you should rather weep, as they all of them say that I am wick[ed] and corrupt, and that I am an ungrateful child – so [I] suppose it must be true! Ah, why did you leave me[?] I loved you so dearly, and you were so fond of me, – the others all hate me; am I then, to thank them for their hatred? That would only amuse them, and the[y] would laugh at me. Yesterday it was Christmas Da[y] – they made each other presents, but not one of them thought of you, Uncle Reed – (*She falls on her kn[ees]*) although it is your birthday, today; you gave them all the wealth they roll in; but they do not think of you. Oh, Uncle Reed, I can bring you nothing but my tea[rs] – I have nothing else, but accept them – I weep with love and gratitude – and they say I am ungrateful – Do y[ou] believe it, Uncle? No, no, you do not believe it. (*Music ceases.*)

[Scene 2]

Jane, Tom

Tom (entering from left): {God} bless me! If I didn't think so! Jane, what [are] you doing here? You come in here, where you are forbid[den] to set foot! One can't leave you to yourself for a momen[t.] What are you doing now?

Jane (jumps up with a wild look, when he enters): I have come to see Uncle Reed on his birthday! I did so, Tom, because nobody else thinks of him.

Tom (perplexed): What say …… is it really today?

Jane: Yes, the day after Christmas Day, which was never forgotten while Uncle Reed lived, and used to make presents to everyone in the house.

Tom (as before): But Jane, he died five years ago! … really one can't think of everything … why, it's an age since that happened.

Jane: Five years! Yes you are right indeed, it *is* an age. What a happy child I was then! Before Uncle Reed died, I knew not that good people die and that a poor orphan can be so wretched.

Tom: I know you had, nevertheless, at that time, lost both your father and mother.

Jane (shaking her head sorrowfully): I never knew my parents. Uncle Reed took me in his arms, and was so tender and kind! While he live[d] I felt not that I was an orphan! (*With a wild burst of emotion*) Oh! Uncle Reed, where are you gone? When will you come and take me away with you?

Tom (sorrowfully): Come, Jane, come! Now you are beginning the wild talk again, to which you have accustomed you[r] self since you had the fever last year! (*Kindly*) No[w] you are getting naughty again.

Jane: Why don't you scold me as you used to do? W[hy] don't you drive me away? Why don't you beat me, as Mrs Reed has ordered you to do?

Tom (perplexed): Because you are no longer a child … because you are a big girl, now.

Jane: Oh, that is not the reason; I have grown older, if you will, but I am still a helpless, ignorant child. The r[ea]son is you dare not, because you have not forgotten the night I was locked up in the room where Uncle died, a[nd] from whence you carried me out, next morning, like a corpse. Now you are frightened of killing me.

Tom: I am afraid of making Mrs Reed hate you stil[l] more than you yourself have done and … well, I consider it my duty to spare you, because your nerves … (*he pauses*). Come along with me, Jane. Only think if anyone were to come and find you here

Jane (with defiance): I won't go.

Tom: Jane! … (*In a supplicatory tone*) Now be good, and don't grieve me.

Jane: Ah, Tom, do not scold me, you know not what I suffer.

Tom: Why what a strange girl you are! Now you are good again, but before …

Jane: I cannot help it, Tom! You are so often unkind to me, and so seldom indulgent! Do let me stop here a little! Nobody thinks of the books here, today. I should also like to keep my Christmas, and read, for an hour! It is so long since I had a book in my hand, because Georgine locks them all up. Let me read a little, Tom, it is the only pleasure I have!

Tom (in conflict with his feelings): I should like you to have the pleasure, but, if anyone saw you …

Jane (hastens to a bookcase, takes out a book quickly and says joyfully): No one, no one shall see me! here it is! Hume's History of England! (*She comes back with a face beaming with joy.*) Do you see, I made no mistake, I knew where to find it. (*Hastens to the window, which has a very broad sill, places the chair against it, and jumps on the chair. Sits on the sill, and says joyfully.*) Just look, Tom, now I shall draw the curtains so that nobody can see me, and then I can sit quietly, and study the history of my country. (*Pleased*) That will do beautifully, won't it? I ought to know something, and they won't let me learn anything at all.

Tom: Well, then, have your own way! I shall come and fetch you in an hour's time … don't stir, and think of me, if you don't of yourself. You know Mrs Reed!

Jane (draws the curtains before her in such a way that she cannot be seen):   Don't be afraid; I'll be as quiet as a mouse.

Tom (aside):   Now Mrs Reed may scold as much as she likes – I haven't the heart to deny the poor creature the only pleasure I can do her, and at Christmas, too. (*About to go; left*)

[Scene 3]

The former

Enter John from door in back scene; he is very elegantly dressed

John (roughly): Tom, what are you doing here? stop here!

Tom (perplexed and frightened): I have not time, Sir.

John (in a commanding way): You shall stop, I want somebody to talk to. Uncle Wytfield, who has returned from Spain, talks nothing but nonsense that no sensible person can stand, and Georgine sits as stiff as though she had swallowed the poker, and makes grimaces like a fine lady, when I only shoot a bread pill at her!

Tom: But it is not proper for you to sit and shoot bread at your sister. Miss Georgine is older than you, and you ought, therefore to show her the respect she is entitled to.

John (throws himself down on the sofa, with his hands in his pockets, and stretches out his legs): Respect! for her! – I do not respect anyone, not even Mama. They will, all of them, one day, be dependent on me, as this wretched Jane Eyre is, now, on my mother! When I am of age, and take possession of the Estate, then I'm the master here, and he who does not obey my orders, and do what I want, will rue it! Don't forget that, Tom.

Tom (dryly):   Yes, but that won't be just yet awhile.

John (jumping up): You bore me, Tom ... you don't amuse me at all! What a pity Mama has forbidden Jane to come here ......

Tom (as before): Yes, it really is a pity you have nobody to plague. Are you not ashamed of yourself, John, to beat the poor child, as you have done so often! Is that proper for a young gentleman of your position?

John: I beat her because I hate her! But it is some time since I thrashed her last, and then she both scratched and bit me, the beastly cat!

Tom: So she did, but then she was in a state of desperation because you struck her with a hammer, and the poor girl had nothing else to defend herself with.

John: She had no right to defend herself at all, when I struck her, for I am the master here, and she is only a beggar, who eats our bread. (*Looking at the curtain*) But what's this! ... Look how the curtain's moving.

Tom (looks also at the curtain, frightened): Yes, you're right! Come, young gentleman, let us go; perhaps it's the ghost.

John (triumphantly): The ghost? Not a bit of it; there must be someone behind. I bet
it is the cat herself – (*running to the curtain, which he throws aside*)
Right, by Jove! What are you doing here, you beast? (*Aside*) Good
heavens! Didn't I just think so?

*Jane (sits, as before, on the window-sill, with her feet on the chair, holding the book
on her knee with both hands; she has a wild look, she trembles in every limb, and
stares at John in a threatening way.)*

John (recedes somewhat abashed): Well, what are you staring at me for? Why don't
you answer? Why do you hide yourself here, to frighten people? I'll
pitch you down, if you don't answer me at once, you beast. (*Stretches
out his hand to take hold of her*)
Jane (as before): Don't touch me, John! A year ago, I was still a cat and scratched
you, because I would not let you kill me with a hammer, but now I'm
bigger!
John (laughs scornfully): I suppose you think I dare not beat you now? You shall soon
see ... (*Goes towards her*)
Jane (with flashing eyes, but without moving): If you do that, John, I shall not scratch
you (*she jumps from the window-sill to the ground*) but I will kill you!
So you had better let me be!
John (receding, frightened): Oh, ho! I dare say you'll take care not to do that.
Jane (calmly): Yes, if you don't beat me.
Tom: (takes her kindly by the hand): Come along with me, Jane.
Jane (without taking her eyes from John): No, *he* shall go first.

[Scene 4]

The former

Enter Mrs Sarah Reed and Henry Wytfield

*Mrs Reed (a tall lady upwards of 40 years of age, proud, repulsive and dark; very
elegantly and splendidly dressed, her manner calm, cold and not
without dignity)*: What is the matter here? (*Sees Jane, and turns away
with a look of considerable disgust.*) What is that creature doing here?
... How can she dare ...
John (going to her): Mama, Jane has hidden herself behind the curtain, and she
threatens to kill me, if I come near her!
Mrs Reed (trying to control herself): Why did you have anything to do with her? It
is your own fault, you have not done as I told you. – (*To Jane*) What
do you want here?
*Jane (who, from the moment Mrs Reed entered has stood trembling and motionless;
looking down, softly)*: I was reading, Aunt Sarah.

Mrs Reed (with self-control, but still coldly and seriously): Have you not been forbidden to come into these rooms[?]

Jane: Yes.

Mrs Reed: How can you then dare to secrete yourself here, when you know my orders?

Jane: Georgine and John have locked up all the books, likewise those which Uncle Reed was so kind as to give to me. You have given me an attic, where it is cold and wretched. I longed so dreadfully for a good book, and here it is quiet and warm.

Henry (shaking his head; to Mrs Reed): Sarah, let her read!

Mrs Reed (gives him a threatening look; then says in the same tone as before to Jane): You could have asked me for a book, then you would not have been disobedient.

Jane (with a sharp look): I did not come here on account of the book{s} alone.

Mrs Reed: What did you come for, then? To listen to what was going on here, I suppose?

Jane: No, but to visit Uncle Reed (*pointing to the picture*) and to send him a grateful thought, as I have no flowers to adorn his portrait with, on his birthday.

Mrs Reed (startled, biting her lips; aside): The serpent.

Henry (with a look of astonishment at Mrs Reed): Yes – it really is the day after Christmas day! In my brother-in-law's time, it was always a great festival here; but now, it seems to be quite forgotten.

John (puffed up): It's a long time since Papa died; one can't always be thinking of that.

Mrs Reed (commanding): Silence! (*To Henry*) I can understand perfectly well, that Jane Eyre remembers this day; my late husband was always spoiling her, and that is how her stubbornness and obstinacy originated. (*Looking gloomily at her*) Have I not forbidden you to curl your hair? Do you not know that Georgine cannot bear it? This mode of dressing the hair, is only fit for the daughters of high families, like my Georgine, who are meant to command, but not for those who, like yourself, are destined to serve and obey. Why do you do this? Answer!

Jane (putting her fingers dreamily through her hair): I did not know my hair had been dressed; I do nothing with it, Aunt Sarah, but it curls naturally. My hair is so stubborn and it will not set otherwise.

Mrs Reed: Then your hair is an emblem of your character! Did you threaten to kill John?

Jane (calmly): Yes, if he beat me again, as he did before.

Mrs Reed: Then beg his pardon!

Jane (looks down, without moving)

Mrs Reed (with a piercing look): You won't?

Jane (calmly): No.

Mrs Reed: You will not beg his pardon?

Jane: Yes, when he has begged mine first, for all the abusive names he has
               heaped on 'the beggar'.

Mrs Reed (to Wytfield): Do you hear, Henry, do you hear? (*To Jane*) Go.

Jane (holds her head down, and is about to go)

Mrs Reed: Put the book down, first.

Jane (turns round and puts it on the table)

Mrs Reed: You will only come here *once* more; but I shall send for you first.

Jane (looks inquiringly at her)

Mrs Reed: Go, and let me be rid of the sight of a wicked and ungrateful
               creature!

Exit Jane, left (with head down)

John (triumphantly to Tom): Well, I must go and tell Georgine this at once. How it
               will amuse her. (*Runs out of door in back scene*)

Tom (follows him shaking his head:– Exit)

[Scene 5]

Mrs Reed, Henry

Mrs Reed (her exasperation breaking out): Now you have seen and heard her, the
               serpent, who has disturbed the peace of this house, ever since she set
               foot in it. Can you now conceive what I have suffered in fulfilling the
               duty my husband was unreasonable enough to impose on me? Thank
               {God} \goodness/ it is now over.

Henry: I have been away from here too long to \be able to/ comprehend all
               the details of this case, at so short notice, but so much I can see: that
               this poor orphan has received but a very indifferent education, and is
               suffering under your hatred.

Mrs Reed: Yes, I hate her! I may, possibly, not have understood how to bring her
               up, or would not understand it; I only know that this creature has grown
               up among us, as a weed and a perfect plague to me and my children,
               and I have been a conscientious fool for putting up with it so long! I
               have tried everything to make her obedient and tractable but she is

incorrigible – \she hates my children and defies me/ – she must go, as
I can only have peace in my house again in this way, for she is as like
her mother, as she possibly can be, and every bit as stiff and obstinate
as she was.

Henry (shaking his head): To the best of my recollection, you had a similar antipathy
for her mother.

Mrs Reed: And was I not right? She has covered our name with shame; she ran
off with a poor naval officer, married this creature who squandered her
fortune, and, some few years afterwards, she was a beggar, a penniless
widow! I can't tell you what I suffered, the evening she came to our
house, with her child, and the weak-minded, romantic Reed received her
with open arms! I was obliged to put up with the sight of her, I had to
nurse and attend her, until death released me of this martyr! I breathed
freely, I imagined my cup of bitterness was drained; but I deceived
myself – \the worst was still to come/ ; she had left the child to his care!
Then you went to Spain, and knew not what a cross I was called on to
bear! Reed was a severe, obstinate man, and I dared not let him suspect
how much I hated the little wretch he was so passionately fond of! He
made a perfect idol of the child, could sit for hours \together/ with her
on his knee, playing with her hair and listening to her prattle! For her
sake, he neglected his own children; indeed, when they all three of them
had the Scarlet fever, he sat, day and night, by Jane's bedside – his only
thought was for her, and he left his own children to me and their fate! I
was obliged to submit in silence; even when death suddenly overtook
him, his last thoughts were with this horrid creature, for he made me
take an oath that I would never abandon the child, but consider it as
entitled to the same rights as my own! The same rights! This beggar!
Thus, in his last moments, he heaped a fresh burthen on my shoulders;
but I have borne it long enough for my conscience not to smite me for
throwing it off, so as to breathe freely again in my own house, after the
lapse of fourteen long years!

Henry (astonished): But what do you intend to do with her?

Mrs Reed: I shall send her to the Establishment at Lowood; I have settled with the
Director, who was here yesterday, and I expect him, every minute, to
fetch her.

Henry: The Establishment at Lowood? Is not that an Orphan Asylum, a kind of
charity school supported by voluntary contributions, in a very unhealthy
neighbourhood, forty miles from hence?

Mrs Reed (coldly): It certainly is an Orphan Asylum. I am not acquainted with the
locality, but I know that young girls are brought up, there, in humility
and the fear of God, and that they learn to do something useful. I am to
pay £18 a year for her, there, and will pay this sum, in advance, for four
years. Jane Eyre will receive the education suitable for her station, and,
from thence, she can look out for a place either as servant or governess,

according to the way she may avail herself of the four years she has before her. In this way, I believe I confer a real benefit on her, and fulfil my duty at the same time.

Henry: It is somewhat late to take this step, Sarah. Some years ago, she might have been able to stand so terrible a change, but at present, she is too old to be sent to such an establishment. Besides, it seems to me that, in this {way} manner, you do not keep the promise you made to your late husband: he certainly cannot have wished she should have been brought up at an Orphan Asylum.

Mrs Reed (bitterly): No, that is certain! According to his ideas, the first educational establishment in London, would not have been good enough for her, and, if he had had time to make a Will, he would, doubtless, have remembered her liberally to the detriment of his own children! But God is just, and willed it otherwise. (*Turning quickly to him*) For the rest, if, as it seems, you do not approve of my plan, you are quite at liberty to provide better for her future welfare. I leave her to you, with pleasure.

Henry: You jest at my expense, Sarah. You must remember that you had nothing before Reed made a rich lady of you, and that I am a soldier without fortune. My circumstances do not allow me to provide for this orphan.

Mrs Reed (coldly): Then you had better leave her to the fate I have marked out for her. I am commended, by the whole county, for what I have done for this strange child, and I believe I merit the praise.

Henry (shrugging his shoulders): It is well for you, if your conscience do not say the reverse!

Mrs Reed (*is about to give a sharp reply*)

[Scene 6]

The former, Tom, Blackhorst; afterwards Jane

Tom (comes in from door in back scene): If you please, Ma'am, Mr Blackhorst wishes
          …

Mrs Reed (enlivened): Ah, he is welcome; call Jane Eyre!

Tom: I have sent James for her; she will be here directly. (*Goes and opens door for Mr Blackhorst*)

Enter Blackhorst (dressed in black, in a sort of clerical costume, about 50 years of age; he is submissive towards Mrs Reed, but his features are hard and cold.)

Blackhorst: You allowed me, Madam …

Mrs Reed (whose expression, when he enters, suddenly changes, and becomes mild and affable): You are very welcome, my dear Sir! (*Goes to the sofa, and points to a chair by the side of it*) I have been quite longing for you.

Blackhorst (sits down, after having bowed to Henry): You are really too good, Madam.

Mrs Reed (sanctimoniously): Yes, I may say I have longed for you, for I see, in you, the servant whom the Almighty has ordained to lead erring hearts, with firmness, to the right path.

Blackhorst: Sometimes even with harshness, Mrs Reed, when harshness is the only remedy! God Himself has indeed chosen me for such a servant, and I will praise Him, if, by His goodness, I may succeed in leading the young lamb back, which, notwithstanding all your charitable deeds, of which you wrote me, has strayed from the flock.

Mrs Reed: I considered it my duty to name this lamentable fact, to lighten your task.

Enter Jane (from left entrance; remains standing near door)

Mrs Reed (perceives her, and beckons her to approach): Come here, you shall not say I have spoken ill of you behind your back.

Jane (astonished, approaches timidly)

Mrs Reed: I have done, for {you,} Jane Eyre, what {God} \we are/ commanded {us} to do for the fatherless. Since she was two years old, she has lived under my roof, she has shared everything with my children, and has been brought up with them. But the seeds of my benevolence, have fallen on barren ground, (*with a deep sigh*) for she has no heart! She is ungrateful [–] she tells falsehoods and is a hypocrite, and I feel that for her future welfare, it is necessary that she should be under the care of a stricter person than I am.

Blackhorst: What you tell me is perfectly dreadful! But you need be under no apprehension whatsoever. I have already softened many a youthful disposition, \many a hardened heart./ With God's help I shall likewise succeed in this case, though it is already somewhat late, in bringing the young lamb back to the fold.

Mrs Reed: Jane Eyre. You see this excellent gentleman. From this time forward he will take charge of your future welfare. In a few days, you will leave for the Institution at Lowood, where I have settled for your remaining for four years.

Jane (with a burst of joy): Indeed? Shall I really leave here?

Mrs Reed: I suppose you heard what I said.

Jane: You will send me to a school?

Blackhorst: Where young girls are taught to fear God.

Jane (looking at him from top to toe): You can spare yourself that trouble, Sir, for Uncle Reed has taught me that – I fear and love God, who mercifully takes me away from this house – but tell me, Sir, what *else* can I learn there?

Blackhorst (much surprised): You can learn much there, Miss, if you have the inclination.

Jane: Oh, I have the inclination, and I am persevering! I will learn everything, everything that can make me independent of other people's benevolence, which consumes my soul like fire.

Blackhorst (severely): The first thing you will be taught, Miss, is humility, for only an humble mind is fit for an Orphan Asylum like ours, which is supported by the benevolence of others.

Jane (shuddering): An Orphan Asylum? You send me to an Orphan Asylum, Mrs Reed?

Mrs Reed (coldly): It is the most fit place for you, and where you can be educated according to your prospects for the future.

Jane (looking up at the portrait): Do you hear *that*, Uncle Reed? They disown your child, your Jane, and an Orphan Asylum is to be her home! Let it be so! I will not be wicked again, as they called me here, for, even if I be persecuted and tortured by hatred, it will only be strangers that hate me, and not those who call themselves my relatives.

Blackhorst (clasping his hands): Good Heavens! {Gracious God!} How can a child speak thus of its benefactors?

Jane (starting): Benefactors! – Do you hear, Uncle Reed!

Blackhorst: Will you permit me, Mrs Reed, to retire! I have already seen and heard enough to cause me to lament that you did not entrust this young girl to our care, years ago. You have been by far too lenient, you have not even told me the whole truth! (*He has risen and will go.*)

Jane (whose chest heaves violently, steps quickly in his way): No, Sir, she has *not* told you the whole truth! But you shall hear it from me, you shall know me better, before I follow you, and turn my back on this house for ever. It would be the death of me, if I could not once express what has been raging within me for years, and I would never do it behind hind her back! (*Pointing to Mrs Reed*) – Mrs Reed told you I was ungrateful – this is *not* true! I never forget a kindness, and the least demonstration of goodness makes a deep and lasting impression on my heart. (*She turns to the portrait.*) *You* know it, Uncle Reed – Mrs Reed has {told} said to you that I tell lies and am a hypocrite; it is not true! If I could lie, I should say: 'I love Mrs Reed, she has been kind to me, she has been a mother to me'; if I could dissemble, I should weep to you and lament that I was thrust out of this house, for I know it would be to my advantage with you! But I tell you there is nothing in the world, I execrate like this woman, whose words and looks have been as daggers to me, ever since I began to talk and understand; the thought of my leaving this house and that I shall never see her and her wicked children again, fills me with joy, and whatever vicissitudes may be in store for me, I will never come back to her again \and never call her Aunt, more,/ even though I could thereby, acquire all the wealth and happiness this world can offer. (*Turning to Mrs Reed*) For you have treated me, for five years, with the most cold-blooded, heartless cruelty – and God knows I have never done you the least harm ...

Mrs Reed (overcome by surprise and fear): How dare you say so, in this gentleman's presence?

Jane (passionately): How dare I, Mrs Reed, how dare I? Because all I say is true – you think my heart is of stone, and that I require no kindness, but I do want kindness, and am accustomed to it. A little kindness would have made me good, and for a little kindness I would have worshipped you, as I did Uncle Reed! But you have no compassion in you, you know not what mercy is! On my death-bed, I shall remember the evening when your wicked son, without the least cause, struck me to the ground with a hammer, when, bleeding and desperate, I was defending myself, and you afterwards had me dragged into the room, where Uncle Reed's corpse had once lain, and which, Tom says, his spirit still haunts; I have not forgotten how, one long, terrible night, you kept me locked up there in the dark, although I was half dead with pain, and cried: 'Aunt Reed, have mercy on me!' Oh, all the world shall know what your mercy consists of. You left me in there, in a state of despondency, and cared not that the doctor afterwards said you had ruined me for life. If I am wicked, you have made me so! You are just what you call *me*: a hypocrite – you are what is still worse, you are a perjuress ...

Mrs Reed (terrified, and no longer able to contain herself): Jane!

Jane (furiously, and without heeding the interruption): A perjuress to the dead, for I was present when you swore to my poor Uncle, that you would treat me like your own children, have the same affection for me and never forsake me, and you have brought me up with hatred, banished me from the rooms you and your children live in, refused to have me instructed with them so that I might grow up in ignorance – and now you thrust me into an Orphan Asylum, now that I am too old to learn, and too young to be left to myself. This is the way you have kept your oath – and when, in the next world, you meet him (*pointing to the portrait*) and he asks you: 'How have you treated my sister's orphan child, and how have you kept your oath?' then you can tell him 'I have *ruined* the orphan child and I have *broken* my oath!" (*To Blackhorst*) Now you can take me away, and see if you can rectify the injury that hatred has done me.

(She hastens out of centre door in back scene.)

Mrs Reed (sinks back in the sofa, trembling violently, and hides her face. Blackhorst looks at her, embarrassed, and follows Jane. Henry approaches Mrs R. and shrugs his shoulders.)

Curtain falls quickly

Act II

There is a suppressed interval of eight years between Acts I & II.

A Room at Thornfield Hall, decorated in a heavy style, as at the close of the 17th century. Furniture Rococo style. Three doors in Back scene, the middle one being the chief entrance; the one to the right (of actors) leads to Rowland's rooms, and that to the left, to the Library. In the first coulisse to the right of actors, is a window; in the first to the left, a splendid Mantlepiece, over which is Rochester's escutcheon carved in marble; on the mantlepiece, two silver candelabra, with candles lighted, and several vases with flowers; large fire, before which a sofa, and a small marble table. Opposite, to the right, a similar table, and two arm-chairs. In background to the right of centre door, is a table with tea-things, the urn and tea-service of silver; at the left of centre door, a chair. On both of the small tables are also lighted candles.

Scene 1

Sam, Mrs Judith Harleigh, discovered

Sam (a man between 50 and 60 years of age has just placed the flower vase on the table): Well! Everything's in order now. I think he'll be satisfied, if he comes and takes his tea here.

Judith (arranging the tea-table): Yes, why should he not be so?

Sam: He was in a dreadful temper when he arrived, and went to his room at once – and although he had been aw[ay] for eleven months, he did not speak to anyone but Grace Poole, with whom he shut himself up.

Judith (sits quietly down in the arm-chair to the right): He is master in this house, and can do as he pleases. His fancies are nothing to anyone but himself, and you know why he speaks to Grace Poole first.

Sam (in an important way): I certainly do know, and I consider myself his lord[ship's] faithful and discreet servant.

Judith: So you are, Sam. But he has not even confided in me, his kinswoman! But I do not mind that, for he is master here!

Sam (angrily): And then he tumbles down here, without having written a word about it.

Judith: Yes, he has always done so, since he came back from India; but what in the world, is the matter with you, today, Sam, you are so dreadfully ill-tempered.

Sam (grumbling): Oh, you know very well, Mrs Harleigh! My old woman, Lea, was everything for you, but since this stuck-up Miss Eyre has come to Thornfield Hall, no one cares for us.

Judith: You are both of you very silly people! We may all consider ourselves fortunate that the young lady has come here, for, with the exception of the few weeks Lord Rochester spends here, since he came into the estate, we were all alone in this solitary castle, as on a desert island, but now it is quite different, since that sweet girl, with her lovely eyes, enlivens us all. Has she not relieved us of all the trouble we had with little Adèle whom his lordship brought with him from France? In three months, she has contrived to master that wild and spoiled child, whom no one, not even his lordship himself could manage in two years. She is always accom[m]odating, obliging and good-tempered, and never inquisitive, and that says a good deal for her, Sam! I know what I had to endure from the inquisitiveness of the last governess, until at last, I got rid of her! And I thank God daily, for sending us this sweet girl. Do you understand that, Sam!

Sam (sarcastically): Good Heavens, Mrs Harleigh, how you do go ahead, you must be quite out of breath! I only hope his lordship may be as pleased with her as you are, or the pleasure will be short, as well as sweet.

Judith: I do hope he will be respectful to Miss Eyre, for, if she leaves us too, he can have his little Parisienne educated where he pleases – I shan't get him any more governesses.

Sam (inquisitively): Do you know, Ma'am, where he got hold of that child, and whom she belongs to?

Judith (dryly): No, I have never asked him, and it is no business of mine. (*The sound of a bell is heard at a distan[ce.]*)

Sam (startled): It is his lordship.

Judith (listening): He only rang once – it's for the footman. (*Another ring*) No, it's for you – quick, Sam!   (*Sam hurries out of side door right*)

Judith (alone): It does not concern me, unless he rings three times, but still I don't suppose he will come in here. But, if he did so? If he wanted to see the new governess. How tiresome Jane is not here! To think that just today, I should have missed the postman from Milcote. Now the poor girl has gone herself, with my letter to the post-office in Hay Lane. I ought not to have allowed her to do it. It is already pitch dark! (*Walks backwards and forwards*) But who could have thought to see Rochester here, today, just as though he had fallen from the clouds! … And the poor girl has nearly two miles to walk … I hope to goodness no accident has happened to her!

[*Scene 2*]

Judith, Jane

Jane (looking in at door in back scene): {What, are you here?} Ah, good evening!

Judith: Thank God you are back at last! Where have you been? I was in a dreadful state about you.

Jane (in a dark blue dress buttoned high up to the throat. Her hair parted. More colour on her cheeks, than in preceding Act; holds herself more upright, it is also necessary that the actress, by means of shoes, be taller than before. She appears contented, without being too lively. She advances kindly to Judith): Your letter is posted, Mrs Harleigh. I have only been to my room to put my cloak and muff away, and as I did not find you in yours, I asked Lea, whom [I] saw in the corridor, where you were. (*Looks around her with wonder*) But how light and comfortable it is here. Even flowers on the chimney-piece! What do all these preparations mean, Mrs Harleigh?

Judith: They mean that Lord Rochester has come home unexpectedly, while you were away.

Jane: Lord Rochester? You don't mean to say so? … Did you know …

Judith: Nobody knew anything \about it/ before he was here. That is just what he always does.

Jane: But what a wonderful day! I thought all the adventures were over, and now they seem to begin in earnest.

Judith: Adventures? How so? Have you …

Jane (laughing): Yes, I certainly have – and you may be sure it was a strange \one/ {adventure}! The air was so fresh, this afternoon, the snow creaked underfoot {the long walk did me good}, I ran on quickly and got rather tired, so I sat down on the stone bench on the hill, about half a mile from Hay Lane, looked over the fine winter landscape, and thought to myself: How rich Lord Rochester must be! for you once told me that all the land I could see from thence, belonged to him! On a sudden, I heard the tramp of a horse on the hill, and, immediately afterwards, an immense Newfoundland dog sniffed about me; I got frightened, and started up, and, at the same moment, a gentleman on horseback galloped up, and his steed, on seeing me, reared and stumbled, and fell backwards with his master under him!

Judith: Good gracious!

Jane: I heard a loud cry, then a dreadful oath; I was terrified, and stepped forward, when the rider said to me, in a deep, sonorous voice: 'If you are not an {bogy} \evil spirit/ or frightened of my horse, give me your hand, that I can get away from the crazy brute.' I was rather shy, but tried to be bold, and succeeded. I helped him up, but he was scarcely on his feet before he had firmly hold of the bridle, and cried: 'Up, Mesrour, up!'

Judith (frightened): Did you say: Mesrour?

Jane: Yes, and he understood the cry, for he made a vigorous effort, and got up. The first thing the wild man did, was to give the beautiful horse a blow with his riding-whip, which caused him to rear again. 'You must be punished for it,' said he coldly, 'why did you throw me'?

Judith (anxiously): Well … what happened then?

Jane: Then he tried to mount, but he had sprained his ankle, and it seemed to pain him. I said 'Can I do anything for you, Sir? I *shall* be happy if I can assist you. He looked so extraordinarily sharp and almost disdainfully at me, and then said dryly: 'Then lend me your shoulder, if you are not afraid of sinking under the weight!' I smiled, and did as he wished, standing very firmly on my feet, and it was necessary, for he placed a hand as heavy as lead, on my shoulder, rested on it, and jerked himself into the saddle in a minute. Without thanking me he rushed across the heath, like the wind, with the dog before him! (*Wittily*) Wasn't that a regular Winter's Tale?

Judith: My poor girl! Do you know who the horseman was? He was Lord Rochester himself!

Jane (frightened): Lord Rochester! On horseback?

Judith: Yes, it is one of his peculiarities. He always leaves his carriage behind in some village \and comes here on horseback/ without our knowing when he is coming, or from whence. It seems, this time, that his ride has done him no good.

Jane: Oh dear, oh dear! That is a bad prospect for me!

Judith: Now I understand why he immediately went to his room. His foot must pain him, and he does not like people to see him suffer – that is also one of his peculiarities.

Jane (attentively): Peculiarities? You told me before, when I asked you how I had better behave to him, that he had no peculiarities.

Judith (perplexed): Yes, that is to say … I meant that it is easy to get on with him, if one leaves him to himself; but of course he has his own way of behaving, like every one else.

Jane (musing): His lordship is certainly not very polite; I have had a proof of that already.

Judith (after some struggle with herself, goes quite close to her): Now, I never wished to speak of this to you, my dear child, for I do not like gossip; but now it is necessary that I should speak, for I love you too well, not to wish that you should make a favourable impression on his lordship. Lord Rochester is the younger son of the house, and was poor, whereas his brother was to have been heir to the whole of the property. They agreed tolerably well, when a mysterious circumstance caused a rupture between them. I do not know what happened, for I lived, at the time, at an old hunting-seat that belongs to the family, but this much I do know, that the old Lord was obliged to separate the brothers for ever, and therefore he sent the present Lord Rochester to the West Indies; there he lived in positive oblivion, until a few years ago, when he came into the estate by the sudden death of his brother. As he has passed half his lifetime away from home, and Spanish Town in Jamaica, as you may imagine, is no place to acquire high manners, he is a little uncouth in his behaviour, but that is all. Otherwise he is, in his character and ideas, a perfect gentleman, and, since he has come here, he has been quite a father to all the poor and distressed in the whole county. (*Looks around her mysteriously*) I only recommend you one thing, dear: you told me, the other day, you had heard some strange laughter in the Hall.

Jane (shuddering): Yes, a most singular, unearthly laughter, as of one risen from the dead, Mrs Harleigh, which seemed to come from the third floor in the tower, and, in the silence of the night, could be heard in my room. I assure you, it made my blood creep.

Judith: Well, you know, too, it is poor Grace Poole, that faithful servant, who is subject to such fits.

Jane (looking steadily at her): Yes, so you told me, and you also said that she was ordered never to leave the tower after dark; nevertheless, I met her, just now, on the stairs, and, as I went through gallery, I heard the shocking laughter again.

Judith (frightened): What do you say? (*Calming herself*) Yes, that is true! Grace Poole was with him.

Jane (attentively): With him? With Lord Rochester?

Judith (confused): I don't know … I think so. But – take care, dear, not to speak to anyone about it, and don't appear to take any notice of Grace Poole. (*Kindly*) It is for your own good I advise you to do so.

Jane: Thank you, Mrs Harleigh, I shall \not forget/ {attend to it.} … (*quietly*) Here she is.

[Scene 3]

The former, Grace Poole

Grace Poole (enters from side door right. She is an elderly woman, clad in a dark woollen gown, and white apron; on her head, a common white cap, which closes round her face; \her physiognomy serious/ her manner and tone firm. She makes no superfluous movements): Mrs Harleigh, his lordship will take tea here.

Judith (pleased): Oh, I am very glad of that! Who is with him now?

Grace: Adèle and Dr Spenley, who has just been sent for, because Lord Rochester has met with an accident.

Judith (with a side look at Jane): Good gracious, is it anything very serious?

Grace: I don't know, he never complains – have you everything ready for tonight?

Judith: Everything is in order.

Grace: His lordship wishes to see the new governess at tea. (*Going*)

Judith: Very well! (*calling*) Grace!

Grace (stopping): What do you want?

Judith (meaningly): Too much noise, by far too much noise!

Grace (coldly): I dare say I shall be able to keep order.

(*Exit through centre door in back scene*)

[Scene 4]

Judith, Jane

Jane (who has not ceased to look at Grace – aside): This is very strange!

Judith: It is a good sign, that he comes in here – he cannot have hurt himself very much! – Hark, is not that Adèle's voice?

Jane: Dear me, has her nurse not got her to bed, yet?

Judith: Oh, as long as Lord Rochester is here, no one can get her to bed! \(*Startled*)/ Good gracious! I think that is his heavy tread – can it be him already? (*Goes to right door, listens, then goes to the tea-table, and lights the spirit lamp under the urn*)

Jane (aside): My heart beats! I am the cause of his misfortune; he must have a singular character, if he have not already a prejudice against me. (*She goes to the back of the room*)

[Scene 5]

The former. \Enter/ Lord Rowland Rochester, Adèle. After them Sam.

Adèle (holding Rowland by the hand, is a child eleven years of age, plainly, but elegantly dressed, lively and joyful): Look, Rowland, there is my good Miss Jane.

Rowland (40 years of age; his face bespeaks vigour, his brow earnest, almost harsh; he is strong, dark hair and a black crinkled imperial. He is clad in a velvet coat trimmed with sable, underneath, he has a plain modern costume, and, on his head, a modern red velvet cap. His manner of speaking is abrupt and commanding, his face has sometimes, a wild expression, which soon disappears. On entering he has low[er]ed his head, and looks neither at Jane nor at Judith. Laconically to Adèle): That will do, Adèle, be quiet! (*Goes limping over the stage to the sofa*) Sam!

Sam (quickly): Yes, my lord.

Rowland (pointing to the sofa): Push that nearer the fire! In this old rooks' nest neither furs nor fire keep out the cold. (*He bites his lips and takes hold of his knee involuntarily.*) The devil! – Sam, give me your arm!

Sam (running up to him): Yes, my lord!

Rowland (leans on him, goes to the sofa, and sits down with difficulty): That will do, push the table this way!

Sam (moves the little marble table \quickly/ to the sofa)

Rowland (places his arm on table, and rests his head on his hand): Now you may go.

Sam (says, in passing, to Judith \quietly and/ sarcastically): Now it's your pet's turn.
   I wish you joy!   (*Exit centre door*)

Rowland (falls into a brown study)

Adèle (who kneels before him, pats one of his hands, which hangs down): Are you
   angry, Rowland?
Rowland (shortly): No.
Adèle (coaxing): Have you brought something for me?
Rowland (shortly): We shall see if you deserve anything.
Adèle (jumps up and claps her hands): Oh yes, I have deserved a great deal! (*running
   to Jane*) Have I not, Miss Eyre?

Jane (places her hand on Adèle's mouth, and bends down to her whispering).

*Rowland (gives Jane a look as though he expected an answer. As Jane does not
   move, he addresses himself \to Judith/ saying dryly)*: Good evening,
   Aunt Judith!
Judith (in the same tone): Good evening, Lord Rochester! (*Goes somewhat nearer*)
   You have had an accident?
Rowland: Yes, that's always the case, when I come here.
Judith: How did it happen?
Rowland: A confounded witch made Mesrour shy.
Jane (aside, merrily): Well, I call that candid.
Judith (timidly and perplexed): It must certainly have been much against her will.
Rowland: That's immaterial to me! (*Suppressing his pain.*) The effects are the
   same. – Tea!
Adèle (running up): Give it to me, give it to me! I'll give him the cup. (*She jumps
   round Judith.*)
Judith: No, certainly not! You'll spill the tea over the carpet – I know you. Miss
   Eyre, will you, please, hand the cup! (*She points to Rowland, and gives
   her the cup; whispering something to her, then she gives Adèle her tea;
   she sits on one of the chairs in the background, and drinks it.*)
Rowland (aside): The new governess does not seem to be intrusive. She is either very
   timid or very cunning.

*Jane (puts the cup on a silver tray, and goes modestly, but without timidity, to the
front, \to Rowland/ and offers it him)*

Rowland (abruptly): On the table.

Jane (puts the cup on the table)

Rowland (looking at her): Ah, by Jove, good evening! Why it's the Bogy!

Jane (bows)

Rowland: I hope you've not been bewitching my tea, as you did my horse.
Jane (looking calmly and modestly at him): I am afraid, my lord, that it was more Mesrour's fault, who was frightened of my ugliness, than mine, for I have no knowledge of witchcraft.
Rowland (looking at her astonished): Oh, indeed! Take a chair.

Jane (goes to the Arm-chair to the right)

Rowland (aside): She's offended about the 'confounded witch'. (*In a contemptful tone*) Vain, like all the rest. (*Aloud.*) Put your chair nearer to me.

Jane (places the chair quietly near the foot of the sofa, so that she sits nearly opposite him)

Rowland (aside): She is not the least timid. (*Aloud*) You are the new Governess?
Jane: Yes, my lord.
Judith (who has been in a state of anxiety, a short distance off, comes quickly forward): At your service, Lord Rochester! She is, and I thank God, daily, that we have her.
Rowland (dryly): Has the young person had tea?
Jane: Yes, thank you.
Rowland (to Judith): Then take your tea, Aunt, and sit down there, (*he points to the chair to the right at the other side of the table*) and be quiet.

Judith (takes her tea with her, without \showing/ the least displeasure, and sits where he bids her; she takes out her knitting, drinks from time to time, but listens continually to the conversation.)

Adèle (comes forward again): My own dear Rowland, what have you brought [with you] for me? Do tell me!
Rowland (dryly to Jane): Has she deserved anything?
Jane: Yes, my lord.
Rowland: Then go to my valet, and let him give you the little box.
Adèle (joyfully): Oh thanks, a thousand thanks! (*She considers.*) But have you brought a present for my governess too?
Rowland (with a suspicious look at Jane): I don't know.
Adèle: Then I will give her some of mine – may I not, you'll allow me to do so.   (*Exit running out of side door right*)

The former, without Adèle.

[Scene 6]

Rowland (with a sharp look at Jane, as before): Did you expect a present, Miss? Are you fond of presents?

Jane (calmly): I do not know. I have [never received] any presents, much less expected one.

Rowland: You are not so candid as Adèle. She demands her presents clamourously, and does not hide her joy.

Jane: Adèle takes advantage of your friendship for her, and wants only what she is accustomed to; she tells me you never come here, without a number of presents for her. But, if I should try to find a reason for expecting a present from you, I should be much embarrassed, as I am quite a stranger to you, and, as yet, have done nothing to merit your kindness.

Rowland (gloomily): Do not trifle with an excess of modesty. I have examined Adèle since I have been back, and am astonished at the progress she has made; she has learned more English, in the short time you have been here, than she did in two years previously.

Jane (bowing and pleased): Thank you, my Lord, now I have received *my* present!

Rowland (looks pleased at her, takes his cup and drinks): Hum! (*Becomes more and more attentive*) What is your name?

Jane: Jane Eyre.

Rowland: You have only been here three months.

Jane: Yes, my lord.

Rowland: And where do you come from?

Jane: From the Academy at Lowood, twenty miles from Milcot.

Rowland (in a tone of pity): From the Academy at Lowood! How long were you there?

Jane: Eight years.

Rowland: Eight years? Then you must have a constitution of iron, for, to the best of my knowledge, the pupils, at that charitable institution, are quite starved and tortured into praying and working, by that hypocrite Blackhorst. That is why you looked so odd, when I saw you on the hill, today. But what were you doing at Lowood all that time?

Jane: I was a pupil there, for four years, and, as nothing further was paid for me, I was teacher there, during the remainder of the time, with five pounds a year.

Rowland (in a half compassionate, half scornful tone): Hum! How did you come to my house?

Jane: I saw, in a newspaper, that there was a vacancy for a governess, at Thornfield Hall; I felt I was capable of undertaking the duties of a better engagement, and forwarded my testimonials to Mrs Harleigh, who sent for me at once.

Judith (proudly): And that was the wisest thing I ever did in my life.

Rowland (with an enquiring look at Jane): Who {God} knows.
Judith: I don't understand …
Rowland (makes a sign with his hand for silence): Yes, yes. Don't you put yourself
        out, Aunt Judith! (*To Jane*): As you were educated at Lowood, you
        must be an orphan.
Jane (seriously, but without being sentimental): I never knew my parents.
Rowland: But have you no brothers or sisters …
Jane: I never had any.
Rowland (impatiently): And had you no relations, an uncle or aunt …
Jane: I had a good uncle, but he is dead, now I have none.
Rowland: None, not any at all?
Jane: There was an uncle on my father's side, who went to America – but I
        have never heard from him; I am alone in the world.
Rowland (with a sarcastic smile): But not helpless, it seems.
Jane (looks at him with astonishment): Your lordship will pardon my not having
        understood your last observation.
Rowland (pointing with a smile, to his forehead): You have good resources here. Now,
        Miss – (*in an illtempered tone*) what is your name?
Jane: Jane Eyre
Rowland: Ah, I forgot – Miss Eyre. What did you learn at Lowood? do you play
        the piano?
Jane: A little.
Rowland: Just as I thought. 'A little' – like every other schoolgirl! Can you sing
        too?
Jane (without showing any annoyance): Yes, a little – but only when I am alone, and
        no one hears me.
Rowland (still looking sharply at her): Are the drawings, Adèle showed me, done
        by you?
Jane {(without showing any annoyance)}: Yes, my lord.
Rowland: Have you any more of them?
Jane: My portfolio is in the library, where I was working today.
Rowland: Fetch it.

Jane (rises)

Rowland: That is to say … (*with an effort*) I shall be obliged if you will fetch it;
        you know I can hardly move.

Jane (goes)

Rowland (calling after her): If the portfolio only contains copies, you can leave it
        where it is.
Jane: Your lordship will be able to judge when you see them. If they are good
        or bad, you will, at all events, perceive, that they are originals; I have

never been able to represent what did not originate with myself. (*Exit side door left.*)

Rowland (looking after her): Hum! She is a proud witch! Now, I suppose, she'll come with some nice rubbish.

Judith (who has difficulty to conceal her annoyance): I do not think so. When Jane Eyre says she can do a thing, you may depend she can.

Rowland: Oh, Aunt, you have been spoiling this little person to such an extent that with all her seeming modesty, she is ready to burst with pride; I never saw such a creature in my life!

Judith: And you certainly never will again, my lord, if you drive her away from the Hall.

Rowland (dryly): She will think twice, before she goes! That jump, from £5 a year at Lowood, to £30 at Thornfield, is not so bad.

Judith: Do pray be careful! Anyone, who can stand Lowood for eight years, must have some strength of mind, and strong minds are not to be trifled with.

Rowland (shrugs his shoulders scornfully)

Jane (comes back with a large portfolio, which she lays open before Rowland.)

Rowland: Sit down.

Jane (sits down)

Rowland (turning the papers in the portfolio): These are water colours; you paint?

Jane: Yes, my lord. I could only express my *thoughts* with the pencil – but I require colours to represent my feelings.

Rowland (who cannot conceal his astonishment, continues to look into the portfolio): What singular ideas! Here is nothing to be seen but the billows of the sea troubled by a storm – a white arm clings to a half-shattered mast at the mercy of the winds and waves. On the mast is a raven holding in his beak, a costly bracelet, which he has stolen from the lifeless arm. There is no living thing to be seen, on this spacious sea, but the bird – and yet all is life and animation! Where did you get this idea from?

Jane: From my own head.

Rowland (looking at her): From that small head of yours?

Jane: Yes, my lord.

Rowland: Does it contain more of that sort of thing?

Jane: I hope there is something better than that.

Rowland (seizes a fresh drawing, supports his head with his hand[,] leans over the table, and looks at the drawing astonished; he touches his cap as by chance, takes a side look at Jane, takes it slowly off, and puts it by the side of him.)

Judith (aside): She has gained the day – he takes his cap off!

Rowland (raises his head, shakes his hair from his forehead and speaks to her quickly):
Were you happy when you did these drawings, Miss Eyre? They all
seem to illustrate a melancholy and grave imagination.

Jane: I lost myself in a world of thoughts, and was happy so long as I was
painting, although the contrast between my ideas and the work of my
brush, vexed me constantly, and I perceived, with sorrow, that I had
not the ability to represent what I wished.

Rowland (looking at the drawing): At all events, these drawings by a pupil at Lowood
are certainly very remarkable – they are full of poetry. (*He seizes,
another, and becomes more and more eager.*) Who taught you to paint
the wind? – What a storm rages over the heath –. Where did you see
Latmos? – for this is Latmos – but what on earth can possess you, that
your brain can create such bubbles? (*Stops suddenly short, as though
he were alarmed at what he had been saying; his tone and manner is
immediately changed, and he pushes the pictures aside*) Now I shall not
be able to sleep for all this stupid nonsense, or shall be dreaming about
it. It must be late! (*He afterwards takes up the portfolio again.*)

Judith: It is past eleven o'clock, my lord.

Rowland: How is it, Miss Eyre, that you have not yet had Adèle put to bed? Do
you want to make new rules, in this old castle? (*He goes, {but} stands
still, and bites his lips with pain.*) Confound the leg! (*Half smiling,
half angry*) That will remind me of your odious beaver hat, for some
days to come, Miss Eyre! Good night! (*Walks, with apparent difficulty
out of side door right, with portfolio underarm*)

*Jane (who has stood up when he rose, looked at him calmly and earnestly, and
continues to observe him in the same way)*

Judith (with much anxiety): What can be the matter now? There is something wrong
again!

Jane (thoughtfully): I don't think so.

Judith: Why not?

Jane (coming to herself again): You said Lord Rochester had no peculiarities, and
that it was easy to get on with him! I think he is full of peculiarities,
and that it will be exceedingly difficult to please him.

Judith: But you did not seem to be afraid of him.[14]*

Jane (again with her thoughts): I don't know – he seems to me like a lion; it is all
over with him who cannot look at such an animal without fear. It gave
me courage.

---

14   * Page 33 wrongly inserted at this point – sense continues from p. 32^V to p. 34.

Judith: Dear me. You compare his lordship with a wild beast. Alas! I was afraid he would not please you.

Jane (gaily): How do you know that? He pleases me just as he is, and I believe that, when he is once accustomed to the 'confounded witch', and the 'odious beaver hat', I shall succeed in giving him satisfaction! Now let us go quietly to bed – I shall sleep well tonight, for {I am} we are no longer alone in this solitary castle; we have a stern protector, but one we can depend on.

(*Exit Jane and Judith through centre door in back scene*)

Act III

[Scene 2]

Same decorations

Jane discovered

Jane (standing alone at a window, looking thoughtfully out): Yes, out there it is spring! But here, in this gloomy castle, it is silent as the grave. One morning at breakfast, they told me his lordship had gone away. It is now twelve days ago, and he has not returned. I wonder where he is now? (A pause) Hum! ...... What is that to me? This singular character puzzles me incessantly, as an enigma I could wish to solve, but dare not! It is wonderful how heav[ily] his presence weighs on all who surround him, and yet I am n[ot] frightened of his lordship; on the contrary, it seems to me the place is very lonely without him.

Judith (behind the scenes): Make haste, Lea! Light all the fires and open windows.

Jane (listening): Open the windows? What can that mean? ... She's coming in here. Well, I must not be inquisitive, it is n[ot] becoming.

Enter Patrick & Judith

Judith: Sam! Sam! Where are you? (*To Patrick*): You say in an hour, Patrick?

15**Patrick (in riding dress)*: Yes, it will not be longer; his lordship is following close on my heels, and the others are coming behind him in a carriage.

Judith (hurriedly): But it is really too bad that we do not know these things sooner.

Patrick: They did not think of it before this morning.

---

15 * Material from p. 33 continues here.

Judith (sees Jane): Ah ... Miss Jane, I'm glad you're here! Go and dress quickly, and
make yourself as handsome as possible. Go to your room at once. I have
sent the parcel up. Yes! Don't be astonished \but make haste/ for there's
no time to be lost, dear! You see they will be here in an hour!

Jane: But why? What am I to dress for?

Judith (hands her an open letter): There it is! Read for yourself! I must get hold of
that grumbling Sam. I say, Sam! Where are you all gone to. (*hurries
out of side door left*)

Jane (looks, with surprise, after her, opens letter, and reads): 'I shall arrive, with my
visitors, an hour after you have received this letter. Please put the guests'
chambers in order also for ladies. The accompanying silk dress is for
the governess, who will make tea for the company; I wish to see her
respectably dressed for my visitors. – Rochester' (*somewhat piqued*)
Hum; '*the Governess*' – of course he cannot remember my name. (*To
Patrick*): So ladies are coming?

Patrick (smiling): Yes, Miss, and very handsome ladies too ... I mean the young one;
as far the old one ... well, that's a matter of taste, but, if she weren't a
lady, I should not think much of her.

Jane (smiling): But you seem to think a good deal of the young one, Patrick?

Patrick: Yes, Miss, and I am not the only person, who does so.

Judith (comes back): There, everything is in order now ... well dear, is not Lord
Rochester a duck? You will see how nicely the pink silk dress will
become you.

Jane (calmly): I shall not put it on, Mrs Harleigh.

Judith: What, you won't put it on? His Lordship sent for it himself, from
London, didn't he Patrick?

Patrick: I should think he did! Lady Clarence's maid's measure was taken for
it; her figure is just like yours.

Jane: Indeed! And who is Lady Clarence?

Judith: Oh, she is a young, proud and handsome widow whose husband has left
her a great name, but only a small property, a few miles from hence.

Jane (dryly): Then I suppose there will be a wedding here?

Judith (laughing): Yes, if it only depended on the lady. She tried her arts on his lordship
already three years ago, when he came back from France; but it was no
good – he does not notice such things.

Patrick (again smirking): Ah, ha; this time he certainly does notice it, ma'am.

Judith: Don't stand there chattering, Patrick! I tell you it is of no use.

Patrick: And with your kind permission, ma'am, I tell you it *is* of use! His
lordship has paid all his visits in the neighbourhood, and was only one
day at each place – but, at Clarence House, they made such a deal of
him, that he stopped there a whole week ... and his lordship and the
sweet young lady sang together, like two larks, and now he is coming
home with both mother and daughter! Several other guests are also
invited, and, if there is not something in the wind, why ...

Judith (shaking her head): I can't think that.

Patrick: Why not? Because he is forty years old? At that age, we men begin to go ahead in earnest, and if one o[f] us gets spooney on a pair of cheesey eyes, it's all up with him! I have only known his lordship for two years, bu[t] my firm conviction is, that there will soon be a marriage. Shall we make a bet?

Judith: Oh, let me be! – you had much better go down an[d] get the stables in order for the visitors' horses.

Patrick (going): They'll soon be something more than visitors.

                                                        (*Exit through door in back scene*)

Judith (uneasily): What an obstinate fellow to dare to maintain such [a] thing! Oh, it is not true, it can't be true!   (*Exit door in back scene*)

[Scene 3]

Jane (alone): And why should it not be true? … If he really did marry. (*Shakes her head thoughtfully*) \Hum …/ I don't know how it is, but I cannot possibly picture to myself Lord Rochester as a bridegroom. (*Smiles*) It seems to me as though he must devour everything that gives itself up to him unconditionally, either from love or hatred, according to the humour he may be in at the time. (*She starts*) Hush, there he is. I know that commanding step; (*smiling*) it is just as though he were vexed that the very earth he treads on, should dare to resist him.

[Scene 4]

Rowland, Jane

Rowland (comes quickly in from a door in back scene, in an elegant riding dress, with his hat on his head, and whip in hand; he speaks loudly, with a gloomy look): But where the deuce, are they all? … (*Sees Jane, and his tone becomes somewhat milder*) Ah, good evening, Miss Eyre.

Jane (bows): Good evening, my lord! (*About to go*)

Rowland (throws his hat and whip on the table; in a half vexed, half goodnatured tone): Are you running away from me again \already/?

Jane (stops): I do not run away from anyone, my lord.

Rowland: Well then, stop here; I have just something to speak to you about, and am glad I met with you first, for I have though[t] of several things, on the way, that I ought to have gold you of long since. During the past week, I have had so much worry with my tenants, that, to tell the truth, I had quite forgotten you. (*Throws himself on the sofa, and looks at he[r] astonished*) You have not put on your new dress?

Jane: No, I thank you, my lord.

Rowland ({starting up} \hastily/): And why not?

Jane (still calm and modest): Because I would not raise myself above my station, and because I would not wear colours that do not suit my appearance. I thank you again, and shall manage to be '*Respectably dressed*' without misapplying your goodness.

Rowland (in a sharp tone): You have read my letter to Mrs Harleigh.

Jane: She gave it me to read.

Rowland: You are offended because your plain dress does not please me.

Jane: No, my lord.

Rowland: You are displeased {because you do} and will not understand that, in this gloomy castle, the eye requires light and gay colours, or you are too proud to accept presents.

Jane (looks astonished at him): My lord ... I ...

Rowland (in a tone of decision, without heeding the interruption): I know you, although I have as yet, spoken but very little with you. Under your simple modesty is a good lump of pride. You just act after your own fancy. I am too matter-of-fact, too commanding for you? Life in India, and the falseness of mankind have made me bluff, and I hurt your feelings with my downright ways? Why do you look so strangely at me? What are you thinking of?

Jane: I was thinking, my lord, that there are not many masters, who take the trouble to ask their dependents, whom they pay, whether their feelings are hurt, or otherwise.

Rowland (surprised): Their dependents, whom they pay, you say? ... Hum! ... But I had nearly forgotten why I rode on so fast, that I got the start of an hour. I have constantly regretted that I was not candid with you as soon as I became acquainted with you; but the reason is that there is something secretive about you. You judge me, without doubt, wrongly, and I wish to justify myself before the others come. I am today, in a commanding mood, and that is a feeling which is {just as} very rare with me{, as going to church}. Listen, therefore, attentively, for I do not know when I may converse with you again.

Jane (who cannot believe her senses): But, my lord ...

Rowland (in a decisive manner): You are Adèle's governess – what are your ideas as to my connexion with this child?

Jane (concealing her astonishment): I have no ideas on the subject, my lord. I never enquire into the affairs of my employers.

Rowland (looking sharply at her): Miss Eyre, you have had your thoughts about it! You speak by far too little not to think a great deal! You thought that Adèle was my child.

Jane (looking downwards): And even if I did think so, to whom are you answerable for it.

Rowland: To no one – except you, who are shut up with her in this dismal castle. You have the right to ask; 'Whose child am I bringing up?' It is but just. – I can tell you, then, that Adèle is an orphan, and I have every reason to believe that she is the offspring of illicit connexion. I have a sacred duty, to a deceased relative, to perform, in taking care of her education, and I therefore fetched her here from Paris – but I am not her father – {but I am not her father}.

Jane (breathing deeply): Then, your behaviour to her is so much the handsomer.

Rowland (carelessly): Pooh! We are not talking of that. You now know, Miss Eyre, that you are probably spending your time and talents on an illegitimate child. I consider myself bound to explain this to you, because, in a few minutes, visitors of distinction, will arrive, who will make your acquaintance. You know how to educate \you have learned much/ you can easily have a much better position in some high family with legitimate daughters, and there shall be no impediment to your advancement.

Jane (with sparkling eyes): Do you really think, my lord, that such prospects could induce me to forsake this unhappy child, whom I love, and who is not answerable for the faults of her parents? Can there be a more enviable position than that of mother to an orphan? Oh, my lord – I myself am an orphan, and I know, that no greater curse can be on the head of an innocent child, than that of being without father and mother. (*Very impressively*): I thank you for your noble candour! I shall, if possible, love Adèle still more than before, I will form her character – for it is only want of love that hardens the heart of a child; I will love her three times as much, as no one loves her but me, and will never forsake her – (*stops suddenly and looks enquiringly at him*) unless you should dismiss me, my lord.

Rowland (who has looked at her with astonishment, says with respect and warmth combined): You have an excellent character, Miss Eyre, and I take you at your word. You promise me not to go away, until I dismiss you? (*Stretching out his hand*) Do you agree to this?

Jane (placing her hand in his, with an agreeable smile): With pleasure, my lord!

Rowland (looks at her with astonishment): Why, bless me, you're smiling ... that's something new, I thought you were not able to do so.

Jane: My lord!

Rowland: It is just as though a ray of the sun were on you. You must do that oftener, Miss Eyre! (*Behind the scenes, noise of wheels, and crack of whips; it gets dark*)

Rowland (starting up): Good heavens, here they are already! It is now evening, and I am not yet dressed. (*Vexed*) I have been talking a great deal too much. (*Abruptly*) Will you receive them, Miss Eyre, and keep them company, for a short time, until I come back! (*In going he stops short, and adds in a more agreeable tone*) That is to say, I shall be glad, if you will do what you dislike so much, and that is, to talk a little to my visitors, will you?

Jane: With pleasure my lord.

Rowland (going): And – people do think so much of appearances – *(overcoming his feelings, in a tone of supplication)* you will afterwards put on the {silk} pink dress, will you not?

Jane (without defiance, but firmly): No, my lord – that must be as it is.

Rowland (angry, going): Well, then, let it be so. I can't make you handsome by force! *(Exit quickly, side door left)*

Jane (alone, looks thoughtfully after him): What a strange, wonderful, but honourable man! *(Stands with her head down, lost in thought)*

[Scene 5]

The former. *Enter/ Sam, Judith, Georgine, Mrs Reed and Francis.*

Sam (opens door in back scene, and comes in with two candelabra \with lighted candles,/ which he places on table in front. Stage becomes immediately light. – Music)

Judith (goes forward): Will you please step in here; your rooms are not quite {ready} warm yet.

Mrs Reed (comes in accompanied by Francis. She has on an elegant travelling dress, a long, black cloak trimmed with fur, a small grey hat, and black lace veil. Time has caused her hair to turn grey, her face pale and thin, and her features still more gloomy and sharp, than in Act I; her deportment and walk only, are unchanged. She goes, while Georgine talks, towards the front, and sits down in a chair to the left. To Francis): Thank you.

Jane (who has remained standing in the front, has turned to the visitors; when she discovers Mrs Reed, she starts, as though she had been struck by lightning; the further they advance towards the front, the more she recedes, step by step; she trembles violently, presses her hands convulsively to her chest, and stares wildly round her as at a ghost; as Mrs Reed sits down, she says): Mrs Reed *(overcomes, by degrees, the hatred which rages within her, and steps, unobserved, round the table, and, from thence, to the background)*

Georgine (in an elegant travelling-costume of dark velvet; velvet hat and feather, and a costly boa picturesquely thrown round her neck; her stature is tall and imposing, her walk firm, but, nevertheless, graceful; her whole manner shows that she moves in good society. She looks around): It is very kind of you, ma'am *(to Judith)* to undertake Lord Rochester's duties, and receive his guests. His lordship must be busy?

Jane (from background, softly): That is Georgine! So it is she – *she* that is to be the wife of Rochester!   *(Music ceases)*

Judith (who immediately the visitors entered looked anxiously for Rowland): His lordship probably did not expect you so soon; he will immediately … *(makes a sign to Sam, who hastens out to right)*

Francis (ironically): One might really think Lord Rochester made an exception to the
    rule and spent time on his appearance.

Georgine (with a look of disdain at Francis): You seem to take Lord Rochester for a
    London dandy! No, he is not the slave of fashion.

Francis (with bitterness): My lovely cousin seems to study the character of her adorer,
    very carefully.

Georgine: No, on the whole, it is not worth the trouble! But I make an exception
    with a few of the details, because it is a pleasure to solve problems.

Francis (turns away from her and goes to Mrs Reed)

Jane (aside):   She seems to know him.

Georgine (throws herself into an armchair; in a haughty tone): Mrs Harleigh, I hope
    you will have the goodness to see that our rooms are soon got ready
    for us, for we are very tired.

Judith: I will do so immediately, my lady. (*Exit quickly out of door in back
    scene*)

[*Scene 6*]

Georgine, Mrs Reed, Francis, Jane

*Mrs Reed (who, at the commencement, has looked around her without taking interest
    in anything, becomes, by degrees, restless, as though she felt ill; during
    the dialogue, she unties her hat, and places it by the side of her; under
    her hat, she has a black lace cap. Her uneasiness increases, she at last,
    places her hand on her chest, as though she had difficulty in breathing,
    lets her cloak fall back, and draws her hand across her forehead.)
    (Music begins again)*: How warm and oppressive it is here.

Georgine (throwing off her boa): It is indeed, but it is your own fault, Mama, for we
    never can wrap up enough for you. You forget that it is spring.

Mrs Reed: And yet I am always cold.

Georgine (abruptly): That's because your blood is so cold, Mama (*Takes her hat off
    quickly, and throws it on the table by the side of her; her curls fall over
    her cheeks, she puts them back from her face impatiently*): It is really
    insufferably hot here.

Francis (in a low voice, bending down to her): It is your conscience, Georgine, that
    sends the blood to your head.

Georgine (laughing scornfully): My conscience? Ha, ha, ha!

Francis: That laughter is not natural. You can't deny that you liked me, that
    you raised my hopes before this Croesus came back. You do not love
    him!

Georgine: One often deceives oneself as to one's sentiments.

Francis (bitterly): Although I do not possess a Thornfield Hall, still I have enough for us both, and an unblemished name – Do you know what they accuse this Rochester of?

Georgine: No, and I do not wish to know it, either.

Francis (aside, desperately): But I will make sure of it, or I will not live.

Mrs Reed (with increasing uneasiness): Good Heavens, what is the matter with me?

Georgine (looks at her with astonishment \and rises/ – rather coldly): What ails you Mama?

Mrs Reed: I don't know, but since I entered this room I have been troubled with a dreadful fear, as though a disaster awaited me.

Georgine (carelessly): Good gracious.

Mrs Reed (rising): I tell you, Georgine, there is something uncomfortable, something dreadful about the air here! Let me go away, before a misfortune happens to us.

Georgine (with a smile of contempt): But Mama – what nonsense this is.

Mrs Reed (her hand on her forehead): It is no nonsense – I am ill.

Georgine (to Francis): Would you please call Tom; he can bring Mama a smelling bottle.

Francis: (turns to door in back-scene, and sees Jane): Ah, here is somebody! – will you be so good ...

Jane (who has struggled with herself, now approaches: her manner is modest, but firm): Can I be of any service to you, my lady? Lord Rochester told me to receive you.

Georgine (proudly): Indeed, that was very polite of his lordship. (*Measures her with a look of contempt*): And who are you to whom he has condescended to entrust with such a commission?

Jane: The governess in his lordship's house.

Georgine (scornfully): The *governess*?

Mrs Reed (who started with terror at the first words of Jane, listens to them without the courage to turn; at last, trying to command her feelings, she turns to her, and gives a shriek.) (Sudden change in music): Ah! I thought as much.

Francis (looks at her with surprise)

Georgine (astonished): What is the matter?

Mrs Reed (between her teeth): The hated one is near me.

Georgine (quietly): But do calm yourself! I don't understand you.

Mrs Reed (seizes her hand convulsively, and draws her to her; softly): Are you blind? Don't you see Jane Eyre?

Georgine (with a hasty look at her): Good gracious, yes.

Mrs Reed (softly): She will make use of her rights against us.

Georgine (after another look at Jane): She won't, if I know Jane Eyre rightly.

Francis (who, with increasing astonishment, has been looking at the party, says to Jane): Do you know these ladies?

Jane (calmly; she looks coldly at Mrs Reed, and their looks meet): No, Sir, this is the first time I see them.

Mrs Reed (starts)

Georgine (softly): You are right – it is Jane Eyre!   (*Music ceases*)

Francis (aside): This is astonishing! – They are evidently quite upset.

[Scene 7]

The former. \Enter/ Rowland.

Rowland (elegantly dressed, looks happy, greets all, and seems quite another man to what he formerly was): Ah, my lovely amazon, my amiable visitors. You have exceeded my expectations, and thereby deprived me of the pleasure of doing my duty as host. You are heartily welcome! (*They all bow.*) There is a shade on your brow, Lady Georgine; I trust I am not the cause of it. (*Shakes her hand*)

Georgine (drawing her hand away): Certainly not, Lord Rochester! (*With an ironic smile*): I only fear that your celebrated Mesrour will suffer in the public estimation, when it is known that you rode from Clarence House at the same time we left it, and that our poor carriage-horses have overtaken the fastest steed in England.

Rowland: Mesrour is less to blame than his master …

Georgine: You confess, Lord Rochester …

Rowland: I confess that, on the way, I had thoughts which were quite new to me, and therefore involuntarily caused my horse to walk.

Jane (aside):   Dear me!

Georgine (in a triumphant tone): That seems as though we were obliged to excuse and forgive you. (*Gives him her hand*) I will do so.

Rowland (kisses her hand): You are too handsome, when you are happy, for a frown to be allowed to remain long on your face. (*As though he suddenly remembered Jane*) But I hope you have been sufficiently well received not to miss the host.

Georgine (shrugging her shoulders with contempt): Who should compensate us for your absence? This young person? We do not even know her.

Rowland (with a look of vexation at Jane): Has she not introduced herself to you?

Jane: I had no opportunity, my lord.

Rowland (introduces her, without much ceremony): Miss Jane Eyre, Adèle's governess.

Georgine (sharply): Adèle? Ah, that is true, the little French girl you brought three years ago from Paris! So this little Parisian harlequin is still in the land of the living.

Rowland: Yes, certainly she is.

Georgine (with a forced smile): One might really have reason to ask: does this or that still exist at Thornfield Hall? For, when you are away, it is just as though the place were sealed up. I do believe the air must give account where it comes from, before it is allowed to pass through the keyholes! But I thought Miss Ellen Warner brought up your little protégée?

Rowland: Miss Eyre has been here for five months.

Mrs Reed (who has controlled herself – coldly): Really? – In what does she instruct the child?

Rowland (rather surprised): Well, in foreign languages, music, in short everything that is usually required of a governess. Miss Eyre paints, besides, and that much better than amateurs generally do.

Georgine (displeased): The character you, who are so difficult to please, give of her, really astonishes one. But Miss ... (*considering*) yours is rather an uncommon name, and I cannot quite remember it – where did you acquire all this knowledge?

Jane (dryly): At Lowood Asylum, my lady!

Georgine (looks down on the ground)

Mrs Reed: I was not aware that such worldly things were taught at that orphan asylum. I have always heard that the pious Dr Blackhorst only instructed his pupils in humility and religion, and taught them to work.

Jane (drily): So he does Mrs ... (*To Rowland*): Pardon me, my lord, but I have not the pleasure of knowing the lady's name ...

Rowland (biting his lips): Ah, I forgot – Mrs Reed.

Jane: Mrs Reed m[a]y be sure that, at Lowood Asylum, I learned all that Dr Blackhorst himself has ever learned, and that I am grateful to her, who framed this instruction for me.

Rowland (laughing): Miss Eyre, you are very easily satisfied. I do not know the circumstances, and, therefore, cannot tell how it happened; but so much I do know: that the party, who sent you on that voyage of discovery, cannot have loved you much!

Jane: I don't think so either, my lord, but it has been to my advantage, nevertheless.

Mrs Reed (aside): Oh the wretch!

Georgine (to give another turn to the conversation): But – I am really astonished that you paint as well! (*Smiling archly at Rochester*): Are you not somewhat partial, Lord Rochester?

Rowland (drily): Towards Miss Eyre! I cannot see what should induce me to be so! You shall judge for yourself. (*Goes quickly towards his room*)

Jane (follows him timidly): Oh, my lord, I implore you ...

Rowland (with a look of severity): No affectation, Miss Eyre.   (*Exit*)

Jane (stands in background, looking down)

[Scene 8]

Francis, Georgine, Mrs Reed, Jane. Afterwards Rowland.

Georgine (to Mrs Reed): Don't you think it strange that Lord Rochester takes so much trouble to convince us that this young person has talent?

Mrs Reed (looking straight before her): I never had any doubt as to her talents.

Georgine (in a low voice): Mama, you betray yourself.

Mrs Reed (as waking from a dream; in a low voice): Be careful, – this reptile does not lie on our path for nothing.

Francis (who has been looking at Jane, with increasing attention; aside): What does this mean? What can be the matter with the girl? there is something wrong here.

Rowland (comes back with the portfolio in his hand; goes to the table, at right hand side, opens portfolio, and says): Well, Lady Georgine, will you look at these drawings. They are really wonderful, for a schoolgirl from Lowood.

Jane (with an involuntary movement, imploring): My lord! …

Rowland (with an angry look): What do you want?

Jane (looks on the ground and stands motionless)

Georgine: Will you allow me to postpone the pleasure of examining these chefs d'oeuvre till tomorrow? Mama is not well, and I require rest myself.

Rowland (closing the portfolio, and turning quickly to her): What, you will not come down into the hall, where everything is in readiness for you?

Mrs Reed: I thank you, my lord, it is too late today. I am getting old; we have had a long drive, and I require rest:– come Georgine.

Francis (offers his arm to Mrs Reed): Will you allow me to accompany you, Mrs Reed?

Mrs Reed (taking his arm): Thank you, Sir Francis! (*Aside*) She or I, – one of us must retreat.   (*Exit slowly with Francis*)

Rowland (to Georgine): So you reject my society, this evening, Lady Clarence? Are you still angry with me?

Georgine (with a coquettish smile): This evening, I only require your arm, so as not to lose my way in this enchanted castle; tomorrow, when we have slept on it, we will see whether we can still be angry with you. (*Takes his arm*)

Rowland: You are no longer so, I can see it in your face. (*In a somewhat careless way; going*): Miss Eyre, you may go to bed – there is nothing further, today.   (*Exit with Georgine through door in back scene*)

[Scene 9]

Jane (alone; she has watched Lord Rochester's behaviour with astonishment and subsequent uneasiness; she breathes fast, her eyes flash, she looks long and silently after him): Today? ...Who can tell ...perhaps for ever! Is that Lord Rochester? He who let me wait two whole months for a word and a smile? Is this the mysterious being, whose thoughts seemed to me as a treasure buried in the bowels of the earth? (*Shakes her head*) No it cannot be him – or he is in love! – And it is Georgine who has so changed him! – What a serpent I have trodden on, since these evil spirits of my childhood again appear before me, and awaken all my bad feelings! (*Sees the portfolio*) Ah – my pictures! Now I could ... (*Goes to the table to take it, but starts back, listens and lets her arms drop*) There he is again! He has left her very soon ...

[Scene 10]

Enter Rowland, Sam

Rowland (in an earnest tone to Sam, as they enter): Mind that everything is {ready} quiet, here in the castle. The ladies require rest. I saw Grace Poole in the corridor ...
Sam (rather perplexed): I don't know anything about it, my lord.
Rowland (sharply): I did see her, although she slipped by me very quietly – what is she doing here, at this time of night?
Sam: I suppose the strangers have attracted her here.
Rowland: You mean it is inquisitiveness! (*Impressively*) Mind she does not commit any indiscretion! Tell her so, and drive her to her room.

Exit Sam (Centre)

Rowland (in going towards his door, to the night, sees Jane; starts): What are you doing here? (*Folds his arms and looks searchingly at her*) I ordered you to go to bed, Miss Eyre – Why did you not obey?
Jane (looking down): I was not sleepy, my lord.
Rowland: Not sleepy? It seems to me, you are stopping here to watch me.
Jane (about to answer sharply, but thinks better of it, and says calmly): Do[es] your lordship order anything further?
Rowland (angrily): No.

Jane (bows and goes)

Rowland (calling after her): Ah, by the bye, what do you think of Lady Clarence?
Jane (stops – without concealing her astonishment): I don't know, yet.

Rowland: Indeed? – It seems to me you examined her pretty closely.

Sam (comes back again, remains standing in the background, and listens with astonishment)

Jane: Yes, I saw her, but, if I am to say what I think of a lady, I must know what she is – not how she looks. Goodnight, my lord!

                                    (*Exit quickly out of door in back scene*)

Rowland (in front): She always has the last word! Not an inch does she give way, with her infernal humbleness. (*Stamps with his foot*) I never knew a more insufferable creature! Who can tell what she is brooding over now? Where is the key to this locked heart? Not even affronts can make her speak out. (*Turns to go, and discovers Sam*) Sam! – What do you want here?

Sam (who has remained standing in the background): I'm waiting for your lordship to go to bed, that I may put out the lights. It's blowing hard, my lord, and one can't be careful enough.

Rowland (draws a long breath): You say it blows? Yes, you're right. The wind whistles down the chimneys – a nice sound, when one want to go to sleep. (*Going*) Did you find Grace Poole?

Sam: No, my lord, she must have gone up long since.

Rowland (at the door): And my visitors?

Sam: They are all gone to bed.

Rowland: Very well, I'll follow their example – (*aside*) that is to say, if I can.

                                    (*Exit side door right*)

Sam (goes to the lights, and begins extinguishing them): Well I never! If I hadn't seen it with my own eyes I wouldn't have believed my senses. The proud nobleman hactually condescendin' to chum with such a Charity hussy. And she contradicts him quite cool, and when he goes on so, that we others are tremblin' and feels quite funny, why, she turns her back on him, and leaves him quite up a Gum tree! (*Remains standing in middle of stage, and clasps his hands*) We who is acquainted with all his secrets and piccadillies, *we* should try this sort of thing on … oh, my! Why I do think he'd collar us, and empty us out o' window! – She must certainly be acquainted with Witchcraft, for any 'cute man, hable to take a clear view of the case, must be of hopinion that no good can come of it. So that's my honly consolation under such a trial! (*Has put all the lights out, except the last, which he takes out of the socket*) What a hollaballoo the wind makes in the chimbley! It'll be a rough night for Grace Poole. (*Pauses in going*) They says he'll get spliced to that 'ere big lady. If that was only true, she would make short work of that Miss Heyre, but I'm afraid he'll never marry!   (*Exit side door left*)

(Music during the following)

(Darkness. Stage vacant for a few moments. Wind howls, but in distance.)

[Scene 11]

Jane (alone, looks cautiously in at the door in the back scene, and then comes forward): It is as silent as though I were the only living being in this large castle. *(She carries a small flat candlestick, with light half burned down \and holds her hand before it/.)* Thank God no one has seen me *(Goes to the small table, and puts the candle down)* I was not quite without fear, while slipping down stairs, for it seemed to me, as though a dark form hovered before me, through the corridor, to the door of his chamber. It must have been my \own/ shadow that alarmed me – How childish! *(Looks about searching)* I cannot sleep before I have my drawings safe. *(Discovers portfolio on table, and hastens to it)* Oh, here they are, how lucky he forgot them! – Oh my treasure, my only spiritual property he would expose to her! Her eyes, those daggers that murdered my childhood, should look at them with ridicule! No, I take what belongs to me. *(Violent gust of wind; she takes the candle from the table, and turns round quickly; this movement extinguishes the light in her hand, – lets it fall in her fright. – Darkness)* How dreadful! – my light has gone out! How wretched it is here in the dark … hush …I hear someone out there again! …(*Starts*) But have I lost the use of my senses? … It seems as though somebody were feeling his way along the corridor! … Now it has ceased …All is still again … I suppose it was only the wind … it must have been … what nonsense this is! Because a gust of wind, from the chimney, puts my light out, I am seized with a fit of trembling, so that my hair is ready to stand on end – and at Lowood, a storm has often lulled me to sleep. Fie, for shame! If Adèle were to behave so childishly, I should scold her, and now I am trembling with fear. *(Gropes about, in the dark, towards back scene)* It is absurd; I must try to find my way, through the lonely passages, up to my room! *(In going to door in back-scene, suddenly a hoarse, unnatural laugh is heard, twice, which seems to become more distant. Jane stands as though she were rivetted to the spot, and the portfolio falls from her hand.)* Good Heavens! There is that frightful laughter again! Grace Poole! terrible woman! How can you dare carry on your demoniacal ways here? Can no one, but I, hear that sound, which seems to come from the infernal regions? *(Listens)* All is quiet again. I hear nothing, but the distinct beating of my heart! … I dare not stop here, but the thought of going makes my blood creep. God Almighty help me from hence. *(She hides her face and stops a moment, as petrified; then raising her head)* But what is this? what a suffocating vapour surrounds me!

Why it's smoke! (*With a loud cry*) it is fire! (*Turns towards back scene*)
There, it strikes brightly through the door! (*Rushes to right hand door,
pushes both sides of it open, thereby disclosing a room lighted up by
red fire; clouds of smoke roll forward*) The door of his room is open! It
burns there! (*Rushes into the room, and disappears to the right; is heard
calling at various distances*) My lord! … My lord – Lord Rochester
– rise, or you will be killed! Do you hear? Fire!

Rochester (behind the scenes): What is it? … What's the matter? … Do let me be!

Jane: For God's sake, wake up! make haste, there's not a moment to lose, get
                up, quick!

(*Stage remains vacant, the red light in the background vanishes, during the discussion,
by degrees, and, at last, goes quite out, so that it gets dark again as they enter*)

(*Music ceases*)

[*Scene 12*]

Enter Rowland & Jane

*Rowland (in a costly silk dressing-gown; his hair hangs about his face and neck, as
though it were wet; one arm is round Jane's neck, and his head rests on her shoulder;
walks slowly and unsteadily*)

*Jane (has put one of her arms round his waist, to support him; in the other hand,
        she holds a silver candlestick with light; she is pale, but firm and
        energetic)*: {Here} \This way/ my lord! The air is purer here, and you
        are half suffocated. (*Takes him to the sofa*) Lie down, and try to come to
        yourself! I will call the servants. (*He sits down; she is about to go.*)

Rowland (breathes heavily): No, no, silence! Not a word … don't stir from hence!
        (*Seizes her arm convulsively*): Do you want to wake my visitors? … I
        should be the gossip of the whole country.

Jane (places the candlestick on the marble table): But, my lord, the fire …

Rowland: Hang the fire! You extinguished the little bit of fire, the bed-curtains,
                in a minute by pulling them down, and you nearly drowned me with
                the water-jug.

Jane: I was obliged to do so, my lord, else you would have been burned alive!
                You did sleep so very soundly.

Rowland (comes subsequently to himself): I suppose I was stupefied by the smoke.
        (*Considering*) I had thrown myself \half/ undressed on the bed, and
        began reading. Sleep overcame me, and I forgot to put out the light,
        so the flames …

Jane (in a firm tone): That light (*pointing to it*) is innocent; it was burning quietly at
        the head of your bed; but the curtains at the foot of it were in flames,
        and the door, leading to the passage, was wide open.

Rowland (surprised): Wide open? – Then I must have forgotten to shut it.

Jane: And a criminal hand took advantage of it for your destruction.

Rowland: Yes, yes, it must be so! But … who should … (*Looking at her*) Who do you think committed such a crime?

Jane: Grace Poole, my lord.

Rowland (seems to breathe more freely): Yes, yes, Grace Poole.

Jane (with horror): That woman, who laughs so horridly, seems to me a perfect fiend.

Rowland (in a tone of jest, to conceal his emotion): Very likely! Therefore you are a perfect angel, Jane Eyre, for without you, I should have been burned! Now, be sensible, and forbear talking – if you are able – about this stupid business! Do not betray me to my guests!

Jane (looking at him with surprise): I will be silent, if you desire me to be so.

Rowland (commanding): I do desire it, Miss Eyre! – (*Milder*) Promise me, likewise, that you will not seek to investigate this affair – that is to say, if your curiosity allow you.

Jane (seriously): I am not curious, my lord, and shall make no enquiries – but (*looking steadily at him*) won't you have this woman punished?

Rowland (dryly): That is my business

Jane (takes her light up from the floor, lights it from the one that burns, and says dryly): Very well, my lord! (*About to go*)

Rowland: One thing more! What did you want here, at this time of night?

Jane (collecting herself quickly, and taking her portfolio): My drawings, my lord.

Rowland (astonished): Indeed? – Hum! So you will not trust them to me?

Jane: Yes, to you – but no-one else.

Rowland: What? Lady Georgine is not to see them, then?

Jane: No, my lord. (*About to go*)

Rowland (aside, and seeming amused): That's comical. (*After a struggle with himself*) You are going without shaking hands with me! Have I offended you so much, this evening?

Jane (stops, but does not move from where she is standing)

Rowland (almost commanding): Well, give me your hand, and don't be so refractory.

Jane (goes calmly to him, and gives him her hand): There, my lord!

(Music to end of Act)

Rowland (grasps her hand, first with one hand, then with both): That's right! I thank you Jane Eyre.

Jane (draws her hand slowly back): There is no cause, my lord, I am no heathen that allows people to burn, when a can of water can save them. But, on one or two occasions, you said it was my fault that Mesrour fell with you, – so now we are on equal terms, my lord!

Rowland (with an impassioned look at her): We have been so, long ago – you must
have felt that, I should imagine. (*Grasps her left hand quickly, holds it
firmly in his own, and lays his arm on her shoulder*)

Jane (starts and stands motionless)

Rowland: You little girl, you really have the courage of a man[,] and the tact of a
woman! My pulse is hammering, and I'll be bound the blood does not
flow one bit faster through her veins, so little does she care for having
saved me.

Jane (head suddenly droops and she tries to withdraw her hand)

Rowland (starts without letting go of it): What! … How's this? … Yes, by Jove … there
i[s a] pulse to her very fingers' ends! … The light shakes in her hand!
… (*Joyfully*) her blood is more frank than her face – it betrays her.
Jane (withdraws her hand by force): Good night, my lord!   (*Rushes out C.*)
Rowland (stretching forth his arms after her): Little School-girl – you are more
dangerous, than you yourself think for! Jane Eyre, I very much fear it
would have been better for you, if you had let me burn[.]

(*Goes to his room*)

Curtain falls quickly for change of scene.

Act IV

[Scene 3]

*A large magnificently furnished drawing-room. To the right and left in front, small
divans with small tables before them. A little further back, likewise divans and arm-
chairs in various places, without too much regard to order. In Back-scene is a glass
door, and two windows looking onto a terrace with aloes; a few steps, from the terrace,
lead to the garden. Fine landscape in distance. Centre door closed. In background to
right is a sideboard with cups and silver services.*

*Rowland, Georgine, Mrs Reed, Francis, Col Clawdon, Edward Harder, Lady Clawdon,
Jane, Adèle, Sam discovered*

*(The ladies in elegant morning dress. A Servant and Sam go round to the visitors,
with trays, and take their cups.)*

*Sam (takes the empty cups to Jane, who pours into them[;] as this is the second time,
none of the visitors take anything)*

Georgine (turns the leaves of a large album, which lies before her on the table): I am quite charmed with this Indian album. I suppose the drawings are done by yourself, Lord Rochester[?]

Adèle (sits dressed up, on a little stool at Georgine's feet)

Rowland (leans over the corner of sofa towards her): There are all after nature, Lady Clarence!

Georgine: But it is quite incomprehensible to me, that you can live in our cold England after having resided so long in that wonderful land. There is so much life and cordiality in India, and how rich the verdure, and grand the scenery – they say, it is tr[ue] that, in India, there is a snake behind every bush.

Rowland (smiling): And you think that species of reptile does not exist in England likewise?

Georgine: At all events, they do not hide themselves behind plants. (*Goes to Edward, with whom she speaks in a low voice*)

Mrs Reed (works at a piece of embroidery, and occasionally takes a sly look at Rowland and Georgine): But very often behind books.

Rowland: How so?

Mrs Reed (bitterly): Well, there is a species of serpent that finds its way into fine houses, where they coil round the inmates, and very difficult it is to get rid of them, when once they have taken up their quarters there.

Rowland (pretending not to understand her): Indeed! To what class do these reptiles belong?

Mrs Reed: To that of teachers and governesses, which are so much the more dangerous, because they inoculate their venom to the young {persons} people entrusted to their care.

Jane (in a high-necked green silk dress of plain make and becoming, gives Mrs Reed a sharp look)

Rowland: Hum, perhaps you have gone through something of the sort yourself?

Mrs Reed (rather embarrassed): I beg your pardon, Lord Rochester, if I have failed to catch your meaning?

Rowland: Well, I mean that experience only, can justify anyone in pronouncing so harsh a judgment.

Lady Clawdon: Mrs Reed is right. One cannot be too careful in the choice of governesses.

Adèle (who sits and listens attentively, and looks at Georgin[e] with admiration): I have a nice kind governess, haven't I, Rowland[.]

Rowland (dryly): Yes, you have.

Adèle (jumps up, and clings to Georgine): You must also have had a good and kind Mi[ss] Jane, for a governess, as you are so lovely. I shall be [so] too, shan't I?

Georgine (pushing her away): You are creasing my dress, child, go away! – By the bye, Lord Rowland, I always thought you were not very fond of children.

Rowland (stretches out his hand to Adèle, who stands quite amazed, and draws her to him): More I am.

Georgine: What caused you then, to take this French doll under your protection? Where did you get hold of her?

Rowland (kindly to Adèle): Go to Miss Eyre, my child.

Adèle (goes dejectedly to Jane, and throws herself into her arms crying)

Rowland: I did not get hold of her, I inherited her, like this castle, my gardens, my park – (*takes a look at Jane, who is kindly occupied with the child*) and I am well satisfied with the whole.

Georgine (bites her lips; tries to give another turn to the conversation): Your park, Lord Rochester, is the most enchanting place imaginable – In summer, it must be quite a paradise.

Rowland (sarcastically): Yes, and that without snakes.

Georgine (sharply): Are you quite sure of that? – But these clumps of immensely high trees, this fine river and the old castle with its towers, have a truly romantic aspect. The six days we have spent here, have vanished as a dream.

Rowland (complimentary): I hope you will say the same of many others.

Georgine (sentimentally): Oh that will be very easy – for you always have fres[h] surprises in store for us. Where are you going to take us tod[ay?]

Rowland: Ah, unhappily, I have, today, so much business to atten[d] to, that I must request you to excuse me, at least for a few hours. Lord Clawdon has promised to do the honours of the house for me, during this time, and take my visitors to the ancient abbey. It also belongs to my possessions, and was erected by Henry VIII.

Georgine: Oh, that will be delightful, and Lord Clawdon will be our cicerone?

Francis & Edward: We will all be so.

Lord Clawdon (who is playing at Chess with Francis, says, sarcastically, making a move): Your ladyship must, unfortunately, content yourself with us.

Georgine (laughing): Oh, I dare say I shan't want any of you, when I once begin to think of Henry VIII, for, the fact is, he is one of my pets, and I have the greatest possible veneration for the jolly old tyrant.

Francis (disdainfully – making a move): Lady Clarence must be quite inconsolable that he has gone to his departed forefathers, for, if he still lived, she would, perhaps, have married him.

Jane (rises and prepares to go)

Rowland (looks commandingly at her, and then turns to Georgine): Lady Georgine would *not* have done so.

Jane (sits down again, and holds her head down)

Georgine (with life): Why not? Yes, certainly! For, if Henry VIII was rather tyrannical, he was a *man*, nevertheless.

Mrs Reed (who has been continually contemplating Rowland searchingly, and not taken much part in the conversation): Heaven {God} preserve you from such a husband!

Georgine: And why, Mama? According to my ideas, a man is very insignificant, if he have not something of the devil about him.

Lord Clawdon & Edward (laugh)

Francis (with a sharp look at Rowland): That's very near at hand!
Lady Clawdon (very gravely): Dear me!
Rowland (kisses Georgine's hand lightly): Bravo! (*Looks after Jane*)

Jane (sits motionless, without seeing him)

Georgine (becomes more and more lively): On my life, I am tired to death of these fashionable dandies – these poor \sickly/ creatures who take so much trouble with their killing faces, their white hands and thin waists, as though a man should have anything to do with beauty, as though it were not woman's prerogative, her dower, her natural heritage! – but a man is always handsome, when his motto is only: Strength, Mind, Honour!

Rowland (having again had a hasty look at Jane, who appears not to take the least interest in what is going on): There is a fine idea, Lady Georgine.

Georgine (rising): I'm handsome, I know, and have a right to be so; when I marry again, I'll have a protector in my husband, not a rival – he shall not divide his affection between me and the figure he sees in his looking-glass; for him, only *one* beauty shall exist, and that shall be *mine*! Am I not right, Lord Rochester?

Rowland (seizes her hand): You *are* right! But only a lady like you can think and demand that.

Francis (aside): By the Gods, she merits the punishment that awaits her.

Sam (who has been away, comes in again, and whispers something to Jane)

Jane (approaches): My lord, the carriages are at the door.
Rowland: Then I hope the ladies will not be too long at their toilettes, for you have a long way before you, and much to see, and I shall expect you at dinner.
Georgine: Oh, we shall soon be ready, come, Mama.
Mrs Reed (rises): You must really excuse me, I am afraid of the cold easterly wind.

Georgine: You are certainly the only one who wishes to be excused. Who will go with me?

Lady Clawdon, Lord Clawdon, Francis, Edward: We will all go!

Georgine: I knew you would! Let us go, and try to enjoy ourselves, without our host.

Rowland: You will succeed but too well.

Georgine (half aside, with a very expressive look): I am not quite sure of that! *(As she turns to g[o] she perceives that her bootlace has come undone.)* Oh, dear, my bootlace is untied. *(Throws back her curls, and beckons to Adèle)* Come, dolly, and do your duty.

Adèle (comes forward and looks at her): What do you want?

Georgine (impatiently): What [do] I want? I want you to tie my bootlace, to be sure!

Adèle (shaking her head): I'm not going to do that.

Rowland (irritably): Adèle! – obey!

Adèle: No – she is only handsome, but not good, I shan't do it.

Rowland (petrified, with a look at Jane): What does this mean?

Mrs Reed (coldly): This is Miss Eyre's way of bringing up children.

Georgine (measures Jane with a long look): She has certainly not learned submission of her.

Rowland (sadly): It really does not seem so!

Jane (in a modest tone, and with steady look at Mrs Reed): I have only been with Adèle for five months, and you know, Ma'am, that it often requires several years to make up for neglected education. *(To Georgine)* Forgive the child, and allow me to make amends for her fault. *(Puts, quickly, one knee to the floor, and ties the strings)*

Sam (shows savage joy)

Rowland (makes a movement as though he would stop her; fold[s] his arms; breathes deeply, and turns his eyes away, as though he could not bear the sight of this)

Georgine (is so astonished that she does not think of preventing he[r]): You are really too good!

Jane (rises, bows, takes Adele's hand, and goes towards background with her; seriously): Go to your room, Adèle.

Adèle (goes, with head down, out of side door right)

Georgine (softly to Rowland): Well, stern despot, I must say you have trained your serpent beautifully! one might almost be frightened of you … if … one cared less for you!

Rowland (finds difficulty in commanding himself): You are really most amiable …

Georgine (in a tone of reproof): Oh, Lord Rochester!

*Francis (has meanwhile taken a pocket-handerchief from off the sofa and hands it to
        Georgine; approaching her)*: Here is your handkerchief, Lady Georgine
        – Lord Rochester will allow me to begin to act the 'galant homme' at
        once. (*Offers his arm to Georgine; which she takes, after having waited,
        in vain, for Rochester to object*) I hope you do not intend to give all
        your day to Henry VIII, my lady.

*Rowland (gives his arm to Lady Clawdon, and goes with her, out of side door {left}
Right; the others follow)*

Francis (softly): This castle, too, has its mysteries, which it may interest *you* to become
        acquainted with.

Georgine (looks at him with astonishment)

Francis (continues aloud): They are all waiting for us, we must go at once!
Georgine (in turning round, touches the arm of Mrs Reed, who has also risen to go):
        Good bye for the present, Mama, au revoir!

*(She goes first, with Francis, Edward follows, Lord Clawdon and Mrs Reed come
last; he offers her his arm, but she refuses it politely; he follows with the rest, who
all go out of side door right.)*

*Mrs Reed (follows slowly afterwards; as she comes by Jane, she stops suddenly,
        without looking at her, in conflict with her feelings, she turns round,
        and says coldly)*: Jane Eyre, I must speak with you.

(Music)

Jane (starts as Mrs Reed speaks to her): With me?
Mrs Reed: Will you come here in an hour's time, when all is quiet in the castle?
Jane (looking calmly at her): I will.
Mrs Reed (goes slowly out of side door left): Very well
Jane (looks steadily after her): She wants to speak to me, to *me*? What can she want
        of me? Have we two not yet done with each other? (*Places her hand on
        her forehead*) To think that I cannot find the reason of what took place,
        that terrible night! Grace Poole still goes about here, as usual – what
        claim can she have on his forbearance? Is he afraid of that dreadful
        creature … what secret that must not come to light, can be locked in
        this castle, or rather in Lord Rochester's breast? … Oh! (*presses her
        hand to her chest*) now I begin to understand … Georgine governs him
        completely … he did not mind seeing my humiliation, nor did he stir
        an inch, to prevent it … quiet … quiet, tortured heart … you have not
        even the right to break.

(Music ceases)

[Scene 2]

Enter Jane, Adèle

Adèle (putting her head in at the same door she went out of, looks anxiously round,
then runs trembling, to Jane, and throws her arms round her crying):
Oh, Miss Jane, save me!

Jane (looks with mild reproach at her): Adèle, did I not tell you to go up to your
room?

Adèle: Oh, you must not be angry with me:– Sam kept me back! He took me
into the room down stairs, and threatened that Rowland would lock me
up in the east tower, because I had been rude to his sweetheart.

Jane (pained, sits down): Sam is a very wicked fellow; you be quite easy, Lord
Rochester is not a tyrant, you know that. Now don't cry.

Adèle (wipes her eyes): Yes – but Sir Francis' servant said that Rowla[nd] locked up all
the people, he is angry with, in the tower, as he does with his Lady!

Jane (starting): What – Whom?

Adèle (low and secretively): His Lady! He said everybody knew, that Rowland's Lady
was imprisoned in that tower!

Jane (in a firm, commanding tone): This is a thing you must never repeat, Adèle, for
it is a falsehood. Hush … there he is!

Adèle (imploring): Is that Rowland? … Oh, do come with me, then; I am so
frightened!   *(Runs out of the glass doors to the garden; Exit)*

Jane (following): Wait a moment.

[Scene 3]

Enter Rowland {Jane}

Rowland (meeting her): Are you here, still, Miss Eyre, will you not drive out with
the others?

Jane (quite calm again): I remained here to beg you, my lord, to excuse me. Adèle
must stop at home – it is a punishment she has deserved; but I do not
like to leave the child to herself when she has done wrong.

Rowland (looks searchingly at her): And I suppose you think I have no claim on you
for my visitors, and that you have already done enough for them.

Jane: At all events I know that they will not miss me[,] and I am indispensable
to Adèle.

Rowland (rather reproachfully): To Adèle? Hum … To no one else?

Jane (quickly): Oh yes, to poor Mrs Harleigh, for, at present, the whole burden is on
her shoulders.

Rowland: To no one else?

Jane (calmly): To no one, my Lord.

Rowland (turns away unwillingly): And … you have nothing to say to me?

Jane: No, my lord.

Rowland: Nothing to ask me about, Miss Eyre?

Jane: I shall never ask you about anything, for I am sure you would always tell me what I ought to know, without my asking, and that any questions, on my part, would not obtain information of – what you yourself desire to conceal.

Rowland: You are very subtle, Miss Eyre; and yet there is a question which, since the other night, is always on the tip of your tongue – one to which you have a right to expect an answer – (*impatiently*) why don't you ask? Is it not worth while? Are you not a woman, and, consequently, inquisitive, since you do not want to know why it was wished I should be burned to death – or have you forgotten that night?

Jane: If I said yes, I should tell a falsehood, my Lord, and I never do that.

Rowland (gloomily): So you will not ask, and you have nothing to say to me – (*looks straight at her*) nothing at all?

Jane: No; not now, perhaps later.

Rowland: Later! Indeed! But if I told you, now … (*Stops, walks a few paces and steps, on a sudden, up to her*) What should you say, if I were, all at once, to marry?

Jane (without showing any emotion): I should say you did {quite} right, my lord.

Rowland: Indeed? It would be quite immaterial to you?

Jane: No, my lord, I should be glad if you were happy.

Rowland (with an almost painful look at her): Really? (*In conflict with himself*) I say, Miss Eyre … you … (*Collects himself, and says dryly*) you can go.

Jane (bows calmly, and goes. Exit.)

Rowland (stamping his foot in a rage): She goes! Not a word, not a look betrays her thoughts! This Sphinx drives me mad!

[Scene 4]

{Rowland} Judith (enters by the same door as Jane went out of)

Rowland: Ah, it's you, Aunt! Are my tenants here?

Judith (much excited, but tries to command herself): No; but I have come to say a serious word to you.

Rowland (surprised): Oh ho! You do look serious; but I have something more important to do, than to listen to you, Aunt.

Judith: I think not! You well know that I never try to pry into your secrets, or give you advice – you will, therefore, see that I must have a special reasons, if I now do both! Now, do listen attentively to me. – When, after your Brother's death, you came into your Estate, and, immediately afterwards, gave orders, that the lightest rooms, in the east tower should be got ready for a visitor, and one dark night, you brought a veiled woman there, whose face none of us have yet seen – and ordered that nobody but Grace Poole should wait on her, and that she should provide liberally for all her requirements, I never asked a single question. You bid me not to let anyone know of the presence of the lady, and never to make any enquiries about her – I obeyed in silence, I kept your secret as faithfully as though it had been my own. Have I done so, or not?

Rowland (impatiently): You did your duty.

Judith: I did so without repining at the want of \that/ confidence which an old relative of your house might well have expected! My nights were often disturbed by the insane laughter which resounded through the solitary castle, and, in the daytime, I have had enough to do, to keep down the curiosity of the servants – you have *never* heard me complain, Lord Rochester! – but now you are working against me, and yourself expose the secret I have so carefully kept – you let a number of useless visitors into the castle ...

Rowland: I was obliged, sooner or later, to open my house to my neighbours, not wishing to encourage the absurd reports that are afloat in the county.

Judith (in a tone of decision): And I have come to let you know that these reports will soon be verified. This morning, very early, Grace Poole heard someone moving about the tower, and, when she opened the door, one of the visitors' servants was outside on the landing, who, in all probability, had been there all night, listening. He made off, when he saw her; but, this morning, Lea heard their servants telling each other stories in the kitchen, which I would not repeat for the world! You ought to know this, Lord Rochester, for you shall not blame me for divulging your secrets, when you yourself ...

Rowland (interrupting her): You need not fear such an accusation from me, Aunt Judith, for no one can betray – what they do not know!

Judith (turns away offended)

Rowland (goodnaturedly): Never mind, Aunt, I know you are an excellent woman, and that, as long as you have the management of my house, it is all right, and I am grateful to you for it!

Judith (breaking out): You're nothing of the sort, Lord Rochester, you think that money settles everything; but that is not what I care about. I want a kind heart at my time of life, and a cheerful face to enliven this gloomy place, as a gleam of sunshine – I had found this, and it gave me fresh life! But now you are driving Jane Eyre away, and I shall be alone and forlorn again. (*Strives to suppress her tears*) This is too much for me – it is cruel and unworthy of you.

Rowland (astonished): Who told you I was driving Miss Eyre away? I never thought of such a thing!

Judith: You never thought of such a thing? Well, Miss Eyre does.

Rowland (turning quickly to her): She dares not.

Judith: She dares not! We shall see! Did I not tell you, the first day {she} you came, that it is no use trying experiments with strong-minded people? Goodness know[s] what you are about with the poor thing! You send for her, whenever she is absent from the breakfast or tea-table, and, when she comes, you act as though she did not exist at all, and look quietly on while that arrogant Lady Georgine lets the dear angel tie her bootlace! That wicked Sam has told me all about it. I wanted to comfort her, when I met her outside just now – she did not see me – but I saw

          …

Rowland (fast): What did you see?

Judith: That she was a pale as a sheet, and that the tears were streaming down her cheeks. Then I saw how it was! They wanted to humble Jane Eyre, but they had not succeeded! She will leave! Believe me, I know her proud, sensitive character! Do make her stop, for the poor child's sake, and your own likewise.

Rowland (suppressing his emotion): Have you now fully executed your commission?

Judith (looks at him with horror): My *commission*? … Do you really imagine … (*much wounded*) oh, how unworthily you think of me and that noble girl! I pity you that you no longer, can understand a mind like Jane Eyre's. Let her go away. There is a curse on this house, and it is no home for her – and, if I have said anything that displeases you, let me accompany her. I shall be glad to go! One service I will yet do poor Jane Eyre; I know she weeps for you, because she looks up to you as a sort of superior being – but I shall make it my duty to acquaint her, that Lord Rochester does not deserve her tears; that will render the departure from hence very much less painful to her.   (*Goes quickly away*)

Rowland (calling after her): Judith – what are you going to do? (*Stops*) No!

Judith (waits expectant at the door)

Rowland (in a firm, commanding tone): Go and do what you like.

Exit Judith (impetuously)

Rowland: Let it be so! It must come to a crisis somehow. It's best as it is! … perhaps it will make her do something which will serve me as a clue. (*Exit door in back scene*)

[Scene 5]

Enter Mrs Reed (by same door from which she left. Looks around her.)

Mrs Reed: She is not come yet. (*Walks backwards and forwards*) She lets me wait for her. (*Lays her hand on her forehead, as though she had a fever*) Oh! ... it is hard to be obliged to come and meet her! But I must, there is no help for it! I cannot make out what is going on between her and Lord Rochester, but I can see there is something, and I cannot share Georgine's foolish confidence, as long as that serpent is between him and us. (*Excited*) With what pride she humbled herself before Georgine! ... Oh, she is very dangerous! ... (*Pauses*) I know she hates me, but hatred for hatred! I will speak without reserve.

[Scene 6]

Enter Jane {Mrs Reed}

Jane (pale, but calm, as one who has formed a resolution): You wished, Mrs Reed.
...
Mrs Reed (calmly): Approach... we will talk without hypocrisy. Time has no effect on characters like ours. We have hated each other, we hate each other still, and shall continue to do so. Dissimulation would be unworthy of us, and can only make us despicable in each other's estimation.
Jane (calmly): You hate me, Mrs Reed, and will, I regret to say, always hate me; but you do wrong in comparing your character with mine. You are older than I am, and cling to prejudices once formed, even when you see yourself that they are unjust, but I was then so young ...
Mrs Reed: You look just as you used to do; you have grown older, but you still have the same pale, disagreeable face, the same dark eyes which used continually to pursue me and my children with their wicked look. Oh, that silent face recalls, to my mind, the whole of that terrible time. What have not I, what have my poor children not gone through! Why did Reed heap this burthen on me, that plagued me from year's end to year's end, daily and hourly! – How relieved I felt when you were gone, and now, you are again before me, you, who have caused my conscience to torture me, and made me all but a criminal!
Jane: What? I ... How have I done this?
Mrs Reed: You have done so, therefore I shall hate you till doomsday, and you will likewise have the same feeling for me; therefore it is impossible that we two live under the same roof ... but rejoice, Jane Eyre! th[at] rich Mrs Reed {has} \is/ now {become} poor.
Jane (confounded): Good gracious! But how can you have become poor?
Mrs Reed: I was obliged to give, to my dear John, all I possessed; at least I sold

Gateshead, and went to live at Georgine's. I am still there, for I have nothing at all left – John has squandered everything.

Jane (clasping her hands): Oh, the rascal!

Mrs Reed (starting): He is my own son, and living in London is expensive – I could not bear the thought that he should want for anything. (*Pause*) Now I have only Georgine left, and when she marries Lord Rochester, I stop here. Do you see, Jane Eyre, that you must leave!

Jane (painfully): Oh, Mrs Reed! I have seen that long ago: but that it is you, who drive me from this home likewise, that the eight years at Lowood did not satisfy you, that it is you, who, for the second time, thrust the poor orphan on the world – this is hard, Mrs Reed!

Mrs Reed (quickly): You are not poor, you are richer than I am, if you yourself will.

Jane (staring at her): I don't understand you.

Mrs Reed (without looking at her): After you had been some time at Lowood, I received a letter from Madeira, from your Uncle Tybald Eyre. He requested me to let you go over to him; he said he had become rich, and would make you his heiress, if you would go and live with him there.

Jane: Good gracious! And why have I never heard anything of this letter?

Mrs Reed (as before): Because I could not bear the thought that you should be living in prosperity, while Georgine and I were getting poorer every day … and because I could not forgive you for putting me to the blush in the presence of Dr Blackhorst and my Brother! I have never been able to forget that you, who were silent, for so many years, suddenly spit your venom over me and my children, and said that you never would call me Aunt, more, and that there was nothing in the world you execrated so much as me! I have never been able to forgive you for that, and this is the reason why I still hate you unceasingly.

Jane (mildly): I have forgiven and forgotten, long ago, all the wrongs you have done me – do the same, Mrs Reed!

Mrs Reed (rising): Yes, when you leave here, Jane Eyre!

Jane (looks straight before her)

[Scene 7]

{The former.} Enter Henry Wytfield, Rowland.

(As Henry comes in, Rowland is seen out on the terrace; he opens the glass door, and stands still, astonished.)

Henry (enters in travelling costume): Ah, you are here, Sarah!

Mrs Reed (turns quickly round): Henry! You bring bad news.

Henry: I'm afraid so. (*Looking at Jane*) But we are not alone.

Jane (grasps his hand and says heartily): It is Jane Eyre who greets you, my dear
    Uncle Henry!

Henry: Are you Jane Eyre? Yes, by Jove, it is you!: and here, with you, Sarah?
    … So you are reconciled to each other?

Mrs Reed (scarcely hearing what he says): You come from Clarence House; have
    you any letters from John?

Henry (producing a letter): Not from him, but I cannot delay it longer … you must
    know all, Sarah, for perhaps the danger may still be averted.

Mrs Reed (trembling): Danger? What danger?

Henry: You never would listen to me, when I warned you, and were always blind
    to the faults of that dissolute fellow. I cannot spare you from hearing
    what is the result of your obstinacy. John Reed has absconded after
    having forged Bills of Exchange for £1,000, which must be cashed, if
    our name is not to be branded.

Mrs Reed (faints, and Jane catches her in her arms)

Jane: {God Almighty} Gracious Heavens!

*Rowland (who is about to enter, stops short on hearing Jane's exclamation, and
retires a few steps)*

Henry (hastens to Mrs Reed and he and Jane take her to the sofa to the left)

Jane (rubs Mrs Reed's hands and forehead): Aunt Sarah, compose your mind! Aunt
    Sarah, hear me!

Henry (softly): Ah – the unhappy woman does not yet know the worst – it is more
    than probable that John has committed suicide.

Jane (clasps her hands): Great God!

Henry (sternly): Say rather: just God! for she atones for the wrongs she has done
    you.

Jane (in tears): Oh, say not so. Her hatred was a disease, which Uncle Reed perhaps
    engendered by his immoderate affection for me!

Mrs Reed (moves and looks up): Ah.

Jane: She lives! (*In a wild and comforting tone*): Aunt Sarah, how do you
    feel?

Mrs Reed: You call me Aunt – you once swore you would never do so again.

Jane (weeping): I was then a wild and unmanageable child, and did not then know
    how badly I behaved to you … Aunt Sarah, forgive me.

Mrs Reed: I sent you to Lowood, although I had promised my husband to treat
    you as my own child … I did not keep this promise … I wronged you
    twice, and therefore, I have nothing to forgive. It is a misfortune, that
    you were ever born.

Jane (hiding her face in her hands): Yes, you are right!

Mrs Reed (rises): Something awful has happened ... I feel it here, here! (*Presses her clenched fist to her chest*) My heart burns like fire. I have loved nothing in the world but John, and he only could harrow my feelings to this extent. (*With a cry of anguish*) John is dead!

Jane (timidly): But ... you have a daughter yet.

Mrs Reed (starting up): Yes, yes! And she must be rich and happy! – Therefore you must go!

Rowland (stands with his arms folded, and makes a movement as though he began to understand what was going on)

Mrs Reed (with trembling hand, takes a pocket-book from her pocket, and opens it, saying): Your Uncle lives and awaits you ... There, there is his first and *second* letter ... I have kept them carefully ... I always thought the time would come when I could free my conscience of this burthen! And now the moment has arrived! Take these letters and go ...

Jane (taking letters): I will go, Aunt Sarah! if you will give me your blessing before I leave. (*Stretches out her arms towards her about to seize her hand*)

Mrs Reed (shuddering): My blessing? You hated John, you once wished to kill him. No, I cannot give you my blessing ... it would be blasphemy! ... But you go for Georgine's happiness ... you have my best wishes – I cannot say more, (*breathes heavily*) no, I cannot say more!

Rowland (with a movement of the hand, as though he had formed a resolution, retires)

Mrs Reed (continues): God alone is just, He will make peace for us. (*She is nearly sinking down, and supports herself on Henry's arm; he gives his hand to Jane and makes a sign to her.*)

Exit Mrs Reed (side door left, supported by Henry)

Jane (stands as though petrified, and exclaims in wild despair): Hatred, always hatred; never a spark of affectio[n] for the poor orphan! (*Looks after Mrs Reed*) What an unhappy being I am; I will go my solitary way between millions of human beings, to a far country, to a new hemisphere, to the only one, in the wide world, who cares for Jane Eyre! (*With stern resolution*) I am his! (*As she turns round, Rowland comes in through centre door.*)

[Scene 8]

{Jane, Rowland}

Jane (perceiving Rowland): Ah, there he is! It is the will of {God} Heaven!

Rowland (approaching): Where are you going, Miss Eyre?

Jane (in a resolute tone): I was looking for you, my lord.

Rowland: It must be the first time you have done so.

Jane: I have never yet had occasion to ask you for anything.

Rowland: To ask me for anything? – You? What can I do for you?

Jane: I request your permission to leave here, my lord.

Rowland: And why do you ask my permission to do what depends entirely on yourself and your own free will?

Jane: I promised you that I would not leave here before you dismissed me.

Rowland: Oh, ah, now I remember! Yes, you're right. Well, if you want to go, I dismiss you.

Jane: I thank you, my lord.

Rowland: But what causes you to form this sudden resolution? You are silent? I fancy, however, I can read your thoughts in that mute countenance of yours – Judith has told you I'm a monster, that I keep a poor woman imprisoned here, and that that woman is my wife!

Jane (calmly): She has not said so, but others have.

Rowland: And you connect the rumour with what occurred that night – it has occasioned gloomy thoughts, unpleasant doubts, on your mind, and confused your opinion of me, is that not so?

Jane: No, my lord. I knew it was all falsehood.

Rowland (suppressing a burst of joy): Indeed, and what has convinced you of that?

Jane: My esteem for you, my lord, and this esteem shal[l] be my support, when I am alone among strangers.

Rowland: This is kind, this is handsome of you, Miss Eyre, and in order that you may not be deprived of that support, eve[n] if we are to be separated for ever, there shall no longer be anything uncertain between us. – Fate or chance has disclosed to you a secret, which {nodody but we two} \you alone shall share with me/ and t[he] Justice of the Peace of this County{, understands}. You do not ask – and I therefore trust you with it the more readily. That demon, who would have burned me alive, is not Grace Poole, as you thought, – it is a Lunatic to whom I must show forbearance, and whom I have not dared to entrust to the care of anyone but Grace Poole, for she has disgraced the family name … she is …

Jane (clasping her hands convulsively; with tremulous voice): Lady Rochester!

Rowland: Lady Harriet Rochester!

Jane (looks down and stands motionless)

(Pause, during which Rowland watches her nervously, as though he expected an answer; he then remains with arms folded)

Rowland: She was my first, and, until a few months since, my only, love! I was the younger son, and, therefore, poor, but we loved each other, and she became my fiancée. I was sent to London for a year – when I returned, she had just been married to the rich heir, whom she had preferred to poor Rowland – she became …

Jane (in violent conflict with her joy, shouts): Your *brother's* wife?

Rowland (repeats slowly): My brother's wife – I should have killed him the same night \but they bound the young Cain/; my father declared I was mad, and had me taken on board a ship, and I did not come to my senses until I got to India – but my belief in {God and} my fellow creatures, was at an end, and I did not regain it. – My father died, my brother went with her to the continent, and, at last, I heard that *she*, too had died there – that did not affect me, I could not even forgive the dead. – Years elapsed, when I one day, received the intelligence that my brother had died. Death had made sad havoc among the guilty ones; I returned to England, took possession of my estate, and heard that Arthur, who had robbed me of my intended, had bee[n] fearfully punished. She had disgraced our name, and Arthur had taken her to the continent to conceal the shame. He was dangerously ill in Geneva, and, when he recovered – the wretched woman had gone off with a handsome Pole.

Jane (looks horrified and confused)

Rowland: Arthur wrote to Englnd, in order to hide his sham[e,] that his wife was dead, but, with strict secrecy, he followed the fugitives, and in less than a year afterwards, he met them in Paris. \In her presence/ He ran the seducer through the body, tore the child she had in her arms, from her, took it to an educational establishment, and brought her herself to England, in a state of insanity, when he shut her up, wit[h] her attendant, Grace Poole, in a castle, belonging to the family, situated in a forest. Arthur charged me, in his will, to take Adèle – that was the name of the forlorn child – to England, to bring the insane woman here, where the air is purer, and to keep secret the stain on our family. You know, Miss Eyre, how I have fulfilled this duty up to the present time.

Jane: I also know how you have been recompensed for your good actions, my lord – this woman wanted to murder you.

Rowland: It was not meant for me. She does not know that her husband is dead, and, with hateful instinct, she fancies I am her husband, and seeks to revenge herself on me, for the death of her lover. Thus she took advantage of the short absence of Grace Poole, to set fire to my bed, and, had it not been for this wretched woman, I should never have known, Miss Eyre, the manful courage that your delicacy and refinement of appearance conceal.

Jane (thoughtfully): Thus you have been the guardian of a woman who has deceived you, and father to a child whose mother marred your happiness. This is most noble of you, my lord, it is more than noble, it is sublime!

Rowland (dryly): It was not my intention, Miss Eyre, that you should criticize my conduct, but I did not wish you to blush when you thought of your former – employer. But – perhaps you will not leave now?

Jane:　　　Indeed I shall, my lord ... without fail (*vehemently*) this very day!

Rowland (looks sharply at her): Then that can't have been the reason why you wanted to go?

Jane:　　　No, my lord, it is not – I did not believe you had done anything wrong.

Rowland (scrutinizing): But why do you wish to leave? Because this woman, who hates you, your Aunt, desires you to do so?

Jane:　　　Mrs Reed? – No, I had resolved to do so some time previously.

Rowland:　Indeed? – How was that?

Jane:　　　You told me you intended to marry.

Rowland:　Fine, I do intend to marry, and that very soon.

Jane:　　　Then Adèle will be sent to a boarding-school, and won't require a governess.

Rowland (nodding): Hum; very likely. Georgine is not very fond of children, and you won't want to be in my wife's way, I suppose? She is too proud for you?

Jane (in a low tremulous voice): Not exactly on that account. I only feel I shall not be wanted here, when you are married, my lord \or 'I shall be out of place, here'/.

Rowland:　You may, perhaps, be right; I think so myself. But ... where do you intend to go? You have no situation.

Jane:　　　A situation has been found for me – I am going to my Uncle at Madeira.

Rowland (still calmly and seriously): Madeira? Hum. That is a long way, Miss Eyre!

Jane (scarcely audible): Yes ... a long way!

Rowland:　It is certain that a young lady of your sense and fortitude, does not trouble herself about difficulties or obstacles! But ... the Atlantic Ocean will be between you and your country ...

Jane (breathing heavily): The Atlantic Ocean ... yes ...

Rowland (mildly): And between – us!

Jane (softly as an echo): Between us!

Rowland:　We shall never hear from each other more.

Jane:　　　Never more!

Rowland:　We shall never see each other again!

Jane (trembling): Never – never again! (*Bursts into tears*)

Rowland (calmly): Why do you cry, Miss Eyre?

Jane (suppressing her tears): I love Thornfield, it was a blessed and happy home for the forlorn orphan. I have not been trampled on here, as I was for so many years before I came; here, I awakened to a fresh life; I have not lived here with low-minded people but in the society of those I love and respect; here I beca[me] acquainted with you, Lord Rochester! I see the necessity of tearing myself away from all this, but I feel as though [I] should die over it! Pardon me then, if I cry, my lord. (*Hides her face in her hands, sobbing*)

Rowland: That's all very true; but if it is so hard for you to lea[ve,] why not remain?

Jane (all at once lets her hands drop, turns quickly to him and says; with sparkling eyes): Remain with you … when you marry?

Rowland: Certainly. You can't stand the separation – so you must stop!

Jane (trembling; she {gets} becomes more and more vehement; until she resumes her original manner): But I tell you I must go away; I may be able to bear the separation, but, to live here longer, is absolutely impossible to me! Do you think I could endure the feeling that I was nothing to you but a supernumerary whom you kept from motives of charity? Do you take me for an automaton, for a \mere/ machine without sense or feeling? Do you think, because I am poor and friendless, that I have neither heart nor mind? Your pride deceives you – I have just as much heart and soul as you, and I understand you better than anyone else here, for they none of them resemble you – but I do {resemble you} my love; I feel there is something in my mind and heart, in my blood and nerves, which is congenial with you, which unites me with you mentally! {And had God blessed me with a little beauty and much wealth, it would certainly be as hard for you to see me go, as it is for me to leave you.} I am well aware that what I say is not in accordance with the ideas of human beings in general; it is not the earthly portion of me, but my spirit which speaks with yours, as though we had already passed the gates of death, and {our souls were before the Throne of God, equal as they are}-we stood within the precincts of eternity, equal as we are.

Rowland (whose chest heaves violently, and who has stood motionless, so as not to interrupt her, throws, suddenly, his arms around her, and presses her to him): Equal as we are! You are right \my/ little Jane!

Jane (astonished, but not deviating from her former tone, remains standing in this position): Yes, I am right – and yet not right, for you are married, or as good as married, to a being whom you never can love in earnest, for she is far beneath you! And now … release me. I have told you what [I] had to say, and now I can go where I will!

Rowland (pressing her tighter to him): No, Jane Eyre, it is too late for that! For the net is around you – now you are caught.

Jane (tears herself quickly away): I tear the net asunder! I am free, and my will is independent[.]

Rowland: And do you think I will let you go now, after having spoken in tha[t] way to me? (*Throws both arms round her*) Do you know I can break you like a reed, my little girl, before I let you go from me?

Jane (stands motionless in his arms, and looks calmly at him): You can, my lord; my
        body is weaker than yours, but my mind is stronger, and my mind is
        my own.

Rowland (looks at her ardently): Oh, how well she knows me, and how truthfully
        she speaks! I wi[sh] to take this powerful, refractory, noble spirit,
        which would escape fro[m] me, were I to destroy the cage wherein it
        is confined. (*Pushes her a[way] from him*) Well, then, your own will
        shall decide your destiny, Jan[e] Eyre! At last you have opened your
        mind to me – now you shall know mine. Since I saw you for the first
        time, since I perceived in you a character so much resembling my own,
        I struggled against y[ou,] poor creature, with all my might and main,
        but in vain, for, wi[th] irresistible force, you have drawn my soul to
        you; it is yours, my he[art] is yours, what I am, and what I possess are
        yours – take, therefore, the least of what remains, my hand! (*Stretches
        forth his right h[and] towards her*)

Jane (retreats a few steps): Oh, \jest/ {trifle} not with me in this trying hour.

Rowland (trembling with impatience and emotion): Jane – come hither to me!

Jane: I cannot, my lord, your fiancée is between us.

Rowland (fervently): I have no fiancée.

Jane: Then you have deceived Georgine, who loves you. .

Rowland: Georgine loves nothing but herself – and my property.

Jane: Why did she come here, then?

Rowland: To give me the key to your firmly closed heart! Obstinate girl! I intended
        that jealousy should help me! I have never spoken of love or marriage
        to Georgine. No one has any claim on my heart but you, my re-fractory
        school-girl! (*Getting more and more vehement*) I will have you! Poor
        and insignificant, forlorn and orphan as you are, I will have you, and
        no other! Don't look so disbelievingly at me (*imploring*) Jane, receive
        me as your husband, but quickly, don't take time to deliberate – say:
        'Rowland, I will love you, Rowland, I will be your wife!' Say it at once,
        or, it's all over with me.

Jane (trembling in every limb): {Are you} \Can he be/ in earnest? ... Rowland's
        wife – I ? I ?

Rowland: You and no other! Will you?– What?

Jane (in tears): Ah Rowland, my lord – my world – I am yours! (*Throws herself into
        his arms*)

(*Music to end of Act.*)

Rowland (embraces her in ecstasy): And I shall never let you go! (*Pause*)
                          [Scene the Last]

{*The former.*} Enter *Francis, Georgine. Lord Clawdon, Lady Clawdon, Judith, Mrs
Reed.*

Francis (sarcastically): Beg pardon, Lord Rochester – we really did not dream we
should come at such an inconvenient time, and witness ...

Rowland (turns proudly to the visitors): That with pride and joy I announce to you
that I have become engaged to Miss Eyre.

All (with astonishment): Engaged to Miss Eyre?

Mrs Reed: Shameful! I thought as much. (*Hides her face in her hands and stands
motionless*)

Rowland (embraces Jane): Yes, my bride, my wife, my treasure which my strong arm
hereafter shall protect – and God who has caused the hand of hatred
to lead the orphan to the embrace of love, will protect two beings who
require, for their happiness, nothing but themselves – (*embracing
Jane with one arm, and stretching the other towards heaven*) and His
blessing!

(*Tableau. Georgine with a look of contempt at Rowland, gives Francis her hand, which
he presses to his lips. J[u]dith shows her joy. All the others express their sympathy in
variou[s] groups. Jane has clasped her hands, and seems to pray.*)

Jane Eyre

or

Poor Relations

A Drama in a Prologue and Four Acts

founded on

Charlotte Brontë's Novel

by

'James Willing' & Leonard Rae
1879

Editor's Notes

The Text

The text exists in a single hand-written copy in the Lord Chamberlain's Collection of Plays in the British Library (Add. MS 53222.B) (see Figure 14). It is written on one side only of heavy, faintly-ruled cream paper of foolscap size, in a small, clear hand throughout except for the first three pages of Act III, which are in a larger, elegant copperplate script. These pages do not appear to have been inserted, since the small hand continues on the same sheet. The paper is in double folded sheets which have been stitched together but are now loose. Right-hand pages are numbered, originally beginning with the first inside page, but the title page has later been numbered '1' and all subsequent numbers changed, running from 1 to 62. The last two pages are badly crumbled at the right-hand edge but no essential meaning has been lost.

Part of the title is obscured by the licence ticket, which bears the number 149 and the following details: 'Name of play: "Jane Eyre" or "Poor Relations" Drama 4 Acts; Theatre: Park; Date of Licence: September 9 1879'. The title page also specifies 'Fee paid £2.2/–'. The title page reads:

[Jane Eyre]
or
Poor Relations
A Drama in a Prologue & 4 Acts
founded on Charlotte Bronte's Novel
Jane Eyre
By James Willing & Leonard Rae

From J. Douglass.
Park Theatre
August 20th 1879

The Lord Chamberlain's Day Book has no additional information except 'Date of Licence Sept 9, Date of Entry Sept 17'.

The text is generously but eccentrically punctuated, and where dashes appear together with commas or full stops I have removed whatever appears to me most redundant. Apostrophes are generally missing for possessives but present for plurals, and also appear in other odd places (eg ti's, whils't); I have normalized these. I have replaced full stops by commas and vice versa where the sense demands it. Question marks and exclamation marks are often indistinguishable and I have used whatever seems to fit the sense best. Capital letters sometimes follow dashes in mid-sentence, but not consistently, and so I have not preserved this usage, and have also removed some other capitals from the middles of sentences.

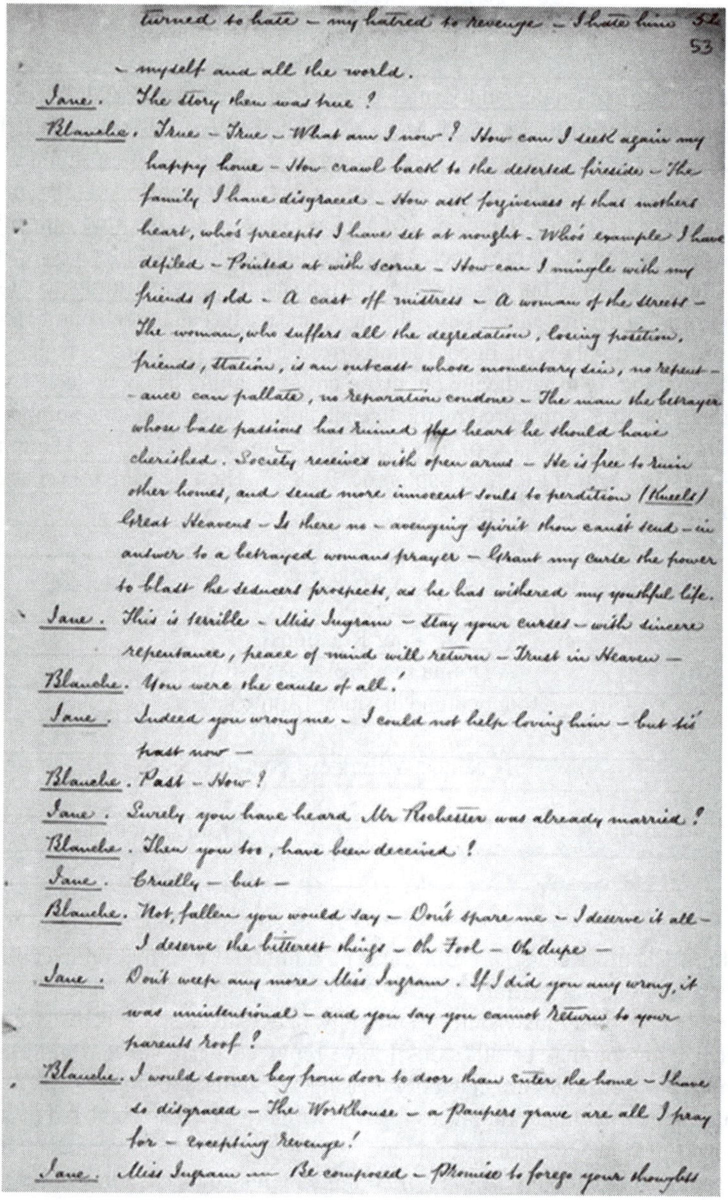

turned to hate – my hatred to revenge – I hate him 52 53
– myself and all the world.

Jane. The story then was true?

Blanche. True – True – What am I now? How can I seek again my happy home – How crawl back to the deserted fireside – The family I have disgraced – How ask forgiveness of that mothers heart, who's precepts I have set at nought – Who's example I have defiled – Pointed at with scorne – How can I mingle with my friends of old – A cast off mistress – A woman of the streets – The woman, who suffers all the degredation, losing position, friends, station, is an outcast whose momentary sin, no repentance can palliate, no reparation condone – The man the betrayer whose base passions has ruined the heart he should have cherished. Society receives with open arms – He is free to ruin other homes, and send more innocent souls to perdition (Kneels) Great Heavens – Is there no – avenging spirit thou canst send – in answer to a betrayed womans prayer – Grant my curse the power to blast the seducers prospects, as he has withered my youthful life.

Jane. This is terrible – Miss Ingram – Stay your curses – with sincere repentance, peace of mind will return – Trust in Heaven –

Blanche. You were the cause of all!

Jane. Indeed you wrong me – I could not help loving him – but tis past now –

Blanche. Past – How!

Jane. Surely you have heard Mr Rochester was already married!

Blanche. Then you too, have been deceived!

Jane. Cruelly – but –

Blanche. Not, fallen you would say – Don't spare me – I deserve it all – I deserve the bitterest things – Oh Fool – Oh dupe –

Jane. Don't weep any more Miss Ingram. If I did you any wrong, it was unintentional – and you say you cannot return to your parents roof?

Blanche. I would sooner beg from door to door than enter the home – I have so disgraced – The Workhouse – a Paupers grave are all I pray for – excepting revenge!

Jane. Miss Ingram — Be composed – Promise to forego your thoughts

Figure 14 Facsimile of page 53 of the manuscript of Willing's *Jane Eyre or Poor Relations* (1879), including Blanche Ingram's account of her seduction by John Reed. Reproduced by permission of the British Library: Add. MS 53222.B

Figure 15   Cartoon of Mr John Douglass, who wrote *Jane Eyre or Poor Relations* (1879) under the name 'James Willing'. Douglass was also manager of the Standard Theatre, Shoreditch, where the play was performed in 1881. Reproduced by permission of Camden Local Studies and Archives Centre

The Playwright(s)

The title page attributes the play to 'James Willing and Leonard Rae', but was actually written by John T. Douglass (see Figure 15),[1] who presents himself merely as the theatre manager. The explanation of this can be found in one of James Willing's obituaries:

> He was the son of the James Willing who founded the well-known advertising agency which bears his name, and when seventy years old was still 'James Willing, Junior', for his father lived to be nearly ninety years of age. [...] I don't know that 'James Willing, Junior', ever wrote a play, although I see that some of the obituary notices say that he did. What I *do* know is that for some few years Mr. Willing enjoyed a vicarious reputation as author – or part-author – of several of the sensational dramas produced at the Standard

[1]   The cartoon in Figure 15 is reproduced from an unidentified cutting in CLSL. It is signed 'AB', *The Entr'Acte*'s regular artist, but the Newspaper Library at Colindale lacks the volume for 1883 in which it probably appears.

Theatre, Shoreditch. And it came about in this way. James Willing was an intimate friend of John Douglass, then lessee of that theatre. In the year 1882 Mr. Douglass seemed, curiously enough, to be obsessed by the notion that the name of 'Douglass' on the Standard playbills as author meant bad luck for any play presented, always excepting the annual pantomime. He also was firmly convinced that the name of

> *'James Willing, Junior.' Meant Good Luck.*

And hence it fell out that [a number of plays] were all announced as 'by James Willing'.[2]

This explanation perhaps accounts for the cautious wording of a first-night review of *Jane Eyre*, when the strength of the play's situations, we are told, 'insured for Mr James Willing a cordial reception when he acknowledged on the final fall of the curtain the compliment paid to the adapter'.[3] A cartoon in *The Entr'Acte* in 1882 shows Mr James Willing, senior, saying to his son, 'What! Disgrace your family name, Jim, by writing plays! What next?' – both men, however, are shown with a knowing smile.[4] Willing is named on only four manuscripts in the Lord Chamberlain's Plays, including this one.

John T. Douglass, on the other hand, was a prolific playwright with almost eighty plays to his name in the Lord Chamberlain's Collection. He was the son of the John Douglass named as manager of the Standard Theatre on the poster in Figure 18. The Douglasses were a very numerous theatrical family, and when John T. Douglass succeeded his father as manager of the Standard Theatre, there were six or seven Douglasses employed in the theatre. His nephew, Albert Douglass, says that John T. Douglass was 'undoubtedly the leading spirit of the Standard Theatre – being responsible for the staging of all the plays, and author of many most successful dramas'. He excelled in pantomime production.[5] A.E. Wilson confirms that 'No theatre could have had a more inspiring chief'.[6]

He wrote his first play for the Standard in 1864 at the age of 22. Wilson writes that

> It was perhaps as an inventor and producer of sensational melodrama that his skill and ingenuity were best shown.
>
> Year after year the audience was thrilled and entertained by dramas which, though crude in literary form and more often than not preposterous and naïve in their stories and characterization, had the merit of introducing scenes of realism depicting disasters on sea and land, floods and rainstorms, ceremonials and pageantries and the festivities and occurrences of everyday life. Many of them were based on topical events.[7]

---

2   Unidentified clipping dated in ink (?) 26 July 1915 (NYPLPA: BRTC).
3   *Daily Telegraph*, 29 August 1879 (CLSL: HC).
4   *Entr'Acte*, 9 December 1882, p. 8. The caption is 'The Two Obadiahs', an ironic reference to puritanical attitudes. Unfortunately, the journal is too fragile for reproduction.
5   Douglass, p. 20.
6   Wilson, p. 124.
7   Wilson, pp. 118, 128. Pp. 129ff give many examples of ships sinking, balloons rising, real horses etc.

Leonard Rae does seem to have been a playwright, with five other plays licensed by the Lord Chamberlain, but he does not appear in any of the standard dramatic reference works, and his name does not appear on any of the printed material associated with *Jane Eyre*. Advertisements, playbills and reviews all refer solely to Willing,[8] which is the practice I shall follow.

Theatres and Performances

Willing's play was an unusually successful one, perhaps because of clever management by its author-manager, J.T. Douglass. In London, it appeared successively at two of Douglass's theatres, the Park Theatre, Camden Town (1879)[9] and the National Standard Theatre, Shoreditch (1881),[10] and then at the Surrey Theatre (1882).[11] It also toured the north of England, appearing in Leeds and Bradford in 1882,[12] and possibly in Oldham in 1879.[13]

The Park Theatre, 1879
There was an unusual delay between the date of Douglass's application to the Lord Chamberlain, on 20 August, and the granting of the licence on 9 September, and this perhaps explains why the first performance, on Wednesday 27 August, precedes the date of licence.[14] The play attracted considerable attention; it was favourably reviewed in the London *Times* and the *New York Times*.[15] The Park Theatre run continued into October.[16]

The Park Theatre was relatively new in 1879, having opened in 1873 (see Figure 16). It was well placed to attract both a high-class audience from the Regent's Park area, and a lower-class audience from Tottenham Court Road:

---

8   A review in *Entr'Acte*, 6 September 1879, refers to the adaptation as 'by Messrs. Willing and Percival' (p. 11).
9   Playbill for Wednesday 27 August 1879 (BPM). The play was followed by a 'Comedietta, entitled 'The Day After the Wedding', including characters called 'Colonel and Lady Freelove'.
10   *Times*, 19 April 1881, p. 4 col. A.
11   Playbill in Theatre Museum (4–15 December 1882). The play was followed by 'the Favourite Comedy Drama, entitled *We All Have Our Little Faults*'. The play was also advertised in *Era*, 2 December 1882 and *Entr'Acte*, 2 and 9 December 1882, pp. 2.
12   See below for details.
13   See head-notes to Paul's play for details.
14   Playbill for Wednesday 27 August 1879 (BPM). It is advertised in the *Daily News* for 27–29 August and in the *Referee* on 24 August for 'Wednesday next'.
15   *Times*, 1 September 1879, p. 6, col. B; *NYT*, 14 September 1879, p. 7.
16   *Era*, 24 August–5 October 1879; see also *NYT*, 28 September 1879 p. 2.

one could take the two divisions of society as being represented by the smart York and Albany Inn to the west of the theatre, and at the top of Park Street and by the Mother Red Cap, a busy tavern patronised by the lower classes at the bottom of Park Street. Apparently the theatre endeavoured to provide facilities for both classes. 'Luxurious stalls, comfortable private boxes, and a spacious balcony or dress circle awaited those who could afford to pay the higher prices of admission, whilst a "singularly roomy" pit was placed at the disposal of playgoers who limited their expenditure to two shillings for the lower and sixpence for the upper part of a playhouse'.[17]

Its management was taken over in 1878 by the Douglass brothers, John Thomas and Samuel Richard,[18] and an article in 1879 notes that they 'appear to be in a fair way to rescue it from the Slough of Despond into which it had been plunged by incompetent management'.[19] *The Daily Telegraph* confirmed that

> West-end playgoers who wish to enlarge the circle of their experiences might advantageously at this time pay a visit to that comfortable and commodious theatre at Camden Town, which, under the energetic management of the Messrs. Douglass, [...] supplies the inhabitants of a now populous region with a constant round of entertainments throughout the year.[20]

They made an energetic team, since Richard Douglass was a noted scenic artist. A review of the 1879 *Jane Eyre* notes that 'the scenes were admirable, one representing a wild Yorkshire wold under snow being particularly excellent and picture-like',[21] and *The Times* also notes 'the striking scenery'.[22] Albert Douglass records that in those days, 'the scenic artist was repeatedly called before the footlights, not only on the first night, but at every subsequent performance during the run of a play'.[23]

Stella Brereton (Figure 17), who played the part of Jane at the Park Theatre, was the wife of Richard Douglass,[24] and a regular performer at the Park, Standard and Surrey Theatres, where she excelled in pathetic roles such as Little Em'ly and Florence Dombey.[25] At the Park Theatre, she 'won golden opinions for the charm of her sympathetic Jane Eyre'.[26] *The Era* was also enthusiastic, noting that the 'playful, outspoken, frank, fearless nature of the heroine was represented with perfect truth

---

[17] Reynolds, p. 39, quoting *Daily Telegraph* 2 June 1873.

[18] Howard, p. 170. The Park Theatre burned down in 1881.

[19] CLSL: HC: unidentified clipping ('...*ic News*'), 15 March 1879.

[20] *Daily Telegraph*, 9 October 1880 (CLSL: HC).

[21] *ISDN*, 6 September 1879, p. 602.

[22] *Times*, 1 September 1879, p. 6, col. B.

[23] Douglass, p. 24.

[24] Douglass, p. 23.

[25] *Sporting and Dramatic News*, 25 December 1880 (CLSL: HC). This article mentions a 'front page' portrait which is probably the source of Figure 17.

[26] *Sketch*, 5 May, 1897, p. 58; see also HCT clipping: *Age*, 28 October 1882.

Figure 16   Interior of the Park Theatre, Camden Town, where Willing's play was first performed in 1879. Reproduced by permission of Camden Local Studies and Archives Centre

Figure 17   Etched portrait of Stella Brereton, who played Jane in Willing's 1879
               play at the Park Theatre. Reproduced by permission of Camden Local
               Studies and Archives Centre

and consistency [...] There was not the slightest indication of the "melodramatic"
heroine'.[27] *The Times*, while approving her 'fresh and sympathetic rendering of the
title role', carps a little about her pronunciation of words such as 'capreecious' and
'umberella',[28] but nevertheless the *Backstage* website confirms that Brereton later
acted in high-class roles, including Shakespeare, at other London theatres including
the Garrick.

Fanny Addison, who played the madwoman, elicited mixed horror and
admiration:

> The very difficult impersonation of the maniac wife enabled Miss Fanny Addison to
> achieve a triumph of realism. There are many opinions as to how far the representation of
> such scenes should be carried on the stage, and it must be confessed that Miss Addison's
> delineation of this fearful creature would hardly have borne to be elaborated to a greater
> extent. The fiendish glare of the eyes, looking as if they were about to start from the head,
> the wild, disordered appearance, the fearful clutching of the hands, and the unearthly
> tones, made one fancy for a moment that an inmate of Bedlam had broken loose and was
> revelling at the Park Theatre in the very worst paroxysms of insanity.[29]

---

27   *Era*, 31 August 1879, p. 12.
28   *Times*, 1 September 1879, p. 6, col. B.
29   *Era*, 31 August 1879, p. 12.

Addison, born in 1847 of a theatrical family, had made her mark playing the part of Rosa Dartle in Halliday's *Little Em'ly* at the Olympic Theatre in 1869.[30] According to the *Weekly Dispatch,*

> so completely did she identify herself with the terrible *Rosa Dartle*, and so vile and powerful was her invective, that the audience, forgetting the courtesy due to a lady, and oblivious to the canons of criticism, actually hissed her *because* she acted so extremely well.[31]

Amy Steinberg, who played Blanche Ingram, was the wife of John T. Douglass.[32]

The Adelphi Theatre, Oldham, 1879
It seems likely that Willing's play was taken to the Adelphi Theatre, Oldham, for the week beginning 13 October 1879, in place of the play by T.H. Paul which was licensed for that date. Details can be found in the head-notes on Paul's play.

The National Standard Theatre, 1881
Willing's play was advertised at the National Standard Theatre, Shoreditch, for 18 April 1881, but despite 'having achieved an enormous success', it was taken off in early May.[33] The Standard Theatre was the principal theatre in Shoreditch, and John Douglass, senior, became its lessee in 1848; the building in which *Jane Eyre* appeared was, however, constructed in 1867. The press was full of extravagant praise of this new theatre, which had a seating capacity of 3,000.[34] Figure 18 shows a poster for this theatre, now called 'The New National Standard', boasting that it was 'acknowledged by the press to be the largest and most elegant theatre in Europe'. The 'Mr John Douglass' described as 'sole proprietor' was our playwright's father, and Wilson states that he 'built the later Standard Theatre after his own design',[35] but a contemporary account confirms that 'Mr Douglas, jun., the son of the proprietor, has the chief merit of design in this very commodious and well-proportioned theatre'.[36]

---

[30] Pascoe, pp. 2–3.
[31] Quoted in Pascoe, p. 3.
[32] Douglass, p. 22. Edward Price, who played Rochester, died in 1895 at the age of 55 (*EA&A*, 1896, p. 86).
[33] *Era*, 16, 23 and 30 April and 7 May 1881; see also *ISDN* 16, 23 and 30 April and 7 May 1881, and *Referee*, 24 April 1881, p. 3.
[34] Howard, p. 222. Wilson quotes some of these descriptions (p. 120).
[35] Wilson, p. 56.
[36] *Daily Telegraph*, 21 December 1867, p. 5; descriptions can also be found in *Builder*, 28 December 1867, pp. 941–2; 1 January 1876, p. 4; *ISDN*, 5 July 1879, is less enthusiastic.

In 1874 John T. and Richard Douglass took over the management of the theatre from their father, who died in 1879.[37] J.T. Douglass,

> a member of a family of Victorian amplitude, was lucky in being able to command the services of quite an army of other Douglasses [...] Every nook of the theatre from the front of the house to behind the scenes seems to have had its Douglass in charge.[38]

John T. Douglass was widely recognized as having improved not only the physical environment of the theatre but also its standard of performance. An *Illustrated London News* preview in 1867 expects 'to find the most elevated views governing the course of the management',[39] and the opening night raised only a little critical caution:

> A more beautiful, commodious and comfortable temple of the drama it is difficult to conceive and it constitutes in itself a sight well worth seeing. [...] True, the kind of drama which the audiences attending the theatre best appreciate is not perhaps adapted to suit the very intellectual playgoers who rejoice in the 'legitimate' [but] the boxes are occupied by an audience whose evident respectability would do credit to any theatre in the metropolis.[40]

Although 'it usually kept a good stock company' the Standard 'was the first of the East End houses that attracted the stars from the west and West End plays',[41] and 'the theatre was splendidly equipped for the accommodation of the most illustrious visitors. Its resources were almost unlimited and certainly superior to those of many of the houses further west'.[42] Richard Douglass, the scenic artist, played a large part in this success, 'excelling in the painting of landscapes and still-water scenes, during a period in which the art of stage decoration of the realistic, photographic kind was possibly at its highest'.[43]

Davis and Emeljanow, drawing on contemporary police reports, show that the 'Standard drew tradesmen, mechanics, their children, and silk weavers from Spitalfields', with a high proportion of Jews among the audience, but there was little evidence of disorder or depravity in this theatre.[44] In 1869 the *Entr'acte* congratulated the Douglasses:

---

37   Wilson, p. 124. John Douglass sen. was manager from 1848 to 1861 and 1864 to 1874;
     John T. Douglass and Samuel Richard Douglass were joint lessees from 1874 to 1884
     (Howard, p. 222).
38   Wilson, p. 124. Wilson states that Douglass sen. was 'one of a family of twenty-one
     children', most of them 'connected with the theatre' (p. 56).
39   *ILN*, 16 February 1867, Vol. 50, p. 170.
40   *Theatrical Journal,* quoted in Wilson, p. 121.
41   Baker, p. 408.
42   Wilson, p. 122
43   Wilson, p. 125.
44   Davis and Emeljanow, pp. 48–9, 51.

Figure 18   Poster for the Standard Theatre, Shoreditch, where Willing's play was produced in 1881. Reproduced by permission of V&A Images/Victoria and Albert Museum

The management of this house has completely demonstrated the fact that the population of the eastern districts of the metropolis is quite able to appreciate plays of the highest class when represented by artists of real ability. When a dramatic poem like 'Manfred'... attracts immense audiences to a house situated in Shoreditch, it is sufficient proof that people at the East-end can enjoy works that do not depend for their interest on the apotheosis of a thief, nor upon the introduction of a real pump or of a real potato-gun. Anyone glancing round the dress-circle of the National Standard might well ask himself if he had not by some misconception entered a new West-end theatre built with a view to eclipsing Drury Lane.[45]

Albert Douglass confirms that it attracted 'the residents of Hackney and Kingsland (very opulent districts then) [...] And what an audience! – keen – critical – pulsating with life and eager to seize every point'.[46]

The actress Bella Pateman, a regular and 'beloved' member of the company (famous for her performance of "Lady Isabel" in "East Lynne"')[47] played the part of Jane in the National Standard performances.[48] Albert Douglass is enthusiastic about her performance, but Joseph Knight is less so, describing her performance in another play as 'terribly artificial' so that 'the wheels and springs of her art are always open to the observer'.[49] Alice Raynor, who played the young Jane in this performance, played the adult role in the northern tour and at the Surrey Theatre in 1882.[50]

North of England Tour, 1882

Willing's play was performed by 'Mr Douglas's London Company' at the Theatre Royal, Leeds from 12 to 14 July 1882,[51] and was reviewed, with bland approval, in *The Era*.[52] This Theatre Royal was built in 1876 in the ashes of the former Royal Amphitheatre, taking its name from an earlier Theatre Royal in Hunslet Lane, which had burned down the previous year.[53] The following week the play moved to Bradford,

---

45 Davis and Emeljanow, p. 53, quoting *Entr'acte*, 10 July 1869.
46 Douglass, p. 45.
47 Douglass, pp. 52–3.
48 *Times*, 19 April 1881, p. 4, co. A.
49 Knight, p. 174.
50 *Era*, 15 and 22 July and 9 December 1882; *Yorkshireman*, 22 July 1882, p. 60.
51 *The Yorkshire Post and Leeds Intelligencer*, 12–14 July 1882. *Yorkshireman* (15 July 1882) reports that *Jane Eyre, or Poor Relations*, 'which was here some eight months ago, is on a return visit', but I have found no evidence of the earlier visit. I am grateful to Shirley Bastow for bringing this performance to my attention and providing a copy of the notice.
52 *Era*, 15 July 1882.
53 Preedy, pp. 10, 12–13, 15–17; *Discover Leeds* (accessed 23 May 2005) documents the complicated history of the Leeds theatres. Preedy has pictures of the Theatre Royal; Abbey House Museum has a model of its auditorium in store, which the staff kindly showed me.

where it appeared at Pullan's Theatre of Varieties from 17 to 22 July 1882.[54] *The Yorkshireman*, though guarded in its estimation of the play, nevertheless feels that 'the mounting of the piece reflects great credit on Mr Pullan'.[55] Pullan's Varieties was built in 1868 as a music hall: 'a large wooden building 120ft. long by 72ft. wide and reputed "to hold 3,000". [...] Great "Stars" of the music hall firmament who appeared at Pullan's Music Hall included Blondin (The Hero of Niagara)'.[56] In this context, a drama of the quality of *Jane Eyre*, performed by a London company, was clearly an ambitious undertaking, but it seems that this was one of the very first performances in a theatre which had re-opened on 15 July after being 'vastly improved' by new decoration and an enlargement of the stage.[57] *The Era* claimed that the play 'is known to the habitués of the house, having been here some months ago' with 'nearly the same' company, but I have not found any evidence of this earlier visit. The reviewer found the plot 'interesting', the dialogue 'smart and effective' and the staging and scenery 'very satisfactory'.[58]

Surrey Theatre, 1882
In December, 1882, Willing's play was back in London, at the Surrey Theatre, 'for Two Weeks only';[59] a playbill dated 4–15 December 1882 announces Willing's 'Romantic, Interesting, and Sympathetic Drama'.[60] A lengthy *Era* notice effectively reproduces the Park Theatre review of 1879,[61] adding that

> the acting of the piece at the Surrey is not, except in one instance, up to the standard of that which has been witnessed in connection with it elsewhere, and consequently some of the interest is sacrificed, some of the business becomes tedious, and there is a temptation among the irreverent gods to ridicule that which should prove most impressive. The exception alluded to is in the character of the heroine, which finds a really able exponent in Miss Alice Raynor.[62]

The Referee is more generous, adding that 'Miss Lizzie Claremont [as] the maniac wife [...] shrieks beautifully',[63] and *The Stage* expands on this, arguing that

---

54 *Bradford Daily Telegraph*, 17–22 July 1882; I am grateful to Shirley Bastow for bringing this performance to my attention. See 'Reception' for an account of *Bradford Daily Telegraph* review (22 July 1882).
55 *Yorkshireman*, 22 July 1882, p. 60.
56 Mellor, pages not numbered.
57 *Era*, 15 July 1882, p. 9; also *Yorkshireman*, 15 July 1882.
58 *Era*, 22 July, 1882, p. 9.
59 *Era*, 2 December 1882; see also *Entr'Acte*, 2 and 9 December 1882, p. 2, and *Referee*, 3 December 1882, p. 3.
60 London Theatre Museum.
61 See *Era*, 31 August 1879, p. 12.
62 *Era*, 9 December 1882, p. 6.
63 *Referee*, 10 December 1882, p. 3.

Miss L. Claremont gives a remarkable instance of versatility and power in her double of Mrs Reed and Rochester's mad wife. Anything more literally blood-curdling than her screams and pantomime in the mad scene would be difficult to conceive; her performance is truly tragic.[64]

The Surrey Theatre may have been past its prime by 1870,[65] but its 1882 audience, unlike the 1867 audience described in this volume, was at least listening to the actors![66]

Reception of the Play

The Park Theatre debut of the play was immediately successful: by 7 September, the management boasts that 'the Public, by nightly crowding the Theatre, have endorsed the unanimous opinion of the Press that "Poor Relations" is one of the most exciting Dramas ever produced'.[67] *The Illustrated Sporting and Dramatic News* agreed, finding in Willing's version 'all those melo-dramatic elements which keep an audience excited and interested in the progress of the incidents from beginning to end'.[68] *The Referee* confirms that

Willing has done his best to pile up the agony, and has gone in for something startling in the way of realism. But Park audiences I fancy can do with a strong flavour to their dramatic dishes, and so perhaps I ought not to object.[69]

Other parts of 'the Press', however, had some reservations about the sensational plot, the unnecessary comic interpolations, and some aspects of the writing. *The Graphic* critic feels that the adaptor 'has handled his materials with some skill', but nevertheless,

the piece has little refinement about it. The incidents are of the startling exciting kind; and Mr Willing has introduced dialogue which certainly does not add much to the literary value of his play. Mr Rochester's habitual associates here seem to be persons of strange manners. [...] The gentlemen tell the ladies they are escorting home in a shower that they 'like rain, for it makes the girls cling to your arm so tight'.

The reviewer also objects to the 'silly conversation' about the clock which is introduced 'on the very brink of the serious *dénouement* of his piece'.

---

64 *Stage*, 8 December 1882, p. 9.
65 Davis and Emeljanow, p. 31.
66 Cf. *Daily Telegraph*, 27 December 1867, p. 3.
67 *Era*, 7, 14 and 21 September 1879.
68 *ISDN*, 6 September 1879, p. 602.
69 *Referee*, 31 August 1879, p. 3.

The play generally, however, is a more meritorious production than might be inferred from these drawbacks. Indeed, the prologue is an excellent example of the art of clear exposition of the basis of a story; and tokens of genuine dramatic art are elsewhere conspicuously displayed.[70]

Another reviewer praised 'the scene between John Reed's forsaken mistress, and the girl she has formerly scorned, being pathetic to a degree'.[71]

Most reviewers, however, focused on the part written for the madwoman. *The Times* found that

> the play abounds in strong situations and is sensational in the highest degree. The maniac wife is played in the most forcible and realistic way by Miss Fanny Addison. If the art which forbids Medea to kill her children in public permits the horrible creature to appear at all, she must be presented as Miss Addison shows her.[72]

The Entr'Acte described the adaptation as 'of a somewhat flesh-creeping and melancholy kind', and predicted that audiences unfamiliar with the novel would be dissatisfied with the muted ending. Nevertheless 'lovers of the horrible and ghastly [...] will be pretty certain to be well-pleased with this piece'. This reviewer, while finding Stella Brereton 'excellent', found Fanny Addison's madwoman '*the* feature of the performance':

> the cries and screams of this maniac woman – [...] made before the audience are permitted to see her – are so real, that a sense of relief is obtained when she makes her appearance, though her entry is made in such a style as would not in an ordinary way be calculated to becalm.[73]

The Era thought the play contained

> details likely to jar upon the feelings of a modern audience. For example, the fearful appearance of the maniac wife in one scene almost curdles one's blood by its appalling realistic character, and the incident of the brother rushing from the mad woman's chamber with his hand torn and bleeding cannot be otherwise than startling and somewhat repulsive.[74]

A retrospective article in 1897 speaks of the absence of classical restraint in this 'great sensation drama':

> Mr Willing had apparently forgotten the Horatian maxim not to exhibit horrors *coram populo*, for the wild appearance of Rochester's maniac wife, and the bloodstained hand

---

70   *Graphic*, 30 August 1879, p. 199.
71   HCT clipping: *The Age*, 28 October 1882.
72   *Times*, 1 September 1879, p. 6, col. B.
73   *The Entr'Acte*, 6 September 1879, p. 11.
74   *Era*, 31 August 1879, p. 12.

of her brother, Richard Mason, were both considered to overstep somewhat the limits of stage realism as marked out in far-away 1879.

This commentator did, however, approve of Willing's changes to the plot:

> The second [act], the most dramatic in the play, had an effective conclusion, differing considerably from the analogous passage in Charlotte Brontë's work; the marriage being prevented, not by the declaration in the church, but by the intervention of Mason, who proclaimed the truth just as his frenzied sister was rushing in upon Rochester and Jane, the latter already decked out in her bridal attire.[75]

The Standard Theatre production of 1881 was briefly reviewed in *The Times*[76] and at more length in *The Stage*, which generally approved of Willing's adaptation – including the comic interventions – singling out for special mention Fanny Addison's 'vividly lifelike' performance in the role of the madwoman.[77] The play was also reviewed during its tour of the north of England, a Bradford critic commenting particularly that 'Mr. F. Percival was very amusing as the "Rev. William Brocklehurst"'.[78] This was clearly a difficult part to play well. A retrospective review judges that 'the character is a badly drawn one, and it would take a very clever actor, indeed, to reconcile an intelligent audience to the inconsistencies of the Chadband-Stiggins-Brocklehurst given us in the adaptation'. The reviewer recalls that Brocklehurst's peculiarities 'were exaggerated to the borders of absurdity by its original impersonator',[79] and *The Era* confirms that this actor, Mr Odell, had 'lent himself to positive vulgarity to win the applause of the gods'.[80]

Uniquely among the plays in this volume, Willing's version has been analysed in a twentieth-century academic journal, and from a feminist point of view. Helena Michie, in 'There is No Friend Like a Sister', focuses on Jane's relationship with Blanche Ingram:

> While in the novel Jane comes to a sense of herself as heroine and subject in the context of a heterosexual teleology that allows her to end her narrative alone with Rochester and her son, the play, in constructing an alternative family for Jane that is based on sisterhood rather than marriage, brings to the foreground the novel's vexed and ambivalent preoccupation with relations between women.[81]

---

75   *Sketch*, 5 May 1897, p. 58.
76   *Times*, 19 April 1881, p. 4 col. A.
77   *Stage*, 29 April 1881, pp. 7–8, p. 8.
78   *Bradford Weekly Telegraph*, 22 July 1882. I am grateful to Shirley Bastow for providing a copy of the review.
79   HTC: unidentified review of performance at New-Cross Public Hall, Saturday 15 October, 'some forty years' after the first showing.
80   *Era*, 31 August 1879, p. 12.
81   Michie, p. 401.

Distinctive Features of the Play

- The Prologue at Gateshead is in addition to the four acts, unlike Birch-Pfeiffer's play, but is otherwise similar: Jane forgives her aunt, but not vice versa.
- Rochester's guests are Ingrams and Eshtons, with the addition of John Reed.
- Brocklehurst (who does not appear in the Prologue) is comic and inflated, a vehicle for satire against hypocritical charities.
- Rochester is distinguished by his respect for Jane despite her poverty.
- Jane refuses fine clothes.
- John Reed is Rochester's rival for Blanche Ingram.
- Rochester proposes to Jane and her 'equal as we are' speech is omitted.
- Jane's flight from Rochester is explicitly to protect her 'honour'.
- Brocklehurst, who takes Jane in after her flight, also offers marriage.
- Blanche Ingram elopes with John Reed, who abandons her; a contrast is drawn between her 'fallen' status and Jane's purity (see Figure 14).
- Jane offers half her wealth and 'sisterhood' to Blanche.
- The scenes at Fearndean [*sic*] are a crescendo of activity with:
  o a farcical interlude in which Brocklehurst describes a clock and Rochester thinks he is talking about Jane;
  o John Reed's attempt to steal Jane's legacy;
  o Rochester's revelation that he has only pretended blindness to test Jane's devotion.

Jane Eyre or Poor Relations by James Willing

Characters in Prologue

Mrs Reed
Georgina
Jane Eyre   } Children
John Reed
Miss Abbot

Characters in Drama

Fairfax Rochester
Mr Brocklehurst
John Reed
Colonel Dent
Lord Ingram   } Guests
Mr Eshton
Mr Mason

Jane Eyre
Blanche Ingram
Mary Ingram
Dowager Lady Ingram
Louisa Eshton
Amy Eshton
Grace Poole
Bertha Mason
Mrs Fairfax
Geogina Reed
Adèle

Prologue

Mrs Reed, Georgina and Eliza discovered

Mrs Reed: It's of no use seeking a quarrel. I know Jane's temper well enough.
Georgina: Little upstart. Having children of your own, I wonder how you could burden yourself with your husband's sister's child.
Mrs Reed: My dear Georgina, all regrets now are useless. I have repented my promise ever since I made it. She was Reed's sister's child and a great favourite with him; in his last illness, he had it brought continually to his bedside; and but an hour before he died, he bound me by vow to

keep the creature. I would as soon have been charged with a pauper brat out of a workhouse: but he was weak, naturally weak. John does not at all resemble his father; I am glad of it: John is like me and like my brothers.

Georgina: She's always quarrelling and a regular little fiend of a temper. Look at her the other day when you put her in the Red Room for her impertinence; she waited until we were all asleep and then, shaking the door violently, screamed at the top of her voice – she had seen a ghost all on purpose to frighten us. If she had been in pain one would have excused it, but she only wanted to prevent our sleep. I know her wicked tricks.

Miss Abbot: I suppose you locked her up because she was a naughty girl.

Mrs Reed: Exactly. You see I have a very difficult duty to perform, and not by any means a pleasant one in bringing up this girl – in my family. She has neither talents or application excepting for mischief. And she is always quarrelling with my own children – on the occasion Georgina was mentioning the little fury shrieked so loudly and worked herself into such a passion that she became delirious and we had to send for a doctor to her.

Miss Abbot: Your family physician?

Mrs Reed: No, indeed – I sent to the apothecary who usually physics the servants when any of them are ailing – I must have been mad to promise Reed to take care of her.

Miss Abbot: Mr Reed has been dead about nine years I think?

Mrs Reed: Yes –

Georgina: And knowing how deeply Mamma feels his loss, that little wretched Jane would insist on saying that she had seen uncle Reed's ghost because the Red Room was the one in which he died. Oh, she is artful. That girl will come to a bad end, she's no gratitude in her.

Mrs Reed: Mr Lloyd the doctor has suggested me sending her to school. I have therefore communicated with Mr Brocklehurst of the Lowood Orphan Schools – and he has signified his attention of calling on me with respect to Jane – and I shall be sincerely pleased to see the back of her.

Miss Abbot: Well, I must say I have before told you, Mrs Reed, my opinion about the child – She's an underhanded little thing. I never saw a girl of her age with so much cover.

Mrs Reed: Why should she think herself on an equality with my daughters and my son because I kindly allowed her to be brought up with them? Miss Abbot, my children will have money at my death – she will be a beggar, a dependent on strangers as she now is on me – but her obstinate spirit and pride prevents her trying to make herself agreeable to her benefactress.

Miss Abbot: I wonder you don't beat her well.

Mrs Reed: I have – I do – but it's no use trying to flog out of the body that which is born in the flesh – the girl is wicked and deceitful to the backbone.

Jane looking in at back

Jane Eyre: Please, Aunt Reed, may I come in the room?
Mrs Reed: Don't call me Aunt Reed until you have learned to behave yourself better.
Jane *(meekly)*: I've been trying to be good.
Georgina: Don't tell lies, Jane. How do you know what my feelings are?
Mrs Reed *(strikes her)*: Take that and that – don't be so pert – there is something truly forbidding in a child taking up her elders in that manner.
Georgina: Her elders and her betters.
Jane: My betters – Yes that story is always ding-donged into my ears – but Aunt Reed – Mrs Reed – I do try to be good – indeed I do, though it seems the more I try, the more often I'm called wicked.
Mrs Reed: No snivelling – be seated somewhere, and until you can speak pleasantly, remain silent – come Georgina and Miss Abbot, let us go into the drawing room. This girl's presence is hateful to me, I cannot brook deceit.   *(goes out L.C. door)*
Georgina *(following)*: And I hate liars. *(Jane looks at her.)* Oh, I don't mind your looks, we don't believe in crocodile's tears or vile tempers.
Miss Abbot *(follows)*: Say your prayers, Miss Eyre, when you're by yourself, for if you don't repent something bad might come down the chimney and fetch you away.
Jane: If you're good people I shouldn't care to be fetched away by any thing good; Eliza and Georgy always do right and John calls his mother names and yet he's his mother's darling boy – but everything I do they call me naughty for however much I try to be good.

Enter Dr Lloyd

Dr Lloyd: Yes, certainly, I can find my way – so here you are. Well, missey, how are you today? Come here, Miss Jane. Your name is Jane is it not?
Jane: Yes, Sir, Jane Eyre.
Dr Lloyd: Well, you have been crying, Miss Jane Eyre; can you tell me what about? Have you any pain?
Jane: No, Sir.
Dr Lloyd: What made you ill yesterday? Did you have a fall? – fall – why, that is like a baby again!
Jane: I was knocked down, but that did not make me ill.
Dr Lloyd: The fall did not make you ill; what did then?
Jane: I was shut up in a room where there is a ghost, till after dark.
Dr Lloyd: Ghost! What – you are a baby after all! You are afraid of ghosts.
Jane: Of Mr Reed's ghost I am: he died in that room, and was laid out there.

Dr Lloyd:	Nonsense! And is it that makes you so miserable? Are you afraid now in daylight?
Jane:	No: but night will come again before long: and besides – I am unhappy – very unhappy, for other things.
Dr Lloyd:	What other things?
Jane:	For one thing, I have no father or mother, brothers or sisters.
Dr Lloyd:	You have a kind aunt and cousins.
Jane:	But John Reed knocked me down, and my Aunt shut me up in the Red Room.
Dr Lloyd:	Don't you think Gateshead Hall a very beautiful house? Are you not very thankful to have such a fine place to live at?
Jane:	It is not my house, Sir; and Abbot says I have less right to be here than a servant.
Dr Lloyd:	Pooh! you can't be silly enough to wish to leave such a splendid place.
Jane:	If I had anywhere else to go, I should be glad to leave it; but I can never get away from Gateshead till I am a woman.
Dr Lloyd:	Perhaps you may – who knows? Have you any relations besides Mrs Reed?
Jane:	I think not, Sir.
Dr Lloyd:	None belonging to your father?
Jane:	I don't know; I asked Aunt Reed once, and she said possibly I might have some poor low relations called Eyre, but she knew nothing about them.
Dr Lloyd:	If you had such, would you like to go to them?
Jane:	No; I should not like to belong to poor people.
Dr Lloyd:	Not even if they were kind to you?
Jane:	No.
Dr Lloyd:	But are your relatives so very poor? Are they working people?
Jane:	I cannot tell. Aunt Reed says if I have any, they must be a beggarly set; I should not like to go a begging.
Dr Lloyd:	Would you like to go to school?
Jane:	John Reed hates his school – but what he hates I might like – he hates me, he does – I should like to go to school.
Dr Lloyd:	Well, well; who know what may happen? The child ought to have change of air and scene. (*To himself*) Nerves not in a good state.

Enter Servant with John Reed

Dr Lloyd:	Is that your mistress, nurse? I should like to speak to her before I go. (*Exit*)
Servant:	Miss Jane, come upstairs and take off your pinafore – Mrs Reed wants to see you directly – come.
Jane:	But I want to read, please.

John Reed: Don't you hear, Ma' wants you, you have no business to take our books, you little rat, you are a dependent, mamma says: you have no money, your father left you none; you ought to beg, and not to live here with gentlemen's children like us, and eat the same meals we do, and wear clothes at our Mamma's expense. Now, I'll teach you to rummage my bookshelves: for they *are* mine; all the house belongs to me, or it will do in a few years.

Jane: Mercy – let me alone – I'll go quietly, I will.   (*Exeunt*)

Enter Mrs Reed and Mr Brocklehurst

Mrs Reed: Then it is understood, Mr Brocklehurst – Miss Eyre joins your Establishment at Lowood.

Mr Brock: A patron of that noble institution. We will see to her moral and intellectual culture –

Mrs Reed: I should wish her to be brought up in a manner suiting her prospects, to be made useful, to be kept humble; as for the vacations, she will, with your permission, spend them always at Lowood.

Mr Brock: Your decisions are perfectly judicious, madam; humility is a Christian grace, and one peculiarly appropriate to the pupils at Lowood; I, therefore, direct that special care shall be bestowed on its cultivation amongst them. And, madam, I don't allow the principal even to thwart my pet theory. The other day I found two of the girls had dared to have one extra clean tucker each in the week – I severely reprimanded them – fancy the extravagance – two extra tuckers to be washed – but the greatest act of disobedience to orders, I have yet to relate. In settling accounts with the housekeeper I found a luncheon of bread and cheese had been served to the girls twice during a fortnight which the principal accounted for by saying, the porridge of the children's breakfast had been so dreadfully burnt they could not eat it. Now, Madam, as I have explained to you, my plan in bringing up these girls is, not to accustom them to habits of luxury and indulgence, but to render them hardy, patient, self-denying. Should any little accidental disappointment of the appetite occur, such as the spoiling of a meal, the under or over dressing of a dish, the incident ought not to be neutralised by replacing with something more delicate the comfort lost, thus pampering the body and obviating the aim of our institution, which ought to be the improvement of the spiritual edification of the pupils, by encouraging them to evince fortitude under any temporary privation. A brief address on these occasions should be substituted for the breakfast, wherein a judicious instructor would take the opportunity of referring to the sufferings of the primitive Christians, to the torments of martyrs. Ah, madam, if we put bread and cheese, instead of burnt porridge, into these children's mouths, we may indeed feed their little bodies – but what do we do for their little souls?

Mrs Reed:	Won't you take a glass of wine?
Mr Brock:	With pleasure; thank you, Madam, I feel rather weak; I will take a glass of wine. (*At luncheon*) I have studied also how best to mortify in them the worldly sentiment of pride and, only the other day I had a pleasing proof of my success. My second daughter, Augusta, went with her Mamma to visit the school, and on her return she exclaimed, Oh, dear Papa, how quiet and plain all the girls at Lowood look, with their hair combed behind their ears, and their long pinafores, and those little holland pockets outside their frocks – they are almost like poor people's children; they looked at my dress and mamma's, as if they had never seen a silk gown before.
Mrs Reed:	This is the state of things I quite approve; had I sought all England over, I could scarcely have found a system more exactly fitting a child like Jane Eyre. Consistency, my dear Mr Brocklehurst, I advocate consistency in all things.
Mr Brock:	Consistency, Madam, is the first of Christian duties, and it has been observed in every arrangement connected with the establishment at Lowood: plain fare, simple attire, unsophisticated accommodations, hardy and active habits: such is the order of the day in the house and its inhabitants.
Mrs Reed:	Quite right, Sir. I may then depend upon this child being received as a pupil at Lowood, and there being trained in conformity to her position and prospects?
Mr Brock:	Madam, you may: she shall be placed in that nursery of chosen plants – and I trust she will show herself grateful for the inestimable privilege of her election.

Enter Jane

Mr Brock:	So this is the little girl respecting whom you have applied to me – What is her age?
Mrs Reed:	Twelve –
Mr Brock:	Your name, little girl?
Jane:	Jane Eyre, Sir.
Mr Brock:	Well, Jane – and are you a good girl?
Mrs Reed (shaking her head):	Perhaps the less said the better, Mr Brocklehurst.
Mr Brock:	Sorry indeed to hear it! She and I must have some talk. Come here – no sight so sad as that of a naughty child, especially that of a naughty little girl. Do you know where the wicked go after death?
Jane:	They go to – a pit full of fire.
Mr Brock:	And should you like to fall into that pit, and to be burned there for ever?
Jane:	No, Sir.
Mr Brock:	What must you do to avoid it?

Jane: I must keep in good health, and not die.

Mr Brock: How can you keep in good health? Children must die. I hope that sigh is from the heart, and that you repent of ever having been the occasion of discomfort to your excellent benefactress.

Jane: What is a benefactress, Sir? Everybody says that word to me – what does it mean, benefactress?

Mr Brock: Well, I cannot better explain the meaning of the word than by reminding you of yours – Mrs Reed to you has been a benefactress.

Jane: Oh, then benefactress means something disagreeable.

Mrs Reed: Mr Brocklehurst, I believe I intimated in the letter which I wrote to you three weeks ago, that this little girl has not quite the character and disposition I could wish: it will be necessary to guard against her worst fault, a tendency to deceit. I mention this in your hearing, Jane, that you may not attempt to impose on Mr Brocklehurst.

Mr Brock: Deceit is, indeed a sad fault in a child, it is akin to falsehood and all liars will go to – mustard, thank you – she shall be watched, Mrs Reed; I will speak to Miss Temple and the teachers. She shall return with me today. What say you, Madam – I myself will see her into the coach and give her into the care of the guard – and will write to Miss Temple to say she is to expect the new girl – in half-an-hour I will return for her – au revoir. Madam – little girl, here's a book called "The Child's Guide" – read it, especially the account of Martha Gibbs, a naughty child, addicted to falsehood and deceit.

(Exit D.L.)

Mrs Reed: Now, Jane – get out of the room – put on your bonnet and shawl. I shall be rid of you this day, and Lowood School will have a worthy addition to the strings of paupers already there.

Jane (goes R.H. burning with rage): I want to speak to you aunt.   *(Exit Jane)*

Mrs Reed: Don't Aunt me – go out of the room, return to the nursery.

Re-enter Jane

Mrs Reed: Go out of the room and return to the nursery until Mr Brocklehurst is ready to take you to school.

Jane: Speak I *must*. I am not deceitful: if I were, I should say I loved *you*; but I declare I do not love you: I dislike you the [worst] of anybody in the world except John Reed; and this book about the liar, you may give it to your own girl Georgina, for it is she who tells lies, and not I.

Mrs Reed: What more have you to say?

Jane: I am glad you are no relation of mine: I'll tell everyone that you treated me with miserable cruelty.

Mrs Reed: How dare you affirm that, Jane Eyre?

Jane: How dare I, Mrs Reed? Because it is the *truth*. You think I have no feelings, and that I can do without one bit of love or kindness; people think you a good woman, but you are bad; hard hearted. *You* are deceitful!

Mrs Reed: Out of my sight – unless you'd draw down a curse upon your head – Mr Brocklehurst, Mr Brocklehurst, take her away at once – I feel anxious to be relieved of a responsibility that has become unbearable.

Mr Brock (shaking Jane): The spirit of the evil one reigns in this little form. Ungrateful girl. It will be my duty to warn my scholars against you – to warn them you are a cast-away. The teachers will be required to watch you – keep their eyes on your movements – weigh your words, scrutinize your actions, and your fellow scholars must be warned to avoid your company – for you are worse than many a little heathen who says its prayers to Bramah – you are a liar.

Jane: Oh, pray don't say that.

Mr Brock: It is the truth – Heavens, would you try to corrupt me into telling a lie – my pupils must be prevented from associating with such an odious little viper – from one who has repaid the kindness and generosity of her benefactress by an ingratitude so bad, so dreadful that at last her excellent patroness was obliged to separate her from her own young ones lest she might by example contaminate their purity – we shall crush that spirit, we shall combat the demon – come Miss Eyre – you must be taught, you are a dependent, a pauper.

Jane: Goodbye, Aunt Reed – forgive me – I'm not a liar – I'm not deceitful, indeed I'm not – say goodbye once?

Mrs Reed: No – begone, ungrateful girl, and never let me see you more.

Jane: What would Uncle Reed say to you if he were still alive?

Mrs Reed: What?

Jane: My uncle Reed is in Heaven and can see all you do and think – So can my poor Mamma and Papa – though you have never loved me, Aunt Reed – and though you wish me dead and won't say good bye – I say it to you, Good Bye, and when I say my prayers – I'll still say, Heaven bless Aunt Reed.

Act I

Scene 1

Thornfield Hall

Mrs Fairfax and Jane Eyre discovered

Mrs Fairfax: How do you like Thornfield?
Jane: I like it very much.

Mrs Fairfax: Yes, it is a pretty place, but I fear it will be getting out of order unless Mr Rochester should take it into his head to come and reside here permanently – or at least visit it rather oftener – great houses and fine grounds require the presence of the proprietor – what do you think of Mr Rochester?

Jane: You said he was not strikingly peculiar.

Mrs Fairfax: Well –

Jane: I think him changeful and abrupt – an uneven temper – our first meeting three months ago did not greatly dispose me in his favour.

Mrs Fairfax: Oh, when you met him in the Hay Lane, when his horse had thrown him – I never heard all about that – at all events he, usually so reserved, said you showed great courage in holding his restive horse until he could remount – he seemed quite taken with your tact and presence of mind – said you were a woman of sense – and that's more than he ever said to me and it's six years I've been in his service.

Jane: And he thanked me by saying I was the cause of his accident – besides the coarse tone in which he asked my name and the sneer – when he learned I was only a governess – 'twas bitterness itself.

Mrs Fairfax: I believe that was put on – no doubt he may appear rude to a stranger but I am so accustomed to his manner I never think of it and then if he has peculiarities of temper – allowance should be made.

Jane: Why?

Mrs Fairfax: Partly because it is his nature and we can none of us help our nature – and partly he has painful thoughts, no doubt, to harass him and make his spirits unequal.

Jane: What about?

Mrs Fairfax: Family troubles for one thing.

Jane: But you told me my little pupil was his ward – has he any family?

Mrs Fairfax: Not now, but he has had – or at least relatives – well, his father had some misunderstanding and I believe was not quite fair to him – he is not very forgiving, he broke with his family, and now for many years he has led an unsettled kind of life since the death of his brother – I don't think he has ever been resident at Thornfield for a fortnight together, until you came here, when he seems suddenly to have found pleasure in talking French with you – his brother died without a will and left him master of the estate – (*with meaning*) he used to thoroughly shun the old place.

Jane: Why should he shun it?

Mrs Fairfax (evasively): Perhaps he thinks it gloomy –

Jane: There is some mystery there. I feel sure of it.

Mrs Fairfax: Why?

Jane: You either are ignorant or conceal the real nature and origin of Mr Rochester's trials – don't you remember when I first arrived, when you showed me over the mansion and how I was startled by a dreadful laugh – that seemed to proceed from some demon – you told me it was Grace Poole – who is she? and why does she always live here? – you know her – you spoke to her – cautioned her to be quiet.

Mrs Fairfax: She was at Thornfield before I came – she is a person we have to sew and assist Leah in her housemaid's work – not altogether unobjectionable in some points, but she does well enough.

Jane: Does she get good wages?

Mrs Fairfax: Yes, I wish I had as good.

Jane: Is she a valuable hand?

Mrs Fairfax: Ah! – she understands what she has to do – nobody better and it is not every one could fill her shoes, not for all the money she gets. But Mr Rochester has written to say he will bring over some friends today – friends from the Leas, I believe there is quite a party assembled there; Lord Ingram, Sir George Lynn, Colonel Dent and others – when these fine fashionable people get together, they are so surrounded by elegance and gaiety, they are in no hurry to separate, and Mr Rochester is so talented and so lively in society, that I believe he is a general favourite with the ladies, and Mr Rochester well knows the ladies at the Leas. There are Mrs Eshton and her three daughters – very elegant young ladies indeed; and there are the Honourable Blanche and Mary Ingram; most beautiful women, I suppose – indeed Miss Blanche Ingram came here to a Christmas Ball and was considered the belle of the evening.

Jane: And this beautiful and accomplished lady you say is not married.

Mrs Fairfax: It appears not.

Jane: But I wonder – no wealthy nobleman or gentleman has taken a fancy to her – Mr Rochester for instance – he is rich is he not?

Mrs Fairfax: Yes, but then you see there is considerable difference in their ages. But between ourselves I expect marriage will be the end of Mr Rochester's visits to the Leas, and Miss Ingram – you've dropped your work Miss Eyre – but here's your pupil coming – I'm glad she has taken to you so kindly – her guardian Mr Rochester is very pleased with the progress she has made – dear me there's Miss Adèle she's running over the flower beds – oh, Miss Adèle, Miss Adèle –

Jane: Her guardian, Mr Rochester – my pupil's guardian – for some weeks I thought it might be his daughter – but he is not married – not even a widower – she calls him Mr Rochester. This is certainly an agreeable change from Lowood School – those eight years of servitude – an age seems to have elapsed since the day which brought me first to Lowood. I have never quitted it until now. All my vacations have been spent at School. I have had no communication by letter or message with the outer world, School Rules, School duties, School habits, notions and voices and places and phrases and costumes – This is all I know of existence after seven years of routine – I am now free – Mr Brocklehurst – that petty tyrant – that terror of the poor Children of Charity – he did one good deed to tell against the years of misery he cost me – when he gave me my testimonials from the School – he has left since I did – and [to] think my advertisement for governess should have been so soon answered – Mr Rochester seems pleased with me – he is a strange man – absent, gluff – I thought him ugly when I first came here – but since his manners have changed, his features improved – Aunt Reed – can I ever forgive the wrong you did on a helpless, friendless child, one who was confided to your care and home – whilst the house you found her was amongst strangers – the bread she broke – provided by Charity. '*A young lady accustomed to tuition (I had been a teacher two years) is desirous of meeting with a situation in a private family where the children are under fourteen. She is qualified to teach the usual branches of a good English education, together with French, Drawing and Music. Address J.E., Post Office, Lowood, Somersetshire.*'

Adèle: Well governess – ah ma gouvernante – my dear you speak my language as well as Mr Rochester does; I can talk to you as I did to him, on the ship that brought us to a huge city, with very dark houses and all smoky, not at all like the pretty clean town I came from.

Jane: Adèle, with whom did you live when you were in that pretty clean town you speak of?

Adèle: I lived long ago with mamma, but she's gone to Heaven. Mamma used to teach me to dance and sing, and to say verses. A great many gentlemen and ladies came to see mamma and I used to dance before them, or to sit on their knees and sing to them; I liked it.

Jane: I wonder who her parents can be!

Enter Rochester & Mason W.E.L.

Rochester: I tell you Mason, it's of no use. I know your anxiety – but think of the anxiety and responsibility in the matter if harm came to you.

Mason: Harm, fiddlesticks, besides I've been before – but, however, if you think it advisable – I'll go to London and see my ship in and then return later on. I've some correspondence from Jamaica I think will interest you – devilish good bargains on hand.

Rochester: Not the first time I've made *good* bargains in Jamaica, eh – Mason?

Mason: Why? How you do run on the same string – you're not the only victim in the world – Ha! Ha! Who is the Lady? Governess I presume, as I see her with your protégée – not a bit like you Rochester.

Rochester: What matters – you'll stay tonight I hope, won't you?

Mason: No, I'm for Town by the coach as early as possible – strange, Rochester, that governess of yours reminds me of some face I've seen abroad – where did you pick her up? Some poor relation perhaps?

Rochester (R): No! Mrs Fairfax advertised for a governess – she seemed a good sort of girl, known better days, superior sort of person.

Mason (L):	Ha! Ha! – Rochester – no tricks – no more French opera dancers.
Rochester:	By heavens, Mason – silence, she is here in a position of trust. Beneath any gentleman's roof her dependence would and shall be her safety – what devil's mission has brought you to England?
Mason:	Pastime. To see how you were getting on – have you any money – eh? If not I shall look in again before I leave – I'm on a very special mission – Mr Brocklehurst, our new vicar here, has asked me to give him a call, and then I set sail for Jamaica.
Rochester:	If, for the sake of appearance, one must keep in with the parson – by the bye – Brocklehurst – here – Miss Eyre?
Jane:	Yes, Sir –
Rochester:	Wasn't Brocklehurst the name of the man who directed the School at Lowood?
Jane:	Yes, Sir.
Rochester:	And you girls probably worshipped him?
Jane:	Oh, no.
Rochester:	You are very cool! No, what, a novice not worship her priest! That sounds blasphemous.
Jane:	I disliked Mr Brocklehurst, and I was not alone in the feeling. He was a harsh man, at once pompous and meddling; he cut off our hair; and for economy's sake brought us bad needles and thread, with which we could hardly sew.
Mason:	That was very false economy – but Rochester – how will your fashionable friends the Ingrams the Marmadukes and others relish a stingy parson? stingy brothers are bad enough – eh, Rochester – Ha! Ha! You like Thornfield – eh? *(Exit L.)*
Rochester:	What is there in this young girl that so enthrals me – that so rivets me to her presence – is it her simplicity – her candour – I can't say it's her beauty – and there is the simple loving expression in her eyes tells me I am not repulsive to her – or is she indifferent to me – no – I seem compelled to draw her out – is it her dependence – her poverty – Fairfax you are getting foolish – yet somehow Thornfield has lost its gloom for me – since Adèle had a governess. You examine me, Miss Eyre, do you think me handsome?
Jane:	No, Sir.
Rochester:	Ah! By my word! there is something singular about you, you rap out a round rejoinder, which, if not blunt, is at least brusque. What do you mean by it?
Jane:	Sir, I was too plain: I beg your pardon, I ought to have replied that tastes differ.
Rochester:	Will you consent to dispense with a great many conventional forms and phrases, without thinking that the ommision arises from insolence?
Jane:	I am sure, Sir, I should never mistake informality for insolence: one I rather like, the other nothing freeborn would submit to, even for a salary.

Rochester: I envy you your peace of mind, your clear conscience – nature meant
me to be, on the whole, a good man, Miss Eyre: one of the better sort,
and you see I am not so – yet I am not a villain, but only hackneyed
in all the poor petty dissipations with which the rich and worthless try
to get on life. When fate wronged me, then I degenerated. I wish I had
stood firm – Heaven knows I do – dread remorse when you are tempted
to err – Miss Eyre: remorse is the poison of life.

Jane: Repentance is said to be its cure, Sir.

Rochester: It is not its cure. (*Jane going*) Where are you going?

Jane: To Miss Adèle.

Enter Adèle

Adèle: Monsieur, je vous remercie mille fois de votre bonté: – C'est comme
cela que maman faisait, n'est – ce pas, monsieur?

Rochester: Pre-cise-ly, and comme celá, she charmed the English gold out of my
British breeches pocket. You must know, Miss Eyre, that Adèle's mother
was a French opera dancer – named Céline Varens, towards whom I once
entertained a grand passion – and Céline returned it, at least she said so,
with [such] superior ardour that I installed her in an Hotel – gave her
a complete establishment of servants, carriages, cashmeres, diamonds
– in short I began the process of ruining myself in the orthodox style
– like any other spooney – I had or I deserved to have the fate of all
other spoonies – strange that I should choose you for the confidante of
all this – but you with your naivety were made to be the recipient of
secrets.

Jane: You flatter me – am I so excellent a confidante?

Rochester: One of the best, because I believe the truest – well, one evening I
happened to call when Céline did not expect me – she was out – I
awaited her return on the balcony – I sat down; took out a cigar – I will
take one now if you will excuse me – suddenly a carriage drew up at
the door – I recognized it as the one given to Céline, she alighted – I
was about to call out – when a figure jumped from the carriage after
her, cloaked and with a spurred heel – (*pause*) you never felt jealousy,
did you, Miss Eyre?

Jane: I, Sir – I –

Rochester: Of course not – I need not ask – because you *never* felt Love – your
soul sleeps – the shock is yet to be given that shall awaken it. But to
proceed. I closed the casement after recognizing the intruder – entered
the chamber where the couple had gone – liberated Céline from my
protection, gave her notice to vacate her Hotel – so ended, as I thought,
my dream – but unluckily the Varens, six months before, had given me
– this girl Adèle whom she affirmed was my daughter – I took the poor
thing out of the slums of Paris, and transplanted it here – Mrs Fairfax

	found you to train it – but now you know that it is the illegitimate offspring of a French opera girl, you may think differently of your post and protégée (*rises*). You will be coming to me with notice that you have found another place and beg me to look out for another governess.
Jane:	No, Adèle is not answerable for either her mother's faults or yours – I have a regard for her – and now that I know who she is – in a sense parentless – as I am myself – forsaken by her mother – and owned only out of charity by you – I shall cling closer to her than before –
Rochester:	But see our visitors – I must meet the ladies – bye the bye – look well at my choice – you will acknowledge – Fairfax Rochester has taste. *Exeunt L.U.E.*
Jane:	It's true then – what is it to me? If true or false, what interest to me? Jane Eyre, fool – to think you are gifted with the power of pleasing him – a gentleman of family – a man of the world – and I a dependent, despised by my rich relations – a novice – I must not forget it – it does good to no woman to be flattered by her superior, who cannot possibly intend to marry her, and it is madness in all women to let a secret love kindle within them which if unreturned and unknown must devour the life that feeds it.

Enter Misses Mary & Blanche Ingram, Lady Ingram, Amy & Louisa Eshton, Colonel Dent, Lord Ingram, Mr Eshton & other guests; Blanche Ingram on Rochester's arm, Mary on the other, Miss Eshton on John Reed's

Rochester (laughing):	Really, Miss Ingram, there's no denying you any request.
Blanche:	I never take a denial. You see, I have been spoiled – been used to have my own way in anything and I flatter myself I know how to take my own part and enforce obedience to my slightest wish.
John Reed (to Miss Eshton):	I must tell him.
Miss Eshton:	No, pray don't – Mr Reed?
Rochester:	What's that, a remark on me – well, let's hear it?
John Reed:	A lady who shall be nameless, suggested Mr Rochester must be happy – a thorn between two white roses.
Rochester:	Ha! Ha! Some ladies might have reversed the saying and call it a rose –
Mary:	Certainly not, Mr Rochester, where would they expect to find thorns – but at Thornfield.
Omnes:	Very good – very good. (*Miss Ingram retires & chats with J. Reed*)
Adèle:	Bonjour M[es]dames, et vous messieurs, je vous souhaite une reception agreable.
Blanche:	What an odious little puppet –
Mary:	How came that brat here? Get out of the way.
Lady Ingram (whispers to them):	My dears, that is Mr Rochester's ward, the French girl I was speaking of.
Blanche:	Mr Rochester – what a charming little thing.

Mary: What a love of a child.

Jane: And this is Miss Ingram, this is to be Rochester's bride. He doesn't look at me now, whilst surrounded by the halo of beauty and riches. Yet I feel pleasure in regarding him like the thirst [a] perishing man might feel who knows the well to which he has crept is poisoned, still he stoops and drinks the divine draught.

Blanche (to Rochester): Mr Rochester, I thought you were not fond of children.

Rochester: Nor am I.

Blanche: Then, what induced you to take charge of such a little doll as that – where did you pick her up?

Rochester: I did not pick her up, she was left on my hands.

Blanche: You should have sent her to school.

Rochester: I could not afford it; schools are so dear.

Blanche: Why, I suppose you have a governess for her: I saw a person with her just now – has she gone? Oh, no, there she is by that tree. You pay her, of course; I should think it quite as expensive – more so; for you have them both to keep in addition.

Jane: Will Mr Rochester glance my way; no, the magnet holds him – I am but the negative pole.

Mary: You should hear Mamma on the chapter of governesses – Blanche and I have had, I should think, a dozen at least in our day, half of them detestable and the rest ridiculous with their sallow half-starved look.

Rochester: I don't find Miss Eyre either ridiculous or half-starved – she has certainly a rather careworn look.

John Reed: How do you spell your governess's name?

Rochester: Eyre. Jane is her Christian name.

John Reed: I knew a Jane Eyre once, not much good of her, used to be at Lowood School, she is a distant relation of mine.

Rochester: That must be the same, she came from Lowood, will you see her?

John Reed: Oh hang it, Rochester you haven't brought me here to meet all my poor relations, I'm not interested in the products of ragged schools.

Blanche: Oh do, please, change the subject; if governesses, ragged schools and paupers are your only topics of conversation – Why ta – ta –

Mary (going): Sooner than be plagued with a lot of poor people after me I'd emigrate to Timbuctoo.

Jane: So that is John Reed, bitter and spiteful as a boy, cruel and revengeful as a man.

Blanche: Mr Rochester, do you mind accompanying us to the next mothers' meeting; that clergyman is an old bore, makes us waste hour after hour stuck round a table with a lot of antiquated old cats making clothing for the widows and orphans, for some unfortunate people who had no business to have had widows or orphans – Ma makes us go, because it is fashionable, because the Wiltons, and the Greys, go and we can't be out of the swim.

Rochester: Mr Brocklehurst is going to leave us.

Blanche: Good news for his congregation.

John Reed: If I mistake not – Brocklehurst used to be at Lowood – oh, Miss Ingram – I left London to escape my creditors, and I arrive at Thornfield to meet my poor relations and a meddling idiot of a clergyman, who used to be my horror as a lad.

Enter Mr Brocklehurst

Mary: Oh – Mr Reed, you should see our clergyman on horseback –

John Reed: Does he ride well?

Mary: He falls off better.

John Reed: Do you ride?

Mary: Not much – Blanche does –

Rochester: Yes, Blanche adores the Hunt –

Blanche: Indeed I do love the stirring sport. It puts fire into the blood – to guide the steed and curb his temper is a trial worth undergoing – then as he urges on his wild career, the hedges seem to fly away – no brooks or obstacles can stay his course – the hounds are loosed – the huntsmen join the cry – Tally Ho – Tally Ho – there's music in the sound of the sturdy hoofs – there's fire in every sportsman's breast – as like a lightning's flash they clear the fields – the woods and streams, ne'er drawing rein or staying pace until the brush is taken and the prize is won.

Mr Brock: Good day, ladies, good day, gentlemen. Mr Rochester, I have accepted your offer for this evening as it may be the last I shall pass at Thornfield – after a blameless life, after the multitudiness reforms I have introduced at Thornfield I am to be superseded by a younger man, by some beardless boy, by some unfledged B.A. from College – all the societies I have started will lose their head, the meetings of mothers will lose their Father and the great Anti-Social, Grand Junction Temperance Society, will cease to exist and have the water cut off – (*brings out petition*) glad to have your name to this most deserving case, three wooden legs in one family and all owing to drink, mother deserving woman, only once convicted and that when in self defence, she put her youngest child on the hob, instead of the cradle, since becoming a teetotaler she is aware it was wrong. Miss Ingram, you might subscribe to this – a Society for supplying chignons to the ladies of Central Africa.

Mary: We are very sorry, Mr. Brocklehurst you are going to leave.

Blanche (to Lady Ingram): Oh, Ma, didn't Mary say that as if she meant it.

Mr Brock: And after the reforms I have introduced – when I came to this diocese I found the incumbent preached his sermons to meagre congregations whilst whenever his curate, a young man, ascended the rostrum, all the pews were occupied by the young ladies of the district. I reformed this. I discharged the young curate and I introduced an aged man, toothless and spectacled, with an impediment in his speech. This effectually put a stop to the congregation of maidens, for I'll guarantee no church in the city of London is more deserted than Mr Brocklehurst's at Thornfield. I have subdued the vanity of the district. I have driven the poor beyond the boundary, I have forcibly extracted the tithes. I have raised the rents, I have lowered the revenues, I have done my duty in every station of life. I have had six children since I came to reside here, and yet I am superseded – excuse this tear –

Rochester: Sorry to see you so affected.

Mr Brock: The sympathy of the congregation is the chief stipend of the Vicar.

Rochester: Mr Brocklehurst, I find this subscription list is headed by you for five guineas.

Mr Brock: My duty –

Blanche: Mr Brocklehurst is down for five guineas.

Mr Brock: Clergymen must set the example.

Mary: And in mine!

Mr Brock: Charity begins at home.

Lord Ingram: Haw, in mine six little Brocklehursts and each supposed to have contributed sums from one guinea to one shilling.

Mr Brock: Train up a child in the way it should go – (*pause*) isn't Mrs Brocklehurst down?

Rochester: Let us look, my Lord? (*Shakes his head*)

Mr Brock: That's a mistake – would you kindly put it down for me – Mrs Brocklehurst – three guineas.

Lord Ingram: And alter the total.

Mr Brock: No – don't alter the total.

Blanche: Oh – I see – these lists will all be added up without Mr Brocklehurs[t's] contribution.

Mr Brock: Yes – It looks well to head the list – I put my name down on everything as an example – on principle – but –

Mary: It looks charitable and it's cheap –

Rochester: Ladies, I'm afraid we shall have a wet evening. Do you see the clouds yonder – a storm is brewing – we had better seek the shelter of the house.

Jane (to Adèle): Come, Adèle – I will see you in – my poor heart will break.

                                        (*Exit L.H.*) (*Noise of rain*)

Lady Ingram: Dear me, it's commencing to rain.

Blanche: We shall get wet through – and I've only got my thin shoes on.

Rochester: Stand under the trees, whilst we fetch some umbrellas from the house – come gentlemen, volunteers this way.

Lord Ingram: We'll go with you – haw! what a confounded nuisance having to get wet running after the ladies.   (*Exit with Rochester & Eshton*)

Mr Brock: Rain – I never travel unprovided for (*Brings out oilskin mackintosh*) – ladies I require an umbrella.   (*Exit R.H.*)

Blanche: Send the governess for our cloaks and umbrellas.

Lady Ingram: And the pattens.

Mary: And my goloshes.

Blanche: Oh, of course she's gone – like all the class thoroughly lazy – oh, Mr Rochester has sent her out. Come here –

Enter Jane with cloaks & umbrellas

Blanche: Here's my cloak, put it round me, make haste – do.

Mary: Do stir yourself – Mr Reed, how proud you must be of your relations – she moves like a tortoise.

Blanche: As lazy as she is high.

John Reed: What's bred in the bone you know –

Lady Ingram: Oh, there's a drop of rain down my neck – my umbrella.

Mary: One for me.

Blanche: Of course you've got one (*snatches it*) give it to me – rain will make you grow – I'm sure a few inches would be an advantage – don't stand staring there – come Mr Reed.

John Reed: Ah, Blanche, there's something nice in a shower of rain – it makes the girl on your arm cling all the tighter for it – as one umbrella for two –

Blanche: Plague on that girl, she's quite upset my collar – servants are dreadfully annoying. Where can Rochester loiter – he's a husband worth spooning for.

Brocklehurst crossing from R. to L.

Mr Brock: Confound it, took the wrong road. The idea of those ladies being frightened at a few spots of rain – I don't fear a shower – umbrellas are an useless expense.   (*Exit L.U.E.*) (*All off*)

Jane (sitting under tree): Why do I sit here – why do I linger in this storm? – if I should die here Heaven knows I had not intended to love him – I have tried to forget his position and mine – oh, Mother – Mother – why is dependence branded as a crime and poverty as a reproach? – (*pause*)

Lightning & Thunder

Music

Enter Rochester hurriedly with cloak & umbrellas

Rochester:.   What – all gone – just as well or they'd have been soaked – (*sees Jane*) – what, Miss Eyre – here alone – why, you'll catch your death of cold – here, take my cloak and umbrella, or better still, take my arm – and I'll hold the shelter.

Jane: Oh, Mr Rochester – what will your rich friends say – let me go in alone!

Rochester: They will say and think what they please, conscience shall be my guide, and that tells me Fairfax Rochester always treats a lady with the respect due to her sex, even if she is other fellows' – poor relation.

Scene 2

A Chamber in Thornfield House (doors R.H. & L.H.)

Enter Mason R.H.

Mason: Yes, I must be satisfied, I have left my name below – Rochester knows how to treat his friends – and I don't see why I shouldn't be amongst them – this little business over and I'll return to the drawing room – Grace – Grace – one moment – High – (*Exits slowly L.H.*) (*Pause*)

A fearful scream is heard off – scuffle off stage

Mason (without): Help, Help, Help, Will no one come – Rochester for the love of Heaven.

Rochester rushes on R.H

Rochester: Heavens – what has he done – I'm coming, I'm coming. (*Noise etc.*)

Enter hurriedly Jane, Miss Ingram and Omnes R.H.

Blanche: What's the matter – where's Mr Rochester?

Mary: What awful event has occurred? Speak – let us know the worst!

Rochester re-enters laughing & with a candle

Rochester: Ha, Ha, – pray don't pull me down or strangle me, I'll – all right, a mere rehearsal of 'Much ado about Nothing' – ladies please keep off – return to the drawing room, remember the hour – Mrs Fairfax allowed some of the servants to ret[ire] earlier than usual, and one has had the nightmare, that's all – she's an excitable, nervous person – she construed her dream into an apparition or something of that sort – now then, come along and we'll get back to our concert – gentlemen, have the goodness to set the ladies the example – Miss Ingram, I am sure you will not fail in evincing superiority to idle terrors. Don't stay too long in the chill gallery – come – it makes me laugh to see how scared you all looked – you'll say there's a ghost at Thornfield next – allons mes amis. (*All exeunt excepting Jane*)

Rochester (aside): I want you – have you a sponge in your room – fetch it and return
directly – come friends? (*Long pause*) (*Groan heard*)

*Jane returns with sponge & basin of water. A demoniacal laugh heard, Ha, Ha, Ha.
Mason calls 'Grace – Grace Poole'.*

Jane: What mystery is this? – Grace Poole – someone calls her – who can
it be? – How still all appears – Nothing stirring. (*Piano is heard very
indistinctly as if a dance was going on in the drawing room – faint
laughter now & again*) Dancing – joy on one floor – and a mystery
– perhaps a crime, here – and I am an accomplice – innocent – but,
who's there?

Rochester (entering): Have you any salts – volatile salts?

Jane: Here, Sir – and the sponge and basin. (*Rochester locks door R.H. then
goes to L.H. door, brings out Mason, his coat off & bleeding from the
throat, places him in a chair, bathes his forehead*)

Rochester: You don't turn sick at the sight of blood.

Jane: I think I shall not – I have never been tried yet.

Rochester: Hold the candle, now the salts. (*Sponges Mason's wound*)

Mason: Is there immediate danger?

Rochester: Pooh, no – a mere scratch – don't be so overcome man; bear up! You'll
be able to be removed by morning I hope – Jane!

Jane: Yes, Sir

Rochester: I shall have to leave you in this room with this gentleman whilst I
calm my guests below; you will sponge the blood as I have done, if he
feels faint you will put the glass of water on that stand to his lips, and
your salts to his nose – you will not speak to him on any pretext – and
Richard – it will be at the peril of your life if you speak to her; open
your lips – agitate yourself – and I'll not answer for the consequences
– remember no conversation. (*Exit R.H. door*)

Jane: What crime is this, that lives incarnate in this sequestered mansion
and can neither be expelled nor subdued by the owner? What mystery,
that breaks out, in blood, at the deadest hours of night? What creature
is it that, masked in an ordinary woman's voice and shape, utters the
sound, now of a mocking demon, and anon of a carrion-seeking bird
of prey?

Rochester re-enters R.H.

Rochester: Now, my good fellow, how are you?

Mason: She's done for me, I fear.

Rochester: Not a whit! – courage! You've lost a little blood; that's all, but how is
this? The flesh on the shoulder is torn as well as cut. This wound was
not done with a knife: there are marks of teeth here!

Mason:	She bit me, she worried me like a tigress, when you got the knife from her.
Rochester:	You should not have yielded – you should have grappled with her at once.
Mason:	But under such circumstances, what could one do? (*Shuddering*) And I did not expect it: she looked so quiet at first.
Rochester:	I warned you – be on your guard when you go near her – besides you might have waited till to-morrow, and had me with you – it was mere folly to attempt the interview to night, and alone.
Mason:	I thought I could have done some good.
Rochester:	You thought; yes, it makes me impatient to hear you, but, however, you have suffered, and are likely to suffer enough for not taking my advice; so I'll say no more.
Mason:	She cursed me and said she'd kill me.
Rochester:	Come, be silent, Richard, and never mind her gibberish, don't repeat it.
Mason:	I wish I could forget.
Rochester:	You will when you are out of the country; when you get back to Spanish Town, you may think of her as dead and buried – or rather, you need not think of her at all.
Mason:	Impossible to forget this night!
Rochester:	Now, Jane, go down stairs and see how the visitors are getting on. Apologize for my absence if any remarks are made – but not without – then return here.
Jane:	Yes, Sir. (*Exit R.H.*)
Rochester:	I'll see to this indiscreet young man – now, Mason – come, rouse up man – be of good cheer – you are better now, we shall have to get you off as quietly as possible, and it will be better, both for your own sake, and for that poor creature yonder. For your sake I have striven to avoid exposure, and I should not like it to come at last – where did you leave your furred cloak? You cannot travel a mile without that, I know, in this cold climate. Jane!

Jane enters

Rochester:	Run down to Mr. Mason's room, the one next mine, and fetch a cloak you will see there. What a mercy you are shod with velvet, Jane! a clod-hopping messenger would never do at this juncture. Now, Jane, trip on before us away to the back stairs, unbolt the side door, tell the driver of the Post Chaise you will see in the yard – or just outside, for I told him not to drive his rattling wheels over the pavement – to be ready, we are coming: and Jane, if any one is about, come to the foot of the stairs and give me a signal. (*Exit*)
Mason:	Fairfax!

Rochester: Yes, what is it?

Mason: Let her be treated as tenderly as can be for my sake!

Rochester: I do my best – I have done and will still – yet would to Heaven there was an end to all this! (*Exeunt L.H.)*

Scene 3

The Drawing Room at Thornfield Hall. Folding doors leading to supper room C. Door L.C. & Door 1st Entrance L.H. Window 1st Entrance R.H. with a recess – Piano 2nd Entrance R.H. Ottoman – Fireplace L.H. – Very beautifully furnished.

As scene opens someone is playing Piano & another finishing last verse of song – guests hanging about, some turning over music.

Omnes: Thank you Miss Eshton.

Lord Ingram: Charming really.

Mary: What a thin voice.

John Reed: And how out of tune – but –

Blanche: Charming nevertheless.

Mary: Now it's over.

Enter Rochester & Jane L. I. E.

Blanche: Mr Rochester, I thought you had forgotten your guests.

Mary: There's that stupid governess again.

John Reed: Can't she be sent off, we don't care about our conversation going the rounds of the kitchen.

Mary: I noticed her, I am a judge of physiognomy, and in hers I see all the faults of her class.

Rochester: What are they Madam?

Mary: I will tell you in your private ear.

Rochester: But my curiosity will be past its appetite; it craves food now.

Mary: Ask Blanche, she is nearer to you than I.

Blanche: Oh, don't refer him to me. I have just one word to say of the whole tribe; they are a nuisance – not that I ever suffered much from them; I took care to turn the tables. Henry, do you remember those nursery days?

Lord Ingram: Ya'as, to be sure I do – and the poor old stick used to cry out – oh, you villains childs! – and then we sermonized her on the presumption of attempting to teach such clever blades as we were – when she was herself so ignorant.

Blanche: I move the introduction of a new topic.

Rochester: Miss Ingram – deign to favour us with one song?

Blanche: Are you particular to my mother tongue?

John Reed: We prefer the daughter's tongue to her mother's.
Blanche: Here's a little thing I learnt in Germany (*plays*). No – its useless, I can't
                 accompany myself – here, Mary – (*Mary plays, Blanche sings German
                 song. After 1st verse*): Oh, bother, I've forgotten my German.
Mr Rochester: Try something – A la Mode de Paris.
Blanche: You help me then – Mr Rochester, your commands are law – what a
                 splendid guide and counsellor you would make.
Mary: Oh, I am so sick of the young men of the present day! Poor puny things
                 not fit to stir a step beyond papa's park gates: nor to go even so far
                 without mamma's permission and guardianship.
John Reed: Ah, Blanche – there's one heart always ready to do you homage.
Blanche: You're a tease – (*aside*) now which is sincere? I always fail to grasp
                 Rochester – when that charity-school governess is present – pshaw – but
                 Mr Reed is – since report says he is a wild sort of fellow – but perhaps,
                 it lies – and after all a reformed rake generally makes the most devoted
                 of husbands – whenever I marry (*pause*) I am resolved my husband
                 shall not be a rival, but a foil to me. I will suffer no competitor near the
                 throne; I shall exact an undivided homage; his devotions shall not be
                 shared between me and the shape he sees in his mirror. Who'll oblige
                 by singing?
Lord Ingram: Dy'e think the governess can?
Blanche: Oh, no, she looks too stupid for that.
Mary: If this was an organ – she might blow the bellows, that's about the
                 extent of her accomplishments.
Jane: He has hardly said a word to me – how can I ever rival beauty such as
                 hers – vain hope.
Rochester: You don't seem happy, Miss Eyre – rather vexed?
Jane: No, Sir, none can be vexed – when admiring.
Rochester: My future bride, Miss Ingram – a man must love such a handsome
                 noble, witty, accomplished lady.
Jane: Probably she loves you.
Rochester: Probably (*aside*) my person or my purse.

Enter Mr Brocklehurst

Rochester: Now, Mr Brocklehurst, we are all anxiety.
Omnes: Oh, Mr Brocklehurst will oblige us.
Mr Brock: Where'ere I take my walks abroad. Good evening, ladies.
Blanche: Try Dr Watts, or the 22nd Psalm – get your night caps ready.
Rochester: Cruel as beautiful, Blanche.
John Reed: Charming always.
Mr Brocklehurst sings: 'Village Blacksmith'.
Omnes: Very good –

[Lady] Ingram: Dear me – ladies, are you aware it's 12 o'clock – we must really say good-night, Mr Rochester, gentlemen are of later hours.

Blanche: Well, good-night, Mr Rochester.

Mary: Good night – good night, Mr Brocklehurst – no more ghosts, Mr Rochester – did you ever walk in your sleep?

Rochester: Not that I am aware of – besides – I sleep tonight at the bottom of yonder corridor, in this wing of the house.

Mrs Fairfax rings bell – servants enter with lights & show off guests in different directions

John Reed (to Blanche): Pleasant dreams to you, Miss Ingram –

Blanche (bashfully): Good night, Mr Reed. If it were a race a race between the two and love alone the stakes – Mr Reed might win – but as it is – Mr Rochester can turn the balance with his gold – I'm not well tonight. Mary.

Lady Ingram: What ails you, my pet.

Blanche: I'm jealous – can't you see it – awfully, madly, grievously jealous
                                                                    (*Exit C. door*)

Rochester: Good night – Miss Eyre – the guests have been merry – they are full of jests and gaiety.

Jane: Yes, Sir – Good night, Mr Rochester.

Rochester: If I ever require your services again like this evening?

Jane: I'll try at least to do all you wish.

Rochester: I will try you – if all these people came in a body and spat at me, what would you do, Jane?

Jane: Turn them out of the room, Sir, if I could.

Rochester: But if I were to go to them, and they only looked at me coldly, and whispered sneeringly amongst each other, and then dropt off and left me one by one, what then? Would you go with them?

Jane: I rather think not, Sir; I should have more pleasure in staying with you.

Rochester: To comfort me?

Jane: Yes, Sir, to comfort you, as well as I could.

Rochester: And if they laid you under a ban for adhering to me?

Jane: I should care nothing about it.

Rochester: Then, you could dare censure for my sake?

Jane: I could dare it for the sake of any friend who deserved my adherence as you, I am sure, do.

Rochester: Good night my – Miss Eyre – I feel I cannot rest tonight.
                                                                    (*Exit with light*)

Jane: What a beautiful night, and how hushed seems everything around – I can almost hear the beatings of my heart – why does it beat so loudly – am I happier than at Lowood? Yes – am I happier than at Gateshead – he, John Reed here – the libertine – his mother's hope. Mr Brocklehurst told me he had been in prison for debt, a roué in society – and [I] find him here – a visitor in this house – does Miss Ingram know his true character? or does she waver between Mr Rochester and him – no – there is no choice. How strange it seems – tush – I am getting foolish again and, I declare, a tear – I'll stay here a little in the moonlight before going to rest – rest – and dream – of blighted hopes – ambition unfulfilled – a love rejected. (*Falls asleep)*

Rochester's door opens carefully & the Maniac runs across – looks round, sees Jane Eyre, about to strike her with fire irons – then goes to folding doors & lights a brand from the fire & returns to door L.H. & disappears – Centre door opens

Grace Poole enters & rushes after her – brings her back, struggling – they go through Centre doors & slam them – the sound awakens Jane – who starts & listens –

Maniac laughs outside: Ha, Ha. Ha.

Jane: Who's there – that cry – the same I heard this evening – merciful powers – protect me – (*kneels)* – ah, what a singular smell – Grace Poole's laugh too – is she possessed with an evil one – I'll seek Mrs Fairfax – ah – there's something wrong – (*Bursts door open L.H.)* Mr Rochester's door is open – and Heavens the bed is on fire – awake, Mr Rochester. Awake.   (*Exits)*

Jane runs back followed by Rochester

Rochester: In the name of all the elves in Christendom, is that Jane Eyre? What have you done with me, witch, sorceress? Who is in the room besides you? Have you plotted to kill me?
Jane: I will fetch you a candle, Sir; thank Heavens you are safe. Somebody has plotted something: you cannot too soon find out who, and what it is.
Rochester: What has happened? Who has been in my room?
Jane: I saw your curtains in flames – who did it I cannot tell – but I heard that dreadful laugh – and I threw the water over the burning curtains.
Rochester: You heard an odd laugh? You have heard that laugh before – or something like it?
Jane: Yes, Sir: the woman who sews here, called Grace Poole – she laughs in that way. She is a singular person.
Rochester: Just so – Grace Poole – you have guessed it. She is, as you say – singular, – very. Well, I shall reflect on the subject – meantime, I am glad that you are the only person, besides myself, acquainted with the precise details of to-night's incident – say nothing of this to anyone – I ask you for secrecy – you can now retire.

Jane:	Good-night, then, Sir.
Rochester:	What, are you quitting me already, and in that way?
Jane:	You said I might go, Sir.
Rochester:	But not without taking leave; not without a word of acknowledgement, not, in short, in that brief, dry fashion – why – you have saved my life! saved me from a horrible and excruciating death! at least shake hands? I have a pleasure in owing you so immense a debt. I cannot say more: but you: it is different:- I feel your benefits no burden, Jane. My Jane –
Jane:	Good-night again, Sir. There is no debt, benefit, burden, in the case.
Rochester:	You would do me good in some way; I saw it in your eyes when I first saw you – my cherished preserver, good-night my – that is Miss Eyre (*pause*) Jane, I have something of importance to say to you – something that had better be said now – you'll remember, Jane, when rumour intimated to you that it was my intention to take Miss Ingram to my bosom, it was you who first said to me, that in case I married Miss Ingram – both you and little Adèle had better leave. In about a month I hope to be a bridegroom, and in the interim, I shall myself look out for employment, and an asylum for you.
Jane:	Thank you, Sir – I grieve to leave Thornfield.
Rochester:	I regret it, as I have known you and –
Jane:	And I have known you. It strikes me with terror and anguish to feel I absolutely must be torn from you for ever. Yet I see the necessity of departure, it is like looking on the necessity of death.
Rochester:	Where do you see the necessity?
Jane:	Where? You, Sir, have placed it before me.
Rochester:	In what shape?
Jane:	In the shape of Miss Ingram; a beautiful woman – your bride.
Rochester:	My bride! What bride? – I have no bride!
Jane:	But you will have.
Rochester:	Yes; I will! – And your will shall decide your destiny – I offer you my hand and heart, and a share of all my possessions.
Jane:	Don't jest with a woman's heart.
Rochester:	I ask you to pass through life at my side – Jane, I summon you as my wife: it is you only I intend to marry – Jane – consent to become my wife.
Jane:	Your bride stands between us.
Rochester (rising):	My bride is here. (*Clasping her*) Jane, will you marry me? I could not marry Miss Ingram – I love you more than life. Fashion I despise – you, poor and obscure, and small as you are – I entreat you to accept me as a husband.
Jane:	What me, poor Jane! who has not a friend in the world but you – not a shilling but what you have given me.
Rochester:	Will you be mine? Say – can you love me?

Jane:	Can I? – Do you truly *love me*?
Rochester:	I do, and if an oath is necessary to satisfy you, I swear it –
Jane:	Then, Sir, I will marry you.
Rochester:	Come to my heart, my own darling one, make my happiness as I will make yours – it will atone – I will guard, cherish and solace you – I know my maker sanctions what I do – for the world's judgement, I wash my hands thereof – for man's opinion – I defy it – *she shall be my wife*.

Act II

Scene 1

Jane:	Now, Mrs Fairfax, tell me candidly, am I not carrying out your plan to the letter?
Mrs Fairfax:	And don't you find it advantageous? When Mr Rochester told me you were to be his wife – of course I was very much surprised.
Jane:	But that's so long ago now.
Mrs Fairfax:	Three months preparation is none too much for such a serious business.
Jane:	But, Mrs Fairfax, you must admit you were mistaken.
Mrs Fairfax:	No, I gave you good advice – try and keep Mr Rochester at a distance – I said – distrust yourself as well as him –
Jane:	Why did you say that?
Mrs Fairfax:	Because, you are young and so little acquainted with men – you cannot be too careful – besides – equality of position and fortune is often advisable in such cases – gentlemen in his station are not accustomed to *marry* their governesses – although I knew you were a pet of his – there are times when, for your sake, I have been a little uneasy at his marked preference, and have wished to put you on your guard – I knew such an idea would shock, perhaps offend you; and you were so discreet, and so thoroughly modest and sensible I hoped you might be trusted to protect yourself.
Jane:	Never mind that now – to-morrow sees the end of your anxiety.
Mrs Fairfax:	To-morrow makes the governess the mistress.
Jane:	I can hardly [believe?] the last hours of courtship are maintained – by this time to-morrow, we shall be far off on our way to London. Mr Rochester has written the labels for my boxes.
Mrs Fairfax:	I'll go now and see the finishing touch given them – bye the bye – your wedding veil is in the cupboard, there – I could never have thought it – he is a proud man – are you sure he is going to marry you for love? –
Jane:	Mrs Fairfax – for what else – he will *marry* me be sure of that.

Mrs Fairfax: It seems so strange – will he *marry* you – I am sorry to grieve you – but in this case I do fear there will be something found to be different to what either you or I expect.

Jane: Why – am I a monster? Is it impossible that Mr Rochester should have a sincere affection for me?

Mrs Fairfax: No, and I dare say Mr Rochester is very fond of you – but – ah well – time will show.

Jane (looking at labels): Mrs Rochester. Wendover Hotel. London. Mrs Rochester! She does not exist: she would not be born till to-morrow, and I will await to be assured she has come into the world alive, before I assign to her all that property.

Enter Rochester C. door

Rochester: Well, my smiling pretty bride – how charming you look. Is this my pale, little elf? This little sunny-faced girl with the dimpled cheek and rosy lips – and the radiant hazel eyes?

Jane: It is Jane Eyre, Sir.

Rochester: Soon to be Jane Rochester – in a few hours, Janet – do you hear that? You blushed, and now you are white, Jane: what is that for?

Jane: Because you gave me a new name – and it seems strange.

Rochester: Yes, Mrs Rochester; young Mrs Rochester – Fairfax Rochester's girl-bride.

Jane: I am your plain Quakerish governess.

Rochester: You are an angel – a sylph – ten years since, I flew through Europe half mad, with disgust, hate, and rage, as my companions: now I shall revisit it healed and cleansed, with a very angel as my comforter.

Jane: I am not an angel, and I will not be one till I die: Mr Rochester, you must neither expect or exact anything celestial of me – for you will not get it, any more than I shall get it of you: which I do not at all anticipate.

Rochester: What do you anticipate of me?

Jane: For a little while you will perhaps be as you are now, and then you will turn cool, and then you will be capricious. Yet after all, as a friend and companion, I hope never to become distasteful to my dear master.

Rochester: Distasteful! and like you again! I think I shall like you again and yet again: and I will make you confess I don't only *like*, but *love* you – with truth, fervour, constancy.

Jane: You are not capricious, Sir?

Rochester: To women who please me only by their faces, I am the very devil, but you please me by your heart. Your influence is sweeter than I can express. Why do you smile, Jane?

Jane: I was thinking, Sir, will you have the goodness to gratify my curiousity, which is much piqued on one point? –

Rochester: What? Curiosity is a dangerous petition: it is well I have not taken a vow to accord every request –

Jane: But there can be no danger in complying with this, Sir.

Rochester: Utter it, Jane: but I wish that instead of a mere enquiry into, perhaps, a secret, it was a wish for half my estate.

Jane: Why did you take such pains to make me believe you wished to marry Miss Ingram?

Rochester: Is that all? Thank Heaven, it is no worse! I may confess even though I should make you a little indignant Jane. Well, I feigned courtship of Miss Ingram, because I wished to render you as madly in love with me, as I was with you, and I knew jealousy would be the best ally I could call in for the furtherance of the end.

Jane: Did you think nothing of Miss Ingram's feelings, Sir?

Rochester: Her feelings are concentrated in one – pride: and that needs humbling – were you jealous, Jane?

Jane: Never mind, Mr Rochester: it is in no way interesting to you to know that – answer me truly once more. Do you think Miss Ingram will not suffer from your dishonest coquetry? Won't she feel forsaken and deserted?

Rochester: Impossible – Miss Ingram has both been forsaken and deserted – yet not through me – three months since, when she heard of our engagement – she flew into a violent temper and vowing vengeance on all my sex – determined to spite me by showing she was not in want of an admirer – the tempter found her, so I hear, in the shape of Mr John Reed – and three days after our engagement was made known – she left the Leas, and eloped with Mr Reed.

Jane: He married her?

Rochester: I hope so – Mr Reed was not a marrying man – I fear she has become his mistress and midst the gaiety and vice of a London life, her wayward and proud spirit will for a time have its sway – until he, tired of his plaything, will cast it aside in the gutter and seek a new love elsewhere.

Jane: That is very sad – Mrs Fairfax is right – men are not to be trusted.

Rochester: What, not I?

Jane: Seriously, I may enjoy the great good that has been vouchsafed to me, without fearing that anyone else is suffering the bitter pang of jealousy I myself felt a while ago?

Rochester: That you may; there is not another being in the world has the same pure love for me as yourself – for I lay that pleasant unction to my soul, Jane, a belief in your affection. I will attire my Jane in satin and lace, and she shall have roses in her hair – I will cover the head I love best with a priceless veil.

Jane: And then you won't know me, Sir; and I shall not be your Jane Eyre any longer, but an ape in a harlequin's jacket. You need not look in that way; if you do, I'll wear nothing but my old Lowood frocks to the end of the chapter. I only want an easy mind, Sir; not crushed by crowded obligations – do you remember what you said of Céline Varens? – of the diamonds and cashmeres you gave her? I will not be your English Céline Varens. (*Sits at table to eat*)

Rochester:	You don't eat?
Jane:	I cannot.
Rochester:	Is it because you have the prospect of a journey before you, Jane? that takes away your appetite.
Jane:	I cannot see my prospects clearly, Sir; I hardly know what thoughts I have in my head. Everything in life seems unreal.
Rochester:	Except me: I am substantial enough: – touch me?
Jane:	You, Sir, are the most phantom-like of all: you are a mere dream. Listen! you were from home last night? I had a dream last night, I dream't that Thornfield Hall was a dreary ruin – the retreat of bats and owls – I saw you like a speck on the white track lessening every moment, insuperable obstacles seemed to separate us.
Rochester:	Now, Jane is that all?
Jane:	All the preface, Sir; the tale is yet to come; on waking, a gleam dazzled my eyes: I thought – oh, it is daylight! but I was mistaken: it was only candle light. Sophie, I supposed, had come in. There was a light on the dressing table, and the door of the closet, where before going to bed, I had hung my wedding dress and veil, stood open: I heard a rustling there. A form emerged from the closet; it took the light, held it aloft. Mr Rochester, this was not Sophie, it was not Leah, it was not Mrs Fairfax: it was not – no I was sure of it, and am still – it was not even that strange woman Grace Poole.
Rochester:	It must have been one of them.
Jane:	No, Sir. The shape standing before me I had never seen at Thornfield Hall before; it seemed, Sir, a woman tall and large, with thick and dark hair hanging down her back. I know not what dress she had on: whether gown, sheet, or shroud, I cannot tell.
Rochester:	Did you see her features?
Jane:	They were fearful and ghastly to me – oh, Sir, I never saw a face like it! It was a discoloured face – it was a savage face. I wish I could forget the fearful look.
Rochester:	Ghosts are usually pale, Jane.
Jane:	This, Sir, was purple; the lips were swelled; the brow furrowed; the black eyebrows widely raised over the blood-shot eyes. Shall I tell you of what it reminded me?
Rochester:	You may.
Jane:	Of the foul German spectre – the vampire!
Rochester:	Ah!
Jane:	Sir, it removed my veil from its gaunt head, rent it in two parts and flung both on the floor, trampled on them. Afterwards, It drew aside

the window curtains and looked at me, the fiery eye glared upon me
– she thrust up her candle close to my face, and extinguished it under
my eyes. I became insensible from terror.

Rochester: Who was with you when you revived?

Jane: No, one Sir, but the broad day. Now, Sir, tell me who and what that
              woman was?

Rochester: The creature of an over-stimulated brain; that is certain.

Jane: I wish I could believe that, since you cannot explain to me the mystery
              of [my] awful visitant.

Rochester: And since I cannot do it, Jane, it must have been unreal.

Jane: But, Sir, on rising this morning, I saw what gave the distinct lie to my
              hypothesis, – the veil torn from top to bottom in two halves!

Rochester: Thank Heaven! That if anything malignant did come near you last
              night, it was only the veil that was harmed – oh, to think what might
              have happened! (*Pause*) Now, Janet, I'll explain to you all about it. It
              was half-dream: a woman did, I doubt not, enter your room: and that
              woman was – must have been – Grace Poole. When we have been
              married a year and a day, I will tell you more, but not now. Are you
              satisfied, Jane?

Jane: Yes – Yes.

Rochester: Your wedding morn. Just a nap, Jane, and then robe yourself for the day
              – the clergyman will be ready early – a trusty watchman is on guard
              – your husband – watching at your door.

Jane: He is my whole world – my more than world – my love – my life
              – almost my hope of Heaven.   (*Exits R.H.*)

Rochester: How I love this day: how I love the sternness and stillness of the world
              under this frost. I like Thornfield now, its antiquity, its retirement; its
              old crow trees and thorn trees; and yet how long have I abhorred the
              very thought of it; shunned it like a great plague house! How I do still
              abhor – ah – what was that – I seemed to be arranging a point with my
              destiny. She stood there, by that beech trunk – a hag like one of those
              who appeared to Macbeth on the heath of Forres. You like Thornfield,
              she seemed to say – like it if you can! Like it if you dare! – But I will
              like it – I dare like it, – and I will keep my word: I wish to be a better
              man than I have been; than I am.

Mrs Fairfax laying breakfast things

Rochester: Is John getting the carriage ready?
Servant: Yes, Sir.
Rochester: Is the luggage brought down?
Servant: They are bringing it down, Sir.

Rochester: Go you to the church, see if Mr Wood (the clergyman) and the clerk are there: return and tell me. Jane!

Enter Jane

Rochester: Ah lingerer. My brain's on fire with impatience and you tarry so long – is the carriage ready?

Servant: The horses are harnessing.

Rochester: We shall not want it to go to church; but it must be ready the moment we return: all the boxes and luggage arranged and strapped on, and the coachman in his seat.

Servant: Yes, Sir.

Rochester: Jane, are you ready? There are no groomsmen, no bridesmaids, no relations to wait for marshal: none but Mr Rochester and his bride.

Jane: I haven't much appetite this morning.

Rochester: Nor I – this very day bid farewell to single life – after the ceremony, my angel – I shall bear my treasure to regions nearer the sun – to French vineyards and Italian plains.

Jane: Treasure – angel – no flattering.

Rochester: Forgive me – am I pardoned – one reconciling kiss. It is your time now, little tyrant, but it will be mine presently: and when once I have fairly seized you, to have and to hold, I'll just – figuratively speaking – attach you to a chain like this – (touching his watch guard). Yes, bonny wee thing, I'll wear you in my bosom, lest my jewel should tarnish – come Jane Eyre – now to become Jane Rochester.

Scuffle without; Mason enters struggling with Maniac. She throws him down & brandishes knife. Rochester and Grace Poole throw themselves on her [and] pinion her. Jane in fright.

Mason: Help – Rochester – Help!

Rochester: Thousand furies, Mason – take her hence – away – away.

Mason: It's too late.

Jane: Merciful Heaven – that fearful form – Edward, speak – who is this demon?

Mason: This demon is that man's wife!

Jane: His wife!

Rochester: Lost! Lost!

Mason: She is Bertha Mason.

Maniac: Ha! Ha! Ha!

End of Act

Act III

[Scene 1]

A tract of snow

Enter Rochester hurriedly

Rochester: She has gone – fled – fled from me – before I could explain – oh Heavens
above – I did wrong not to tell her all beforehand but I was fearful my
treasure would escape me – oh Jane, Jane – my wife – yes – yet I have
a wife – a fiend, a demon – a scourge – Jane saw my wife – beheld
the sole conjugal embrace I am ever to know – why did Mason release
that fiend – just as my hopes were about to be realized – Jane – Jane
– the echo of the hill alone answers me – I must find her, I cannot let
her leave – I was told a female answering her description was on the
road – for four whole days I have sought her in vain – she has taken
nothing with her to protect her from the cold – her money, jewels all
left behind, what can my darling do. Penniless, unprotected and alone,
the thought is madness – Jane – Jane (*Rochester calls*) you must hear
me.

Enter Mason R.H.

Mason: Rochester here – still seeking her? is it not enough you have blighted
her life – but you must now seek the destruction of her soul? Rather
let her leave and forget you and thank Heaven was in time to prevent
the execution of your project in justice to your wife.

Rochester: My wife – your sister Bertha Mason – a lunatic – a frantic dangerous
maniac's hate – the gambols of a demon – those are the endearments that
are to solace my leisure hours. I feared the truth would be known and
always will be – but I'll shut up Thornfield Hall: I'll nail up the front
door, and board the lower windows; I'll give Mrs Poole two hundred a
year to live here with *my wife*, as you term that fearful hag: Grace will
do much for money and she shall have her son, the Keeper at Grimsby
Retreat, to bear her company, and be at hand to give her aid, in the
paroxysms, when *my wife* is prompted by her familiar to burn people
in their beds at night, to stab them, to bite their flesh from their bones,
and so on as you well know. Oh my experience has been heavenly if
you only knew it – I had a charming partner – pure, wise, modest – you
can fancy with *my wife* how happy I must have been but hence, let me
never set eyes on her or you again; I have a right to deliver myself from
if I can; of the fanatic's burning eternity I have no fear: there is not a
future state worse than this present one – let [me] break away, and seek

a home in the grave – Jane – Jane – where are you?   (*Exit*)

Mason: I must follow or he may do himself a mischief; how he hates his lawful
wife. Yet how he loves Jane Eyre!   (*Exit*)

Enter Brocklehurst

Mr Brock: The golden fortune has deserted me – my living gone – my cash
decreased – my family increased – my duties augmented, and still I
cannot prosper, I am alone – £50 a year, with six huge mouths to feed,
six graduating forms to clothe and six pairs of feet to be shod is not
the most luxuriated stipend – yet I live – my poor wife is no more, my
schools have lost their principal and with that loss £30 a year allowed
by the Vicar has fled my house – ah, Where e'er I take my walks abroad
–

Jane outside

Jane (outside): Oh save me!

Mr Brock: What's that, a woman's voice – (*goes & brings her on*). Poor young
thing – you'll catch your death of cold sitting in the snow. –

Jane: Alas – Sir, I am starving.

Mr Brock: Starving – that's nothing – at my house we look forward to the time
when we can get used to it and live on balmy breezes – why it's Miss
Eyre – my teacher from Lowood.

Jane: You know me – Mr Brocklehurst – oh, thank heaven I have found a
friend –

Mr Brock: How came you here – this is not the condition I expected to find Mr
Rochester's bride – you don't look as if you were only four days
married.

Jane: I am not married – I am not a bride – I was an ardent expectant woman
almost a bride – but now a solitary girl again – my life a blight. My
prospects desolate – my hopes dead – Mr Brocklehurst – Mr Rochester
has deceived me – he has a wife living!

Mr Brock: And he wanted another – I always \thought/ that man had pluck – but
tell me –

Jane: My love is shivered – Mr Rochester is not to me, what he has been,
for he is not what I thought him – I do not ascribe vice to him – I will
not say he has betrayed me – but he has lied to me, and I must go – he
has a wife living. And my love would be a crime – I left Thornfield,
hurried away I hardly knew whither – I slept on a stone last night, in
the fields the night previously – where to go I know not – neither do I
know where to get another meal.

Mr Brock: Well, we haven't much, Miss Eyre, but you shall have a meal if I have
to go without myself.

Jane: Oh thanks, but cannot I work for you – anything – cannot I teach – haven't
              you a school – something that I can do – to earn my living.

Mr Brock: What can you do?

Jane: I will be a dressmaker. I will be a plain work-woman; I will be a servant,
              a nurse girl, if I can be no better.

Mr Brock: Mrs B is dead, so nurse girls I hope will not be required.

Jane: Then I shall have to – but I don't pay rates and taxes.

Mr Brock: No, not that – for I'm a rate payer – but Jane – a thought strikes me
              – you loved Lowood – the life there I mean.

Jane: No, Sir – and yet –

Mr Brock: You were a teacher.

Jane: Ah! –

Mr Brock: You were a good one too – well will you join my schools – teach the
              young Charity Children – poor cottagers' daughters – neither very large
              or clean – will you take the place of my defunct Araminta?

Jane: I will – I accept it with all my heart.

Mr Brock: It's not mentally degrading – but it is not elevating – the salary is £30 a
              year – and with my fifty – we may again hold up our heads – and swim
              clear of bread and water – come, Jane, I'll apply to the Vicar at once
              – testimonials from Lowood – oh, let us be joyful, joyful – that is, I'll
              be joyful.   (*Exit L.*)

Jane: Oh, Rochester – why did you deceive me – he wished me gone – we are
              parted for ever now – I shall never cross his path again or be a barrier
              to his lawful love.   (*Exeunt L.H.*)

Scene 2

Interior of the Curate's house

Jane seated at table

Enter Mr Brocklehurst

Mr Brock: Then we will consider that settled. I have been down to the Incumbent
              and he has sanctioned the employment of my new governess – I hope
              you are better after your nap – and not to lose any time I have arranged
              [for] you to commence your duties today.

Jane: So soon, Sir. Well, I'm ready.

Mr Brock: I wouldn't hurry you, but the allowance does not begin until the duties
              –

Jane: I am deeply grateful to you, Sir. You have rescued me from starvation
              and offered me a roof to shelter – you shall find I am neither unmindful
              of your generosity or slow to acknowledge it. I will commence my
              school duties at once – (*aside*) it will serve to quiet this rising at my

heart, to blot out the remembrance of sorrow, guide my thoughts from him – the one whom I so deeply love – the one who has so cruelly wronged me.

Mr Brock: There is my joy in the house – there is plenty in the hand – an extra £30 a year income. But is it not only a temporary increase? She may leave – yet who knows I am a widower – I am handsome. The roses are still on my cheeks and my limbs still rejoice in the suppleness of youth – were she of my mind we might unite the incomes – she might become Mrs Brocklehurst the 2nd – united incomes £80 a year – behold the joyful picture – on the other hand, a new wife might bring a new six mouths to feed, six extra suits of clothes to provide, six extra pairs of boots, and no extra income – behold the warning – I'll chance the wife – and trust to providence for the rest.

Enter John Reed door L.F.

Mr Brock: Mr Reed, this is indeed an honour. –
John Reed: I want you to serve me, Mr Brocklehurst.
Mr Brock (aside): Everyone seems seeking my services.
John Reed: I have travelled from London to see you – are you quite alone?
Mr Brock: Quite –
John Reed: You are surprised to see me?
Mr Brock: Yes, – and not pleased.
John Reed: How so? (*Sits R.*)
Mr Brock: Ugly stories were circulated about Miss Ingram and you –
John Reed: People indeed will gossip – what did they say?
Mr Brock: – That you had eloped with her.
John Reed: Ha, Ha, – that she had eloped with me you mean – well the fact is – the girl was spoony on me – clean gone and of course under those circumstances a man makes his own bargain.
Mr Brock: Bargain – (*Sits L.*)
John Reed: Yes – bargain.
Mr Brock: There's not much bargaining in taking a wife.
John Reed: Wife! – who's taken a wife?
Mr Brock: You haven't – you – Miss Ingram –
John Reed: Blanche Ingram's not my wife – why the village idiots didn't imagine I'd married the spoony girl?
Mr Brock: Well, I believed you had – don't call the village idiots because they in their ignorance perhaps, expected Mr John Reed to act as a gentleman – (*rises*).
John Reed: What does it matter to me, what they think – we'll change the subject – I have not seen Blanche Ingram (*rises*) for more than a month – I left her in London – she begins to have concientious scruples about her conduct and because I remonstrated – she asked me to marry her – of

course I couldn't do that, so one word led to another and we parted. But my business with you is to put you in the way of earning money.

Mr Brock: Honestly?

John Reed: Yes – I want you to sign a paper for me – you must know I've nearly come to the end of my tether – funds are short – and there's about twenty thousand pounds left me by a relative – at least it comes to me providing we can prove the death of his niece; now this latter you can certify – now you can assist me – the relative's name is John Eyre, of Madiera and Jamaica, and the neice whose death I want to prove is Jane Eyre!

Mr Brock: Jane Eyre!

John Reed: Yes, she was at Lowood with you, some two years since. I sent to Madeira to say she died at Lowood and now they want proof of that – I found all the deeds amongst my mother's papers after her death. If she were alive and tried to prove her claim, I'd throw them in the fire before she should touch a penny – give me a pen and ink?

Mr Brock: But she is not dead!

John Reed (giving notes): Did Jane Eyre die at Lowood?

Mr Brock: Notes – money – it means freedom, independence.

John Reed: Here's the paper – I repeat – didn't Jane Eyre die at Lowood?

Mr Brock: What shall I do – she is alive still.

John Reed: Someone of that name may be – but the Jane Eyre – the one – didn't she die at Lowood – no-one will ever question you on the subject. *It is between ourselves*, there is £500 for your signature – didn't Jane Eyre die at Lowood?

Mr Brock (timidly): No! She's alive now!

John Reed (papers all on table): Come, sign – she's dead?

Mr Brock: She's dead – no, I can't – the lie sticks in my throat – Jane Eyre is now under this roof – take back your money – take back your pride – Jane Eyre, who was at Lowood, is living still – I accept my poverty and honour – at Lowood we were weak in victuals, but strong in morals.

John Reed: Fool – idiot – none will ever know it – none can prove against you.

Mr Brock: Yes, a conscience!

Enter Jane: during this, seizes papers & stands C.

Jane: And I have the papers also – Ah John Reed – Answer – Is Jane Eyre dead now?

John Reed: Fool – dupe – but you must have your claim – I am not defeated yet – I leave you *(aside)* but not for long – when that Parson's gone – be warned, Jane Eyre.   *(Exit L.H.D.)*

Mr Brock: I can't speak to her now – I feel ashamed I could ever have entertained an idea of wronging her. Miss Eyre – I'm going to the schools – will you accompany me?

Jane:	Not yet – I'll follow you.
Mr Brock:	We ought to unite our incomes now – £20,000 and £30 pounds on her side and £80 per annum on mine – whene'er I take my walks etc. (*Exit D.F.*)
Jane:	My uncle dead? Left me rich – if not for me – why did John Reed keep the document back – what is this? Aunt Reed's handwriting – Eternity is before me – seek Jane – Jane Eyre – tell her all – all – A letter, with the Madeira mark, and dated three years back. 'Madam ... Will you have the goodness to send me the address of my niece, Jane Eyre, and to tell me how she is; it is my intention to write shortly and desire her to come to me at Madeira. Providence has blessed my endeavours to secure a competency; and as I am unmarried and childless, I wish to adopt her during my life, and bequeath her at my death whatever I may have to leave. I am, Madam &c &c John Eyre, Madeira.' What is this mystery? I cannot fathom it.

Enter J. Reed

John Reed:	At last alone – Jane Eyre – you know me – as a boy you remember my temper – as a man I have not improved – I am less likely to be trifled with. I come to demand my property – those papers.
Jane:	They are not yours – how is it this letter [is] dated three years back, and I have never heard of it?
John Reed:	Because I disliked you too fixedly and thoroughly ever to lend a hand in lifting you to prosperity. I could not forget your conduct to my mother, Jane – the fury with which you once turned on her, the tone in which you declared you abhorred her the worst of anybody in the world. I could not forget it; and I took my revenge; for you to be adopted by your uncle, and placed in a state of ease and comfort was what I could not endure. I wrote to him; I said I was sorry for his disappointment, but Jane Eyre was dead: she died of typhus fever at Lowood.
Jane:	You wrote that – knowing it was a lie.
John Reed:	Yes, but it profited me – because I hate you – I sent also to Mr Briggs the solicitor – he wrote to me of a Jane Eyre – he enquired himself – he waited on me, to say that Mr Eyre of Madeira, your uncle, was dead – that he had left you all his property.
Jane:	All?
John Reed:	But you are dead – you cannot prove your identity – so it comes to me – my scheme is matured and do you think I will tamely submit to have my hopes blasted now – no.
Jane:	They are mine.
John Reed:	Bah! You give me up those papers, or by Heavens I have a murder on my hands.
Jane:	Yes, a fitting termination to the life of a heartless seducer.

John Reed:	You upbraid me – Ha, Ha, – my highly moral Jane Eyre – the mistress of Mr Rochester.
Jane:	You lie, I am not his mistress.
John Reed:	You tried to make him commit a crime to marry you, when he had already a wife – you'll come down yet – he turned you out of doors – that's the report.
Jane:	Heavens how unjust.
John Reed:	Give me those papers, Jane Eyre! – You've raised the devil in me – give them to me!
Jane:	Coward to attack a woman!
John Reed:	Give 'em me! (*Seizes her, struggles*)
Jane:	I'll die first – is there no help – I'll raise the village – Help! Help! Rochester – Rochester!

Rochester runs in at door, siezes Reed, throws him round

Rochester:	At last – At last!
John Reed:	Didn't I say right – be happy with your Paramour. (*Business*)
Rochester:	Wretch.
John Reed:	You are a noble example – worthy champion of a cast-off mistress – Ha, Ha, the atmosphere is not clear, immorality abounds – I'll seek purer scenes, unimpregnated with the odour of governesses and married men's mistresses, it serves me right for conversing with a lot of poor relations.
Rochester:	Well, Jane, not a word of reproach? Nothing bitter – nothing to cut a feeling or sting a passion? You regard me with a weary, passive look. Jane, I never meant to wound you thus. If the man who had but one little ewe lamb that was dear to him as a daughter, that ate of his bread and drank of his cup, and lay in his bosom, had by some mistake slaughtered it at the shambles, he would not have rued his blunder more than I rue mine. Will you ever forgive me?
Jane:	Mr Rochester.
Rochester:	You know I am a scoundrel, Jane.
Jane:	Yes.
Rochester:	Then tell me roundly and sharply – don't spare me.
Jane:	I cannot: I am tired and sick. If I could go out of life now, without too sharp a pang, it would be well for me.
Rochester (goes to kiss her, she repulses him):	What! How is this? you won't kiss the husband of Bertha Mason? You consider my arms filled, and my embraces appropriated?
Jane:	At any rate, there is neither room nor claim for me, Sir.
Rochester:	Why, Jane? I will answer for you – because I have a wife already. You have as good said I am a married man – as a married man you will shun me, keep out of my way – just now you refused to kiss me.

Jane:	All is changed about me, Sir; I must change too. Was Adèle to have a new governess, Sir?
Rochester:	Adèle will go to school – I have settled that already, nor do I mean to torment you with the hideous associations and recollections of Thornfield Hall, where the Maniac dwells you call my wife.
Jane:.	You speak of that unfortunate lady with hate. It is cruel, she cannot help being mad.
Rochester:	Jane, my darling Jane, you misjudge me again, it is not because she is mad I hate her. If you were mad, do you think I should hate you?
Jane:	I do indeed, Sir.
Rochester:	Then you are mistaken – every atom of your flesh is as dear to me as my own, your mind is my treasure, and if it were broken, I should not shrink from you with disgust as I did from her – but why do I follow that train of ideas? I was talking of removing you from here. I have a place to repair to, secure from unwelcome intrusion – even from falsehood and slander.
Jane:	And take Adèle with you. She will be a companion for you.
Rochester:	What do you mean, Jane? I told you I would send Adèle to school: and what do I want with a child for a companion?
Jane:	You spoke of retirement, and retirement and solitude are too dull for you.
Rochester:	Solitude! – I see I must come to an explanation. You are to share my solitude. Do you understand? Jane, will you hear reason? if you don't I'll try violence.
Jane:	Sit down; I'll talk to you as long as you like, and hear all you have to say heartily, but I cannot while you are in such a passion.
Rochester:	But I am not angry, Jane: I only love you too well; hush now, I wipe your eyes, you don't love me then? It was only my station, that you valued? Now that you think me disqualified to become your husband, you recoil from my touch, as if I were a viper.
Jane:	I *do* love you, more than ever: but I must not indulge the feeling: and this is the last time I must express it.
Rochester:	The last time, Jane?
Jane:	I must part with you for my whole life: I must begin a new existence amongst strange faces and strange scenes.
Rochester:	You mean you must become a part of me. You shall yet be my wife: I am not married. I shall keep only to you so long as you and I live. You shall go to a place I have on the shores of the Mediterranean. There you shall live a happy and most innocent life. Why do you shake your head? Jane, you must be reasonable or in truth I shall again become frantic.
Jane:	Sir, your wife is living. If I lived with you as you desire, I should be your mistress.

Rochester:	Jane, you forget I am not long enduring. Out of pity to me and yourself –
Jane:	Heaven help me!
Rochester:	I am a fool! I keep telling her I am not married, and do not explain to her why. I forget she knows nothing of the character of that woman – can you listen to me?
Jane:	Yes, Sir, for hours if you will.
Rochester:	I ask only minutes, Jane – it was my father's and eldest brother's resolutions to keep the property together; they could not bear the idea that a younger son should be a poor man. I must be provided for by a wealthy marriage. My father sought me a partner, the daughter of a Mr Mason, a West India planter, with a fortune of thirty thousand pounds: When I left college I was sent out to Jamaica, to espouse a bride already courted for me. Her relations encouraged me; competitors piqued me; she allowed me; a marriage was achieved almost before I knew where I was. I never loved, I never esteemed, I did not even know her. But I married her: gross, grovelling, mole, that I was. My bride's mother I had never seen. I understood she was dead – the honeymoon over, I learned my mistake; she was only mad and shut up in a lunatic asylum – insanity was in the family. My father and my brother Rowland knew all this; but they thought only of the thirty thousand pounds, and joined in the plot against me – with a pigmy intellect she had giant propensities! How fearful were the curses those propensities entailed on me! Bertha Mason, the true daughter of an infamous mother, dragged me through all the hideous and degrading agonies which must attend a man bound to a wife at once intemperate and unchaste – my father died. I was rich enough now – the doctors now discovered that *my wife* was mad – her excesses had prematurely developed the germs of insanity.
Jane:	I do pity you.
Rochester:	She was a helpless, dangerous lunatic.
Jane:	What did you do when you found she was mad?
Rochester:	Friends [advised me] – take her to Europe, place her in safety and comfort: shelter her degradation with secrecy, and leave her. To England I conveyed her – a fearful voyage I had with such a monster in the vessel. Glad was I when I at last got her to Thornfield, and saw her safely lodged in that third story room, of whose secret inner cabinet she has now for ten years made a wild beast's den – a goblin's cell. I hired Grace Poole, as an attendant for her.
Jane:	What did you do when you had settled her here? Where did you go?
Rochester:	What did I do, Jane? I transformed myself into a will o'the wisp. I sought the continent, and went through all its lands. My fixed desire was to seek a good and intelligent woman, whom I could love: a contrast to the fury I left at Thornfield.
Jane:	But you could not marry.

Rochester: I had determined, and was convinced that I could and ought. For ten long years I roved about, living first in one place, then in another – I could choose my own society; no circles were closed against me. I was recalled to England. On a frosty winter afternoon – my horse stumbled in Hay Lane, when I was just in sight of Thornfield – a little fairy – yourself, came to assist me. When once I'd pressed your fair shoulder – all love seemed to return to me – I found you were at my house – I could see you often, I was delighted by your freedom of manner – your winning smile – in short – I loved you.

Jane: Don't talk any more of those days.

Rochester: No Jane, no need to dwell on the past – the future is brighter – after a life of solitude, I have found you – I love you – you are my life – you are my wife – I have no other – no demon – I was wrong to deceive you – I should have asked you a pledge of fidelity – give it me now, Jane? Why are you silent? Jane, I want of you – this promise – say – I will be yours, Mr Rochester?

Jane: Mr Rochester – I will *not* be yours!

Rochester: Do you mean that, Jane?

Jane: I do –

Rochester: Jane – do you mean it now?

Jane: I do.

Rochester (kissing her): And now?

Jane: I do –

Rochester: This is bitter – it cannot be wicked to love me?

Jane: It would be to obey you.

Rochester: Oh, comply, Jane – consider the despair in which you leave me. – soothe me, love me – tell me you love me and will be mine – who in the world cares for you but I? – Who will be injured by what you do?

Jane: I care for myself – Mr Rochester, I love you – but you see before you a woman who prizes honour as the noblest gift bestowed.

Rochester: I am losing my senses – Jane, come with me?

Jane: No, farewell –

Rochester: Farewell, Jane – Heavens –

Jane: Farewell – for ever –! (S*inks into chair*)

Scene 3

A Country Lane. Night.

John Reed: Well, I feel rather better after that short nap. I can get a horse at the next village and then I intend to return and watch my little cousin. If she has looked through those papers, she'll find Briggs's address – she may communicate with him – make an appointment – convince him of her identity, then goodbye to my £20,000 – I'd no idea that little imp was under Brocklehurst's roof – what's she doing there – will she leave him now? I watched the house some hours after dusk – Rochester left her early in the day – mounted his horse and rode away. But she never crossed the threshold (*looks at watch*). By Jove, it's very late, one whole day wasted through my cursed folly – but I must have – those papers back – she must never see the solicitor with those in her possession – that's a rare blaze yonder, I suppose a hay rick on fire – rather in the direction of Thornfield – it's been burning some time – I'd give a trifle if it was Rochester's place – and Rochester and his mistress were in it – and burnt to a cinder – they and the precious documents she stole from me – but I never have any luck in my wishes – now, Jane, I'll have a short excursion to the nearest Inn – come what may – you shall never prove your claim –   (*Exit L.H.*)

Blanche Ingram appears L.H.

Blanche: It is he – John Reed – I saw him hastily cross the road a short time since – I thought I should catch up with him. Ah, he mounts a horse and rides in the direction of the fire yonder – you shall not escape me – you are known – your victim *is* here – I'll follow whilst life remains – I'll dog your steps and cross your path at every turn – justice shall sleep no more.   (*Exit L.H.*)

Scene 4

Interior of Curate's house as before

Jane: Well – here I am ready for School – I have written to Mr Briggs to the address on his note, and begin already to feel the responsibility of independence – I must not neglect my school duties – yet – a knock – who can that be so early?

Opens door – Blanche Ingram enters

Blanche: Pardon me, Miss – my strength is failing – I crave a morsel of bread and a drink of water, and one moment's shelter from this drenching rain – then I will go on my way again – I fear to die yet –
Jane: Die – my good woman! here. (*Gets glass of water*)
Blanche: Though why I struggle to live, I know not, my life is valueless.
Jane: Surely I know that face!
Blanche: Know me – you – ah – yes, your name is Jane Eyre!
Jane: And yours was – Blanche Ingram.
Blanche: And I have received charity from you – charity from your hands.
Jane: This is indeed a change.

Blanche:	Yes, a change – but who wrought the change – whose fault was it that I fled with that villain – yours, Jane Eyre! – The guilt, the sin of my elopement lies at your door – I loved Fairfax Rochester – you, with your smooth face and mock humility, tore his love away, and crushed my heart – John Reed poured into my ears the taunt – I was a jilted woman. Furious at Rochester's preference for you, I threw myself into the tempter's arms – he promised marriage – I, too credulous dupe, believed him, trusted him – loved him – but he robbed me of the choicest jewel of a woman's life – and then flung aside the empty casket – my love turned to hate – my hatred to revenge – I hate him – myself and all the world.
Jane:	The story then was true?
Blanche:	True – true – what am I now? How can I seek again my happy home – how crawl back to the deserted fireside – the family I have disgraced – how ask forgiveness of that mother's heart, whose precepts I have set at naught – whose example I have defiled – pointed at with scorn – how can I mingle with my friends of old – a cast off mistress – a woman of the streets – the woman, who suffers all the degradation, losing position, friends, station, is an outcast whose momentary sin no repentance can palliate, no reparation condone – the man, the betrayer, whose base passion has ruined the heart he should have cherished, society receives with open arms – he is free to ruin other homes, and send more innocent souls to perdition. (*Kneels*) Great Heavens – is there no avenging spirit thou canst send – in answer to a betrayed woman's prayer – grant my curse the power to blast the seducer's prospects, as he has withered my youthful life.
Jane:	This is terrible – Miss Ingram – stay your curses – with sincere repentance, peace of mind will return – trust in Heaven –
Blanche:	You were the cause of all!
Jane:	Indeed you wrong me – I could not help loving him – but 'tis past now –
Blanche:	Past – how?
Jane:	Surely you have heard Mr Rochester was already married?
Blanche:	Then you too, have been deceived?
Jane:	Cruelly – but –
Blanche:	Not – fallen – you would say – don't spare me – I deserve it all – I deserve the bitterest things – oh fool – oh dupe –
Jane:	Don't weep any more, Miss Ingram. If I did you any wrong, it was unintentional – and you say you cannot return to your parents' roof?
Blanche:	I would sooner beg from door to door than enter the house – I have so disgraced – the Workhouse – a Pauper's grave are all I pray for – excepting revenge!
Jane:	Miss Ingram – be composed – promise to forego your thoughts of vengeance and leave your betrayer to answer a higher tribunal.

Blanche: You counsel this?

Jane: Yes – Miss Ingram – suddenly I have learned that I am heiress to my uncle's property.

Blanche: You – the despised governess?

Jane: Yes – I – and you are aware I am without sisters, relations or friends – save one I have lost – Miss Ingram – Blanche, I offer you a home – the independence – the affluence which will be mine – I offer you to share it – I long for the ties of home and friends – Blanche, will you be my sister?

Blanche: Your – sister – am I awake – you pity me – you offer me a home – the companionship of all that is good and virtuous – Heaven bless you – forgive me? – I came here to curse you – and I stay – to bless – to adore you. (*Embraces*)

Jane: There, there – drive out all these bitter recollections of the past – think of the future as a new existence.

Blanche: The future – how shall I ever repay your kindness – stay – ah – I had forgotten, Miss Eyre – Jane – answer me one question – do you still love Mr Rohester?

Jane: What do you mean?

Blanche: Do you still cherish the memory of the man who deceived you? Do you still love Mr Rochester?

Jane: With all my heart and soul –

Blanche: What would you do for him?

Jane: What would you do for the man you loved? –

Blanche: Brave all dangers – sacrifice my life; if needs be –

Jane: So would I willingly.

Blanche: Listen – Jane – last night as I lay on the ground beneath the hedge – I saw a fire reflected on the sky – bitterly cold on the ground, I rose and went towards the spot – and there learned that Thornfield Hall was a smoldering ruin.

Jane: His house? –

Blanche: I pressed on and curiosity led me to enquire concerning it – this is what I heard – the fire broke out at dead of night –

Jane: Always – the fatal hour at Thornfield!

Blanche: Amidst the roaring of flames, a tall female figure was seen at one of the windows – the people saw it was a Maniac – Mr Rochester called her Bertha – he rushed through the burning rooms – he was seen approaching to save her, when with one yell – she sprang from the window and the next minute lay smashed on the pavement.

Jane: Dead – And Mr Rochester – is he alive?

Blanche: Yes – but many think he had better have died.

Jane: How? – speak quickly?

Blanche: Mr Rochester was dragged from the ruins.

Jane: Alive – Thank Heaven.

Blanche:	But with a Broken arm – a cripple.
Jane:	Joy – no worse.
Blanche:	Yes – worse – he is blind!
Jane:	Great Heavens – a cripple and blind!
Blanche:	Jane – do you still love Mr Rochester?
Jane:	I love him now – more than ever –
Blanche:	Jane – sister – come, follow me!
Jane:	Where?
Blanche:	To help the cripple – to give sight to the blind!
Jane:	I'm ready. (*[They] hurry out of door.*)

Act drops quickly

Act IV

Scene 1

Interior of the Library at Fearndean

Rochester discovered sitting in Arm Chair, doctor with him

Rochester:	So, Doctor, if you can manage to keep the secret –
Doctor:	Never fear, Mr Rochester – we medical men are not the most communicative creatures in creation.

Enter Mrs Fairfax R. D.

Doctor:	All you have to do now is to rest – and, Mrs Fairfax, see that his eyes are bathed regularly. We have made him a comfortable as circumstances will allow.
Mrs Fairfax:	He can't expect in a few hours to have as many comforts around him as it took him years to get together at Thornfield – I think if he could only see what is being done for him – he'd approve of all the arrangements – don't you think so, Doctor.
Doctor:	I'm certain he would – good day, Mr Rochester – keep easy in your mind – don't give way to fits of temper – don't be despondent – it's an unfortunate affair – but it might have been worse.
Rochester:	It couldn't have been worse.
[Doctor]:	You might have met the fate of your wife!
Rochester:	Don't mention her, Doctor – I wish I had – I have nothing to live for – Jane has deserted me – don't say wife again please?
Doctor:	Well, well. I'll be quiet – I know the subject was never pleasant to you – Mrs Fairfax – if any visitors should call – any that he has no objection

to – let them come to him – conversation will brighten his spirits and
divert his thoughts from his sufferings – come, Mr Rochester, tread
carefully – lean on me?   (*Exit with Rochester R.*)

Mrs Fairfax: It's no use talking to him – he snubs me – calls me an ignorant old
woman – I was obliged to speak this morning though – when he blowed
me up – I told him I thought he wanted a certain young lady as was
a governess *once* to wait on him – it was all very well for my poor
governess to improve her position by trying to marry a rich handsome
man, but when the handsome figure becomes a cripple and the brilliant
eye loses its fascination – you, fine marm – don't care to be a nurse
– when I was young – girls took their husbands for better or worse – but
now they cling to them in the sunshine, but desert at the first approach
of rough weather – that is not love – the downright old-fashioned true
love twines round the heart like [iv]y round a tree engrafting its roots
so strongly into the sturdier stem – the rougher the storm – the tighter
it clings – that's how I loved once – but the villain jilted me. –

Enter Jane

Jane (entering): What a strange place – how different to Thornfield – will he love me
now? – Here, Mary! –

Mrs Fairfax: Well if you're not the very last person I should have expected to see.

Jane: Yes. You didn't think I should return.

Mrs Fairfax: That I didn't – oh, lor – I had such a bad opinion of you – Miss Eyre
–

Jane: Well you'll change it now, when I tell you I've come to take care of
your patient –

Mrs Fairfax: What, Mr Rochester?

Jane: Yes –

Mrs Fairfax: Ah, that'll about please him, I'm not sorry – when will you begin your
nurse's duties?

Jane: At once – Mrs Fairfax – show me where the things are – the tea things
– the invalid's broth? &c

Mrs Fairfax: Shall I put down your parcel?

Jane: Oh, thank you – stay – haven't you a drawer somewhere – to lock
up?

Mrs Fairfax: There's a spare drawer there.

Jane: That will do – these papers are of great importance to me – (*goes to
drawer*). Why, there's no key here!

Mrs Fairfax: Well, they're no thieves in the house. Is that the way you're going to
begin your duties – calling us all thieves and locking up everything of
value?

Jane: Oh, forgive me – there, I'll leave it as it is – I didn't mean to offend
you.

Mrs Fairfax: Now you'd better come and see the patient. Oh! Here's the Doctor
bringing him back. (*Exit Mrs Fairfax*)
Re-enter Doctor & Rochester

Doctor: Here, Mr Rochester – in your old chair again.
Rochester: Yes – thanks – Doctor, for your assistance – you won't forget what I
asked you?
Doctor: No – rely on me. (*Exit L.H.*)
Rochester (in chair): Give me the water, Mary?
Jane: Will you have a little more, Sir? I have spilled half.
Rochester: Who spoke? Where is the speaker? Whoever you are, be perceptible to
the touch – the voice I know.
Jane (going to him): 'Tis I, Sir – my – Mr Rochester.
Rochester: Her very fingers – her small slight fingers – if so there must be more
of her. (*Seizes Jane & embraces her*) Is it Jane?
Jane: Yes, Sir – bless you, I'm so glad to be near you again.
Rochester: Jane Eyre – my Jane!
Jane: My dear Edward. I am come back to you.
Rochester: I felt that you loved me, and trusted you would not leave me.
Jane: Which I never will from this day.
Rochester: And you are not an outcast amongst strangers?
Jane: My uncle in Madiera is dead and has left me a fortune.
Rochester: But since you are rich, Jane – you now must have friends who will look
after you – and not suffer you to devote yourself to a blind cripple like
me.
Jane: You forget I am my own mistress.
Rochester: And you'll stay with me.
Jane: Certainly, unless you object – I'll be your companion – wait on you.
Read to you. Walk with you – be your eyes and hands.
Rochester: But my seared vision – my crippled strength – I am no better than the
old lightning-struck chestnut tree in Thornfield orchard – what right
would that ruin have to bid a budding woodbine cover its decay with
freshness?
Jane: You are no ruin – one can love you still.
Rochester: But, Jane – I want a wife?
Jane: Do you?
Rochester: Is it unwelcome news?
Jane: That depends on circumstances, or your choice.
Rochester: Which you shall make for me.
Jane: Choose then, Sir – her who loves you best.
Rochester: I will choose at least – her I love best – Jane, will you *marry me*?
Jane (playfully): Yes, Sir – I think I might – if I tried – let's look – yes I think I'd
chance you for a husband.
Rochester: A poor blind man, whom you will have to lead about by the hand.

Jane:	Yes –
Rochester:	A crippled man twenty years your senior whom you will have to be nurse to –
Jane:	Yes –
Rochester:	Truly – Jane?
Jane:	Most truly – dear Sir.
Rochester:	My darling – Heaven bless you, and reward you – my wife!
Jane:	My husband – never to part more. (*Embraces*)

Enter Mr Brocklehurst slowly L.H. – looks out of window

Mr Brock:	There goes £30 a year out of my income – hem – hem.
Rochester:	Who's that?
Jane:	Mr Brocklehurst – The Reverend Gentleman at whose house I was so welcomed and cared for. He offered me a situation as teacher at his schools at £30 per annum.
Mr Brock:	Allow me to observe – this is hard on me – abducting my school teacher – Miss Eyre – the school duties have commenced – the scholars wait their mistress – if they are imitating their teacher at the present time – the sooner the holidays occur, the better for the morals of the[ir] school. (*To Rochester*): What do *you* think of the present I have brought.
Rochester:	Thanks, Sir – thanks – you could not have brought me one I value more (*to himself*) I thank you for the care of her. She is charming.
Mr Brock:	Perfect to the eye at first sight – but the manufacture has been rather (*looking at clock*) scamped – not a good foundation.
Rochester:	How do you know – it's true she was reared in poverty – has her face altered?
Mr Brock:	Not much – excepting there's a scratch under the one –
Rochester:	Her face scratched –
Mr Brock:	You'll excuse it not being better polished –
Rochester:	She is polished – naturally –
Mr Brock:	I never heard anyone say so before –
Rochester:	Never mind her defects, Sir –
Mr Brock:	I thought it would be so useful for you – its merry tick will be a companion for you through the weary nights.
Rochester:	Sir – I'll hear no more – I am satisfied with her as she is.
Mr Brock:	If it don't suit you after a week or so – you can change it for another.
Rochester:	Change – Sir
Mr Brock:	Yes – the man I had her from said he'd change it till you were suited, there she goes.
Rochester:	I don't want her to go, Sir – I want her to stop.
Mr Brock:	Well, you have a funny idea of these things.
Rochester:	Insulting – silence, Sir – or you may find the mischief difficult to repair.

Mr Brock:	Repairs – yes repairs are difficult, but not expensive – there's one of my congregation puts a new spring for 5/ – or entire new movement for £1 – pendulum extra –
Rochester:	Man – what are you talking about?
Mr Brock:	This clock – and you –
Rochester:	I spoke of Jane Eyre.
Mr Brock:	Oh, this is a winding-up arrangement –
Rochester:	Ha, ha, ha, –
Mr Brock:	You'll excuse me, Mr Rochester. (*Exit L.H.*)

Window opens slowly – John Reed enters

John Reed:	Only the blind man, so, so, I'm safe – this is where she placed the papers – now to see what the lock is made of – ah not closed – yes, here they are – ha! – soft – Jane Eyre – now prove your case if you can – I defy you – you cannot do it –

Blanche (in at window): But I can – wretch!
John Reed (locks door): Blanche.

Blanche:	Yes, your victim – who received kindness from the girl you would rob – and who will defend a sister's rights with my life.
Rochester:	Who is that – what is it?
Blanche:	Help – thieves – thieves – help!
John Reed:	Fool – there is none here to detain me. (*Dashes her down and is making to window, when Rochester, who has risen, meets him*)
Rochester:	You lie, John Reed.
John Reed:	Blind idiot, let go –
Rochester:	Never – (*tears off bandage*)
John Reed:	Great Heaven, he is not blind, he sees!
Rochester:	Yes – he can *see* – I was blind even to the one I loved – blind to learn if her love was deep enough to fly to my side as a cripple – but blind no longer to see my darling's heritage stolen by a robber and a scoundrel –

Noise, all doors broken open – Brocklehurst enters

Jane:	Rochester – Edward – you can see.
Rochester:	Yes. Pardon the deception, Jane – my sight is slightly injured but it was given out I was stone blind. And anxious to test the sincerity of your love – I feigned blindness. That was the secret I told you I had, and which I longed to tell you – when you had consented to link your life to one you thought abandoned by the world.
Jane:	Edward – Oh joy –
John Reed:	It seems I'm not wanted here.

Mr Brock:	Young man – you are a superfluous party – I scorn to number you amongst my flock – Miss Eyre – here is a lett[er.]
Jane:	For me – yes from Mr Briggs, he admits my claim – Jane Eyre – is rich – but richer far in the love of the man she loves.
Rochester:	Mr Brocklehurst, I've taken your teacher away – but in honour, I am bound to allow you her salary.
Mr Brock:	I must look forward a bit, and if you are inclined to further the prospects of my little school, when your married, give me your promise, all the little Rochesters shall be educated at my establishment. Mr Reed – that is the way out.
John Reed:	Curse you all – well – Blanche I suppose you'll come with me? – you can't both marry Mr Rochester.
Blanche:	Tempter – I am proof against you now. (*Exit Reed L.H. door*)
Jane:	My home shall be yours, Blanche.
Blanche:	Call me Sister?
Jane:	Sister – dear sister. (*To Rochester*): to Blanche you owe my early presence with you.
Rochester:	My love – my life – to-morrow will see our hands united as our hearts have long since been – my Jane – my darling Jane Eyre.
Jane:	To-morrow, indeed to become, Jane Rochester.

Curtain

Jane Eyre

by

T.H. Paul

1879

Editor's Notes

The Text

The play exists in a single hand-written manuscript (Add. MS 53224. A) in the Lord Chamberlain's collection of plays in the British Library. The Lord Chamberlain's Licence No. is 181, and the licence ticket reads: 'Name of Play: "Jane Eyre" Drama 3 acts / Theatre Adelphi Oldham/ Date of Licence October 13 1879'; the Lord Chamberlain's Daybook has no additional information except 'date of Licence Oct 13 Date of Entry Oct 14'. The title page bears the words 'F. Percival Esq, 14 Dover Street, Piccadilly'.

The foolscap pages of the manuscript (76 in all) have been bound but many are now loose. The text is written in a large, sprawling hand on one side of the paper only; pages 1–17 are on whitish paper, but pages 18–76 are on poor quality paper, very browned and crumbling at the edges; words are missing in some places. Part of Act II is in a different hand, which I have marked with asterisks. Each act has a title page on white paper. The pages are numbered beginning with the title page as number 1; earlier numbering, which starts with the first page of text as number 1, and begins afresh for each act, has been struck out. Act II may be incomplete, since it breaks off in mid-page with Bertha setting fire to the room, and there is no proposal scene between Jane and Rochester, although Act III begins with their wedding imminent. There is no direction for Act II curtain-fall, although Act I ends with 'Picture' and 'Act Drop'; Act III, however, has no marked ending either.

The manuscript seems to have been copied rather than composed. The transcription is hasty and careless (especially in Act III) with some words missing and others illegible or nonsensical; in editing I have silently corrected many obvious errors and supplied words in square brackets where a reasonable guess is possible, but in some cases I have had to leave gaps. Where words are inserted by the copyist, I have indicated them \thus/. Most speeches have no punctuation; others have the occasional dash or comma. There is almost no final punctuation. I have supplied dashes and commas where necessary to make sense, trying to keep the atmosphere of the original as much as possible. I have, however, finalized all speeches with full stops, exclamations or question marks as seemed appropriate. I have removed capital letters from the middle of sentences and supplied apostrophes for abbreviations such as 'won't'. I find the abbreviations for entrance and exit points somewhat obscure (e.g., '2LR'), but have left them as in the manuscript. I have used the predominant forms 'Georgina' and 'Broklehurst' throughout, although 'Georgiana' and 'Brokelhurst' sometimes appear.

The Playwright

The author is not named on the manuscript, and no playbills seem to exist, but Nicoll identifies T.H. Paul as the playwright, with this as his only play.[1] The British Library lists three manuscript plays by Paul, including this one, in the Lord Chamberlain's

Collection. The 'Backstage' web-site, however, lists playbills for ten plays by Paul, many with French titles and seeming to be adaptations, all performed at the Alhambra Theatre (presumably the one in Bradford), but not including *Jane Eyre*. I have not been able to discover anything else about the playwright.[2]

Theatre and Performance

The play was licensed for performance at the Adelphi Theatre, Oldham, on 13 October 1879. An advertisement in the *Oldham Evening Express*, however, suggests that the version of *Jane Eyre* performed in that theatre on that date was a touring version from 'the Globe Theatre, London'. The advertisement as a whole reads as follows:

ADELPHI THEATRE, OLDHAM

To-night (Friday), and every Evening during the week "ASCOT" and "JANE EYRE." Mr. Gillespy, the Manager, has pleasure in announcing that he had Engaged at great expense Francis Percival's Celebrated Dramatic Company, from the Globe Theatre, London, in the latest London Production now being played with enormous success at the principal London Theatres.

The following has been received:–

"St. James's Palace, London. To James Gillespy. – I have read the two plays 'Ascot' and 'Jane Eyre', about to be produced at the Theatre under your management, and have no objection to the representation. – Signed yours, &c., Edward F.S. Pigott. Oct. 11, 1879.[3]

Although the advertisement suggests that both Oldham plays had already enjoyed a successful run in London, this can hardly be the case, since the Lord Chamberlain's licence does not predate the Oldham performance for either play.[4] Although W.G. Wills's *Jane Eyre* was performed at the Globe Theatre, which is claimed as the home of 'Francis Percival's Celebrated Dramatic Company', the Oldham advertisement cannot refer to this play since it was not written until December 1882. In fact, I have found no evidence that Francis Percival was connected with the Globe Theatre or a play called *Ascot*. He does not appear in Diana Howard's list of managers of the Globe Theatre,[5] and although the 'Backstage' website lists 172 entries relating to well-documented productions by Percival, these are predominantly at Her Majesty's and the Haymarket

---

1   Nicoll, Vol. V, pp. 80, 516.
2   Investigations via Adams, *Backstage*, Boase, *Britannica Online*, *DNB*, the Lancashire Archive and Oldham Local Studies Library have all proved negative.
3   I am grateful to Susan Smith at Oldham Local Studies and Archives for providing this information. Edward Pigott was the Lord Chamberlain's Examiner of Plays at the time. (Stephens, *Censorship*, pp. 32–3.)
4   Adams describes *Ascot* as 'a farcical comedy in two acts, by PERCY FENDALL [...] first performed at the Theatre Royal, Oldham, on October 13, 1879; first played in London at the Novelty Theatre, on March 29, 1883, with Miss Florence Marryat and Gilbert Farquhar in the cast' (Vol. 1, p. 84). Nicoll confirms the author and date of first performance (Vol. V, p. 364).

Theatres and there is no mention of the Globe Theatre or *Ascot*.

There is, however, a significant advertisement in *The Era*, 21 September 1879, announcing that Willing's version of *Jane Eyre*, which had been running in Camden Town since the end of August,

> will have to be withdrawn for Twelve Nights, in the height of its success in consequence of an arrangement made, previous to its production, with Mr D'Oyly Carte's 'H.M.S. Pinafore' Company to appear at the Park Theatre on October 13th. Managers having dates vacant either October 13th or 20th are requested to communicate with Mr W.S. Johnson Royal Park Theatre, Camden-town, London.[6]

The coincidence is too great to be accidental, especially when we see that Willing's play was once described as 'by Messrs. Willing and Percival',[7] and that 'Mr F. Percival' played the part of Brocklehurst in Willing's play in Leeds and Bradford in July 1882[8] (though not in London in 1879).[9] It seems almost certain, therefore, that the play performed in Oldham was Willing's rather than Paul's, and that Gillespy, in advertising it, just named the wrong London theatre. What remains mysterious is why Percival submitted Paul's play to the Lord Chamberlain when Willing's was already licensed and in production. Infuriatingly, although Oldham appears regularly in *The Era*'s list of provincial theatres, it does not appear for the week of 13 October 1879.

The Adelphi Theatre, Oldham, was only ten years old in 1879. It was situated in Union Street and had a seating capacity of 1,500. In 1881, when it reopened as The Gaiety, the new management claimed that it 'had been dragged down to the lowest depths of poverty [...] and bad odour',[10] which may explain why Mr Gillespy was so keen to advertise Percival's prestigious London company in 1879.

Reception of the Play

I have not been able to find any reviews of the play.[11]

Distinctive Features of the Play

- The MS is hastily written and possibly incomplete.
- Broklehurst [*sic*] is a comic character.
- Jane is already a teacher at the beginning and answers both Broklehurst and Aunt Reed as an adult.

---

5   Howard, p. 95.
6   *Era*, 21 September 1879, p. 10.
7   *Entr'Acte*, 6 September 1879, p. 11.
8   *Era*, 15 July 1880, p. 10; 22 July 1882, p. 9.
9   Programme for Park Theatre, Camden Town, 27 August 1879 (BPM).
10   June Greaves, *Oldham Theatres*, 1976. I am grateful to Maureen Burns, of the Oldham Local Studies Library, for providing this information.
11   I am grateful to Susan Smith, of Oldham Local Studies Library, for searching the *Oldham Evening Express*, *Weekly Chronicle* and *Weekly Standard* for reviews.

- Rochester is a philanthropist who takes in Jane when she is ejected from Lowood. He loves Adèle and calls her 'darling'.
- The Reeds, already impoverished, are aware of Jane's legacy at the outset.
- John Reed plots to marry Jane and plots with Mason to blackmail Rochester.
- Mason is from the West Indies but met Rochester 'in India'; Bertha is the daughter of an 'India merchant'.
- The appearances of the maniac are exploited in Acts II and III, with snow, fire, and a scene framed in a window (see Figure 19).
- It is Jane who directs Rochester to save his wife and even after her death she refuses to marry him 'out of respect'. Her final agreement to the marriage is not convincingly motivated.
- Rochester refers to Jane's 'angel work' when she offers to help the Reeds.
- The wedding is attended by cheering villagers.

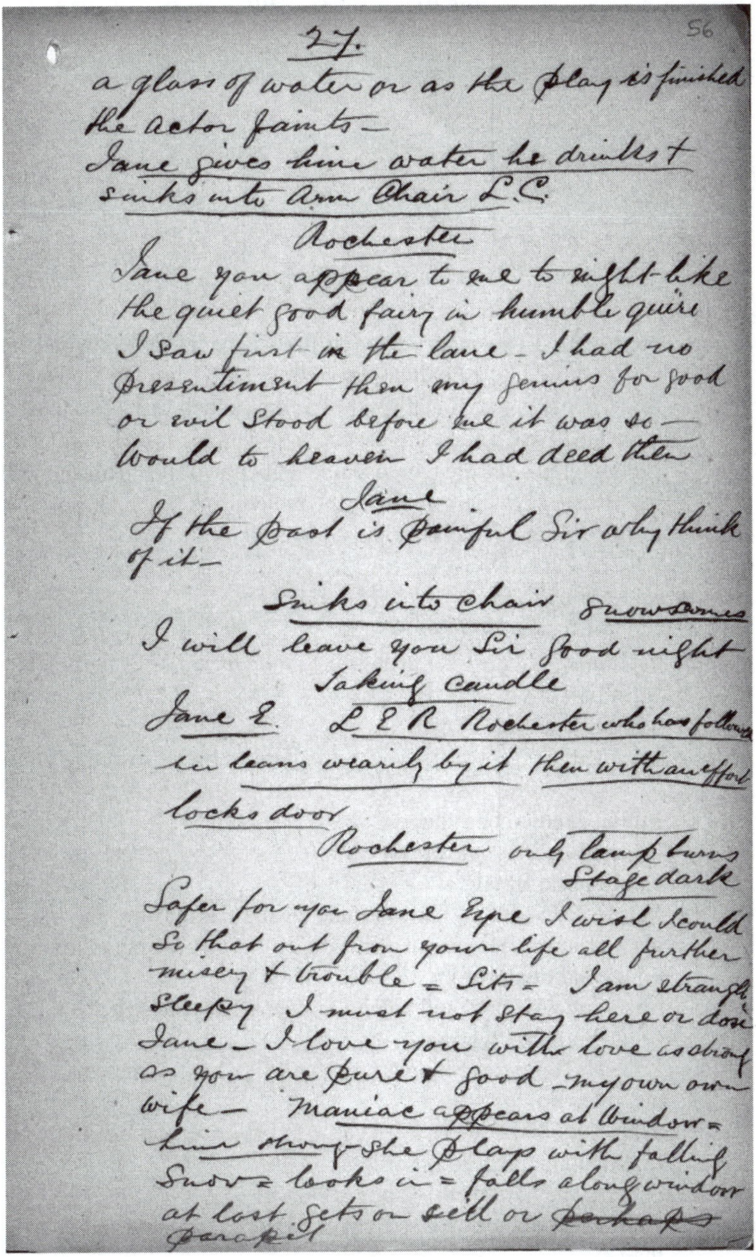

Figure 19   Facsimile of page 56 of the manuscript of *Jane Eyre* by T.H. Paul, 1879, including the sensational appearance of 'the maniac' framed in a window against a backdrop of falling snow. Reproduced by permission of the British Library: Add. MS 53224.A.

Jane Eyre by T.H. Paul

Act I

Scene 1

Landscape

Enter Robert Leav[e]n R & E

Robert (speaking off): Thankee. I'm all right now, I shall find it. (*Looks off L.)* Why there it is, I can read the name from here (*reads*) Lowood Institute (looks more like a Penitentiary) rebuilt by Naomi Broklehurst Hall in this County – well I can't say as I think much of it – so that's where poor Jane Eyre's been shut up for two years & more. I wonder whether she's altered – she did have a temper of her own and no mistake although my Bessie says the way her Aunt and cousins treated her was enough to rile an angel – Hello, what's this little lot –

Girls enter from 2 EL walk across followed by Jane Eyre

Robert (looks and calls in doubt):   Miss Jane (*Jane turns*) I beg pardon ain't you Miss Eyre?

Jane: My name is Jane Eyre.

Robert: I knew it lor bless you – you ain't altered a bit – growed of course and –

Jane: I think I remember you –

Robert: At Gateshead (*Jane starts*) Mrs Reed's (*She shudders*) and you \can/ call to mind Bessie –

Jane: Indeed I can with joy and gratitude for she was the only one who shewed me kindness – hers was the only smile that threw a ray of love and light on the dark days of my miserable childhood.

Robert: She's my wife now and when I tell her what you've just said she'll be proud enough I warrant.

Jane: You shall take some kinder message still – but tell me what brings you to Lowood –

Robert: Your Aunt and cousins have come to look over the Institute and I was told to come up here for orders –

Jane (with an effort): They are well I hope?

Robert: Oh for that matter they're right enough but they nag and quarrel more than ever.

Jane: Robert I cannot listen to such remarks.

Robert: Of course not Miss I ask pardon – Mr John's come with them – he's worse than ever – he is working his quiet dodge now so \as/ to gammon his mother out of some more money –

Jane: Silence – shew respect to those you serve or serve them no longer.

Enter Mr Broklehurst LER comes down C

Mr Brok: What am to infer from what I behold? Answer, Jane Eyre, in the spirit
             of truth – why you have neglected your trust and elected to listen to
             the voice of the male stranger whose raiments have dazzled your eyes
             and blinded your heart to your duty and made you desert the lambkins
             of my flock?
Robert: I beg pardon, Sir, I –
Mr Brok: Menial – for so I judge you by your garments – be silent – Jane Eyre,
             speak and do not by falsehood seek to palliate by paltry excuse –
Jane: Mr Broklehurst you are mistaken – this man is a well-tried honest
             servant and you have no right to insult him if with impunity you can
             me –
Mr Brok: Oh, misguided child raise not thy voice in wrath or ere the sun goes down
             punishment may befall thee! (*to Robert*) Whose servant art thou?
Robert: Mrs Reed's – this young lady's rich relation.
Mr Brok (slightly changed tone): Jane Eyre – repine not, you see you are not forgotten
             by your good and wealthy friends –
Jane: You are mistaken Sir, I am not the object of their visit.
Mr Brok [*illegible*]: In that case neglect your duty no more – follow your charges
             (*Points R*) remain firm to your post and see the girls do not pick the
             buttercups or play at idle games.
Jane: Are they then to have no amusement or pleasure?
Mr Brok: What dreadful words – take this tract, obdurate Jane Eyre, and read it
             with gleesome spirit to my little flock – go – (*Jane Eyre wearily exit
             IER*) (*To Robert*) Here is one for you too – (*gives tract*) it is entitled 'A
             bit of brimstone or a sod in pickle'.
Rochester (calls outside): Hollo! Here, I say, lend me a hand will you!
Mr Brok (looks off IER): A voice raised in distress, a muddy dirty-looking fellow – a
             beggar perhaps or tramp – let us flee from all such – neither lend or
             give to such (*to Robert*) follow me and acquaint me with your business
             here –

Rochester (calls out)

Exit Broklehurst followed by Robert 2EL

Enter Rochester 1ER; he appears suffering from effects of fall

Roch: Christianity and civilization exemplified – that fellow must have
             seen and heard me and yet in spite of the plight I'm in he walks off
             unconcernedly – to the devil with such fellows as he. My wrist hurts
             so confoundedly I –

Enter Jane Eyre 2ER

Roch:	Hollo! where did you spring from?
Jane:	I was in the field by the lane where your horse threw you – he was straying so I took the bridle and fastened him to the gate yonder –
Roch:	Bravo, my heroine, my good fairy of the wood – then you are used to horses, not a farmer's daughter I'm sure –
Jane:	No, I'm a pupil teacher at the institute here. You seem hurt – shall I get assistance for you?
Roch:	No not from there – just take your handkerchief and bind firmly round my wrist (*business*) there, deuce take me but you're a thorough household fairy. Now I must get my horse – have you an umbrella? No stick! Well then I must leave you –
Jane:	I am willing to help you, Sir.
Roch:	Did I forget to ask your leave? – Ah well – I'm in pain, my little teacher, so forgive me, and I'll not forget the governess of Lowood Institute.

(Exit leaning on Jane 2ER)

Enter Mrs Reed & John Reed followed by Georgina & Eliza Reed

Mrs Reed (going L looking off):	You're mistaken, my dear John – it never can be Jane!
Georg:	I really cannot conceive what it can signify whether it is or not – we have done with the low connexion and I presume none of us wish to renew it –
Eliza:	It certainly is not advisable on the score of expense alone – each day brings increase of expenditure and I consider I am sufficiently impoverished by a nearer relative than a cousin (*looks spitefully at John*).
John:	Well, book-keeper, anything else spiteful to say? I'll outlive you if it's only to read the interesting account of the death of the notorious female miser, Eliza Reed – (*Eliza & John quarrel, Georgina laughs*).
Mrs Reed:	Pray cease this bickering, I'll not call it quarrelling – and for such a subject!
Georg:	Indeed yes – absurd –
Eliza:	Rediculous and improfitable! [*sic*]
John (aside):	Perhaps – but still let's say no more about it.
Mrs Reed:	Quite right, my dear John – Georgina is wise in saying we have no wish to renew the acquaintance of your cousin which, as Eliza says, would be unprofitable in every way –
George & Eliza:	Then why bring us here?
John:	You can't call it pleasure!
Mrs Reed:	No, John, you are quite right – your brother is correct, my dears – it is not a pleasure, it is duty!

Georg:	A change, certainly!
Eliza:	Curiosities are expensive –
John:	You would deny yourself the luxury of wondering –
Mrs Reed:	Pray cease – left as this child was to my care, I did my best, but her evil temper would not allow her even to agree with us though as cousins –

Georg:	Cousin indeed – (*Turns up stage R*)
Eliza:	Prospectless and penniless! (*Turns up stage L*)
John (aside):	I'm not so sure of that –
Mrs Reed:	I dare not tell them of Jane's good fortune – the envy, covetousness and greed of my own children might ruin their chance of sharing in the fortune that awaits her – as a child she defied and terrified me but the discipline and usage of Lowood may have made her more tractable –

Enter Mr Broklehurst L; bows obsequiously to Georgina & Eliza who are L. John lights cigar & lounges on bank.

Mr Brok (bowing):	Your servant, ladies.
Georg:	Mama (*Nods superciliously*).
Eliza (who has been looking at contents of purse and closes it quickly):	Mama!
Mrs Reed (turning):	Ah, Mr Broklehurst – delighted to renew our acquaintance. My daughters you have met – my son, John Reed (*introducing; Brok bows*).
John:	That's me – How are you?
Mr Brok:	With gratitude I may say I am well and with pleasant fervour welcome my dear friends – you have come to see the humble work of a weak but worthy servant of Eleemosary [sic] offerings. (*Coughs & points*) This institute was erected –
Mrs Reed:	Yes, we had a circular – but Jane Eyre?
Mr Brok:	Good heart? benevolent fount overflowing with milk and honey for the orphan and the friendless – she has risen through the humble merits of my tuition to a pupil teacher –
Mrs Reed:	But is her temper changed?
Mr Brok:	Dear friend, first let me ask you your views as to her future –
Mrs Reed:	That depends upon herself (*with meaning*).
Mr Brok:	Will you not enter our humble though hospitable if not noble pile – we there can review the past and exchange ideas as to the future.
Georg:	It would be as well, Mama – I am fearfully faint – I wonder wonder if Jane can make me a welsh rarebit?
Mr Brok:	She may have neglected that branch of her education –
Eliza:	Education in many cases of the lower classes means extravagance – meat seven times a week – wicked and preposterous –
Mrs Reed:	My dears, do not discuss (*to Brok*) is Jane out?
Mr Brok:	Yes with the flock in yonder field.

John:	What – sheep-shearing –
Mr Brok:	No, tempering the elements to the rough winds of the youthful minds by reading one of my tracts to my dear little charges.
John:	Oh then, see, [I'll] soon fetch her (*to Mrs Reed*) you and the girls go in the house and I'll trot her in –
Mr Brok:	Ah then, you are old friends.
John:	Oh yes – you ask her, we liked each other – we did – I shall carry the scar she gave me to my grave and she can't forget my simple childish vengeance – if she should why I'll soon call it to her memory, never fear. (*Exit*)
Mrs Reed:	My dears, we'll do as your brother says – if Mr Broklehurst will give me his arm –
Mr Brok (business):	My dear Madam, let us lead the way to the institution which you will be pleased to observe was built or rather rebuilt by me (*walks off describing to Mrs Reed L*).
Georg:	With somebody else's money – (*following L*).
Eliza:	At a very great expense to outlay I'll be bound. (*Exeunt L*)

Enter Jane followed by John Reed

Jane:	John Reed, I beg you will not speak to me – time has not yet taught me to forget your cruel usage to a helpless child.
John:	You are powerful now, are you? and can defy me more than ever, Eh! –
Jane:	Yes I can, and will – for Heaven in its mercy has strengthened my heart – not with revengeful feelings either for my past wrongs or fears for future evil, firm in resolves to neither scorn nor threaten, but content to trust to that power which protects and punishes in its own good time. (*Exit L*)
John:	Well, that shews a better feeling than before for my purposes – more easily worked on – cant takes the place of viciousness – I hate her more than ever but if that precious letter mother keeps so closely to herself and never dreams that I know of is true, Jane Eyre would be worth marrying – I must prevent all chance of her reconciliation with any of my family but myself – then by shewing her a way to change her misery and poverty to affluence and happiness time will then let me mould circumstances to my will – I can't afford to lose a chance so for the present need Jane Eyre shall be my sport and profit. (*Exit L*)

Scene 2[12]*

School room at Lowood – 2 desks R & L – forms – bare walls – raised desk for Miss Temple C. Girls at desks over slates, books etc.

Mrs Reed, Georgina, Eliza, Miss Temple, Mr Broklehurst

A Bell rings as Scene opens

Mr Brok: This, my friends, is our Educational Mill – where we grind into the youthful mind the rudimentary basis of future knowledge –

Miss Temple: I have no reports to make or complaints today Sir.

Mr Brok: Indeed – but I have some enormitie[s] to call your attention to, Miss Temple, and but for the presence of strangers –

Mrs Reed: Pray proceed, Mr Broklehurst, with your discipline – we should prefer to see the usual working of the admirable Institute –

Georg: It's a novelty to us.

Eliza: And not expensive –

Mr Brok: Dear \honoured/ Friends, if you will let me call you so, for are we not fellow workers in the good cause of humanity and truth? I would willingly proceed as you wis[h] but justice will compel me to speak in terms of reproof to one in whom you are interested (*this is spoken down the stage to Mrs Reed*).

Mrs Reed: I should prefer that you did so – it will enable me to judge if I dare take her back to the bosom of my family.

Mr Brok: Then with a double zeal will I test her humility. Hem! (*Coughs loudly and goes to desk*) Miss Temple (*pulls out a long list*) I have here a few complaints and corrections I wish to bring to your notice – the first comes under the head of Domestic Stockings – Hem – I was struck with grief when I saw a quantity of black hose hanging on the line drying in the sun – now from the size of the holes in those stockings I'm sure they have not been mended from time to time –

Miss Temple: They are of an inferior quality –

Mr Brok: Impossible – I bought them myself – attend to it do not give out more than one darning needle to each pupil. Then I see in last week's account there are two extra tuckers – the rule limits to one.

Miss Temple: I gave permission for two pupils to take tea with some friends.

Mr Brok: I was not aware that our pupils had any – I'll see into it – but here is a thing that surprises and pains me – my friends, bear with me, it is very serious (*movement*). I find in the accounts a mention of lunch of bread and cheese twice in the past week – the regulations allow no such meal – whence the invitation – by whose authority –

---

12   * Fragile paper begins here.

Miss Temple: By mine, Sir – each day the breakfast was so ill prepared it could not possibly be eaten.

Mr Brok: One moment – are you aware my plan and rule is to make these girls hardy and able to dispense nay positively despise luxury and indulgence – if accident spoils the meal what a glorious opportunity for causing them to exercise self denial – such an incident should not be neutralized by pampering them – Miss Temple do not let it occur again – a glorious opportunity has been lost by feeding their bodies with bread and cheese and willing by pernicious indulgence their immortal souls –

Miss Temple: Jane Eyre pleaded so hard for them –

Mr Brok: You hear, my dear Madam – Jane Eyre (*looks round*) why she is not here –

Miss Temple: She complained of headache and I gave her leave to remain in the dormitory.

Mr Brok: This is very sad – send for her at once –

Miss Temple (sends off girl R): You will feel faint with the delay, I fear, let me advise some sherry and a biscuit (*Broklehurst goes off taking girl with him*).

Mr Reed: Georgina will you –

Georg: Much pleasure – I'm dying with hunger.

Eliza: I think it might have been offered before.

Broklehurst returns, child carrying tray and four glasses. Broklehurst hands [them] to the ladies and takes one.

Mr Brok: Miss Temple, that child has dirty hands – make a note for punishment –

Enter Jane Eyre R. Mrs Reed & daughters [are] L.

Mr Brok (C): Jane Eyre – I regret to hear of your duplicity and deceit – why seek to hide yourself from your friends under the canopy of a headache?

Jane: You are mistaken, Sir. I am friendless as I have ever been.

Mrs Reed: Jane – do you not see us?

Jane: Yes, and the sight of you reminds me of the agony I suffered as a child at your hands – left to your mercy – how did you fulfill the trust committed to your care? I freely forgive you the cruelties of the past, and only ask to be left in peace in my lonely wretched life –

Mr Brok: What words are these – ingratitude is a black spot on the human heart – has your elevation to the position of teacher made you forget the first precepts taught you, the principles of truth? To overcome the vanity that consumes you I'll ask you the elementary questions before the younger members of the School – Where do the wicked go?

Jane (steadfastly looking at Mrs Reed): To the bottomless pit.

Mr Brok: What is the bottomless pit?

Jane:	A pit full of fire – so pictured by you and such as you to children's minds – but the conscience of the wicked must ever foreshadow the punishment which awaits the evil doer – (*Goes up to place* [?] *Mrs Reed seems overcome*).
Mr Brok:	And what must the wicked do to prevent going there – [Jane's reply is not given] strange unorthodox and obdurate girl – young ladies, I regret you should hear such words – now you see this child – (*draws their attention to girl at desk R, leaving Mr[s] Reed L*).
Mrs Reed:	She is the same as ever, seems to se[e] my thoughts – but she shall not fri[ghten] me into weakness – this letter which [should] give her happiness she shall never [see] (*tears letter*). Now, Jane Eyre,you little know wha[t] your defiance has cost you –

John enters suddenly L

John (takes pieces of letter from her hand): Don't destroy it altogether, it may [be] useful yet –

Mrs Reed:	You know its contents then?
John:	Every word – don't be afraid, I'm not going to tell her though, until she's willing to come to our way of thinking – there, leave it to me, Mother, we must crush her still more, get her turned out from here if necessary – why, you look frightened!

Mr Broklehurst, Georgina and Eliza come down L, business of school going on at back

Mr Brok:	Mr Reed, welcome to Lowood Institute – we will now leave this – (*Child enters L and hands card [to Bro?]*[13]*) *Mr Rochester* (*as he speaks Rochester enters L, mud removed but arm in sling*).
Mr Brok:	Delighted at the honour – permit me to introduce to you, ladies, Mr Rochester, the most recent and liberal donor to our institute.
Roch:	Mrs Reed's know[n] to me already – may I dare hope that I am remembered?
Georg:	Indeed, yes – last season in town we met.
Eliza:	Grieved we were at missing Mr Rochester from our circle – Mama (*aside/) he's from India and wealthy!
Mrs Reed:	Delighted to meet Mr Rochester, whose name is so distinguished – my son – John Reed – (*they exchange bows*).
Roch:	Distinguished? And for what? you do me too much honour, Madam – the giving of a few hundred pounds which does not deprive me of o[ne] luxury or expensive whim scarcely deserves distinction or mention.
Mr Brok:	What we have we value not.

---

13 * Edges of page have crumbled leaving lacunae.

Roch: It is not so in my case – my visit here today proves it, for though I answered your appeal for funds, I have called to see for myself the workings of the place you pleaded.

Mr Brok: My dear Sir, you are quite right – I would there were more like you – you will readily see there is no extravagance here, no waste of substance in idle luxury.

Roch: It appears not – frivolities of life are scarcely the ideas to plant in the minds of those who have to start life depending on their own exertion – such things make the struggle for bread harder to bear.

All: Indeed, yes – (*a buzz of admiration*).

Roch: Have you a girl here called Eyre – Jane Eyre?

Mr Brok (Movement): Oh, Yes – Yes – (*Groans*).

John (to Mrs Reed aside): Now's your time – tell him not to spare her –

Mrs Reed (aside to Broklehurst): Do not mention the relation for the dear girl's sake – I have done with her for ever – I cast her off as a disgra[ce] as you will find her.

Mr Brok: In that case I too have done with her. Excuse me, I am sorry to say it, and it is with pain and regret, believe me, that this roof does shelter the girl you speak of – Jane Eyre – stand out. (*Jane advances R*) There she is, an example, Sir, of the vanity you so justly condemn – Miss Temple, the pupil teacher's hair will be cut and worn from now according to regulation 9 – may I ask your reason for enquiring for her –

Roch: Well, she was in the fields today, she spoke to a man – and –

Reeds: It was her then – we saw her.

Mr Brok (groans): My honored friends and patrons, let me speak a word of warning to my little flock – Dear children, there is an interloper, an alien and not a member of our true flock amongst you – guard against her, shun her, no longer shall she teach you and while she remains here exclude her from you –

Jane: What do you mean? What am I charged with and who is my [accuser]?

John (urges Mrs Reed)

Mrs Reed: I am – you are unworthy in every way for the position you hold, both false and deceitful –

Jane: I am not deceitful – if I were, I should say I loved you and I don't, I hate you –

Mr Brok (explanation to Rochester): This lady has been her benefactress –

Jane: I see your motive – fear not, I do not own you as a relation – I'll never call you Aunt again – the very thought of all your cruelties drives me nearly mad –

Mrs Reed: How dare you affirm that –

Jane: How dare I Mrs Reed? Because it's the truth – you think I have no
                  feelings, that I can do without one bit of love or kindness – but I cannot
                  live so longer! Heaven help me – what shall I do?

Mrs Reed and daughters turn from her

Mr Brok (with severity): Leave this house – th[is] home that you have cast your evil
                  blight upon – Begone!
Jane: Oh, Sir – what have I – do not believe me wicked entirely – at the sight
                  of these enemies of my childhood I was betrayed into passion – I hardly
                  know what I'm saying – Oh Forgive me Sir, Forgive me –
Mr Brok: Never.
Roch: Then she is expelled from Lowood Institute.
Mr Brok: Yes – for ever – my doors are closed against her.
Roch: The[n] mine are open to receive her!
All: What!
Roch: As governess to my adopted child.

Picture
Music[?]
Act Drop

Act II

Scene 1

Thornfield. Handsome chamber, elegant furniture. Doors R & L. Bay window. C.
Middle portion must open to admit entrance to room. Set[tee] by window – Armour
-Stand for [illegible] etc. – long bright Spanish knife – old fashioned hearth fire
burning. R. Piano. View of open country from window – Snow scene. Door 3 L L. 2
L 4 Candelabras about, wax lights & Xmas festoons. 2 LR.

Enter Grace R. She [has] pint measure etc in her hand. Followed by Robert she
points by window.

Grace: Put the rubbish there since you have been told to bring it into the house
                  –

Robert (carrying holly, firs): Rubbish do you call it, wait till you see how Mrs [E]yre
                  will arrange them, then you won't say so –
Grace: Yes I shall, you don't know me.
Robert: What's more – I don't want to, you don't say much, but think a lot I'll
                  be bound – (*He turns to holly etc. Grace gives one glance L and exits*
                  quickly – terrific scream heard. Robert looks up 3 LL.)

Robert:	What's that! – she's gone, it's my opinion she's either a supernatural being, or else she takes too many pints of porter. (*Jane enters R*) Anything wrong, Miss?
Jane:	No, Robert, I trust not. The screams I thought came from here.
Robert:	I believe, Miss, it's that Mrs Poole, she was here not a minute ago and vanished all of a sudden.
Jane:	I will speak to Mr Rochester about it – (*Busies herself with the holly etc*) Robert, send Miss Adele to me –
Robert:	Yes miss – beg pardon, miss but don't it seem strange to have the Reeds here –
Jane:	Strange – not at all – your master has invited them as his guests –
Robert:	But still after them behaving so badly to you, and master thinking such a lot of you –
Jane:	Silence – or serving as I do the same employer it will be my duty to report your remarks to him – Tell Miss Adele to come to me.
Robert:	Yes Miss. (*Aside*) I've offended her, I wouldn't have put my foot in it for anything, for she's – no – she's better than gold, that's what she is – (*Exit R*).
Jane:	I wish I could stifle my own thoughts as easily as silence the remarks of others – what right have I to rebel even by the shadow of a thought against the wishes, free act and will of a man of so noble, generous, honest heart and mind as him I serve – an air of mystery clings alike to him and to his house. I know not, nor do I seek to know the cause except it be to shew my loving gratitude and serve the man whose hand was stretched out to save the orphan and helpless girl from misery and shame –

Enter Adele R. She runs to Jane. (If child can speak, a few lines of dialogue follow.)

Jane:	There, darling – sit there (*ottoman*) and help me with these Christmas signs (*business*). No more lessons for a long time now.
Adele:	What must I do then?
Jane:	Why try to love Papa more than ever –
Adele:	And will you try to? (*Enter Rochester overhearing*)
Roch (R L):	Well said, Adele – the ruling passion of woman's nature is shown by your remark –
Jane:	And that is, Sir?
Roch:	Lovemaking – why, I declare – Jane Eyre you have quite a colour, your cheeks outdo the holly berries – but there, Adele, we must not tease or be troublesome, else kind governess will leave us – (*Child on his knee*) Do you know what today is? – (*Adele shakes head*) Well, it's my birthday – and what have you to give me – (*Adele thinks – puts arms about his neck – kiss*) There again – lavish of her kisses like her – (*puts her from him roughly – Adele holds down her head & runs to Jane*).

Jane: Oh Sir, she thinks you are angry.

Roch: No, no, my little poor child, not with you – not with you – there, darling, see what I have for you – (*puts chain & locket round her neck*) won't you like to go and look in the glass, and see how handsome and becoming it is, eh – (*Adele runs quickly out R*) The floweret is like the root from whence it spring, gold its sole idol, its life, and love – (*Jane Eyre is going Door R*) Where are you going?

Jane: To Adele, Sir.

Roch: She has more attractive metal now, never fear – you are afraid of me because I talk like a sphynx –

Jane: I am bewildered Sir, not afraid –

Roch: Then sit – draw your chair. Miss Eyre, I cannot see you without disturbing my comfortable position – come closer – I have performed the part of a good host, put my guests in the way of amusing each other – what do you think of my choosing your enemies for friends, eh?

Jane: Mr Rochester forgets that he pays for receiving his orders – few masters study the thoughts and feelings of their paid subordinate –

Roch: I forgot the salary – well in consideration of it, consent to dispense with conventional forms and phrases, without thinking the omission arises from insolence –

Jane: Informality I like – and can never mistake it for an insult, but a salary would never reconcile anyone to the latter –

Roch: Humbug – most people submit to anything for money – speak for yourself, and I'll listen and perhaps believe – do you think me handsome?

Jane: No Sir.

Roch: A plain answer indeed.

Jane: I beg pardon Sir, tastes differ, beauty is of little consequence.

Roch: Bah! Don't try to soften the previous outrage – Am I a fool?

Jane: Far from it, sir, but I hope a philanthropist –

Roch: You say that because I don't like the society of children and old women – I have been knocked about by fortune, she has knocked me with her knuckles until I'm as hard and tough as an india rubber ball – and yet ugly and heartless as I am women lay matrimonial snares for me – even your handsome cousin has smiled upon me – well, why shouldn't I marry her – (*Screams of laughter heard – both start – Rochester goes L, listens, returns to chair*). You look scared and afraid –

Jane: I have heard the screams before and,

Roch: And wondered why I could be so foolish as to keep a servant who has fits and makes such horrid sounds – Jane Eyre – sit down, obey your master – tell me then why I should not cheer my lonely life and marry your cousin Georgina Reed –

Jane: I know of none sir –

Roch: Once more quiet – then you cannot possibly have any objection –

Jane: I, Sir – Oh, no, except the day I wish you happiness I must resign my
                 post as governess here –
Roch: And wherefore?
Jane: As a dependent my duty is to honour your guests, but in the event of
                 your marriage with my cousin, I must not – nay will not remain here –
Roch: Well, when the contingency arrives I and Adele must suffer our loss
                 with calmness and becoming fortitude * but you may wish to desert us
                 before then – I'll no longer detain you here under false pretences –
Jane: Sir!
Roch: Yes, I have deceived you inasmuch as your pupil Adele is not my adopted
                 but my own child – you may have guessed it – no. Others less pure and
                 not so intensely ignorant of the world as you are would have done so
                 – Adele's mother was a French opera dancer – in my wildest moments
                 I never thought there was any consecrated virtue about her, more of
                 musk and amber than any odour of sanctity – but still I invested her
                 with fidelity and charm she did not possess. I found her false, so gave
                 her notice to quit the hotel I had taken for her, shot her companion,
                 which provoked her into abandoning her child – no natural claim will I
                 acknowledge on Adele's part to be supported by me, but I could not leave
                 the poor child to sink in the mud and slime of Paris, so I transplanted
                 it here to grow up in the wholesome soil of an English country garden
                 – you have taught, may have learnt to love her, but now you know who
                 and what your protégé is, I suppose you'll beg of me to look out for a
                 new governess – Eh? –
Jane: No – the poor child is blameless – forsaken by her mother and disowned
                 by you, she has more need of my care and love now.

Enter Georgina, Eliza, Broklehurst & John Ree[d]

Roch: Ah, my friends, you look charming (*Broklehurst smiles*[)] – at least the
                 ladies, while you all seem better for your walk (*Broklehurst appears
                 very cold*).
Georg: But we found it dull without you –
Roch: I was forced to forego the pleasure – wealth has its troubles and cares
                 –
Eliza: Ah! but it's nice to be rich –
Mr Brok (sentimentally to Eliza): Money cannot always obtain for us what we value
                 most in this vale of tears –
Roch: You are quite right, Mr Broklehurst, what say you Mr Reed? –
John: My life has taught me another creed –
Roch: I daresay, but your cousin Jane Eyre tries to think differently – (*Jane
                 has been up at window unnoticed till now*). Bye the bye, you did not see
                 her on your arrival – here, Miss Eyre, let me introduce you to your old
                 friends and relatives – (*Jane advances*) – This, as you know, is Adele's

governess, and for the time being my deputy housekeeper, through the illness of Mrs Fairfax – I mention it as your comfort during your visit depends on her – (*Each receives her with silent recognition according to character*). This will never do at [all.] Time [now to forget] and forgive. (*To Broklehurst*) [Can you not] as a Christian minister improve the opportunity by reading a homily on 'Peace & Goodwill.' –

Mr Brok:	If I thought the good seed would not fall on barren soil –
Roch:	Remember, Sir, from rocks and mountains wild flowers grow, *while hidden gems* securely rest unsuspected by us wise judges of each other.
Georg:	Cousin, I bear you no animosity. I am sure in your position you will do your duty and make me as comfortable as you can – (*Gives tips of fingers, Rochester looks at Jane who takes them*) –
Eliza:	I am pleased you are able to earn your own living and trust you are trying to save a little against a rainy day, it's sure to come sooner or later and of course you know you have no one to look to but yourself now your Aunt Reed is very ill and –
Jane:	I am sorry to hear that, how is it you have all left her alone –
Georg:	I couldn't do her any good – she has a nurse and besides (*to Rochester*) I did so long to see Thornfield (*They converse together*).

John (aside): And its owner –

Eliza (aside to Jane): You see it will make such a difference in the expenses and we are so dreadfully impoverished by John's conduct –

John (coming between them): Eh! (*Eliza goes up*) – There, Jane, will you shake [ha]nds and as Mr Rochester says forget the past, [it's?] not because you are a servant I'm [not?] proud to acknowledge your relationship, [?] my fault we have not renewed it befo[re] –

Jane:	I will try my best to forget the past, and wis[h] you happiness in the future –
Roch:	Now, Miss Eyre, if you have welcomed your friends, you will please attend to my guests –
Jane:	Yes, Sir. (*To ladies*) Shall I show you your rooms?
Georg:	Yes – Eliza come –

Eliza (who has been talking apart to Broklehurst): No, I have a duty to which I have devoted myself –

Mr Brok:	Yes, your noble-minded sister accompan[ies] me on a mission of charity – at such a season of the year one must open their heart and think of the starving poor in this inclement weather –
Roch:	Where are you going and what are you going to do?
Eliza:	To the cottages we passed this morning –
Mr Brok:	We purpose leaving a tract at each –
Eliza:	We shall not forget the dinner hour – for the present au revoir – come, Mr Broklehurst. (*[exeunt] 2 LR*)

Georg: Come, Jane, take me to my room and get me some mulled Port – Au Revoir till we meet in the billiard room – don't forget the challenge Mr Rochester.   (*Exeunt 2EL, shewn off by Jane*)

Roch: Ah, John Reed, what a happy man you must be with two such sisters.

John: So wealthy bachelors like you Rochester often think – why don't you marry?

Roch: For many reasons – possibly I may fear the chance of a refusal from the lady I should wish to make my wife –

John (aside): Can he mean Georgina?

Roch: But what of yourself – what's to hinder you from the happiness you would frame for me – you have the advantages of youth and looks –

John: Oh, it's all very well – no advantages in the matrimonial market outweigh wealth and position – besides my health for the last few months has prevented me –

Roch: Marrying – this is news – and who was to have been the happy woman?

John: Well, as it has not come off, we leave it from discussion until it does. (*Turns surlily away*)

Roch: Are you afraid of my poaching? Suppose I were to guess –

Enter Jane Eyre 2EL with packet – Rochester turns & says 'Jane Eyre' – John makes movement of surprise

Jane: Excuse me intruding, Sir, but one of the servants just fetched me to see a gentleman who is now in the grounds waiting for you –

Roch: Waiting to see me – why not shew him in here?

Jane: He refused to enter the house until you had received his message – in case you would not see him, he gave me this packet to hand to you –

Roch: The devil he did. What's his name?

Jane: Mason, Sir – from the West Indies.

Rochester starts

Jane: Why, you turn pale, Sir, are you ill? Let me fetch you some water.

Roch (aside): No, my little friend, don't stir, I've got a (*staggers*).

John (aside): Some secret here – why, what's wrong can I –

Roch (rallying): Nothing, its an attack I'm subject to. (*Aside to John*): One of the reasons I don't marry – (*aloud*): I must see my friend Mason at once, he was always eccentric. I must go now, this packet, you, Jane, take charge of this. I have no time to lock it up – (*aside*): do not leave it about – secure it safely in your own room till I ask for it – (*aloud*): There, I am quite recovered now, excuse me, Reed, I rejoin you directly. (*Goes to Door 2. Screams of laughter heard. Exit calling*): Grace Poole, Grace Poole –

John:	Why, Jane, what mean those horrible screams? Have you heard them before?
Jane:	Yes – but – I don't know –
John:	What! You mean to tell me you've lived in here for months and can listen unmoved to sounds like these?
Jane:	I do not say so and yet for all that I am ignorant of the cause – Mr Rochester thinks –
John:	No matter what he thinks – what does he say?
Jane:	That a servant who has been here for years breaks out in these wild fits –
John:	Desirable party – why does he keep her –
Jane:	I don't know –
John:	There's some secret mystery here – why was he so startled when you told him of his friend –
Jane:	It is not my business or yours John Reed –
John:	Suppose it means harm to you – being here your reputation perilled and character lost for ever –
Jane:	You dare to insinuate or insult –
John:	Neither, Jane – but I am your only male relative, the only one you have in the world that loves you –
Jane:	You love me – your lips pollute the word –
John:	No, don't say that, you'll find me a better fellow than you think for – cousins often marry, why should not we – (*John mistakes her silence.*) I'm not well off but still we can do well in many ways – why that packet might be some value suppose we see –
Jane:	John Reed, stand out of my way. Never dare speak to me again –
John:	If you won't love me, you shall learn to fear me –
Jane:	My heart is filled with scorn and loathing and has no room for fear of such as you – let me pass I say (*R*) insult or molest me again at your peril. (*Exit R*)
John:	We shall see who succeeds in the long run, my charming, amiable cousin – I've crushed you before and I will again or my name's not John Reed. (*Looks after*)

Enter Grace 3EL – pint measure etc. under apron. Touches John's arm – he turns.

John:	Hollo, who are you? What do you want?
Grace:	You are looking after our governess.
John:	Our's? What, are you one of the household?
Grace:	I rather think so, as you will find, if you stay here long enough –
John:	Indeed! what are you?
Grace:	A tried, trusted and confidential servant.
John:	What's that you have? (*Business*) Why, it's beer –

Grace: Yes, don't drink it, its my privilege – at times when I'm peculiar, I like
                  to take my meals alone – I'm privileged –
John (aside):   Now to fathom the secret of Thornfield – then you are an old servant
                  of the family –
Grace: Yes, Sir, and although I'm afflicted the kind master still lets me stay –
John: Bah – (*Turns from her*) A drunken idiot – the mystery is explained – I'll
                  have that packet though Jane Eyre –

Enter Rochester & Mason

Roch: Ah! still here – John Reed – (*introduces*) Mr_Mason whom I met years
                  ago in India. (*They exchange greeting*) – Grace, show Mr Mason to my
                  private study – (*Grace curtseys – shews Mason, who seems bewildered,
                  off 3EL*) You will excuse my friend but he has come over about property
                  he is interested in and I must write immediately – he will rejoin us later
                  on.

Scene gets darker

John: I shall be glad to know him – he must be a good fellow since he seems to
                  have such a hold on you – (*Starts*): by the way, what a singular woman
                  that is whom you sent away just now –
Roch: Oh yes, Grace Poole – well sometimes we make ourselves the victim of
                  our weaknesses knowingly – she's harmless though – (*Screams heard
                  louder than before*)
John: There is nothing harmless in that it means –

Enters all but Jane Eyre, Robert 1E

Roch: It means what is the matter – no danger – a mere rehearsal of Much
                  Ado About Nothing, the poor nervous, excitable servant's in a fit again.
                  (*To Robert*): What now?
Robert: Dinner is served, Sir.
Roch: There you are, don't wait, I must see to this to prevent its occurring
                  again. Shall be with you directly – now help me in my difficulty to support
                  the dignity of my home – (*They move off.*) Thanks, not a word –

When all off 2EL, enter Jane 2ER as Rochester rushes to 3EL

Roch (calls across): Wait here, Jane, you may save me yet –

Grace appears at door – exchanges hurried whisper to Rochester –

Roch: Jane, a bowl of water, and some linen quickly – *(She Exit 2ER.)* –

Enter Mason from 3EL – torn & bleeding – Jane re-enters with bowl etc – Rochester supports Mason to chair

Roch: There, never mind. The water, bandage his hand – (*business*) fool to venture –

Mason: I thought I might do good – I

Roch: It's idle to talk now, *away* at once for all our sakes – or there'll be no peace now – (*Screams – Mason starts*) Come, man try the window – straight to the gate to save time – Carter the chemist will know what is best for the bite of a dog –

Rochester looks at[14]* *Jane and assists Mason to the window. Exit Mason. Rochester watches – Jane stands amazed. Rochester closes window.*

Roch: Heavens, when w[i]ll th[is] end – Jane, you look pale – the danger's past – the enemy is gone.

Jane: That man can harm you, Sir, he dare not –

Roch: Right – little friend, he never will without he knows he can – it is imperative that I should keep him ignorant that harm to me is []possible – I puzzle you – I'll do so no more for you are my friend are you not?

Jane: I like to obey you, Sir, and if you have no more to fear from others than from me you are safe.

Roch: Heaven grant it may be so.

Enter Robert 1EL

Robert: Your guests are anxious for you, Sir.   (*Exit Robert.*)

Roch: Enough – I am free now and will join them. And you, Jane Eyre?

Jane: I am going to hear Adele say her evening prayers.

Roch: Then frame one that she may whisper to heaven for me.

Jane exit to ER

Roch: What's the feeling that overcomes me? I have lived it down till now – Oh God grant it may kill rather than conquer me. (*Enter Robert.*) Lights here and make the house seem gay with merriment and joy and drown the curse. Now for my friends and, as the world says, my future bride.   (*Exit 1EL.*)

Robert lights candles about stage

---

14   * New hand begins here.

Robert: Well, Master does seem strange – he is a good fellow, I'm sure and yet
                  I don't like living in the house – I never look at the curtain without I
                  think – hollo, what's that? Oh, its only the wind –

Enter Grace 2EL – glass of water & decanter on tray

Robert: Hollo, how quiet you are – I never heard you come in.
Grace: No need to make a noise unless you get something for it.
Robert: I don't know how it is, but you always frighten me.
Grace: Fools are easily frightened – (*Robert still lighting & arranging
                  room.*)

Enter John 1EL

John: What's this, more beer?
Grace: No, Sir, it's water for the Governess – who I have to attend to every
                  nigh[t] – least way put this here for he[r] to take with her the last thing
                  – such fads and fancies – (*She place[s] tray on small table R Robert
                  [?].*)
John: *Indeed*! If I was sure that she would drink any of it that packet should
                  at lea[st] be mine – it would be eas[y] to ascertain her room – first[15]*
                  [I] must get the op[i]ate – but – Grace – is there a doctor near here –
Grace: Oh, yes, quite close to the gate – are you ill?
John: No, a neuralgia pain – I was forced to leave the table – direct me to his
                  house.
Grace: Shall I go, Sir?
John: No, my good woman – I know what I require.
Grace: You can see his lamp from the window – (*They go to the window.*) The
                  snow has covered the path that leads to the gate –
John: Why, what are those footprints by the window there? They go right
                  along the way you point – why it's quite close to the ground – I can
                  get out by here –
Grace: No, Sir, go round the door – I daren't let you this way –
John: Hollo – what's frightened you? There's something red upon the snow
                  – it looks like blood – there (*gives mone[y]*) You needn't direct me
                  further – I'll find my way, and solve the mystery of Thornfield [three
                  or four words illegible.]

Enter Jane 2ER

Jane: What are you doing here, Grace?
Grace: I'm going up to my own room directly – did you come here for
                  Master?

---

[15]   * Original hand resumes here.

Jane:	No, why do you ask?
Grace:	Nothing particular except you seemed frightened a bit ago and I thought perhaps you wanted to talk to him about the noises. Do you bolt the door of a night? It will be wiser to do so in case of danger – robbers you know – though we can trust in Providence we must not dispute the means for securing – I'm going to my own room now – Good night, Miss – *(Exit 3EL)*
Jane:	Can it be that meditates evil against me [*sic*]? I must and will speak to Mr Rochester, or the strain will be too much for my mind – and yet should I not bear something for his sake – I'll try, heaven help me, I'll try.

Enter Georgina & Eliza 1EL

Georgina:	By no means a lovely dinner party.
Eliza:	The repast was perfect but an amount of extravagan[ce] which you should see to if you accept Mr Rochester –
Georg:	I'll wait until he proposes, Eliza.
Eliza:	He is sure to do so before our visit is [over?]
Georg:	Well, when he does I think I shall accept him – the place is desirable and his wealth is not in Bank shares or any fluctuatious See [S]aw fund – you, Eliza, shall be my Secretary & Book-keepe[r].
Eliza:	Provided my future husband does not object I may accept such a post –
Georg:	You don't mean to say –
Eliza:	Anything premature – we'll not discuss it further – Jane, open the piano – Georgina let us entice these haughty men from their wine – it will be society for all and a saving of useless expense – *(Plays)*.

John enters hurriedly 2EL. Seeing who is in the room he saunters careless by R as Rochester & Broklehurst enter 1EL. Eliza ceases to play as Rochester enters.

Roch:	Brav[o]! that is, *(entering)* do not let us lose the charms of music it – [soothes] the savage bre[ast] [Edge of page crumbled; difficult to tell where words may be missing.]
Broklehurst (who is slightly elevated):	Harmony shed[s] its soothing ray upon my troubled hear[t] [?] I adore it – pray proceed –
Georg:	Perhaps Eliza's tired –
Eliza:	Spiteful! Ah, dear, you can't play – it is a pity isn't it –
Georg:	Thanks, dear, I'm not fond of display or exertion – do you sing, Mr Rochester[?]
Roch:	Well, no, but our good friend will help me in the difficulty *(to Broklehurst)*.

Mr Brok:	I do not lack the power or the will but tho' the spirit and voice be strong the knowledge of words and melody [are] weak yet still I will join[?] – let us lift our organs and exclaim altogether – Oh let us be joyful –
Eliza:	I will try a little air. (*She sings – business ad lib.*)

Jane has been sitting hidden and unobserved.

Roch:	Jane Eyre, I missed you – play to us –
Jane:	Pardon me, Sir – I was merely waiti[ng] your orders before retiring.
Roch:	No, come, let your friends hear one of your qualifications for the post you hold.
Eliza:	Play your scales, Jane, then –
Jane:	Sir, I beg you'll excuse my staying in this room – (*Takes tray with water bottle & glass on R*)

John is R. Screams of laughter from L. All turn – John, who has been watching opportunity, pours contents of phial in water bottle.

Georg:	How dreadful – I feel quite frightened!
Eliza:	I cannot remain here, Georgi, let us say Good night –
Roch:	Ladies – sorry to lose your society – but you are perhaps tired with travelling – these sounds disturb you – \you/ will not hear the[m] tomorrow – the cause shall be removed – Good night –

Exeunt Georg & Eliz after business

Mr Brok:	Now we are deserted indeed – no mo[re] shall the children of Judea sing – then what are we to do –
Roch:	I have important letters to read and ans[wer.]
John:	What – the packet you received today[?] By the Bye, where's your friend Ma[son?]
Roch:	He's gone.
John (aside):	Yes, but not far.
Jane:	Here is the packet you gave me to mind.
Roch:	Take charge of it (*to [Jane]*). I shall sit here and read my letters, so excuse me for at least the present – I will perhaps join you in the billiard room – if not, Good night – to morrow morning I will prove a [b]etter [h]ost.

Jane strikes bell. Robert enters [and] puts out light.

Roch:	I shall go to bed. (*Goes up [to] arm chair*)
Mr Brok:	Don't apologize – I shall not play billiards –
John:	You should as a commercial of the Church on the Green as well as black cloth there's cannons to be made such things is Flukes and double pockets while sinecures we call the rest [*sic*].

Mr Brok:	I don't understand the game – Good night.

(Robert shews [him] off 2LE)

John: Well, good night – I'll not intrude on your correspondence – I am sure
it's urgent – and to you, cousin Jane, Good night – I am glad you have
so *good* and kind [a] master.

(Exit 2EL. Rochester follow[s] & closes door.)

Roch: Jane, for the love of heaven give me a glass of water or as the play is
finished the actor faints – (*Jane gives him water – he drinks & sinks
into arm chair LC*)

Roch: Jane, you appear to me tonight like the quiet good fairy in humble guise
I saw first in the lane – I had no presentiment then my genius for good or
evil stood before me – it was so – would to heaven I had d[i]ed then!

Jane: If the past is painful, Sir, why think of it – (*Snow comes*) I will leave
you, Sir – Good night!   (*Taking candle Exit Jane LER*)

*Rochester, who has followed her, leans wearily by it then with an effort locks door.
Only lamp burns. Stage dark.*

Roch: Safer for you, Jane Eyre. I wish I could [stamp?] out from your life
all further misery and trouble – (*sits*) – I am strangely sleepy – I must
not stay here or doze – Jane – I love you with love as strong as you are
pure and good – my own own wife –

*Maniac appears at window – hair showing – she plays with falling snow – looks
in – falls along window – at last gets on sill or parapet. Window C flies open – she
crouches, then enters – looks about – at last sees knife – the brightness attracts – she
holds [it] in light by open window – feeling the cold – moves away goes to fire – still
holding knife, takes half-burnt stick – tosses it about as a child would – she gets near
curtains where Rochester sleeps – [br]and starts into a flame – she yells out with
delight –*

Act III

Scene 1

*Exterior of Thornfield House. Built out L – Balcony – Steps return pce 3EL. Backing
Landscape – Church in distance R.*

Mason discovered looking up at house

Mason: No signs of any one about – I'm afraid to ring – she might hear my voice
and break out again – besides Rochester might suspect me – Oh! how I
wish I had never seen John Reed – since that fearful night he has held
me completely in his power and swayed my every act – if I only had
nerve enough to leave here for ever, and make my escape from the man

who is leading me hour by hour into greater danger. Once away I can make terms with Rochester – he has always treated me liberally. I will – I'll go – he shall tempt me no more – (*Is going R – met by John*)

Mason *(aside)*:	Too late.
John:	No reply as yet to our letter?
Mason:	I don't know – I have not seen anyone – besides it's your letter.
[John:]	Miserable fool. What are you afraid of? Haven't we got this man in our power to increase the value of the secret we possess? I have waited until today – and do you think he'll defy us now and run the risk of exposure on this his wedding day for the sake of the paltry sum we ask –
Mason:	But he does not know or suspect that –
John:	You would turn against him – I thought you said he knew you – so why not eh?
Mason:	Because he has always treated me well and kindly, helped me no end of times – while you –
John:	Yes, me – see what I've done for you!
Mason:	Brought me lower than ever eve[r] I imagined I could be.
John:	How so?
Mason:	A weak and vacillating man with fortune at his command beca[m]e a fit prey for you and when driven by desperation and poverty he forgot the ties of gratitude and betraye[d] a noble and generous man.
John:	That's a very pretty sentiment but I've no fine feelings – so I'll ring the bell – and get the answer to our letter – I say ours because you are the 'proof' – failing that cursed packet I fall back on you – I don't seek 'War to the knife' – I'll sink all revenge for the sake of a lump sum down – why man – what do you fear, keep up – in a few hours you will be well reconciled to your own fortune – let the devil take every body else's.
Mason:	Well, if he will agree to anything like your – I mean our terms –
John:	Never fear – here goes to prove it! (*Rings bell*)

Enter Robert

John:	Mr Rochester?
Robert:	What name, Sir?
John:	John Reed –

Robert:	Oh, you left the letter last night – there is no answer and here is your letter – (*Closes door*)
Mason:	There – I knew it – his indomita[ble] will and nerve of iron you will ne[ver] conquer or shake.
John:	That['s?] my work – if I fail I'll call on you – at least we shall thwart his intention and mar his happiness – to say nothing of the revenge I shall have on my cousin Jane Eyre.
Mason:	Your satisfaction is good for yourself but it won't pay the hotel bill here – what am I to do?

John: Why get out – don't go far in case you are wanted – Go! (*Shout[s?]*)

Exit Mason R

John: Fool! he can't think what it is to be a broken man as I am – I've treasured the thought that will stand me in good stead today – now then find the marketa[ble] price – is *going up* – (*Grace at door*).
Grace: Your business Sir?
John: Mr Rochester.
Grace: He can't see you.
John: Won't, you mean – well, I'll wait here – he's bound to pass this way to the church[.]
Grace: But surely on a day like this you'[ll] not trouble him? Won't I tho' – he'll see!
Grace: Your sisters are here – do you wish to see them?
John: Yes, I do, so tell them – their affectionate brother waits for an interview. (*Grace goes in leaving door open.*) Just as well – I might get a trifle out of them to keep me going altho' the big thing may come off yet.

Georgina & Eliza – from house on steps

Georg: We heard you were here.
Eliza: So we came to enquire what you wanted.
John: Can't you guess – money.
Georg: I can't supply you. I have none – if I had I should not be here [to see?] Jane Eyre married to –
Eliza: The man you though[t] safe for yourself – never mind – of course the money [is?] a loss and we suffer by this besides since [now?] we have been impoverishe[d] so much that we could not with wisdo[m] refuse the invite to our relative['s] weddin[g].
John: Well if there's anything to be got out [illegible] you'll have but to the [*sic*]. Can either of you help me – come exercise your sisterly love.
Georg: I have some – I mean money and that's all you want –
Eliza: Why not be careful, John – I can only give you advice –
John: To the devil – (*Eliza screams*).
Georg: I have done with you for ever!   (*E[xit] in[to] house*)
John: Always selfish –

Enter Broklehurst from house
Broklehurst: I heard you were here, dear Miss Reed[.]
Eliza: Yes, I was summoned to a most painful interview – I couldn't discuss it now, I only say 'Bro[ther] John I've done with you for ever'!
                                          (*Exit into house*)
Mr Brok: What can be the meaning?
John: Well – that she is turning against [me] so I suppose we had better go [!]

Mr Brok: I am respected and invited to the wedding – you my friend are as a
                 Black Sheep – you have called the wolf and provoked in the shape of
                 the animal of annoyance you ask for help – why not help the friend
                 [?]
John: I would if I could escape with impunity like you've done.
Mr Brok: Severity – severity – severity. As [blank] I will entice him from here
                 – let us take a stroll –
John: A drink you mean – I'm staying at the 'Bee'.
Mr Brok: Dear John, you may drive forty horses to the pond but not one will
                 drink – but still on certain occasions the *animals will* not be obstinate
                 – let us seek the [blank] and try the milk –
John: And Rum!   (*Exeunt R*)

Church bells heard – Rochester enters from house.

Roch: At last my dream of happiness is realized – in a few hours I'll be far
                 away with all I love and value on earth and so at last burst the bond
                 of misery that binds to the place – the bells ring out then to your peal
                 which sends me echo in my heart of future hope and happiness [*sic*].

Enter Jane Eyre, Georgina & Eliza

*Children from R then flowers. Villagers enter R. Cheer – Broklehurst hastens to help
ladies down steps of house.*

Roch: See, Jane, your friends of former days have not forgotten you –
Jane: Their presence and humble offering indeed make me happy – but another
                 instance of your thought and love –
Roch: The same that shall encompass thee through life – now friend[s] to the
                 Church – (*Enter John R followe[d] by Mason*)
John: Stop –
Roch: At whose command?

John: At mine (*aside to Rochester, who has seen Mason*): – It is not too l[ate]
                 [this is the end of the line & bottom of the page] will you the money.
Roch: To be your victim – Never!
Jane: Rochester, what does this mean?
John: He can't answer so I will – if he marries you it is not legal!
All (general movement): Why?

John: He has a wife already – now, Mr Mason, it's your turn – (*Screams. To
                 Mason*): If you are silent your sister the Maniac proclaims her right!
All: His sister!
John: Yes and his wife –

Maniac appears at open window – Grace rushes from house

Grace (to Rochester): She has \escaped and/ fastened the door of the passage that leads to her cell – the place is in flames and I cannot get near her –

Flames burst out – Maniac on parapet

Roch: What can I do?
Jane: Do? Why, your duty – save your wife!

Rochester makes movement to her – she draws back and points at Maniac. Business until Rochester rushes out of house – figure falls – from return pce.

Scene 2

Front Chamber – Broklehurst supporting Eliza

Broklehurst: Lean on me – you need support indeed at this trying moment – droop not my lilly – you Broklehurst –
Eliza: Oh!
Mr Brok: No – be Mrs Broklehurst!
Eliza: At such a moment –
Mr Brok: That is why I avail myself of it, that I may point a moral and ado[rn a] tale – Eliza, I am no more decep[5 or 6 characters] dwelleth not here – (*Strikes breast*) – When first my eye fell upon thee I wa[5 or 6 characters] resolve at least to try to win the priz[5 or 6 characters] tell me may I call you min[e] and extend my School –
Eliza: Oh! how can you talk to me so – I don't dislike it – but the terrible example we have just seen and loo[k] at the waste of money – the breakfas[t!]
[Mr Brok:]   Then fix an early date it may do for a [5 or 6 characters] to regale our friends with –
Eliza: I can't refuse you – but not a word before Georgina yet –
Mr Brok: I'll not breathe a syllable until our happiness is confirmed – (*about to embrace*)
[Eliza:]   Don't! Oh here comes Georgina!

Enter Georgina L
Georg: A lucky escape indeed for me – but if I had been his victim the law should have punished him –
Mr Brok: He is a wolf with a raging tooth seeking to devour the young lamb –
Georg: I have no sympathy for the young lamb as you call her –
Eliza: An artful designing cat –
Mr Brok: Quite so – the simile is perfect.

Georg:	I shall pack up and leave at onc[e.]
Eliza:	It will never do to stay, altho' it's a sad waste of money –

Enter Grace L

Georg:	Acquaint your master that I cannot remain here after these terrible disclosures –
Eliza:	That we regret coming –
Grace:	The doctor is with him now in the drawing-room – master was taken there and must not be moved yet – as you will have to pass through may I ask you to delay your departure until we can get Mr Rochester to his room –
Georg:	Decidedly not. I'll not remain here a moment more than is absolutely necessary for my own comfort –
Eliza:	I quite agree with you, sister – the dreadful place might corrup[t] any of us –
Mr Brok:	Then let us depart – for fear of contamination – for though my friend we have our armour buckled on we may fall beneath temptation. Let us gird up our loins and pack our portmanteaus – come – I will lead the way. And, my good woman, if you have any regard for yourself, you will not remain here – come my friends – (*Exeunt L*)
Grace:	Indeed – well, as my patient is dead, my work is over, yet still I'll stay to help if possible the man who now is blind and helpless –

(*Exit R*)

Scene 3

Chamber same as Act II

Rochester seated in chair. Jane standing at door dressed as in firs[t] Act.

[*Roch:*]	Jane – Jane – what, gone from m[e?] Then I am indeed alone and helpless, the light of my soul lost to me for, what matters then the[16]* power of night – since she has left me life is dark indeed. (*Sinks back. Jane hands him a glass of water.*)
Roch:	This is not Grace nor – no, no, I cannot be mistaken – speak to me or I shall go mad! tell me I am not dreami[ng!] Is it? Is it? Jane –
Jane:	Yes, Sir.
Roch:	And by now I should have called you Wife – my dream of happiness is over.
Jane:	Thank heaven the waking came to save you from crime – bless and forgive me. I do those whose vengeance spared us both from sin and shame.

---

[16] * New hand begins here.

Roch: Do you turn from me, Jane?

Jane: No, Sir, never in heart, but respect to the dead as well as duty to myself makes me say farewell.

Roch: Respect and duty – cold words compared with love and worship – listen to me – hear my story, if not to forgive, at least to pity me – my father['s] idol was gold and for me, his second son, he arranged a marriage with the daughter of a wealthy Indian merchant – I did not oppose his will and before I was two and twenty I found myself cursed with a wife in whom there was the taint of madness. For years I kept the secret of my misery but at last her conduct and violence through her own excess became dangerous – by the death of my father and brother, I succeeded to Thornfield. I left India and returned to England, bringing with me the wretched woman whose existence I have since then hidden from the world. I sought by travel and dissipation to kill the horrors of my home while my heart was yearning for the holy love of a pure minde[d] and honest wife.

Jane: Do not speak farther I implore – I both pity and forgive you.

Roch: Then why withhold your love from me – let the world and society say and think what it may – can you not defy them and give your life and happiness to me?

Jane: Master – friend – husband – for so by the right of our love you are – do not tempt me to what in after years even you might condemn.

Roch: Then you'll leave me here to die uncared for and alone.

Jane: No, no, I cannot bear to hear you talk so – do not think lightly of me if I cast aside all womanly reason and tell you, as I do, my love for you is unchanged and as great as ever – the world say what it may I will not – cannot desert [you.]

Grace: Mr Mason wishes to see you, Sir – may he come in?

Roch: Yes.

Enter Mason

Roch: Let him speak quickly and be gone.

Mason: I am here to make the only restitution in my power. Here is a letter for Jane Eyre. I know by its contents its value and importance. (*Jane takes letter.*)

[Jane:] It bears a date of more than two years ago.

Mason: Yes – has been kept back by your Aunt that you might never know the wealth your Uncle had left you.

Enter John

John: You miserable thief – you have robbed me – give me back those papers or I'll –

Mason: It is too late to threaten – she knows her good fortu[ne] and can defy
            you – as I do!
John: What – you dare –
Mason: Yes! Weak and false as I've been, I have at last had the resolution to
            do an act of right and justice and save you from further crime –

[Enter Mr Broklehurst]

Mr Brok: I am pained to be the bearer of sad and sorrowful news but this is a
            v[a]l[e] of tears – John Reed, your mother's dea[d] and your sisters are
            poor now, as you are.

Jane business

John: Dead!
Mr Brok: Alas, yes. Flesh is grass/ Grass is clay / We're here sometime / Then
            called away. I will see them to the coach and then depart on my way
            – they are here!

Enter Georgina & Eliza

Jane: Cousins, I am sorry for your loss.
Georg: What – is it possible?
Eliza: And can you condole with us?
Jane: And willing to help you – you look incredulous. I have the power – this
            letter informs me I am rich and you both shall share my property!
Georg & Eliza: Cousin Jane!
Jane: Not a word – forget the past as I forgive it. (*Movement [as] John Reed
            goes toward door*) Stay, John Reed, you need help to save you from your
            worst enemy – yourself. Will you not speak to him? (*To Rochester*)
Roch: Say and do as you will – I'll not mar your angel[ic] work by word or
            deed.
John: Coals of fire – may time prove their worth and my repentence to be
            true.
Jane: And to that same future do we all look for hope and happiness – while
            memory leads us back with tend[er] care to thoughts we love and cherish
            may all pas[t] wrongs and evils be forgotten and cloud no more the life
            and joy of Jane Eyre.

Jane Eyre

by

W.G. Wills

1882

Editor's Notes

The Text

The text exists in a single hand-written copy in the Lord Chamberlain's Collection of Plays in the British Library (Add. MS 53285 E). Figure 20 shows the title page of the manuscript. The licence number is 265 and the licence ticket reads: 'Name of Play: "Jane Eyre" Drama; Theatre: Globe; Date of Licence: Decr. 18th 1882'. The Lord Chamberlain's Day Book has no additional information except 'Date of Licence 18 Dec Date of Entry 19 Dec'.

The play is written in several different hands on one side only of blue-lined foolscap firmly stitched and glued into a booklet; some left-hand letters are lost in the binding. A blank page is left between acts and there are several blank pages at the end of the booklet. Pages are numbered throughout, beginning with the first page, which contains the title and beginning of the text; original new numbers for Act II have been struck out. The title and beginning of Act I is partly obscured by the licence ticket.

For Act I, the hand is large, sprawling but legible and the ink very black; Acts II and IV have a large, round, childish hand; Act III is different again but still large and legible. In Act I, the speakers' names are fully spelt out and centred over the text; elsewhere they are more abbreviated and to the left; in Act III they are underlined in red. I have adopted the more complete versions of names used in Act I. Punctuation is sparse and the same light mark serves for comma or full stop; a double mark could be exclamation mark, question mark, colon or semi-colon. There are very few apostrophes (except in Act III where they are used for plurals) and there are some odd spellings such as 'comeing'. On the other hand, the writer understands French and Adèle's mistakes in English (not taken from the novel) are realistic. In editing for spelling and punctuation I have made as few changes as possible, consistent with clear sense; I have, however, introduced some dashes in place of 'comma splice' or where the sentence is undivided. I have removed capital letters from the middles of sentences except for the emphatic sentence, 'Is that Woman Your Wife?'. Rochester is called 'Fairfax' in Act I, 'Edmund' in Act II and 'Edward' in Act III. Since 'Edmund' is the predominant form, I have adopted this throughout.

The Playwright

Apart from Birch-Pfeiffer, whose reputation lay on the continent of Europe, William Gorman Wills is the only playwright in this collection who was well known during his lifetime, and the only one to have a published biography.[1] Born in Ireland in 1828, the son of the poet James Wills,[2] he was a noted portrait-painter as well as writing plays, novels and poetry. From the 1860s onwards he was living in London and

---

[1]   Wills, 1898.
[2]   Boase, Vol. 3, p. 1395.

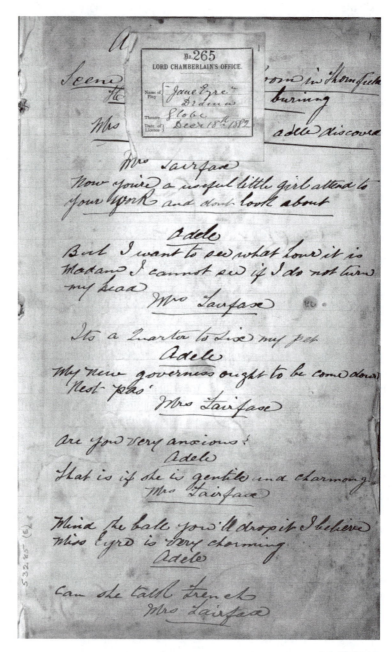

Figure 20 Facsimile of the title page of the manuscript of W.G. Wills's *Jane Eyre*, 1882. Reproduced by permission of the British Library: Add. MS 53285 E

practising all these occupations; his dramatizations were primarily historical dramas and adaptations of novels. Lynton Hudson describes him as 'one of the busiest play-manufacturers of his time [...] a cousin of Oscar Wilde, who had become in effect the resident dramaturge of the Lyceum in that he was the first playwright to draw a yearly salary from a theatre'.[3] The *Backstage* website lists over a hundred items, mostly play programmes, under his name. A contemporary wrote of him that

> his Bohemian life, his impassioned character, his hasty methods of production, gave him in the distance the look of genius. But it was a misleading look ... his pieces are founded upon conceptions which crumble away upon analysis.[4]

He had, however, a genuine talent for the theatre: 'as a deviser of theatrical scenes and situations, Wills had power. His taste was thoroughly commonplace, his language trivial or extravagant. But he could fit eminent actors with telling parts, and was useful as librettist to the scene-painter and stage-manager'.[5]

Wills's *Jane Eyre* was written during a period in which he 'produced with great rapidity a quantity of very inferior work'.[6] It 'was written with great rapidity, for it was intended to take the place at the Globe of a play which was not paying its expenses, and the work occupied only a fortnight'. Indeed, his brother writes, 'the last act was at first very carelessly written' and had to be re-written before it was performed.[7]

The writing in this play reflects the progressive gentrification of theatre audiences during the century, and also the central location of the theatre. The language follows Charlotte Brontë's novel very closely in parts, with a sophisticated terminology and clever jokes. Despite the sensational appearance of the murderous madwoman in Act II, there is little striving for suspense. The play seems to appeal to an audience who already know the story, a speculation born out by the reception of the play (below). There is, however, a notable shift in emphasis, as compared with the novel, from Jane's experiences to Rochester's, for instance in the transfer of a memorable phrase – 'I have stood at the bar of my own conscience' – from her to him.[8]

Theatres and Performances

The play was written for the short-lived Globe Theatre in Newcastle Street, off the Strand (not to be confused either with Shakespeare's Globe or with the Globe on Shaftesbury Avenue), and first performed there on 23 December 1882,[9] with Mrs

---

3 Hudson, p. 64.
4 *DNB*, quoting Augustin Filon.
5 *Cambridge History of English and American Literature*, Vol. 13, Part 1; accessed 9 February 2005.
6 *DNB*.
7 Wills, pp. 186–7. I am grateful to Sarah Fermi for making this passage available to me.
8 Act II; in the novel, Jane is 'Arraigned at my own bar' (Vol. II, Ch. 1).
9 *Referee* (17 December) advertises the play for 23 December; see also *Times*, 19 December 1882, p. 6, col A; *Daily News*, 19 December 1882, p. 4; *Stage*, 29 December 1882, p. 11.

Bernard-Beere, its actor-manager, in the title role (see cover picture for her portrait as Jane Eyre). *The Illustrated London News* announces that 'lo, and behold! our Christmas Eve will be spent with Mrs Bernard-Beere at the Globe Theatre, crying our eyes out over the new version, by Mr. W.G. Wills, of "Jane Eyre"'.[10] The play ran throughout February 1883,[11] but on 4 March, the *New York Times* announced bleakly that '"Jane Eyre" at the Globe is not a success. It will be played for the last time tonight'. *The Referee*, however, offers a different explanation, reporting on 28 January that 'Mrs Bernard Beere [...] has been indisposed in the last week, and has had to seek a change of Eyre, her part as Jane of that ilk being taken by Miss Alexis Leighton'. By 11 February, we find that

> Next week will see the last of 'Jane Eyre' at the Globe. Mrs Bernard-Beere [...] has several times been out of the cast though indisposition, and her health is so precarious that she has resolved to adopt the advice of her medical attendant and seek a fresh supply of vigour in the south of France.[12]

On 17 February, *The Graphic* announces that 'The Globe Theatre closes this evening, Mrs Bernard-Beere's state of health having unfortunately compelled her to relinquish the management of that house'.[13] After a three-week silence the following announcement appears in *The Era*: 'Globe Theatre.– Owing to the continued indisposition of Mrs BERNARD-BEERE, the Theatre is TO BE LET for a short period at a moderate rent. Apply to Mr Charles Kelly, at the Theatre'.[14] A retrospective article on Bernard-Beere in *The Sketch* confirms that her illness had in fact been life-threatening.[15]

The Globe Theatre was built, in 1868, in the excavations intended for a large hotel which was not completed, and was demolished in 1902.[16] Figure 21 shows the newly built interior in 1869. Contradictory accounts exist of its comfort. C. Gordon, writing in 1903, is fairly positive:

---

10   *ILN*, 16 December 1882 (Vol. 81, p. 623). Playbills in Bodleian (John Johnson Collection), BL, BPM and HTC (Stead Collection) show that the play was preceded by a comedietta, also by Wills, entitled *A Fair Encounter*. (Vol. V, pp. 80, 627 lists 23 Dec as the first performance).

11   *Times*, 19 December 1882, p. 6, col. A.; 23 December, p. 8, col. C; 25 December, p. 6, col. A; 29 December, p. 6, col. D; 11 January 1883, p. 8, col. B; 12 and 13 January; 1 and 16 Feb. *NYT* has a notice for 7 January 1883, p. 10.

12   *Referee*, 28 January 1883, p. 3, 11 February 1883, p. 3.

13   *Graphic*, 17 February 1883, p. 178.

14   *Era*, 3 March 1883.

15   *Sketch*, 28 April 1897, p. 28.

16   Banham. Howard (p. 95) also gives this demolition date, though Bergan says 'after World War I' (p. 77).

The proprietor was Mr Sefton Parry, who thoroughly understood the needs of a theatre, and he made a very comfortable little place of this, which afforded accommodation for about 1500 people. Its construction was peculiar: for, taking advantage of the deep foundations of the premises which were in course of construction by the defunct Strand Hotel Company, he made the pit and stage underground, the dress circle and boxes being even with the entrance in Newcastle Street [...] The interior of the theatre was in the form of a segment of a circle, an arrangement which afforded a good view of the stage to all beholders. The roof was domed, and, as it was before the age of electricity, the theatre was lit by a large sun burner in the centre, which also acted as a ventilator. There was nothing gorgeous in the decoration, but it was a pretty little theatre.[17]

Erroll Sherson, on the other hand, recalls that the Globe and its neighbour, the Opera Comique, were known as 'the rickety twins', being 'two uncomfortable, ramshackle houses back to back in that part of East Strand and Newcastle Street which lay between the churches of St. Mary le Strand and St. Clement Danes'. It seems that the whole area was due for demolition and the builders 'deliberately ran up the theatres as cheaply as possible with a view to making large profits' from their destruction. 'Whether this be the fact or not, both these theatres were constructed in the loosest manner and with the greatest disregard for the comfort, or even the safety, of the public.'[18] E.B. Chancellor, in describing the Globe as, on the whole, 'one of the more successful of London's playhouses',[19] seems to be following Gordon, who adds that 'there was scarcely a modern writer of eminence who had not had his plays performed at the Globe'.[20]

Mrs Bernard-Beere, the actor-manager of the Globe, was one of those now-forgotten actresses who had a great reputation in her own time. A widow whose father-in-law was a baronet, she came from a rather higher level of society than usual.[21] Erroll Sherson describes her acting as 'superlative', saying that

with the exception of Mrs. Kendal and Ellen Terry there was no English actress of her day who came within measurable distance of her, and now there are none at all.

She was what is generally described as an 'emotional actress' [with] a magnificent stage appearance, a great emotional power and – what is hardly ever found among modern actresses – a wonderful diction.[22]

Erroll Sherson compares Stella Brereton, who played Jane Eyre 'two years previously at the insignificant Park Theatre in Camden Town', very unfavourably with Bernard-

17 Gordon, pp. 242–3.
18 Sherson, p. 237. *Saturday Review*, 18 June 1887, offers a detailed account of the safety measures at the Globe in case of fire (Vol. 56, p. 95).
19 Chancellor, p. 140.
20 Gordon, p. 244. The Theatre Museum in London has a photograph of the outside of the Globe (annotated '1868–1902 Demolished ') and a plan of the interior 'from "The Box Office", 15 June, 1885'.
21 Pascoe, p. 37.
22 Sherson, pp. 243, 245.

Figure 21   Interior of the Globe Theatre, Strand, London, where W.G. Wills's *Jane Eyre* was first performed in 1882: *Illustrated London News*, 16 January 1869. Image supplied by Hull University Photographic Service

Beere.[23] On the other hand, the *Saturday Review* was very grudging in its praise of Bernard-Beere's later, but very famous, performance as Fedora at the Haymarket, claiming that she had 'not just modelled herself on Bernhardt but has ape[d] every gesture and every movement of the French actress'.[24]

Apart from the cover picture to this volume, there are a number of other portraits of Bernard-Beere. *The Theatre* has a very attractive signed photograph,[25] and *The Sketch* has a number of photographs of her in various roles.[26] The Harvard Theatre Collection has a cartoon signed 'AB' (the regular *Entr'Acte* artist who drew John Douglass in Figure 15).[27] The *Illustrated London News* was by no means the only journal to comment that Bernard-Beere's physical appearance was too striking for the part of Jane, the reviewer regretting that the casting of the play deprived the audience of 'the contrast between the demure governess and the handsome, proud, voluptuous Blanche Ingram', but praising Bernard-Beere's handling of the part. This reviewer describes in lengthy detail the actress's deportment in the scene where 'Jane Eyre has heard the secret of Rochester's life, and she determines to hear it from his own lips'. At Rochester's confession, 'comes scorn, a torrent of dignified denunciation, the grand contempt of a pure and injured woman. It is so lofty, so fine, so true that the man she has loved withers and droops under the sublimated truth.'[28] In this review she is praised as a 'rising actress'.

Fifteen years later, she is described as 'assuredly one of the most brilliant and distinguished English actresses of our time'. This retrospective article in an 1897 issue of *The Sketch* includes an interview, in which she describes the conception, casting and rehearsal of Wills's *Jane Eyre*. It makes fascinating reading, especially in conjunction with the *ILN* review quoted above. We have to remember that Bernard-Beere was a theatre manager as well as an actress; she recalls that her 'first production – Tennyson's play, "The Promise of May"' [–] was 'a dire failure', and she had nothing ready to supply its place:

> However, I yearned to play Jane Eyre, and Charles Kelly, who was with me then, was, of course, the ideal actor for Rochester, so W.G. Wills adapted Charlotte Brontë's great book for us, and we rehearsed the play as he wrote it, in scraps. It was a curious experience, and another was the woman with the maniac laugh. It was necessary to find an actress for the mad wife, but the requisite laugh could not be discovered in the West End. One day, however, Mr Wills came and told me he had found the very laugh we wanted – a wonderful, weird laugh – in Shoreditch, and Miss D'Almaine was engaged. But she would never do the laugh at rehearsal, which rather disconcerted me. However, Mr Wills assured me that it would be 'all right on the night'. The dress-rehearsal came, and I had

---

23 Sherson, p. 247.
24 *Saturday Review*, 12 May 1883 (Vol. 55, p. 601).
25 *Theatre*, NS Vol. 2 (July–December 1880), facing p. 127.
26 *Sketch*, 28 April 1897, p. 28.
27 The Colindale Newspaper Library lacks the *Entr'Acte* volume for 1883.
28 *ILN*, 30 December 1882 (Vol. 81, p. 683).

just finished my scene with Rochester when I heard a hideous, screeching laugh that froze my blood, and affected me so terribly that, instead of merely falling in a pretended faint, I actually swooned away. And so realistically did the woman, playing the maniac, clutch my throat that I retained the marks of her fingers for three weeks. After that, Charles Kelly stood close by every night to protect me, for I never felt safe with that woman.[29]

The *Times* review confirms that 'Miss D'Almaine's wild shriek and the look of insanity in her eye and in her distorted features will not readily fade from the imagination'.[30] It is tempting to believe that this actress from Shoreditch had already acted the part in Willing's play at the Standard Theatre (Shoreditch) in 1881, but *The Stage* review mentions Fanny Addison in that part.[31]

The fate of Tennyson's 'Promise of May', whose failure prompted the writing of *Jane Eyre*, also makes a curious story. Erroll Sherson commiserates with Bernard-Beere, who

> had to contend with a very bad play by the Poet Laureate; with the presence, in a private box, of Mr Gladstone whom the pit and gallery chose to regard with loud outspoken disfavour; [and] with a most unfortunate *lapsus calami* on the part of Tennyson who had innocently allotted to the character played by Herbert Vezin a couple of lines with a double entendre that set the whole house (already inclined to 'guy' the piece) rocking with laughter.[32]

The second night was even worse, as *The Entr'Acte* reports:

> An extraordinary scene occurred last night at the Globe Theatre, during the performance of Mr. Tennyson's drama of 'The Promise of May'. At the conclusion of the opening scene, the Marquis of Queensberry, who occupied a seat in the stalls, rose in his place, and loudly protested against the Laureate's representation of the principles of freethought. After considerable interruption the act was allowed to proceed to its close, but immediately upon the fall of the curtain, Lord Queensberry again rose and, apparently under the influence of considerable excitement, announced himself as a professing freethinker, and once more accused Mr Tennyson of presenting a travesty of the sentiments of the sect to which he avowedly belonged. This unexpected interruption created a considerable disturbance in the theatre, and amid much confusion, during which the speaker was indistinctly heard, it was found necessary to urge the marquis to leave.[33]

---

29   *Sketch*, 28 April 1897, p. 28.
30   *Times*, 25 December 1882, p. 6, col. A. See also *ILN*, 30 December 1882, Vol. 81, p. 683 for a more extended description of D'Almaine's appearance. The Bodleian playbill for the Globe production shows that D'Almaine and Bernard-Beere both acted in the preceding comedietta, *A Fair Encounter*, and a playbill for *The Queen's Evidence* (1886) shows that D'Almaine's first name was Beatrice (University of Kent collection). *EA&A* for 1907 lists 'Mrs D'Almaine' as having died in 1906.
31   *Stage*, 29 April 1881, pp. 7–8, p. 8.
32   Sherson, p. 245.
33   *Entr'Acte*, 18 November 1882, p. 11.

The same issue of the journal has both a long and serious review of Tennyson's play, and a full-page cartoon representing 'Little Set-To Between the Poet Laureate and the Free-thinking Marquis (Queensberry Rules)'; the little marquis, wearing boxing gloves, dances before the looming poet, who gestures vaguely with one hand, his other in his pocket.[34]

The Entr'Acte review decides that 'the best feature of "The Promise of May"' was 'some very pretty incidental music' by Hamilton Clarke, who also wrote the music for *Jane Eyre*. This is the only play in this collection to have specially composed music, and this marks the play as 'superior', especially as Hamilton Clarke was a composer of some repute.[35] He appears in *The New Grove Dictionary* as 'conductor, organist and composer', who

> succeeded Sullivan at St. Peter's, Cranley Gardens, in 1872. He then became conductor at several London theatres and provided incidental music for Henry Irving's Lyceum productions. He also toured with the D'Oyly Carte Opera Company and for a time was principal conductor of the Carl Rosa Opera Company. [...] An expert arranger, he scored some of Sullivan's overtures; he also published a useful *Manual of Orchestration* (London, 1888) as well as some fiction and music criticism.[36]

David Mayer demonstrates how the best 'melodrama was scored and elaborately orchestrated, and the score was carefully integrated with the text and with dramatic action during performance'.[37]

In September, 1883, the play was performed at the Theatre Royal, Manningham Lane, Bradford,[38] which had opened on this site in 1868.[39] *The Era* review notes each performer (including Maggie Hunt as Jane and Charles Kelly as Rochester)

---

[34]   *Entr'Acte*, 18 November 1882, pp. 11 and 8. Unfortunately the volume is too fragile for reproduction. In a series of lectures 'professedly on Shakespeare', T. Hall Caine praised 'The Promise of May' 'as the most remarkable [play] that had been written for many a long day' (*Referee*, 17 December 1882, p. 3).

[35]   Adams, Vol. 1, p. 296.

[36]   Sadie, Vol. 5, p. 914. I am grateful to Sarah Fermi for providing this information.

[37]   Mayer, p. 50. I am grateful to Jean Chothia for bringing this and other works to my attention.

[38]   *Bradford Daily Telegraph* advertises the play for 24–29 September 1883; *Bradford Weekly Telegraph* advertises the beginning and ending of the run. The company is described as that of 'Mr Chas. Kelly'. Playbill in BPM for 27 and 29 September [1883] announces that 'the performance will commence with the Favourite Farce, *Advice Gratis*'. Programme for *Advice Gratis* in the Bodleian (John Johnson Collection) gives the author as Herman Charles Merivale, but Mullin gives Charles Dance. The manuscript is in the Lord Chamberlain's Plays (Add. MS 42944 ff. 819–836b).

[39]   Photographs of the exterior of the theatre can be found in Mellor (pages not numbered), in *Images of Bradford* (anon.), p. 157 and Firth, pp. 108–9.

with polite approval; 'the play was nicely mounted, and the dresses appropriate'.[40] Charles Kelly, who played Rochester at the Globe and in Bradford, was the husband of Ellen Terry, and had a distinguished career.[41]

Reception of the Play

Wills's play was received as in contrast with Willing's, which was still being performed at the 'transpontine' Surrey Theatre on 15 December 1882,[42] with Wills's version appearing on the 23rd. Wills's brother, Freeman, certainly stresses the subdued nature of Wills's *Jane Eyre* in his biography of the dramatist:

> The adaptation of *Jane Eyre* was undertaken for Mrs Bernard Beere in 1882. The plot is compressed into those scenes which pass in or near Thornfield Hall. Mrs Bernard Beere was too tall and debonnaire for the thin, plain, pale little person of the novel; but this on the stage, where the eye has its dominion, was undoubtedly far from a disadvantage.[43] The play strikes – necessarily, perhaps – a very different keynote from the novel; so much that could not be compressed goes to making the latter. One cannot compress a whole atmosphere on the stage. The play is the love story of Jane and Rochester, with the ghost of his mad wife standing between them. The lunatic shriek is heard only once, and the sight that appals the heroine's eyes only once appears; the more sensational features of the novel are also left in the background – the attempt to destroy Rochester, the burning of the Hall, in which the mad woman loses her life and he his sight. It is the sentiment of the story that is woven into the play, and this is done with success and good taste. The public might have liked stronger fare, but the piece held its ground well and gained the sympathy of the best judges by its pure and lofty tone, and entire freedom from vulgar sensationalism. A dramatist with less good taste could have crowded his narrow stage canvas with all the incidents of the novel, and entirely failed by doing so to give its dramatic equivalent.[44]

---

[40] *Era*, 29 September 1883, p. 9. *EA&A* for 1905 (p. 77) lists Maggie Hunt (Mrs Arthur B. Franks) as having died in 1904 at the age of 44.

[41] Pascoe, pp. 229, 231.

[42] Theatre Museum playbill.

[43] The *Times* review also thinks Bernard-Beere's appearance an advantage, since 'it is doubtful whether a theatrical audience could interest themselves in a puny and insignificant heroine' (25 December 1882, p. 6, col. A.). Although *Referee* notes that Bernard-Beere does not realize 'Jane Eyre's description of herself as an unattractive and undersized little woman' (quoted *Daily News*, 25 December 1882, p. 4), a 'Yorkshire correspondent' argues that 'she errs on the right side', since his own encounter with Charlotte Brontë showed her in attractive clothes with hair fashionably dressed (*Referee*, 7 January 1883, p. 3).

[44] Wills, pp. 186–7.

A *Times* review of an early performance also stresses its subdued atmosphere in pointed contrast with Willing:

> The story of 'Jane Eyre' notwithstanding one or two powerful situations, is so much more psychological than dramatic that its production at the Globe Theatre on Saturday night must be taken to indicate a desire on the part of the management to elevate the tone of the stage rather than to gratify popular taste. Mr Wills has treated his subject in a scholarly and refined, but not, it must be said, in a strongly impressive manner. It was doubtless impossible to achieve any different result without treading in the footsteps of a transpontine dramatist who has already vulgarized the story by giving prominence to the episode connected with Rochester's maniac wife. The novel interests us in the fortunes of two characters only, and [...] a dramatist could have no more difficult task than to translate Charlotte Brontë's analytical studies of Jane Eyre and Rochester into such action and movement as the stage demands.

This review plays down even the sensational appearance of the maniac, pointing out that she appears only once, and that 'even such sensationalism as might legitimately have been taken from the novel the adapter has eschewed', relying 'solely upon the pathetic features of Jane's attachment to Rochester, her cruel disappointment [...] her noble resolve to leave him, and her return'. The writer's conclusion is that

> It may be that this adaptation of 'Jane Eyre' will not suit the public appetite, which is accustomed to stronger fare. But on literary and artistic grounds the dramatist and his interpreters have strong claims on our sympathy. It is seldom that a play is presented so simple in its motive, so free from vulgar sensationalism, so pure and lofty in its tone.[45]

The *Graphic* takes a similar line:

> Mr W.G. Wills has written for Mrs Bernard-Beere a new dramatic version of *Jane Eyre*, in which – probably from the adaptor's desire to avoid giving a melodramatic air to Miss Brontë's psychological autobiography – the story is brought down to its barest and most simple form. That the dramatist has not condescended to vulgarise his original in the interest of playgoers of the class who crave for mere excitement is a merit which entitles him to the gratitude of playgoers of refined tastes. On the other hand, he has unfortunately not succeeded in constructing a play presenting the ingenuity of construction and the variety of situations which are necessary in these days for achieving a lasting success upon the stage.[46]

The *Illustrated London News* confirms that the quiet tone of the play did not quite meet with audience approval, while revealing that some of its best effects were melodramatic indeed:

> The dramatist who attempts to touch a novel for the purposes of the stage immediately brings a hornet's nest about his ears. Mr. W.G. Wills, 'the mildest-mannered man that ever

---

45   *Times*, 25 December 1882, p. 6, col. A.
46   *Graphic*, 30 December 1882, p. 723.

scuttled ship or cut a throat', in a dramatic sense, is for ever getting into hot water. [...] Of course he satisfies nobody. Public opinion would have had 'Jane Eyre' treated exactly as Mr. Wills has not treated it. They clamour for the restoration of all that has been omitted. Remembering the excitement of the book, they are greedily anxious for every scene and circumstance. Utterly forgetful of the difficulties of the dramatist, they demand with a loud voice every incident in the career of Jane Eyre, from the moment when she was at school at Lowood to the moment when she is restored to the arms of her blind lover [–] they would have it all, though such a play lasted a fortnight instead of three hours.

In my humble judgment Mr. Wills has done well to confine himself strictly to the story of the loves of Jane Eyre and Rochester, with such elaboration and detail as space would allow, and to discard the more melodramatic moments that would jar with the tone and colour of his work. Not, indeed, that the new play, 'Jane Eyre' is wholly calm and uneventful. There is thought in it, but there is also action. One scene for weirdness has no parallel on the modern stage. It is where Jane Eyre is made to discover the dread secret of Thornfield Hall. With admirable dramatic instinct, this occurs at the very instant when the cup of the heroine's happiness is full. She has scarcely uttered up her prayer of joy for deliverance from loneliness and sorrow ere the unearthly scream and the mocking laugh come as if from the grave to silence the woman's ecstasy. Jane Eyre stands shuddering, motionless in the darkening twilight. Then to her horror she sees a panel pushed aside, and forth creeps that which is more terrible than any ghost conceived by the fevered imagination. It is the mad wife, more beast than woman, who with bitter lips and long claw-like fingers makes for her prey, and crawls to the throat of her fainting rival.[47]

The Stage describes this as 'a scene of thrilling power',[48] and *The People* confirms that 'the effect at the close of the second act when the shrieks and laughter of the mad wife are heard, and her unexpected appearance through the secret door puts the heroine in a passion of fright, was overwhelming'. This reviewer feels that 'of versions of "Jane Eyre" hitherto seen, this is the highest in respect of art'.[49] *The Illustrated London News*, however, suggests a few improvements, preferring that 'a faint and distant echo of the mad woman's laugh be heard in the earlier scenes of the play', and feeling it a mistake to entrust the truth about Mr Rochester's marriage to the Ingrams, who have played a largely comic part earlier in the play. He also finds 'the crude introduction of the Rev. Mr Prior all through the play a dramatic error of even a graver kind'.[50]

There seem to be few critics, in fact, who were whole-heartedly satisfied with the play. *Theatre* magazine calls it

> a curious example of a play which, without being deficient in strong, dramatic stuations, without lacking the poetical sweetness and tenderness [characteristic of its author], still at the conclusion leaves the spectator dissatisfied. It is as though, during the working out of

---

47   *ILN*, 30 December 1882, Vol. 81, p. 683.
48   *Stage*, 29 December 1882, p. 11.
49   Quoted, together with other short reviews, in *Daily News* 25 December 1882, p. 4.
50   *ILN*, 30 December 1882, Vol. 81, p. 683.

the drama, Mr Wills had been conscious of an idea which he has never been able to grasp – a life-study of which he has been unable to get at the heart.[51]

Distinctive Features of the Play

- The play begins at Thornfield, where Jane has a good and easy relationship with Adèle (see cover picture).
- Jane has come to Thornfield from good friends, Mr Prior (a clergyman who wanted to marry her) and his mother.
- There is much emphasis on the Ingrams' sneering at Jane but she rises to it and sees Rochester's love as her vindication.
- There is some emphasis on Rochester's searching of his conscience.
- The maniac is treated sensationally, but there is no foreboding laughter.
- Jane collapses after being attacked by the madwoman.
- All the women (Mrs Fairfax, Grace Poole and the Ingrams) warn Jane to leave the house before the wedding because of Rochester's reputation.
- Blanche reveals the prior marriage; Jane is first unbelieving, then bitter.
- After the fire, Rochester is left alone in poverty.
- Jane's legacy is not mentioned.

---

[51] Quoted in Leonard, p. 763.

Jane Eyre by W.G. Wills

A[ct I]

Room in Thornfield. He[arth with fire] burning.

Mrs [Fairfax and] Adèle discovered

Mrs Fairfax: Now you're a useful little girl – attend to your work and don't look about.
Adèle: But I want to see what hour it is, Madam. I cannot see if I do not turn my head.
Mrs Fairfax: It's a quarter to six, my pet.
Adèle: My new governess ought to be come down, n'est pas?
Mrs Fairfax: Are you very anxious?
Adèle: That is if she is gentile and charming.
Mrs Fairfax: Mind the ball – you'll drop it I believe. Miss Eyre is very charming.
Adèle: Can she talk French?
Mrs Fairfax: Remember that you are to talk English to her and till the company go away and you must keep with her entirely – there's Miss Blanche Ingram complains of you and says you are very troublesome.
Adèle: But her sister, Miss Mary, she says I am very pretty. Ravissante.
Mrs Fairfax: Better be good than pretty.
Adèle: Oh I am tired of {th}dis. When does Mr Rochester return?
Mrs Fairfax: He might be back tonight – he might be back tomorrow.
Adèle: [I] do wish he come, and bring me my new dress.
Mrs Fairfax: Oh, that's what you're thinking of.
Adèle: – Magnificent white dress and pink sash; and bows and I will come down after dinner like von leetle angle. (*Listens*) Ah, here is Miss Eyre.
Mrs Fairfax (rising): Now, Adèle, be very polite – your best manners, pet.
Adèle (murmuring): My new governante.

Enter Jane Eyre, Mrs Fairfax advancing with outstreched hands

Mrs Fairfax: How do you do, Miss Eyre! I hope you like your room – you've had a cold journey – come to the fire. We shall have tea directly. Mr Rochester is away. I am a relation of his and keep house for him – we expect him home every day.
Jane: This is my new pupil.
Adèle: Bon pour Mademoiselle.
Mrs Fairfax: This is your new pupil, Adèle Dupres.
Jane: Not Rochester?
Mrs Fairfax: No. This is a little French girl – a ward of Mr Rochester's whom he brought over from Paris – where he lived for many years.

Servant brings in tea

Mrs Fairfax: Now, Adèle, go and make friends with Miss Eyre. (*To Jane*): She talks English very well.

Mrs Fairfax goes to tea table.

Jane: We must be great friends, Adèle. (*Kisses Adèle on the forehead and sitting, draws her close to her*) Are you very fond of your lessons, Adèle?

Adele: Ah Mademoiselle, I detest them – I do love the dance, the dress, the picture books. Oh, I am triste here.

Jane: It's a big house. I suppose we could play hide and seek here.

Adèle: Non – non – non; there is a ghost in this house.

Mrs Fairfax: Oh, nonsense – silly stories of the servants. You can have your tea on this little table – don't stir. (*Brings table over*)

Adèle: Oh, but it is true – it is true – why den do we bolt our bedroom doors every night?

Mrs Fairfax: There have been some robberies in the house, Miss Eyre, two years ago – and it is a good rule to bolt one's door.

Adèle: We are talking, Madame, Miss Eyre and I, pray do not interrupt.

Jane: Oh fie, you mustn't talk in that way.

Adèle: Can you tell stories?

Jane: Oh, yes.

Adèle: Do tell one!

Mrs Fairfax: Don't tease Miss Eyre. She's tired.

Adèle: Hush – hush – hush. (*To Jane*): Commence.

Jane: Well. I'll tell you an adventure that happened to me this very evening about two miles away from the gate.

Adèle: Tres bien.

Jane: Well, as I was I was coming along the road – taking great care not to slip, you know, the road is covered with ice, and it was growing dark – dark – dark – when what do you think I heard?

Adèle: What?

Jane: I heard behind me a great trot, trot, trot, and a Bow wow of a big dog.

Adèle: Oh – a Bow wow of a big dog!

Mrs Fairfax: Was that this evening, Miss Eyre?

Jane: About half an hour before I arrived, Ma'am.

Adèle: *Avance!*

Jane: Well. I looked round, my dear, and I saw a great black horse.

Adèle: One great black horse.

Jane: And on it was a great dark man.

Adèle: One great dark man.

Mrs Fairfax: You say there was a dog with him, Miss Eyre?
Jane: Yes, there was a large Newfoundland, that followed the gentleman.
Adèle: Eh bien.
Jane: Well, just as he was passing me – clatter – clatter – upon the ice, and I was standing by a gate to get out of his way, the horse gave a great slip on the ice, and down it fell, and the poor man with it – bang!
Adèle: But that is shocking.
Mrs Fairfax: Was he much hurt?
Jane: I really thought he must have been killed at first, but he got up and disentangled himself without assistance – I think he had only a slight sprain, Ma'am.
Mrs Fairfax: Was he coming this way?
Jane: Well, I helped him to his horse, but I think he stopped at a surgeon's in the village.
Mrs Fairfax: A large dark man, you say – dear me, it must be Mr Rochester – I must make enquiries immediately.
Jane: Mr Rochester!
Adèle: Had he a box, with a pretty white dress in it; ribbons and bows?
Mrs Fairfax: To be sure his luggage was sent on to day but I hardly thought he'd come till tomorrow.
Rochester (heard without): Are the ladies in?
Servant (heard without): No, Sir.
Mrs Fairfax: Why, that's his voice in the Hall!

Enter Rochester

Mrs Fairfax: Mr Rochester, I've been so alarmed about you: are you much hurt?
Adèle: Have you brought my cadeau – my present?
Rochester: Ah! this is my heroine of the high road – the pixie who put a spell upon my horse and took his legs from under him! I'm sorry I could not give you an earlier welcome.
Jane/:   I hope, Mr Rochester, that you've quite recovered your hurt.
Mrs Fairfax: Why Edmund, you limp a little!
Rochester: This young lady was my crutch – my prop – if she would lend me her arm now – I might reach my easy chair and we might make acquaintance.
Jane: With pleasure, Sir.
Rochester (to Mrs Fairfax): This is the way we went along, Mrs Fairfax – quite like old friends till I reached my horse. (*Takes a few steps with Jane affecting to be lame then with a laugh walks to his chair*) Thank you, Miss Eyre. I won't play the imposter longer. Any letters?
Mrs Fairfax: One; I put it on the Library chimney piece and for the moment it is mislaid – a foreign post mark.
Rochester: A foreign post mark? Won't you be seated? (*Jane sits.*)
Adèle: Monsieur.

Rochester:	I know what you want, my little French lady – well, I didn't forget you.
Adéle:	Merci beaucoup! Has Monsieur brought a present for Mademoiselle Eyre?
Rochester:	Did you expect a present, Miss Eyre? Are you fond of presents?
Jane:	I hardly know, Sir – I've little experience of them – they are generally thought pleasant things.
Rochester:	Generally thought: what's your opinion?
Jane:	It so much depends upon the giver.
Rochester:	This little woman doesn't think so – a present is welcome from any hand – if you ran up to your room, Adéle, you would find what you love best.
Adéle:	My new robe! (*She skips to the door. Hesitates as she opens it.*) No I have fear – the Ghost! Mrs Fairfax, come with me.
Mrs Fairfax:	You little goose. (*Exeunt*)
Rochester:	I think your name is?
Jane:	Eyre.
Rochester:	And your other name?
Jane:	Jane.
Rochester:	Well, Miss Jane Eyre. You've been very good to me tonight – you've shown courage, coolness and good nature.
Jane:	Now you've given me my present, Mr Rochester.
Rochester:	You've been resident in my house about an hour.
Jane:	Yes, Sir.
Rochester:	And you came from –
[Jane:]	Lowood School in Yorkshire.
Rochester:	Ah. A charitable concern. How long were you there?
Jane:	About eight years.
Rochester:	You must be tenacious of life. Who are your parents?
Jane:	I have none.
Rochester:	Nor ever had, I suppose! You were a sort of wraith or water witch – you spread that damned ice on the road – because I broke through one of your rings – well if you disown your parents you must have some sort of kinsfolk – uncles and aunts.
Jane:	No – none that I ever saw.
Rochester:	And your home?
Jane:	I have none.
Rochester:	Where do your brothers and sisters live?
Jane:	I have no brothers or sisters.
Rochester:	Who recommended you to come here?
Jane:	I advertised and Mrs Fairfax answered my advertisement.
Rochester:	Have you ever lived in a town?
Jane:	No, Sir.
Rochester:	Have you seen much society?

Jane: I once was at Boulogne.

Rochester: Mr Prior is, I think the Clergyman of your parish – he is young – I suppose your ladies of the school worshipped him.

Jane: Not at all, but he and his mother were very kind friends of mine. If they had known I was going away they would have prevented me.

Rochester: A village tyrant – eh?

Jane: A tyranny of fondness, Sir.

Rochester: So you stole a march upon the Reverend Mr Prior – that explains all – I met the reverend gentleman today hot foot – in pursuit – and having had a letter from Mrs Fairfax mentioning your name – I asked him up to the house.

Jane: Oh, Mr Rochester, I am sorry you did that.

Rochester: Well, well, you must meet him now and let the stray lamb take care of the shepherd's crook – I suppose I am the wolf?

Jane: Now, Sir, you know all about me – is my examination ended?

Rochester: I think I know less than when I began. (*He takes from his pocket bundles of letters.*) Now it's your turn – it's only fair, before I read my letters – that you should question me. Have you anything to ask me, Miss Eyre?

Jane: Why do you treat that dear little girl so coldly, Mr Rochester?

Rochester: Because she is nothing to me – because she is the memento of an unhappy time.

Jane: But you have accepted her as your ward – are you just?

Rochester: Well then, I am unjust – go on.

Jane: I have no more questions, Sir.

Rochester: What little interest you have in me. (*Rochester looks over letters*)

Re-enter Mrs Fairfax & Mrs Poole

Mrs Fairfax: I think the Master seems busy, Mrs Poole – I'll choose my time to speak to him.

Mrs Poole: Well Ma'am it's only this – here are all the company coming back and the laughter and noise comes up to us and drives her savage – she's as sly as a cat too.

Mrs Fairfax: She's quiet now.

Mrs Poole: Cause the house is quiet – but it's frightful when the company are here.

Rochester (rising): What are you talking of? (*He advances.*)

Mrs Fairfax: Oh, nothing, Mr Rochester.

Rochester: Damn it, I heard you. Pardon me, Mrs Fairfax. Mrs Poole, I pay you liberally – are you satisfied?

Mrs Poole: Oh quite, Mr Rochester, but –

Rochester: For God's sake then, let me alone. Keep the memory of it from me. Hush there's a stranger here – you must not leave your charge for a moment.

Mrs Fairfax: The foreign letter is found, Edmund – here it is (*gives letter*).

Rochester (takes letter looking at envelope): From Jamaica. Mrs Poole, will you wait
    a moment (*opens letter*)?

Mrs Fairfax (going to Jane): Here is a song Mr Rochester brought. Will you look
    over it – I think it pretty (*gives song*).

Jane: Thank you ma'am. (*Mrs Fairfax resumes her knitting.*)

Rochester (to himself): Coming back from Jamaica – coming here? (*Aloud*): this must
    be stopped. This letter is from Mr Mason.

Mrs Poole: My patient's brother, Sir

Rochester (to Mrs Poole): He wants to come over to see her.

Mrs Poole: It would be a bad sight, Sir.

Rochester: Mrs Poole, take this letter – you are the proper person to satisfy the
    inquiries and tell him from me I forbid his coming here.

Mrs Poole: I'll do so, Sir.

Rochester: I'm afraid you're careless – here's this child talking about a ghost.

Mrs Poole: Me Sir? I'm mute as the grave.

Rochester: Well, well, be temperate – be discreet – good evening.

                                                    (*Exit Mrs Poole*)

*Rochester returns to his chair, and as if thinking, leans his head on his hand – Jane
stares at Mr Rochester. He looks up under his eyes.*

Rochester: Well?

Jane: Well, sir!

Rochester: Why, you've been staring at me.

Jane: I beg your pardon, Sir.

Rochester: Do you think me ugly?

Jane: Yes, Sir, I mean –

Rochester: Never mind the afterthought – you are blunt to the master of the house
    – what do you mean by it?

Jane: Sir, I have only made a blunder and I beg your pardon. I should have
    said that tastes differ – that beauty is of little consequence –

Rochester: Oh, is it?

Mrs Fairfax: Miss Eyre, you mustn't mind Mr Rochester – he's only in jest.

Rochester (rising): Forgive me, Miss Eyre – you are come to a strange house amongst
    strangers – whom you will not find very companionable – so I thought
    we might get at home with one another at once. You will never feel
    yourself as an inferior with me. I'm quite sure you'll receive my orders
    without being hurt by a tone of command – I'm rather a Turk. (*Jane
    smiles.*) What are you smiling at?

Jane: I was thinking, Sir, that very few masters would trouble themselves
    to enquire whether or not their paid subordinates were hurt by their
    orders.

Rochester: Paid subordinates. What, you are a paid subordinate are you? Ah, I'd
                forgotten the salary.
Mrs Fairfax: Here they are, come back from their drive, Edmund.
Rochester (rises): Oh, you'll wait here, Miss Eyre. I must introduce you.
                                              (*Exit Mrs Fairfax & Rochester*)
Jane: Shall I like them? Will he like me – I cannot tell yet. He is so different
                from all I ever met yet – a little rough but kind – he wishes to make me
                at home – that touched me – shall I like all this strange proud company
                and will they like me? This dreadful shy feeling will choke me – where's
                my presence of mind? Ah, here they come.

*Enter Lady Ingram & her two daughters, Blanche & Mary. They advance to Jane
smiling.*

Lady Ingram: Allow me to introduce myself – Lady Ingram – my two daughters.
Jane (bowing): I'm Miss Eyre.
Blanche: We are so sorry you did not arrive in time to join our drive to the
                monastery, Miss Eyre.
Lady Ingram: Mr Rochester told us – we should find a young friend of his just
                arrived.
Jane: I'm just arrived, my Lady, but I'm afraid I can hardly claim to be a
                friend of Mr Rochester. I'm the new Governess.
Lady Ingram: Dear me. I beg your pardon. How very stupid.
Blanche: One of Mr Rochester's jests.
Jane: I'm very sorry you've been misled.
Lady Ingram: Oh, no consequence.
Mary (holding our her hand): I'm very happy to know you, Miss Eyre.
Jane (a little affected): Thank you for your kindness, Miss Ingram.

Jane retires to the roll of music & turns it over.

Enter the two Miss Beechers and Lord Desmond

Desmond: I absolutely deny the charge.
Miss A Beecher: You did – you said both our noses were red – oh, Blanche, he's been
                so impertinent.

Enter Rochester

Blanche: I hope you were very desolate without us, Mr Rochester.
Rochester: Without you, of course – my only relief was fulfilling your many
                commissions.
Desmond: Filled up you time pretty well, ah?
Lady Ingram: She missed you so much.

Blanche:	Oh! Nonsense, Mama.
Desmond:	She's been so cross and unmanageable.
Blanche:	Will you hush. I'm thinking only of business, Mr Rochester.
Rochester:	Madam.
Blanche:	Have you got the lace?
Rochester:	I've got the lace.
Blanche:	Have you sent the box of new library books?
Rochester:	The box has arrived.
Blanche:	No dear naughty novels?
Rochester:	All highly proper.
Blanche:	What, no runaway matches? No divorces? No terrible French heroines? What not one nice naughty book?
Lady Ingram:	You silly girl.
Rochester:	Perhaps one.
Blanche:	Charming.
Lady Ingram:	I should pounce upon it, I can assure you.
Desmond:	A bad child's guide, Rochester, eh?
Blanche:	And the new song.
Rochester:	I think Miss Eyre is looking over it.
Jane:	Oh, I have done with it. (*Brings it over to Blanche*) It seems a pretty song.
Blanche (coldly):	Oh, thank you.
Rochester:	And now, how are you going to reward me for my faithful service?
Blanche:	By singing it at once for you.
Rochester:	That will more than repay me.

[Blanche] goes to piano

Enter Adèle in her new frock

Adèle:	Bon jour Monsieur, et Mesdames.
Blanche:	Oh, what a little puppet.
Mary:	What a pretty dress.
Rochester:	A little imp, just popped up from a trap and shockingly at home.
Jane (coming forward):	Adèle, dear Miss Ingram is just going to sing such a pretty song. Sit over here beside me. A very pretty dress – now be very still.
Blanche (touching the chords):	Good gracious, my fingers are so stiff with the cold I can't play accompaniment. What's to be done? (*Rubs her fingers*)
Lady Ingram:	Surely Miss Eyre is able to play?
Blanche (coldly):	Will you be good enough to accompany me, Miss Eyre? It's quite simple.
Jane:	I play very badly, Miss Ingram, or I'd be very happy.
Lady Ingram (aside):	Dear me! What an unqualified governess.
Desmond:	Let her treat us to the scales.

Lady Ingram: You really must have a competent teacher.
Mary (kindly): Miss Eyre, will you let me take your place?   I'm sure my sister
        should be very much obliged.
Blanche (tossing her head): Not at all.
Rochester: I am, Miss Eyre.

Blanche sings the following song set to simple taking music. Mary accompanies.

The Birth of Love

The dew-[b]ent flowers were sleeping fast
In the pearly light of morn –
When the soft winds whispered it is past
And the infant Love was born.
And the birds sent up a song of praise
Far its charm was all around
And they circled in a giddy maze
As they made the hills resound.
        And they circled in a giddy maze
        As they made the hills resound.

And the wild beast in his tangled lair
Now felt the touch of its wand
And every youth and maiden fair
Rejoiced in the sacred bond.
E'en the big trees nodded in their joy
To the fleeting clouds above
As they mutely said this new born boy
Was the infant God of Love.
        As they mutely said this new born boy
        Was the infant God of Love.

Applause of company at end of song

Rochester: Thank you, Miss Ingram, and now I challenge you to a game of billiards
        to circulate your blood.
Blanche: Done – how many points will you give me?
Rochester: As many as you please.
Blanche: And what will you bet me?
Rochester: What you please.
Lady Ingram: I really must witness this game. Come, we'll all go in.
Desmond: I think I'll follow (*looking at Jane*).
Rochester (jocularly aside to him): No you don't, I'm not going to let you flirt with
        my governess. Come along.

Desmond (aside to Rochester): You reserve that for yourself, eh?

Lady Ingram: Come along – I'll back Blanche.

(Exeunt all but Blanche who returns from the door)

Blanche: Pardon me, Miss Eyre. Will you allow me to ask you a question – I don't mean to be rude.

Jane: Ah, certainly, Miss Ingram, but till I know what you're going to ask –

Blanche: I simply wanted to know what Mr Rochester meant by speaking of you as his friend.

Jane: Certainly not much, Miss Ingram. No doubt he meant kindly.

Blanche: Not to talk of a governess – it was not perhaps the thing to my mother and myself.

Jane: If Mr Rochester offers me his friendship I will respectfully accept it.

Blanche: Pray let me give you a word of advice. Mr Rochester may sometimes forget himself with his social inferiors, but I mean kindly when I warn you you should not forget your place with him.

Jane: My place is beside my pupil.

Lady Ingram (calling): Blanche, Blanche, Mr Rochester is waiting.

Blanche (frigidly bowing): You'll pardon me.   *(Exit)*

Adèle: Ma Foi, is she not beautiful!

Jane: She is beautiful.

Adèle: And magnifique – sa robe –

Jane: Magnificent, dear.

Adèle: Oh, the beautiful flowers – I will put one in my dress.

Jane (to herself): Let me keep a brave heart. Let me keep the tears back. What a kind word and look he gave me.

Enter servant

Servant: Mr Prior wants to see you, Miss; shall I show him up?

Jane: Show him up *(aside)*: Since it must be.   *(Exit Servant)*

Adèle: Shall I go, Miss Eyre?

Jane: No, no, stay.

Adèle: How do I look?

Enter Mr Prior

Jane (advancing with outstretched hand): Forgive me for leaving the school. What – you won't shake hands? Indeed, I grew too miserable.

Prior: It's a grand place this, Miss Eyre. You need not explain – your village home was poor – but your duties lay there.

Jane: Won't you sit down, Mr Prior? No? One can find duties everywhere. I have found mind here.

Prior: You are among grand people here. Your social superiors. They will scorn and insult you.

Jane:	I've felt it already. I'll bear it.
Prior:	I've heard some of them sneer at you as I passed the hall.
Jane:	I can bear that – the pain of this conversation I cannot bear, feeling what I owe you. It is useless – indeed it is useless.
Prior:	We stood to you, Jane, when you had not a friend in the world. You had two faithful hearts to rely upon – my mother's and mine. Come back to us, dear Jane.
Jane:	I cannot – tell me of the village, the School, of your dear mother, but don't press this subject.
Prior:	Confess it was a heartless thing to leave the place without a farewell.
Jane:	I meant it as a kindness – to spare pain to us both. I'll remember you and pray for you – all the same, if you'd allow me to be only a friend, I should not have left my post, though the hardship and poverty were wearing me out. But you would press. You would.
Prior:	Say persecute at once.
Jane:	You would wring my heart with imploring me daily, hourly, for what I could never give – my love –
Prior:	You may have had a distasteful pastor, Miss Eyre –
Jane:	No, no.
Prior:	Here you have a master who is a notorious profligate.
Jane:	Stop there, Mr Prior – I scarcely know Mr Rochester, but I have only experienced kindness, consideration and sympathy.
Prior:	Yes the leopard has a pretty skin, The snake; a playful rattle.
Jane:	I utterly refuse to hear my master maligned.
Prior:	Tell me one thing, Jane – in the village or elsewhere, have I a rival?

Mr Rochester enters, cane in hand

Jane:	No.
Rochester (coming forward):	I hope I'm not interrupting the meeting of two friends. I only want to ask you, Mr Prior, to give me the pleasure of dining and staying for the night.
Prior (stiffly):	Thank you, Sir, but I have my duties at home. I've been impressing upon Miss Eyre – your governess – that my mother's home is open to her. We are much attached to her and I have begged of her to return.
Rochester:	Well, Miss Eyre, will you return with this gentleman or stay with me? or rather with Adèle?
Jane:	I will stay, Sir.
Rochester:	I am glad of it.
Adèle:	And me I am glad (*runs to her and puts her arm round Jane's waist*)

Act II

Library in Thornfield House

Rochester discovered

Rochester: Let me see, t'was two months since I received that letter from Mason. Two months before, he must have written it – no, nearer three – for the voyage and the vessel from Jamaica was in Southampton last Wednesday. What a frightful thing if Mason should come.

Enter Servant

Servant: Did you ring. Sir?
Rochester: That fellow from Southampton is below?
Servant: That Gipsy man you bought the horse from, Sir? He's below in the kitchen, waiting.
Rochester: Show him up.   *(Exit Servant)*
Rochester: Oh the fetters we forge for ourselves – the cannon balls we fasten on our own ankles, till they work to the bone – the idea of meeting that man, a weak amiable gentleman, shakes my nerves to my centre – I have stood at the bar of my own conscience and I've asked the question – Have I a right to be happy as other men? to shake off a terrible incubus and be happy as others? and I have said yes – a hundred times yes – I am acquitted – but if this Mason comes, ruin, and desolation.

Enter Nat Lee

Rochester: Oh! Nat, you come from Southampton. Well?
Nat:.   Well, your honour. I was on the quay for four hours till she come in.
Rochester: The vessel from Jamaica. Well?
Nat: I stood at the gangway and kept my eye on the passengers as they coom ashore.
Rochester: Did you ask the steward the names of the passengers?
Nat: Arterwards. Your honour. I did.
Rochester: Well, did he tell you the name of Mason?
Nat: No, your honour.
Rochester (aside): Thank God! (*Aloud*): Well, you say you watched the passengers. What sort of a man did I tell you to look out for?
Nat: Why, a small gentleman with large dark eyes, a look of colour about him, and black hair rather long and curly.
Rochester: Well, man, did you see anyone like that?
Nat: No, your honour.

Rochester (aside): Safe. (*Aloud*): Now go down stairs, Nat, to my study – you know
           where it is. I've not done with you yet.
Nat (turning at door): Would your honour let me make a few shillings by telling the
           ladies' fortunes before I go?
Rochester: We'll talk of that presently.   (*Exit Nat Lee*)
Rochester: The weight is lifted off my heart. Now I can mix in life and smile and
           plan like all the world around me. There's Blanche's laugh – I'll put
           that young lady's heart in the crucible and test it for alloy.

Enter Blanche, Lady Ingram, Lord Desmond, followed by Mary & Miss Beechers

Blanche: Oh, here he is – you surely are not going away, Edmund, again?
Lady Ingram: It's really too bad.
Desmond: Why, Rochester, you're not going out in all this rain?
Miss Beecher: You'll be positively drowned.
Mary: Washed away.
Rochester (laughing): There's only one here to whom I owe amends – that's to you,
           Blanche. I am obliged to ride over to Mr Bushey, the Magistrate, on
           business and I shall be absent three whole hours, isn't it heartless?
Blanche: I'll pardon you, but I'll never pardon the Magistrate.
Rochester: I'm not going yet, no sentiment till the fatal moment. I'm coming
           back.   (*Exit Rochester*)
Blanche (yawning): What on earth's to be done?
Lady Ingram: My love, Mrs Fairfax assures me there are some pretty costumes in the
           house and we'll have a capital charade, in the drawing room.
Blanche: Well then, Mamma, we might possibly survive till five o'clock – but
           what's to be done after?
Desmond: Egad! I've thought of a word!
All: Tell us – do tell us.
Desmond: Why, Sorrel.
Mary: What does it mean?
Desmond: Why, don't you know – its a plant and the colour of a horse.
Miss Beecher: Capital!
Lady Ingram: Well, my Lord, let us hear – 'sor'. How would you represent that?
Desmond: I[t] don't mean anything.
Mary: And 'rel'.
Desmond: Don't mean anything either. Confound it, I must try again.
Mary (aside): The dear stupid thing.
Blanche: My dear Mamma, this is the third day of the deluge. I am tired of
           everyone, and everything, do tell me what to do.
Desmond: Billiards!
Blanche: Sick of them.
Mary: Where's your French novel?
Blanche: Left the heroine dead and the hero a lunatic.

Lady Ingram (slyly): I know the matter with you, my darling.

Miss Beecher: Her dear Mr Rochester is going away.

Blanche: I'll grow tired of him bye and bye.

Lady Ingram: Much too soon to begin, love.

Blanche: Oh. I suppose I must wait for the honeymoon?

Mary: Nonsense, Blanche, he's never out of your thoughts.

Blanche: Mary, don't be silly.

Mary: Take comfort, poor lamb, her grim ugly blue-beard won't be so long away – he'll come back to it again.

Blanche: How can you be so absurd?

Desmond: If you'd accepted. Me. Miss Ingram. –

Blanche: Your absence might have been a relief, my Lord. Mamma. I've got a capital notion.

Lady Ingram: And what's that, my dear?

Blanche: A delightful, mischevious, splendid idea for a wet day.

Miss Beecher: Do tell us, what – what?

Blanche: You know that proper demure creature Miss Eyre?

Lady Ingram: Oh, the governess?

Blanche: The Governess. Let us get her down, and draw her out – let us bait her. I'm sure we shall have some fun.

Desmond: Drawing the badger, eh?

Mary: Oh, for shame, Blanche!

Lady Ingram: I don't think it quite, a ladylike employment, my love.

Blanche: On the contrary, we'll all be so condescending, and charming. We'll pretend we've had an argument and make her the arbiter, don't you see? I'm quite sure she knows – nothing of history.

Lady Ingram: And I don't think she knows French – a most incompetent person – but, my sweet love, I can't approve.

Blanche: Do you want your sweet love to lie dead at your feet, Mamma? I *must* be amused – (*Rings bell*).

Desmond: I'll examine her in the Globes.

Mary: What do *You* know of them?

Desmond: All the more competent because I know nothing. I'll lay you a pair of gloves, Blanche, the Lady takes the change out of us all, and I hope she may, six against one isn't fair.

Blanche: Done.

Enter Servant

Blanche: Where is Miss Eyre?

Servant: In the conservatory, Miss.

Blanche: Would you tell her that Lady Ingram –

Lady Ingram (aside): My love, I cannot –

Blanche: – that Lady Ingram would be much obliged if she would be so good as to come to the library.   *(Exit Servant)*
Mary: I know if Mr Rochester comes in, he'll stop your baiting.
Blanche: On what plea? Cruelty to animals?
Lady Ingram: Do be careful, Blanche love.

Enter Jane

Blanche: Oh, Miss Eyre, thank you – we've had an argument.
Desmond: Flying at one another.
Blanche: And we've all agreed to appeal to you as the learned person in the house.
Jane: But I'm not learned, Miss Ingram.
Blanche: Oh! That's modesty.
Lady Ingram: I think I understood you to say Miss Eyre, you were clever at embroidery. Would you be so good as to finish that flower?
Jane: With great pleasure. (*Sits at embroidery*)
Blanche: The question in dispute is this. What is the date of the 'Diet of Worms'?
Desmond: We all know that worms are the diet of fish, but it ain't that, Miss Eyre.
Blanche: Can you tell us?
Jane: Do you really wish to know?
Blanche: Of course, we are dying.
Jane: It was in the year (*gives date*).
Miss Beecher: Wonderful. Amazing.
Desmond: Egad (*turning Globe*): Miss Eyre, you can't think how stupid I am. I spend an hour every morning twirling this globe here looking for Great Britain.
Blanche: Of course you are a good French scholar?
Jane: I can talk French.
Desmond: Hams-cat-ska. Deuced hard to get one's tongue round Hams-skat-ska.
Lady Ingram: You've been abroad?
Jane: I was at school in Boulogne.
Lady Ingram: Oh, English-French.
Desmond: Grim Tartary.
Blanche: Donner un plat de *sa* metier! What's that, Miss Eyre?
Jane (promptly): Bad French – *son* métier.
Blanche: I said, '*son metier*'.
Lady Ingram: How can you be so presumptuous? My daughter has had the most expensive masters – impossible!
Blanche (put out): I beg your pardon, Miss Eyre. I am quite correct.

Desmond:	Cochin China. Miss Eyre, could you tell me where to find Great Britain?
Jane:	Oh, if you look to the North West of France, my Lord.
Desmond:	Ah. Thanks, but where are all its little islands? Here are some little dots to the West, like a small eruption. I should know 'em.
Jane:	Probably the *Scilly* Isles.
Desmond:	I've had enough of the Globes for the present.

Adèle bounds in, clapping her hands

Adèle:	De beautiful dresses are found – de drawing room is ready – de Charades!! De Charades!!
Miss Beecher:	Oh do come. Delightful.
Lady Ingram:	Now love, be happy.
Blanche:	Come, I'll lead the forlorn hope. *(Exit all but Lord Desmond)*
Desmond:	I don't pay compliments. I'm not clever enough, but I like clever women. I say, you're a deuced clever one.
Jane:	What, because I knew where to find Great Britain? Why, *you* found Crim Tartary, my Lord.
Desmond:	Eh. And caught a Tartar – eh. Gad! I have you there.
Jane:	You have.
Desmond:	I say! Let's get up a conspiracy – you play up to my lead in the drawing room. What's this? – you say – I found Crim Tartary, and then I say the other thing you know. Deuced good.
Jane:	You can't open a bottle of Champagne twice, My Lord, it gets flat.
Desmond:	Ah, you have *me* there. I say, how in Heaven's name do [you] pass the day? I can't pass the day for the life of me. A fellow can't smoke two dozen cigars in the day, and Rochester's so deuced bad at billiards – it's no fun. How do you pass the day?
Jane:	Well, I read and work, and I teach and I think.
Desmond:	Think, I'd like to try. How do you begin?
Jane:	Well, my thoughts are like a circle, my lord, no beginning and no end.
Desmond:	Egad! my thoughts are like a circle too, that means a nought, you know *(laughs)*. By Jove, I've done it again. We might lead up to that in the drawing room you know.
Jane:	We might.
Desmond:	I'd rather like to pass the day with you.
Jane:	We should bore one another to death, my Lord.
Desmond:	I'd like the death. Now you couldn't suggest to a fellow, Miss Eyre, some amusement on a wet day? Not books you know, I hate books, some little sporting, interesting, amusement, you know, that would last till the dressing bell.
Jane:	Killing flies.

Desmond:	That's like telling a fellow to hunt in July. There ain't any flies in January. Capital game we might have else, you and I. I've won a lot of money on it in India – you put a lump of sugar there, and I put a lump of sugar here, and we see who attracts the most flies in six hours – capital game – we might play for love you know.
Jane:	My Lord, look around you, your mother, and your sisters, and the Miss Beeche[r]s are all gone.
Desmond:	Egad, I thought I was gone too. We'll play that game in the summer, Miss Eyre. Deuced clever. Egad. *(Exit)*

Jane sits in window.

Jane:	Now if I saw Mr Prior's horse coming up the road in the distance, I think I would run upstairs, pack up my things and return with him. He was right – he was right – what is this misery which dogs me, upstairs and downstairs – which gives the venom to my humiliation – poor fool, are you in love? I must weed out this nonsense from my heart. (*Distant merriment heard*) Yes. Yes. Your mirth would be louder and longer if you knew the contemptible weakness of this heart – and yet – and yet she is not worthy of him: he cannot care for her.

Enter Blanche & Rochester, not seeing Jane

Blanche:	But I tell you I can be jealous.
Rochester:	Impossible.
Blanche:	Frightfully jealous – I could be jealous of a canary – I could be jealous of your horse, if you fondled it too much.
Rochester:	I say – quite impossible that you could be jealous.
Blanche:	I am even jealous of the attention you pay to that \prim/ demure creature – the governess – oh, I have watched you.

Jane pulls down blind & rises.

Blanche (aside to Rochester): Send her away.

Rochester:	Miss Eyre, don't disturb yourself. We've no secrets. My horse is being saddled in the yard, and I have some directions to give you before I go.
Blanche:	I think you are very unkind.
Rochester:	Why, my girl?
Blanche:	Going away in this way. What takes you from home?
Rochester:	I've no objection to tell you, and to tell Miss Eyre – it may concern you both. My neighbour and I have speculated very heavily, and this morning I received disastrous news.
Blanche:	Good gracious. Mr Rochester, what will be the consequence of this?

Rochester:	Oh don't be alarmed. By no means ruin. My friends –
Jane:	I'm so glad of that.
Blanche:	Oh, then, it won't affect you at all?
Rochester:	No more than this – I shall be obliged to sell my horses, give up my town house, probably be waited on by a maid in a mop cap, and send my liveried servants to the right about.
Blanche:	Have you informed my mother of this, Mr Rochester?
Rochester:	My dearest Blanche. I thought you were the one to break it to her.
Jane:	You may be happier so, sir, and those around you too.
Rochester:	I have often pictured to myself, if I became a poor man, what a peaceful happy home I might create around me. No stately dinners – no chattering parties – but a ministering loving wife, such as you, Blanche, in your quiet alpaca gown, sharing with me my privations and turning by her sympathy – our common cares into joy.
Blanche (aside):	That wouldn't suit me.
Jane (aside):	How sweet that would be.
Blanche:	I think Mamma must be wondering where I am.
Rochester:	Let us go and find her. *(Exit Blanche & Rochester)*
Jane:	Ah, that humble home with him: how coldly she listened to what brought my heart to my lips – I cannot live here – if she were worthy of him – well – I should, no doubt, have two tigers tearing my heart, love and jealousy, and they would soon make an end of me, but to see daily her unworthiness, and his devotion – I cannot bear it. I must go – oh what a fool I am! I'll set it down *(takes out diary)* I'll write on this page – Jane Eyre – brought up on charity – a poor country school mistress – without family – without beauty – vain – presumptuous – jealous. Now on the other side – Blanche Ingram – birth – beauty – position – accomplishments and the winner of my dear Master's love.

Enter Rochester, quietly. Jane sees him, and closes diary.

Rochester:	Why are you taking notes – you are a spy upon the house! Come let us have a look?
Jane:	No – no – it couldn't interest you.
Rochester:	Oh. You have secrets?
Jane:	One can have private thoughts without having secrets.
Rochester:	Hallo. Look round. Mr Prior's at the window. *(Jane turns quickly. Rochester gently takes diary & pretends to read)*: 'Dreamt of Mr Prior last night'.
Jane (trying to seize it):	Give it back. You must give it back. *(He gives it back.)*
Rochester:	Little friend, you've noticed my tender 'penchant' for Miss Ingram?
Jane:	Yes Sir.
Rochester:	She's a rare one, is she not, Jane?
Jane:	Yes. Sir.

Rochester: She's an armful – a strapper – a real strapper – big, blonde, and buxom.

Jane: Mr Rochester, I got a letter, yesterday, from Mr Prior telling me his kind mother was ill. Here is the letter.

Rochester: Well I don't want it.

Jane: But I want your leave to go for a week.

Rochester: When do you wish to go?

Jane: Early tomorrow morning. Sir.

Rochester: Well. You must have some money – I've given you no salary yet. How much have you in the world, Jane?

Jane (taking out purse): Five shillings. Sir.

Rochester (taking purse, pours money on his hand, chuckles over it, takes out his pocket book): Here.

Jane: Fifty Pounds! I thought you were poor. Sir.

Rochester: Oh did you?

Jane: You only owe me six pounds – I've no change.

Rochester: I don't want change – take your wages.

Jane: Not more than my due.

Rochester: Ah, right, I forgot that you might stay away three months., if you had fifty pounds. Here are three sovereigns – that's plenty.

Jane: Yes, Sir. But now you owe me three.

Rochester: Come back for it, then. I am your banker for forty-seven pounds.

Jane: Mr Rochester. I may as well mention another matter of business to you, while I have the opportunity.

Rochester: Matter of business – I am curious to hear it.

Jane: You have informed me, sir you are going shortly to be married.

Rochester: Yes, what then?

Jane: In that case Adèle ought to go to school.

Rochester: To get her out of my bride's way – I see – not a doubt of it. Adèle, as you say, must go to school and you of course must march straight to the devil.

Jane: I hope not, Sir, but I must seek another situation somewhere.

Rochester (with a comic stare): Of course, and you will ask Mr Prior to get you a place?

Jane: No, Sir, I shall advertise.

Rochester: You shall walk up the Pyramids of Egypt – at your peril you advertise. I wish I offered you only a sovereign instead of three – give me back two, Jane. I have use for them.

Jane: And so have I, Sir. I couldn't spare the money on any account.

Rochester: Little niggard. Give me one sovereign, Jane.

Jane: Not one shilling, Sir – not one penny.

Rochester: Just let me look at the money.

Jane: No, Sir – you're not to be trusted.

Rochester: Jane!

Jane:	Sir.
Rochester:	Promise me *one* thing.
Jane:	I'll promise you anything that I think I am likely to perform.
Rochester:	Not to advertise – trust to me – I'll find you a situation.
Jane:	I shall be glad to do so, Sir – if you will promise that Adèle and I shall be safe out of the house before your bride enters it.
Rochester:	Very well. I pledge my word on it. You go to morrow then?
Jane:	Yes. Sir. Early.
Rochester:	Then you and I must bid good bye for a while.
Jane:	I suppose so, Sir.
Rochester:	And how do people perform that ceremony? of parting, Jane? Teach me. I'm not quite up to it.
Jane:	They say farewell.
[Rochester]:	Then say it.
Jane:	Farewell, Mr Rochester, for the present.
Rochester:	What must I say?
Jane:	Why the same.
Rochester:	Farewell, Miss Eyre, for the present. Is that all?
Jane:	Yes.
Rochester:	It seems stingy. I'd like something else. One might shake hands. There is something, Jane, which makes this farewell difficult for each of us.
Jane:	We have been good friends – I grieve to leave Thornfield. I've not been trampled on – I've not been petrified and I've had a kind master.
Rochester:	Something more than that. Jane, I've a queer feeling with regard to this friendship as if there was a string somewhere under my left ribs, that was joined to your heart, and if we parted overlong, I've a nervous notion I should take to bleeding inwardly – as for you – you would forget me.
Jane:	That. I never should, sir – you know – such a friend as you, Sir, can never be forgotten.
Rochester:	Well, well, we've said Farewell. (*Exit*.)
Jane:	If he knew how hard it is to answer him gaily when my heart is full. Well done, Jane. You've got through it without a sob.

Enter Adèle.

Adèle:	Oh Mademoiselle, that mechant Blanche. Do you know what she said to me?
Jane:	What did she say?
Adèle:	She said that I did not belong to Monsieur Rochester or anyone.
Jane:	Never mind, Adèle. I love you all the better for that. As a child I was just like you – we love one another all the better – shall I tell you a ghost story?
Adèle:	Oh, oui.

Jane:	It's very very short – there was once a great, great, lord and a poor slave girl, and this great Lord sometimes smiled upon the girl, and the foolish girl used to watch for that smile, and long for it – she'd say in the morning to herself, 'I wonder will he smile on me to day', and at night, 'he looked on me today, but did not smile.
Adèle:	Was she a Governess?
Jane:	Hush. They're all coming in.

Mrs Fairfax appears at door.

Jane:	And there's good Mrs Fairfax beckoning for you. Good night.
Mrs Fairfax:	Come, Adèle, (*Exit with Adèle.*)

Enter Lady Ingram, Desmond, Mary, Blanche & Miss Beecher.

Blanche:	Why can't you have the gipsy in here?
Mary:	Oh do have him up in this beautiful moonlight.
Miss Beecher:	It will be so sentimental.
Lady Ingram:	My dear. You're not going to have a great dirty Gipsy up in the library?
Blanche:	Well, we're not going down in the kitchen to him, that's certain, and I positively must have my fortune told.
Desmond:	Let him come up. He's a funny old dog – have him up.

Enter Servant.

Servant:	He's coming up in spite of me, my Lord – he says the master gave him leave to tell the young ladies' fortunes.
Desmond:	And here he comes. (*Exit Servant.*)
Lady Ingram:	How vastly absurd.

Enter Rochester disguised as a Gipsy.

Rochester:	Good even to you gentle folk – good e'en to you and fair fortunes to you all.
Blanche:	That depends upon *you* – be sure to give me a good one.
Rochester:	Eh, my bonny leddy – I've a good will to do so – but that rests with the stars – show me your little palm.
Blanche:	Must I cross it with silver?
Rochester:	Ah, sure a bit o' siller – I'll sit me here (*looks at her hand*). Come round a bit, my Leddy, and let the moonlight on it. Ah, dear heart, bags o' gold and siller and my lord for a bridegroom – the black crow that followed you is a puir fowl not worth the plucking – gold peacocks, and pheasants are your sort.

Blanche:	What nonsense – that's enough for me.
Rochester:	Coom forrad, coom forrad – young and bonny ones, stretching your pretty necks in the darkness. (*All advance except Jane.*)
Mary:	What's my fortune, Sir?
Rochester:	Ah, you ken it well yourself – slybody – there's the cousin. He with the yellow hair and rides the white horse with the hounds.
Mary:	Gracious. How do you know that?
Rochester:	Ah. I knows it all – who'll speer her fortune next?
Desmond:	What will be my fortune at the next Derby, my man?
Rochester:	You back the foal 'Fiddler'.
Desmond:	What then?
Rochester:	Why, you'll lose!
Desmond (aside):	Damn it. I've backed him heavily.
Lady Ingram:	I don't think this is quite right.
Desmond:	Seems to know all about us.
Blanche (to Mary):	How do you feel?
Rochester:	There's anither leddy here – she cant hide fra' me.
Mary:	Oh, Miss Eyre, you must come and have your fortune told. (*Leads Jane forward.*)
Rochester:	Well, you want to know your fortune?
Jane:	I don't care about it – you may please yourself. I don't believe in it.
Rochester:	Why, its like your impudence to say so – I heard it in your step.
Jane:	Did you? You've a quick ear.
Rochester:	Ah, and a quick eye, and a quick brain.
Jane:	You need them all in your trade.
Rochester:	Well I do specially when I get a customer like you. Why don't you tremble?
Jane:	I'm not cold.
Rochester:	Why don't you turn pale?
Jane:	I'm not sick.
Rochester:	Why don't you consult me, *saucy*?
Jane:	I'm not silly.
Blanche (aside):	What nerve that creature has.
Mary:	Hush. (*Rochester lights pipe & smokes.*)
Rochester:	You are cold – you are sick and you are silly.
Jane:	Prove it.
Rochester:	Let me look in your face – stand in the light there. Ye are cold because ye are alone. Ye are sick, because ye see happiness afore yer, at your lips and yer cannot taste it. Ye are silly 'cause ye will not stretch to it.
Jane:	I can't guess riddles – what do you mean?
Rochester:	I'll read your life for yer. Here you are *aloane* wi' all the foine folk around you – like figures in a glass, but there's one o 'em that ye watch, wi' yer doleful ee'n night and morn.
Blanche:	What can he mean?

Rochester: Ye sit in yer winder to watch him. I ken yer habits I ken yer ways.

Jane: You've learnt them from the servants.

Rochester: Where's squire Rochester?

Jane: From home.

Rochester: Well, but he'll come back.

Blanche: Come out of this, for mercy's sake – lets light all the candles. Do give me your arm, Lord Desmond, I'm frightened.

Lady Ingram: Give her a good lecture, my lord, upon her superstition

Desmond (aside): I'll not back 'Fiddler'. (*Aloud*): My dear Miss Ingram, trust me, I'll save you from the bogies.   (*Exit.*)

Mary: Won't you come, Miss Eyre.

Jane: I'm not afraid. I'll wait.   (*All exit but Rochester & Jane.*)

Rochester: Ah, go along with all of you. I hae to talk to you. Ye saw, dearee, how she leaned on the lord's arm. I'd warn Squire Rochester to look out. If the silly lord come back to her now – the puir squire is counted out.

Jane: But I did not come to hear Mr Rochester's fortune. I came to hear my own.

Rochester: Kneel there on the bit stool. I'll read your fortune in your face. Why ye might pick the fruit fra the branch by the stretching of your hand. I saw good fortune herself, put that you wished for on the shelf for you. You've only to take it down. You fancy Mr Rochester!

Jane (quickly): If this is all you're to tell me, Good night!

Rochester: Ah, you silly daft – wi' half an ee' ye could see that Squire Rochester fancies you. That heart is galled wi' this chain that hawds him to the tall bowld faced lass. His thoughts are wi'ye now, fu' of' love as he jogs along the dark road fu' i' love. Ha ye no love for him?

Jane (agitated): Who has told you this? Do you see into people's hearts and secrets? Old man? Yes, I love him – I thought no one knew it – if you know my heart, do you know his? You're mad to say he cares for me. I'll listen to you no longer.

Rochester: Ah, your voice trembles, your step totters. (*Throws off disguise.*) Well, Jane, don't you know me?

Jane: Mr Rochester.

Rochester: No other come back.

Jane: What have I said? I've been in a dream. Oh, Sir, t'was scarcely fair – I hardly thought I should meet you again, in travesty.

Rochester: You shall meet me, Jane, to night, without any disguise. I have found the situation for you. You are to undertake the education of Mrs Dionysus O'Gall's five daughters of Bitternut Lodge. Connaught. Ireland.

Jane (moved): I thought that Adèle and I – it is a long way off, Sir.

Rochester: No matter – a girl of your sense will not object to the voyage or the distance.

Jane: The distance and the sea – a barrier –

Rochester: From what, Jane?

Jane:	From England – from Thornfield – and –
Rochester:	Well? from me –
Jane:	From you, sir (*agitated*). A long way, a long way.
Rochester:	To be sure, and when you get to Bitternut Lodge, Connaught, Ireland – and you must go to morrow, never to return –
Jane:	I wish I'd never come to Thornfield. I wish I'd never been born.
Rochester:	Because you are sorry to leave it?
Jane:	I have known you, Mr Rochester – your kindness. Your company – is what I have reverenced – is what I have delighted in – and the tongue will speak out at last. It strikes me with terror and anguish to feel I absolutely must be torn from you for ever. I see the necessity of departure and it is like looking on the necessity of death.

Rochester (suddenly): Where do you see the necessity?

Jane:	Where? You, Sir have placed it before me in the shape of Miss Ingram – your bride.
Rochester:	My bride! What bride! I have no bride.
Jane:	But you will have.
Rochester:	Yes, I *will*! I *will*.
Jane:	Then I must go. You've said it yourself.
Rochester:	*No* – you must stay – I swear it.
Jane:	I tell you I must go. Do you think I can stay to be nothing to you? Do you think I am a machine without feelings and can bear to have my morsel of bread snatched from my lips and my drop of living water dashed from my cup? Do you think because I'm poor, obscure, plain, that I am soul-less and heartless? You think wrong. I've as much soul as you and full as much heart. If God had gifted me with some beauty and much wealth, I should have made it as hard for you to leave me, as it is now for me to leave *you*. It is my heart and soul now that addresses yours. Not the servant addressing her master – but equal.
Rochester:	As we are.
Jane:	And yet not so, for you are as good as a married man – and wed to one inferior to you. One you cannot love – I would scorn such a union – therefore I am better than you – let me go.
Rochester:	Where Jane – to Ireland?
Jane:	I have spoken my mind and can go anywhere now.
Rochester:	You shall act for yourself. I am no longer engaged to Miss Ingram.
Jane:	No longer? (*Aside*): But what is this to me?
Rochester:	You remember how I confessed to heavy losses before that paragon of fidelity? Her mother acted promptly – I found this letter on my table – very polite – deprecating anything sudden or unpleasant, she had long suspected the state of things – and regretted that the suit of Lord Desmond should have been repulsed – so and so – and Jane, I am free.
Jane:	You play a farce, which I merely laugh at.

Rochester: Do you doubt me, Jane?

Jane: Wholly!

Rochester: You've no faith in me?

Jane: Not a whit.

Rochester (passionately): Am I then a liar in your eyes? Am I so little of the gentleman that I could insult you by such an offer in jest – I love you dearer than life – you poor obscure, dependent – I entreat you to accept me as a husband.

Jane: What, me? Mr Rochester, let me look in your face.

Rochester: Why?

Jane: I want to read it. It's all the world to me to believe you are true, and your offer real. My only feelings to you must be gratitude and devotion.

Rochester: Gratitude!! Jane – accept me quickly. Say Edmund – give me my name – Edmund, I will marry you?

Jane: Do you truly love me? Do you sincerely wish me to be your wife?

Rochester: I do. You do not want an oath?

Jane: Then Sir. I will marry you.

Rochester: Edmund!

Jane: Dear Edmund.

Rochester: Come to me – come to me entirely now – make my happiness – I will make *yours*.

Jane: Leave me alone now, dear – I want to think – I haven't yet conceived my happiness.

Rochester (kisses her. Aside): God pardon me, and man meddle not with me! I have her, and will hold her. (*Aloud*): Are you happy, Jane?

Jane: All too happy.

Rochester (aside): Then it will atone – it will atone. God will pardon me.

(*Exit*)

Jane: He's mine – Jane Eyre's own love is like a king's crown placed on a beggar's head – there never was a wilder, grander, fairy gift in a tale – nothing but death can snatch away this joy – and after all my life of labour and sorrows, God is too just to cut short my blossom'd life. Now come slight and insult on me, would be a sort of luxury – whilst I whispered *he is mine* – he is mine. Keep down, swelling heart, or joy may kill you – no mortal ever lived happier than I – no happiness was ever so cloudless – none can stand between him, and me (*Maniac laugh heard distant*) – Oh, what's that? God protect me, it was like a devil's laugh. (*Laugh repeated almost at door*) Edmund – Edmund – save me – I – I can't escape. What is it? what is it?

Door opens & Madwoman appears, sees Jane, approaches with horrible menaces; with a cry Jane drops on floor, Maniac is about to strangle her when Rochester enters quickly, advances – Maniac gibbers, & points from Jane to Rochester, & to herself. She retreats through door.

Rochester: Grace. Grace Poole – Here! (*Closes secret door*) Jane. Dearest one, you are safe. (*He supports her head on his knee & the company heard without calling*): – Open, what's the matter. What's the matter?

End of Act II

Act III

Library, about 4 o'clock, sunshine dying out and showing again across the books

Mrs Fairfax discovered arranging some books

Mrs Fairfax: Dear me, I don't like the task at all of giving this dear young lady a hint – and she has really been too ill, but I wi[sh] I could get her to leave the house and go home while Edmund's away in London.

Enter Jane

Mrs Fairfax: Well dear, you're up!

Jane: I have been ill.

Mrs Fairfax: You have had a great shock, dear Miss Eyre.

Jane: I remember it dimly. I want to know all about it. Can you tell me? Can you explain?

Mrs Fairfax: Sit down, dear. Sit Down.

Jane: What day is this, Mrs Fairfax?

Mrs Fairfax: Just a fortnight since that distressing evening, my dear.

Jane: The Ingrams are gone.

Mrs Fairfax: They are gone home, and, only fancy, dear, there's likely to be a match between Lord [blank] and the beautiful Miss Blanche.

Jane: Where's Mr Rochester?

Mrs Fairfax: He is [in] London. He ascertained from the doctor that you were only suffering from a nervous shock.

Jane: And he'll be back?

Mrs Fairfax: We expected him yesterday. We don't know what keeps him in London!

Jane (smiling): I think I can guess. Pardon my questions, Mrs Fairfax – and my pupil?

Mrs Fairfax: Adèle is gone to a relations of Mr Rochester's where she will remain, but you will have no difficulty, dear Miss Eyre, in finding a place.

Jane: Thank you, I've found a happy, beautiful place already.

Mrs Fairfax: Oh! Indeed!

Jane: I'll be glad to leave this house.

Mrs Fairfax: You keep looking at that secret door, dear, there's no cause for alarm. (*Jane draws chair to Mrs Fairfax*)

Jane: Perhaps not, but I would implore you to give me an explanation – it's something dreadful.

Mrs Fairfax: Well, dear –

Jane (with hushed voice): Who is this fearful woman upstairs!

Mrs Fairfax: I always understood, my dear, that she was a half-sister of Mr Rochester. I believe a Creole by birth. He has acted very generously towards the poor creature. She has been cruelly treated, I understand in an asylum.

Jane: How was it the company in the house knew nothing of her?

Mrs Fairfax: Naturally Mr Rochester would be very sensitive.

Jane: How is it that she could be loose about the house!

Mrs Fairfax: It has very rarely happened. Once I heard she tried to set fire to Mr Rochester's bed -curtains, when he was asleep – but I mustn't alarm you.

Door opens, Jane starts. Enter Grace Poole.

Grace: How is the young lady?

Mrs Fairfax: A little nervous yet.

Grace: If I were the young lady. I wouldn't sleep another night in this house.

Jane: But why!

Grace: Oh! Many reasons, Miss. Some of them might offend you if I told. The coach passes at six o'clock, Miss. She up there – is dangerous and cunning. I wouldn't stop If I was you.

Mrs Fairfax: How can you frighten her!

Grace: But I would like to frighten her if it would make her catch that coach. If she wants the fare, we could make it up for her.

Jane: If your patient be so dangerous Why do you leave her!

Grace: I've an assistant, and she's quiet now. Her ear's so quick, bless you – that any loud talking or singing comes up to her when I can scarcely hear a sound.

Jane: I am going tomorrow, Mrs Poole. I don't think between this and then there'll be either singing or loud talking. I've a good friend to take care of me – when I go.

Mrs Fairfax: I think he's waiting for you now, dear.

Jane: What! Mr Rochester!

Mrs Fairfax: No dear, Mr Prior.

Jane: Oh! is he come! I'll see him.

Grace: She's got Mr Rochester on her lips.

                                      (Exits with a keen look at Jane)

Jane (rises): I'll go down to him.

Mrs Fairfax: Why should you, dear! I'm going down and I'll send him up. No – no – don't be frightened, that door is fast nailed up. I'll send Mr Prior to you.   *(Exit)*

Jane: There's something chilly about everyone. I wish he were back – my happiness has taken flight, and that dream of the little child three nights always the same – dabbling its hand in the grasses. It always brought me ill-luck – I wish he were back.

Enter Mr Prior – she shakes hand with him

Jane: You don't forget me, dear Mr Prior – two long journeys to see me. Is your mother well?

Prior: I don't think she was ever well, Jane, since you left us.

Jane: Oh, then you shouldn't have left her.

Prior: She bade me come.

Jane: Won't you sit down, Mr Prior? How happy I could fancy you would be in this library all day. Do sit here – see you can turn this little book-stand on its swivel – open some deep book – light your candles – and there you are – happy.

Prior: You seem happy, Jane!

Jane: I am happy. I only want one thing.

Prior: And that – !

Jane: Some confidential friend to tell my happiness to.

Prior: You look pale.

Jane: I've had a nervous attack, Mr Prior. What do you think has happened to me since I saw you?

Prior: I'm very anxious, Jane, to know.

Jane: Spoken like a ghostly monitor – but there is nothing sepulchral in my news – fancy the wildest grandest dream [of] a poor governess. Fulfilled.

Prior: You mean that – !

Jane: Come, come, dear old friend. You know you always thought of me but as a friend and sister – I shall always be so.

Prior: But this news –

Jane: Tomorrow at this hour – I shall be Mr Rochester's wife.

Prior (half aside): Thank God, I am come in time!

Jane: You will be present –

Prior: It is time, Jane, to tell you what has brought me here. It has got about that Mr Rochester has been paying you attentions.

Jane: Well!

Prior: But it's not well, Jane – don't think I am speaking under jealousy.

Jane: I am sure you are not. But you are speaking of what you know nothing.

Prior: Jane, there are ugly rumours about concerning Mr Rochester.

Jane: Vile calumnies – I love him the more!

Prior: They've come to me from such a trustworthy source that I must see Mr Rochester.

Jane: Why not! But it is a pity to worry him and he mayn't be home for hours.

Prior: I must see him – Heaven forbid I should wrong any man unheard – but I must see him – I'll wait in the hall like one of his lackeys for any length of time.

Jane: Oh dear, Mr Prior, you get so excited and fall into that dear sermon-tone. You'll stay with me here, won't you! And I'll tell you all.

Enter Servant

Servant: Lady Ingram and the Miss Ingrams Miss.

Jane: Tell them that Mr Rochester's from home.

Servant: But they want to see you, Miss.

Jane (aside): Their sneers and their scoffs will be pleasure to me now. (*Aloud*): Ask them to walk in.   (*Exit Servant*)

Prior: Jane, if you find him false – without truth – and without honour –

Jane: I know what you'd say – would I come back to the school! I will!

Prior: And trust me, I will never press my suit again. If this happens so, we'll work together as friends! (*Takes hand*)

Jane: As friends!

Prior: I wait below.

Enter Servant

Servant: Lady Ingram and the Miss Ingrams.

Prior passes them, bows, they bow slightly in return. Exit Prior & Servant.

Enter Lady Ingram, Blanche & Mary

Lady Ingram: Good morning, Miss Eyre.

Blanche: Good morning, Miss Eyre. (*Jane bows.*)

Mary (shaking hands): You've been unwell – I hope you've got over your fright.

Jane: Thank you, I'm much better (*all seated*).

Lady Ingram: I understand that your pupil has gone to school.

Jane: A fortnight ago she went to some friends of Mr Rochester's.

Lady Ingram: Oh!

Blanche: I presume, Miss Eyre, you are no longer her governess.

Jane: No, Miss Ingram. (*To Lady Ingram*): Mr Rochester is from home, Lady Ingram.

Blanche: We haven't come to visit Mr Rochester.

Lady Ingram: We were aware Mr Rochester was from home – we have come here from a kindly motive to you, Miss Eyre.

Blanche: In point of fact, to give you a warning.

Lady Ingram: When your pupil has left your care and the pretext for your presence here has ceased – how can you think of remaining here another day, in such a house, Miss Eyre.

Jane:	Mrs Fairfax is here.
Lady Ingram:	Mrs Fairfax is an elderly lady and a relation. Pardon me – if you wish to retain your respectability it is peremptory you should leave this house at once. Till you can secure a new place, Miss Eyre, – ah – I have noticed you are proficient at your needle and as my daughter's wedding with Lord [blank] is coming on, we could give you employment – in – a – making up the dresses.
Blanche:	Not on the same terms as you've had here, of course. We should be very sorry to see you in want.
Mary:	Oh! Blanche.
Jane (aside):	What a luxury there is in their insults now. (*Smiling*): Thank you, my lady and Miss Ingram – you are very kind – I should be too busy and am in no want.
Lady Ingram:	Oh!
Mary:	My mother does not mean to offend you.
Jane:	I am not the least offended.
Mary:	You may always look upon me as a friend, Miss Eyre.
Jane:	Except Mr Rochester, I have found no other friend here.
Blanche:	You mentioned Mr Rochester. Since my mother and sister shrink from letting you [know] what that gentleman is I feel it my duty to let you know. Mr Rochester is a man who has been living under false colours before the world.
Jane:	Miss Ingram!
Blanche:	A dishonourable, despicable, unprincipled man whose life has been one system of hypocrisy.
Jane:	What are you saying, Miss Ingram – can your anger with Mr Rochester –
Blanche:	My anger! I thoroughly despise him – only contempt.
Jane:	How can you descend to such idle slander?
Blanche:	Facts are not idle slander. He is no gentleman – a hypocrite – almost a felon.
Lady Ingram:	Gently, gently, Blanche!
Blanche:	And if you don't know this, all the world knows it. (*Mockingly*): All the world knows it.
Jane:	Miss Ingram. Mr Rochester is not here to answer you – you traduce him behind his back. When you call him hypocrite or a felon, I think you are raving – but – 'Not a gentleman'! There never was a gentleman in the largest sense – if he is not one!!
Lady Ingram:	Don't be angry, Miss Eyre.
Jane:	I am angry. It ill becomes your daughter to call him no gentleman, whom she has loved for his money and left when she heard he was poor.
Blanche:	Miss Eyre. How dare you!

Jane: Not a gentleman! When others wounded a poor dependent he knew how
               to heal the wound – he has no vulgar arrogance which now tramples on
               the humble. He is incapable of the petty insults of patronage – which
               hurts to the quick – his manly kindness – his thoughtful goodness – his
               delicacy for another's feelings and his staunch friendship, don't seem
               known to you – they are to me, and your words are empty spite and
               evil slander. I am glad my indignation has found a tongue to tell you
               so to your face!

Blanche: Don't go yet Miss Eyre – let your extraordinary passion cool down.
               I don't know the relation at present existing between you and Mr
               Rochester – but if you wish to retain a shred of respectability –

Jane: Tell me at once. What you mean!

Mary: Pray do not be shocked, Miss Eyre, at some startling news.

Jane (to Mary): What is it, what is it, I will not believe anything against Mr
               Rochester.

Blanche: A cold fact, Miss Eyre, will be enough for you without comment. You
               are aware of the relation to which Mr Rochester stood to me – '*Mr
               Rochester has a wife alive.*' (*Jane sinks back on chair.*)

Jane: I don't believe it. Impossible.

Blanche: A wife alive – in this house.

Jane: Oh, this is monstrous – you startle me – now I see your mistake.

Mary: Indeed, it is true, Miss Eyre.

Jane: Don't you say it is true, don't you say it – with that kind beautiful face
               of yours (*aside*) or perhaps I should believe it and drop dead.

Lady Ingram: Dear me, what causes this agitation?

Jane: Lady Ingram – I see your mistake – I can explain it – I've learnt from
               Mrs Fairfax's own lips – there is a poor patient – a half sister –

Lady Ingram: Mrs Fairfax has been deceived among the rest.

Jane (sternly): You have made a monstrous charge. What's your evidence?

Blanche: Give me that letter, Mama.

Mary: I respect your loyalty to your friend.

Blanche: This patient, as you call it, has a brother – the news reached him of my
               engagement and he considerately wrote to me to tell me of the state of
               the case. Should you like to read it?

Lady Ingram: The first few lines will explain all. (*Jane snatches letter and staggers
               toward window.*) Most suspicious agitation.

Blanche: Why should we concern ourselves any farther about her, Mama?

Mary: Poor thing! Poor thing!

Jane (returning): What is this letter? Who is this Mr Mason! I'd sooner believe a word
               from Mr Rochester's lips than the cry of a whole slanderous world. I
               don't believe – (*tears letter in two*) some lying enemy.

Blanche: It was a pity you tore it. I was about to ask you to keep it, you seem
               so interested in Mr Rochester. (*Rising*): We'll leave the interesting
               investigation to you – the letter refers you to one 'Grace Poole'. Let's
               hope her evidence will be satisfactory.

Jane: Grace Poole? (*She mechanically takes up letter.*)
Lady Ingram: Good Morning, Miss Eyre.
Blanche: We do not renew our offer, Miss Eyre.
Mary (approaching her & taking her hand): Write to me, Miss Eyre, and remember,
                 I am your friend. (*Jane has seen nothing and heard nothing. Her hand
                 drops dead beside her from Miss Ingram's, the other hand holds letter,
                 her eyes are as if tranced.*)   (*All Exit except Jane.*)
Jane (after a pause): What have they told me, something dreadful is ringing in my
                 ears, a letter, yes – here's a letter (*looks at letter*). It couldn't be. Grace
                 Poole! (*starts from her lethargy into sudden activity*) I must see her. I
                 must know the truth – I must wring it from her.

Grace Poole looks in.

Grace: Hush. This loud talking Miss, is very bad for my patient. I am obliged
                 – (*Jane darts to her side.*)
Jane: Grace Poole, you must answer me. I must know the truth – I've a right
                 to it now, a sacred right, and you must – you shall tell me.
Grace: Tell me your right, Miss, and I may tell you the truth.
Jane: My right. He has asked me to be his wife. I love him beyond all created
                 things – tell me – only tell me that patient is his sister – and I'll love you
                 too. Woman, why are you silent! You've something horrible to tell.
Grace: Well, Miss, you don't seem fit to hear it. So you're to be his wife! Eh!
                 Ah, Miss, I told you to quit the house.
Jane: Say no more (*she seems about to fall*).
Grace: I've said enough. (*Aside*): The bullet has gone to her poor heart. (*Aloud*):
                 Sit there, dear, and I'll bring you some water.   (*Exit*)

Jane seated, silent with the letter in her hand

Enter Rochester. He stands for a second to look at her.

Jane (to herself): He's come.
Rochester (aside): How pale she looks – she's not heard me come in. (*Aloud*): Jane. (*To
                 himself*): Thinking of to morrow, Jane, our wedding day? (*He stops to
                 kiss her, taking her hand.*) What, not a word? You turn your cheek from
                 my lips and draw your hand from mine. What's the matter, my girl?
Jane: Nothing, Sir, that you can cure.
Rochester: Now I look at you, you are pale. Listen to me. Every mile of my long
                 journey I've been thinking of this coming moment, when we should
                 meet – rouse yourself. I have cheer for you – I had your measure for
                 a certain dress – it's come, white as a sunbeam – I have in my pocket
                 here that magic scrap of legal paper – called a marriage licence – throw
                 off this nervous depression, dear – are you angry with me because I'm

a day later than I promised? Today was cloudy – tomorrow will be sunny and lucky is the bride, the sun shines on. (*Aside*): She *is* still under the shock. (*Aloud*): I have something here to make you smile – let me try on this band of gold!

Jane: It is a mockery, Sir, and you know it.

Rochester (taken aback): Jane, who has been talking to you? Who has been setting you against me! I am the victim of many cruel rumours – you will not believe them.

Jane: I have been listening to others and questioning others. I wish only to question and listen to you. Who is that terrible woman upstairs?

Rochester: I knew it. My girl, you are under a sort of spell of terror.

Jane: Terror at what! If what I have heard be true, I don't care what becomes of me – I could wish I'd been killed that night. Despair, Sir, has no fear.

Rochester (after a pause): What have they told you, Jane!

Jane (handing the letter): That! (*Rochester snatches the letter glances over contents.*)

Rochester: The hound! (*Tears letter.*) Jane, dismiss this letter from your mind. There, the infamous thing is in scraps.

Jane: Is that Woman Your Wife?

Rochester: Listen to me, listen to me with that patient, wistful look – I know and love you so well.

Jane: Is that Woman Your Wife?

Rochester: But you don't listen – Oh, Jane – what a change in my life your coming here has made in me – it has been a gentle charm, the daily delight in being kind to you. The sweetness of hearing my name pronounced by your lips. Let no one blame me, my girl, that I loved you – when your very smile was a festival to me. Let none dare blame me!

Jane: Is that Woman Your Wife?

Rochester: Have I ever told you what a wretched life has been mine, till I met you? Some time I will tell you, and your pity for me will kill your blame.

Jane (rising): Oh! Sir, you will not answer me, you turn me off when I am asking you a question of life and death.

Rochester: Sit down. I must be heard. The same act, Jane, that's condemned by man, may be pardoned in God's sight – who knows the heart, has watched all that's been resisted, and fathomed the depth of misery – you ask me have I a wife? Body and soul of me rise in writhing against the avowal. Yes. One who never loved me. One who basely deceived me again and again – brainless – intemperate and unchaste, one whose excesses ended in madness. You've seen her, a wild beast, loathsome and murderous. Do you call that wild beast – a Wife?

Enter Mr Prior with a knock0

Rochester: We are private here!

Prior: I see my fears were groundless – Jane, the haven was always open to you. I will bring you back to it.

Jane: Mr Prior, before we go – look at that gentleman – when you see a face again that looks manly, honest, strong, mistrust it. Let us leave this wretched house.

Rochester: Jane, speak to me. I do not ask your pardon, I no longer excuse myself – I've told you what I am – call me by the name I deserve, but for God's sake, speak to me.

Jane (to Prior): I told you that he had asked me to be his wife – he has deceived me to the last. He has let others tell me the dreadful news – that he has a wife.

Prior: Mr Rochester, it is not my duty to give your conduct its true name, I leave that to your conscience. I have now stepped in between you and your designs. I take the position beside her, as a Clergyman and her only friend.

Rochester: Jane. I can only see you, only hear you. The only excuse I make was my great love for you. Why didn't I tell you this before – because I trembled to lose you – my silence was my great love for you. I thought we should go abroad, that you would be my wife before God, in your own conscience and in a happy strange country. We might have broken a mere human law, but who would be harmed? I should be saved from this horrible doom, and you would have been happy. It was still my great love. Won't you look at me and speak to me?

Prior: You compel me, Sir, to speak more strongly and tell you –

Jane: Be silent, Mr Prior, my grief is my own and I'll tell him what he has done for me. (*To Rochester*): You ask me to speak to you, Sir – what have I to say! but that I have been a poor truthful vain fool, and you have purposed to destroy me, without pity or warning. What have I to say, but that you spread your net well, and I could detect [no] false ring in all your kindness. Oh! Sir, in whom am I to believe, when the one I could have worshipped has proved an enemy? (*Rochester sits with pale face in hands, affected.*) You have done me a bitter wrong, that will follow me through life. Henceforth I'll distrust everything I love, I'll think everything happy must be hollow. The misery you have made for me, I must bear – and – and – when I remember – and – (*She is overcome, as she hears him sob heavily, she runs to him and kneels at his feet.*) My own kind, beloved master, I forgive you heartily and freely.

Prior: Jane, be firm.

Jane: Though we must part, I'll never forget you – don't let my words grieve you, God bless you a hundred times and may he give you peace – my happiness shall be to pray for you night and day. (*Rochester sobs.*) Don't. Don't. Turn your face to me. (*She turns his face gently towards her.*)

Prior: This is weakness, Jane. Come or I must leave you.

Jane: Leave us, my kind Friend, a moment. I'll follow.

Prior: I'll await you below.   (*Exit*)
Jane: My dear Master, we've got to say *Farewell*.
Rochester: What shall I do, Jane! Where shall I turn for a companion, for some
                   life? Think of my misery – you will leave me reckless and drift[ing.]
Jane (kissing his hand): Farewell, and God comfort us both.
Rochester: You are going, Jane. (*Jane goes to door.*)
Jane (standing): I am going Sir.
Rochester: You are leaving me.
Jane: Yes!
Rochester: Oh Jane, my love, my hope, my life, come back!
Jane: Farewell, for both, dear Sir, I must go.
Rochester (starting up): By God, I cannot part with you, and I won't. Duty and
                   honour shrivel up before my love for you! Cling to me, Jane! For you
                   cannot escape me, put your arms round my neck and say you are mine
                   till death part us. (*A shriek and laughter heard. They slowly part as
                   under a spell.*)
Jane (in an awestruck voice): Farewell! Master! (*Approaches door. Rochester stands
                   dazed.*)

End of Act III

Act IV

Porch to a Lodge. Steps to a door. Apple tree in Bloom. – Evening.

Enter Mrs Fairfax. & Servant carrying a table

Mrs Fairfax: Lay it here, James. The sunshine will soon be round here. Now carry
                   round the easy chair – it's in the back garden.

Enter Grace Poole with handkerchiefs just washed. She hangs them on bushes.

Mrs Fairfax: No one calls, Miss Poole, to ask after the poor master. A month after
                   that dreadful event and no cards, no letters.
Grace: As you brew, Mrs Fairfax, so will you bake. Sow the storm and there
                   comes the whirlwind.
Mrs Fairfax: A fine old family mansion burnt to the ground and all the property
                   destroyed.
Grace: Pity, ma'am, that some ugly scandal weren't burnt too with the
                   property.
Enter Jane

Jane: Mrs Fairfax.
Mrs Fairfax (startled): Here is Miss Eyre.

Jane:	What has happened?
Mrs Fairfax:	Have you heard no news?
Jane:	I know nothing except this – that my dea[r] Master is alive and in some dreadful trouble.
Grace:	I thought, Miss Eyre, you would take my advice and quit this place.
Mrs Fairfax:	I had your letter, dear, and you said in \it/ that your purpose was quite unshaken – never under any circumstances to return again.
Jane:	Mrs Fairfax, he has called me – he is in some dreadful extremity – what has happened?
Grace:	Called you, Miss Jane! I know to my certain knowledge your *late* master – couldn't have called you.
Jane (agitated):	My late master – he is not, not dead?
Mrs Fairfax:	No, Miss Eyre, but he cannot have called you – how long have you been here?
Jane:	I have come this moment – I have been travelling all night, and all day – you may call it a dream, Mrs Fairfax, but far away in the Village School – when the children had gone, and I was quite alone – his voice came to me as plainly as I hear yours, and it solemnly bade me come – for God's sake what has happened?
Mrs Fairfax:	If you'd been at home now, dear, you'd have had a letter from me giving you an account of the dreadful trouble we've had here. We have all had a marvellous escape, but the old house is in ruins, and all the property destroyed.
Jane:	Where is *he*?
Grace:	My dear young lady – you cannot see him – it's a pity you've come all this way.
Mrs Fairfax:	He has held to his promise, dear. He has never written to you or attempted to follow you. You should not have come.
Jane:	God would not have allowed that heart-broken call to come to me if it were not right – where is he? I must just speak to him – just answer his call and I will go.
Grace (with a sign to Mrs Fairfax):	He has gone to London, Miss.
Jane:	Good heavens! I've no money, and I'm worn out.
Grace:	Why, you can sleep at the Inn, Miss – it's the second time I've given you good advice. The first time his wife was alive, but there's as much danger to your good name now as then. (*Exit*)
J ane:	Mrs Fairfax, I may have been deceived, but before I return do tell me everything – all that you've told me in your letter – I'm so tired. I'll sit down. His wife is dead?
Mrs Fairfax:	It's nearly two months, Miss Eyre, since you left Thornfield.
Jane:	Well?
Mrs Fairfax:	Mr Rochester had severe losses, and he lived almost entirely alone in his study – no doubt in dreadful depression, after that exposure.
Jane:	My poor master.

Mrs Fairfax: But now indeed is a time when everybody should forgive him and pity him.

Jane: You would tell me he is ruined?

Mrs Fairfax: Listen, dear – it's just eight days ago since I was wakened, at the dead of night, by Mr Rochester's voice – warning me to get up – that the house was on fire – I dressed myself instantly and when I got into the corridor it was filled with smoke – I could hardly breathe. He hurried me along till we were at the top of the grand staircase and then, my dear, we heard that awful laugh upstairs, that so startled you.

Jane: His wife!

Mrs Fairfax: He stopped and bade me go down and escape – 'I must save her', he cried – the upper staircase seemed all aflame, but he seemed to me to rush through it and dissapear.

Jane: I could have sworn he'd do it.

Mrs Fairfax: Yes, it was a noble attempt, for she was a terrible burden, dear. I was forced to run down and escape into the air – and there were the two women servants – all that remained – standing on the grass terrified – we all thought Mr Rochester was lost – as we looked up we saw a dreadful sight – the Madwoman was standing on the roof *alone*, with the glare of the fire on her, and with an awful cry she seemed to leap and disappear – Mrs Poole then came out, very much overcome with the smoke – and told us that her patient, who was very fierce and cunning, had found an opportunity of setting fire to one of the rooms and the dry beams caught like tinder –

Jane: But Mr Rochester?

Mrs Fairfax: I am sorry to say he was very badly injured. He staggered through the smoke and sparks to us, and seemed not to find his way.

Jane: Not blind –

Mrs Fairfax: Well, we have great hopes the sight is not entirely gone.

Jane: And that's what has taken him to London. Thank you, dear Mrs Fairfax. Farewell.

Mrs Fairfax: I know your motive for coming was kind and good, dear, but you've laid too much weight on a dream.

Jane (sadly): It was no dream. It was no dream.

                                                        (*Exit lingeringly leaving bag behind*)

Mrs Fairfax: I pity her from my heart, but nothing would come of it, if they came together – he a poor afflicted gentleman, and she a village schoolmistress.   (*Exit through little gate*)

Slow melancholy music

Enter Rochester from porch

Rochester: It was about sunset yesterday – I heard her voice – Jane's voice – I think the sun is shining and there is a spring breeze. (*He gropes his way down steps with stick.*) They set my chair somewhere about here. (*Sits*) I heard Jane's voice yesterday when I was in my despair, as if it came from fifty miles away, and I called out in an agony – Jane – Jane and I heard her voice – Master, I'm coming! She hasn't come.

Enter Mrs Fairfax

Mrs Fairfax: Well, Sir. You've found your way out?
Rochester: Is the last post in?
Mrs Fairfax: Yes, Sir.
Rochester: No letter?
Mrs Fairfax: Some business letters about the sale, Sir. It's very heartless of the neighbours, Sir, making no enquiries.
Rochester: Two high crimes against society, madam. Poverty and scandal. The first is unpardonable! (*Aside*): No letter – no letter.
Mrs Fairfax: Mr Rochester, I was going to tell you this morning – my eldest daughter has written to me, to offer me a home. I should be very sorry –
Rochester: Quite right – quite right – leave the sinking ship. I'm not so poor, Mrs Fairfax, but that I shall continue your salary always.
Mrs Fairfax: I thank you with all my heart! – Of course you know –.
Rochester: There – there – have you heard anything about Miss Eyre?
Mrs Fairfax: I believe, Sir, she's to be married to Mr Prior.
Rochester (aside): Married – I did not think there was a pang left for me. (*Aloud*): Why not, Mrs Fairfax. Who can blame her? Least of all, I.
Mrs Fairfax (aside): In tears. (*Aloud*): Can I do anything for you?
Rochester: Would you kindly bring me a glass of water?
Mrs Fairfax: You are not in pain?
Rochester: Pain – no.   (*Exit Mrs F. into house*)
Rochester: The light of my eyes has gone indeed – Jane has left me.

Jane enters

Jane (comes down till behind porch – takes up bag): As I leave this place I feel something like a lengthening chain drawing me back – I must go – just – just a last look! (*Sees Rochester.*) My master. They've been deceiving me. But I felt he was near – ruined – blind – alone.

Enter Mrs Fairfax
Mrs Fairfax: If trouble comes of this do not blame me. (*Retires*)

Jane brings water & touches Rochester on the arm.

Rochester: Thank you – give it to me. So you tell me she is to be married? I loved her, Mrs Fairfax – I could never make you understand how I loved her

– I must tell you, Mrs Fairfax, a strange thing that happened to me last evening – a strange thing – I had an impatient fit on me and I thought I couldn't bear my trouble any longer, and in the folly of great trouble – I stretched out my hands, and I cried out – Jane – Jane. Come to me –

Jane:	My beloved master, and I am come!
Rochester:	That voice! am I dreaming! Who is this? Who is this?
Jane:	Will you have a little? –
Rochester:	Who is it – what is it – who speaks?
Jane:	The dog at the gate knew me, Sir – and Mrs Fairfax knew me – I came just now.
Rochester:	Great God – what delusion has come over me? What sweet madness has seized me? Who are you –
Jane:	I'm Jane Eyre.
Rochester:	Where is the speaker? Is it only a voice? Oh, I cannot see, give me your hand or my heart will stop, and my brain burst. (*Jane takes his hand in both hers.*) 'Tis her hand! Is it Jane?
Jane:	Don't you know my voice – God bless you, Sir – I'm glad to be so near you again.
Rochester:	Jane Eyre!
Jane:	My dear Master, I am Jane Eyre – you called me and I am come.
Rochester:	My living dearest – this is certainly her soft hair – this her cheek – but I cannot be so blest after all my misery – it is a dream – such dreams as I have had when I have clasped her once more to my heart, as I do now, and kissed her as thus – and felt that she loved me and trusted that she would not leave me.
Jane:	Which I never will, Sir, from this day.
Rochester:	Never will! says the vision – but I always woke and found it an empty mockery, and I was desolate, and abandoned – my life dark – lonely – hopeless – my soul athirst and forbidden to drink – my heart famished and never to be fed – gentle soft dream nestling in my arms now – you will fly too as your sisters have all fled before you – but kiss me before you go – embrace me, Jane.
Jane:	There sir, and there!
Rochester:	But you must leave me again?
Jane:	Mrs Fairfax has told me everything, and I will not leave you unless you drive me away.
Rochester:	Yes – you understand one thing – by staying with me – I understand another – you pity me. I want more than that – you came to be my [nur]se?
Jane:	Yes, Sir.
Rochester:	But you must marry some day.
Jane:	I don't care about being married. Sir.
Rochester:	You should care. If I were what I once was I would try to make you care – but a sightless block –

Jane:	It's [time], Sir, somebody tried to humanize you, you are grown into a sort of shaggy lion – you've a look of Nebuchadnezzar in the fields about you. Your lunch shall not be grass or nettles.
Rochester:	I thought you'd be revolted, Jane at my poor blind mask.
Jane:	There's the danger of loving you too well for it.
Rochester:	Am I hideous, Jane?
Jane:	Very Sir. You always were, you know.
Rochester:	Humph! I don't know what you've been, but the wickedness isn't taken out of you.
Jane:	I have been with good people – far better than you.
Rochester:	Who the deuce have you been with?
Jane:	Can you see where the sun sets, sir?
Rochester:	I see a dim light.
Jane:	Can you see my hand pass between you and the sun?
Rochester:	I see it.
Jane:	Then you are not blind, Sir.
Rochester:	So you are going to be married?
Jane:	Not that I know, Sir.
Rochester:	What about this Mr Prior?
Jane:	He's a good man, Sir, and a handsome man.
Rochester:	Damn him. Did you love him, Jane?
Jane:	Of course – he was the Clergyman of the Parish.
Rochester:	He wanted you to marry him.
Jane:	He asked me to marry him more than once.
Rochester:	Don't you think you'd better take your hand off my shoulder.
Jane:	I like it there – you'd better push it off.
Rochester:	Ha. Jane. I don't want a nurse – I wanted a wife.
Jane:	Do you Sir?
Rochester:	Yes – is it news to you?
Jane:	Of course. You said nothing about it before.
Rochester:	Is it unwelcome news?
Jane:	That depends on circumstances – on your choice.
Rochester:	Which you shall make for me, Jane.
Jane:	Choose Sir, then – her who loves you best.
Rochester:	I will choose her I love best. Jane – will you marry me?
Jane:	Yes, Sir.
Rochester:	A poor blind man – whom you must lead about by the hand?
Jane:	Yes. Sir.
Rochester:	A crippled man twenty years older than you whom you'll have to wait on?
Jane:	Yes, Sir.
Rochester:	In faith. Jane?
Jane:	In good faith. Sir.
Rochester:	Oh, my love – God bless you and reward you! (*Embrace*)

Curtain

Works Cited

Plays

Anon. *Jane Eyre: A Drama in Two Acts*. British Library Add. MS 53063.F, 1867.

'Courtney, John' [John Fuller]. *Jane Eyre or The Secrets of Thornfield Manor*. British Library Add. MS 43009, 1848.

Birch-Pfeiffer, Charlotte. *Jane Eyre or The Orphan of Lowood, A Drama in Two Parts and Four Acts*. New York: Fourteenth Street Theatre, 1870.

Brougham, John. *Jane Eyre: A Drama in Five Acts adapted from Charlotte Brontë's Novel*. 'The Acting Edition': No. CXXXVL in French's American Drama Series. New York: Samuel French, 1856.

Hering, Mme von Heringen. *Jane Eyre: A Drama in Four [Two] Acts. An Adaptation from a Danish Play*. British Library Add. MS. 53182 N, 1877.

Michély, R. *L'Orfanella di Lowood. Dramma in due parti, diviso in un prologo e tre atti*. Ridotto dal Tedesco. Napoli, 1874. [Copy in British Library shelved at 11715. ee.6.]

Morera y Valls, Francisco. *Juana Eyre: drama en 4 actos y un prólogo*. Arreglado a las Escena Española por F. M. Barcelona: Manero, 1869. [Copy in Harvard Widener Collection, HOLLIS number 005511026.]

[Paul, T.H.]. *Jane Eyre*. British Library Add. MS 53224.A, 1879.

Phillips, Watts. *Nobody's Child: A Drama in 3 Acts*. British Library Add. MS 53061.P, 1867.

'Willing, James' [J.T. Douglass] and Leonard Rae. *Jane Eyre or Poor Relations: A Drama in a Prologue and Four Acts founded on Charlotte Brontë's Novel*. British Library Add. MS 53222.B, 1879.

[Wills, W.G.]. *Jane Eyre*. British Library Add. MS 53285 E, 1882.

Critical and Historical Works

Adams, W. Henry Davenport. *A Dictionary of the Drama*. [1904]. 2 vols projected but only Vol. 1 published. New York: Franklin, 1965.

Agerer, Stefanie. 'Complete List of Theatre Reviews', in Christian Grawe, *Fontane Chronik*. Reclam-Verlag, 1996.

Alexander, Christine and Margaret Smith (eds). *The Oxford Companion to the Brontës*. Oxford: Oxford University Press, 2003.

Anon. *Images of Bradford: 1860–1970*. Bradford: Bradford Libraries and the Breedon Books Publishing Co., 1992.

Baker, H. Barton. *History of the London Stage and its Famous Players (1576–1903)*. London and New York: George Routledge and Sons, 1904.

Banham, M. *The Cambridge Guide to Theatre*. Cambridge: Cambridge University Press, 1995.

Barker, Clive. 'A Theatre for the People', in Kenneth Richards and Peter ThoMSon (eds). *Nineteenth-Century British Theatre*. London: Methuen, 1971.

Bentley, Eric. *The Life of Drama*. New York: Atheneum, 1964.

Bergan, Ronald. *The Great Theatres of London: An Illustrated Companion*. Hong Kong: Prion, 1987.

Boase, Frederic. *Modern English Biography* [...] *Concise Memoirs of Persons who Have Died [...] 1851–1900*. 6 vols. London: Frank Cass, 1965.

Booth, John. *A Century of Theatrical History, 1816–1916. The 'Old Vic'*. London: Stead's Publishing House, 1917.

Booth, Michael R. 'The Acting of Melodrama'. *University of Toronto Quarterly* (October 1964), Vol. 34 (1), pp. 31–48.

————. *Theatre in the Victorian Age*. Cambridge: Cambridge University Press, 1991.

————, Richard Southern, Frederick and Lise-Lone Marker and Robertson Davies (eds). *The Revels History of Drama in English*. 7 vols. London: Methuen, 1975–1978.

Bordman, Gerald and Thomas S. Hischak (eds). *The Oxford Companion to American Theatre*. 3rd edn New York and Oxford: Oxford University Press, 2004.

Bottle, Ted. *Coventry's Forgotten Theatre: The Theatre Royal and Empire*. Westbury, Wiltshire: The Badger Press, 2004.

Bradby, David, Louis James and Bernard Sharratt (eds). *Performance and Politics in Popular Theatre*. Cambridge: Cambridge University Press, 1980.

Brooks, Peter. *The Melodramatic Imagination*. New York and London: Yale University Press, 1976.

Chancellor, Edwin Beresford. *The Pleasure Haunts of London during Four Centuries*. London: Constable and Co.; Boston and New York: Houghton Mifflin, 1925.

Connor, Eleanor. 'Famous Old Theatres of New York: The Bowery Theatre'. *Call Board*, Vol 9 (4), p. 8 (New York Public Library of the Performing Arts, Billy Rose Collection, NBLA +).

Davis, Jim and Victor Emeljanow. *Reflecting the Audience: London Theatregoing, 1840–1880*. Hatfield: University of Hertfordshire, 2001.

Dickens, Charles. 'Amusements of the People'. *Household Words* (1850), Vol. 1 (1), pp. 13–15.

Dauer, Holger. Review of Birgit Pargner's *Zwischen Tränen und Kommerz: Des Rührtheater Charlotte Birch-Pfeiffers, 1800–1868*. (http://iasl.uni-muenchen. de/rezensio/liste/dauer.html).

Douglass, Albert. *Memories of Mummers and the Old Standard Theatre*. London: The Era, n.d. (Foreword dated 1924).

Eagleton, Terry. *Myths of Power: A Marxist Study of the Brontës*. 1975. 3rd edn. Basingstoke: Palgrave Macmillan, 2005.

Easthope, Antony. *Literary Studies into Cultural Studies*. London: Routledge, 1991.

Encyclopedia Britannica. 11th edn Cambridge: Cambridge University Press, 1910.

Evans, Catherine Anne. *Charlotte Birch-Pfeiffer: Dramatist.* PhD thesis, Cornell University, 1982.

Fagg, Edwin. *The Old 'Old Vic' [...] from its Origin as 'The Royal Coburg'.* London: Henderson and Spalding, 1936.

Firth, Gary. *Bradford.* The Archive Photographs Series. Stroud: Chalford, 1995.

Gordon, C. *Old Time Aldwych: Kingsway and Neighbourhood* with maps and illustrations. London: T. Fisher Unwin, 1903.

Hartnoll, Phyllis and Peter Found (eds). *The Concise Oxford Companion to the Theatre.* Oxford: Oxford University Press, 1992.

Howard, Diana. *London Theatres and Music Halls 1850–1950.* London: Library Association, 1970.

Hudson, Lynton. *The English Stage, 1850–1950.* London: Harrap, 1951.

Jackson, Russell. *Victorian Theatre: A New Mermaid Background Book.* London: A. and C. Black, 1989.

James, Louis. 'Was Jerrold's Black Ey'd Susan more Popular than Wordsworth's Lucy?', in Bradby et al., pp. 3–16.

Katz, Ephraim (ed). *The International Film Encyclopedia.* Basingstoke: Macmillan, 1982.

Knight, Joseph. *Theatrical Notes.* London: Lawrence and Bullen, 1893.

Leonard, William Torbert. *Theatre: Stage to Screen to Television.* 2 vols. Metuchen, NJ and London: Scarecrow Press, 1981.

Mander, Raymond, and Joe Mitchenson. *The Lost Theatres of London.* London: Rupert Hart-Davis, 1968.

Martersteig, Max. *Das Deutsche Theater im 19. Jahrhundert: eine kulturgeschichtliche Darstellung.* Leipzig: Breitkopf and Härtel, 1924.

Mayer, David. 'The Music of Melodrama', in Bradby et al., pp. 49–63.

Mayhew, Henry. *London Labour and the London Poor* [1851]. 4 vols. London: Frank Cass and Co., 1861–1862.

Mellor, Geoff J. *Theatres of Bradford.* Bingley: Bookworm, 1978.

Michie, Helena. 'There is No Friend Like a Sister: Sisterhood as Sexual Difference'. *ELH* (Summer 1989), Vol. 56 (2), pp. 401–21.

Mullin, Donald. *Victorian Plays: A Record of Significant Productions on the London Stage, 1837–1901.* New York and London: Greenwood Press, 1987.

Nicoll, Allardyce. *A History of British Drama 1660–1900.* 6 vols. Cambridge: Cambrdige University Press, 1959.

Nudd, Donna Marie. '"Jane Eyre" and What Adaptors Have Done to Her'. PhD thesis, University of Texas at Austin, 1989.

Nudd, Donna Marie. 'Bibliography of Film, Television and Stage Adaptations of *Jane Eyre*'. *Brontë Society Transactions* (1991), Vol. 20 (3), p. 169–72.

Pascoe, Charles Eyre. *The Dramatic List: A Record of the Principal Performances of Living Actors and Actresses of the British Stage: with CriticisMS from Contemporary Journals.* 1879. 2nd edn London: David Bogue, 1880.

Preedy, Robert E. *Leeds Theatres Remembered.* Leeds: The Author, 1981.

Rahill, Frank. *The World of Melodrama*. University Park, PA and London: Pennsylvania State University Press, 1967.

Reynolds, Elizabeth E. 'Recreations and Leisure in St Pancras during the nineteenth century'. Thesis, N.p. 1961. [Copy in Camden Local Studies Library.]

Roberts, Peter. *The Old Vic Story – A Nation's Theatre 1818–1976*. London: W.H. Allen, 1976.

Rowell, George. *The Victorian Theatre, 1792–1914: A Survey*. Cambridge: Cambridge University Press, 1978.

Rowell, George, and A. Jackson. *The Repertory Movement: A History of Regional Theatre in Britain*. Cambridge: Cambridge University Press, 1984.

Sadie, Stanley (ed). *The New Grove Dictionary of Music and Musicians*. 10 vols. London: Macmillan/Grove, 2001.

Sherson, Erroll. *London's Lost Theatres of the Nineteenth Century*. London: Bodley Head, 1925.

Smith, Margaret (ed.). *The Letters of Charlotte Brontë*. 3 vols. Oxford: Clarendon, 1995–2004.

Staedeli, Thomas. 'Portrait of the Actor Olaf Fönss'. http://www.cyranos.ch/smfoen-e.htm

Stark, Susanne (ed.). *Beiträger zur Rezeption der britischen und irischen Literatur des 19. Jahrhunderts im deutschsprachigen Raum*. AMSterdam: Rodopi, 2000; accessed online, 8 March 2005 at http://www.iasl.uni-muenchen.de/rezensio/liste/stark.html.

Stephens, John Russell. *The Censorship of English Drama 1824–1901*. Cambridge: Cambridge University Press, 1980.

———. *The Profession of the Playwright: British Theatre 1800–1900*. Cambridge: Cambridge University Press, 1992.

Stoneman, Patsy. *Brontë Transformations: The Cultural Dissemination of 'Jane Eyre' and 'Wuthering Heights'*. Hemel Hempstead: Harvester Wheatshead/Prentice Hall, 1996.

Strachey, Ray. *The Cause*. 1928. London: Virago, 1978.

Taylor, George. *Players and Performances in the Victorian Theatre*. Manchester: Manchester University Press, 1989.

Thornbury, G.W. and E. Walford (eds). *Old and New London: A Narrative of its History, its People and its Places Illustrated with neumerous engravings from the most Authentic Sources*. 6 vols. London, Paris and New York: Cassell Petter and Galpin, 1879.

Wills, F.C. *W.G. Wills: Dramatist and Painter*. London, Longman, Green and Co., 1898.

Wilmeth, Don. B. and Tice L. Miller (eds). *Cambridge Guide to American Theatre*. Cambridge: Cambridge University Press, 1993.

Wilson, A.E. *East End Entertainment*. London: Arthur Barker, 1954.

Yates, W.E. Review of two works on Charlotte Birch-Pfeiffer by Birgit Pargner. *Forum for Modern Language Studies* (1 January 2005), Vol. 41 (1), p. 112.

Electronic Sources

Backstage: http://www.backstage.ac.uk.
Britannica Online: http://search.eb.com.
Cambridge History of English and American Literature: http://www.bartleby.com.
Discover Leeds: http://www/leodis.org.
Gutenberg-DE Project: http://gutenberg.spiegel.de/autoren.htm.
IASL Online, University of Munich: http://iasl.uni-muenchen.de/rezensio/liste.
Kronologisk oversikt over Halvorsens konsertvirksomhet Del 1 (1864–1883): http://folk.uio.no/oyvindyb/musikk/Halvorsen/registre/kronologi1864_1883.html.
LoveToKnow 1911 Online Encyclopedia. © 2003, 2004 LoveToKnow: http://42.1911encyclopedia.org; http://98.1911encyclopedia.org.
Oxford Dictionary of National Biography: http://www/oxforddnb.com.
PeoplePlay: http://www.peopleplayuk.org.
Theatre Ephemera: www.neiu.edu/~rghiggin/ephem/Ephemera.html.
The Times Digital Archive: http://web5.infotrac.galegroup.com.
WebArchive: http://www/webarchive.org.uk.

Journals Consulted

Bradford Daily Telegraph
Bradford Weekly Telegraph
Builder
Call Board
Coventry Herald and Free Press
Coventry Standard
Daily News
Daily Telegraph
Entr'Acte
Era
Era Almanack and Annual
Examiner
Graphic
Illustrated London News
New York Clipper
New York Spirit of the Times
New York Times
Oldham Evening Express
Oldham Weekly Chronicle
Oldham Weekly Standard
Penny Illustrated Paper
Referee
Saturday Review
Sketch

Stage
Times Online
Yorkshireman
Yorkshire Post and Leeds Intelligencer

Archives and Libraries Consulted

Abbey House Museum, Leeds
Bradford Local Studies Library
British Library
Brontë Parsonage Museum
Camden Local Studies Library: Heal Collection
Coventry Local Studies Library
Houghton Library, Harvard College
Harvard Theatre Collection
Leeds Local Studies Library
New York Public Library for the Performing Arts: Billy Rose Theatre Collection
Newspaper Library (Colindale)
Oldham Local Studies Library
Southwark Local Studies Library
Theatre Museum, London
Yorkshire Archaeological Society, Leeds

Index

Index refers to editorial material. Page numbers in italics indicate illustrations or tables.